A CORRESPONDING
RENAISSANCE

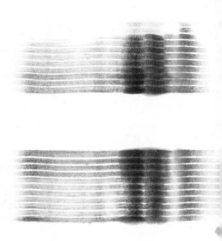

A CORRESPONDING RENAISSANCE

Letters Written by Italian Women

1375–1650

*Translated and Edited,
and with an Introductory Essay by*

LISA KABORYCHA

New York   Oxford
OXFORD UNIVERSITY PRESS

to Gene Brucker

Caro Maestro, Carissimo Amico

Oxford University Press is a department of the University of Oxford.
It furthers the University's objective of excellence in research,
scholarship, and education by publishing worldwide.

Oxford   New York
Auckland   Cape Town   Dar es Salaam   Hong Kong   Karachi
Kuala Lumpur   Madrid   Melbourne   Mexico City   Nairobi
New Delhi   Shanghai   Taipei   Toronto

With offices in
Argentina   Austria   Brazil   Chile   Czech Republic   France   Greece
Guatemala   Hungary   Italy   Japan   Poland   Portugal   Singapore
South Korea   Switzerland   Thailand   Turkey   Ukraine   Vietnam

For titles covered by Section 112 of the US Higher Education
Opportunity Act, please visit www.oup.com/us/he for the
latest information about pricing and alternate formats.

Published by Oxford University Press
198 Madison Avenue, New York, New York 10016
http://www.oup.com

Library of Congress Cataloging-in-Publication Data
  A corresponding Renaissance : letters written by Italian women, 1375-1650 / translated and edited,
with introductory essay by Lisa Kaborycha.
    pages cm
  Includes bibliographical references and index.
  ISBN 978-0-19-934243-3 (pbk. : alk. paper)
  1. Women--Italy--History--Renaissance, 1450-1600--Sources. 2. Women--Italy--History--Sources.
  3. Women--Religious life--Italy--History--Sources. 4. Renaissance--Italy--Sources. I. Kaborycha, Lisa.
  HQ1149.I8C67 2016
  305.40945--dc23

                                                                                    2014042378

Printing number: 9 8 7 6 5 4 3 2 1

Printed in the United States of America
on acid-free paper

Contents

Color plates follow page xv

Map of Italy showing cities and towns of origin
or destination of letters associated with the correspondents

Acknowledgments

When first approached by editor Charles Cavaliere to compile an anthology of Renaissance correspondence for Oxford University Press, I was intrigued. The subject of Renaissance epistolography has attracted considerable scholarly interest in recent years, yet no such collection as he envisioned existed. However, aware of the vastness of the subject matter, I questioned my ability to synthesize such a massive amount of material in a meaningful way. I also believed there was another, perhaps more interesting story to be told about the period and suggested focusing on letters written by women. I am grateful to Charles for his openness to this idea when I proposed it to him, and to the academic reviewers whose many detailed comments and suggestions were crucial in helping me refine the concept of this book. Without Charles's vision and their encouragement this book would never have come into being.

Although this book is the product of many years' study of Renaissance letters, some of it deriving from research I carried out a decade ago for my dissertation on Quattrocento Florentine *zibaldone* manuscripts, as the project grew and developed, it expanded far beyond both the fifteenth century and the Florentine context. It has forced me to leave the familiar territory of Florentine historiography and extend my research into every region of the Italian Peninsula, into the late seventeenth century, and across a variety of disciplines. To pursue these studies I have been fortunate to have access to the unparalleled resources of the library and staff at I Tatti, the Harvard University Center for Renaissance Studies. I must thank first and foremost Michael Rocke, Kathryn Bosi, Angela Dressen, Spyros Koulouris, and Valerio Pacini for their unflagging assistance and expertise.

However, in researching material for this book, the printed and manuscript material I consulted often gave rise to questions for which I had no reliable answers. I reached out to many specialists who responded with generosity, sharing the fruits of their research with me. Philippa Jackson shared with me her detailed notes on the genealogies of Sienese families, and Niccolò Capponi provided advice on searching for biographical material on Florentine elites. Daniel Bornstein, Eleonora Carinci, Giovanni Ciappelli, Jessica Goethals, Gerry Milligan, Natalie Tomas, and Jane Tylus each helped with crucial information from their own research, fact-checking, and/or bibliographical information. All the translations in this book are my own, except where otherwise noted; however, I have had much help in refining them. I was fortunate to have Jonathan Gnoza check all my Latin translations; his expert command of that language brought subtlety and greater depth to those letters than I could have achieved alone. The assistance of Paolo Galluzzi was invaluable: he carefully went over my translations of scientific terminology, correcting my many inaccuracies. Gabriella Battisti, Roberto Bellosta, Kathryn Bosi, Elena Brizio, Monica Farnetti, Roberta Orsi Landini, Raffaele Morabito, Maria Grazia Nico Ottaviani, Mary Bulgarella Westerman, and Gabriella Zarri all aided me in interpreting difficult passages in Italian, whereas Anna Russo assisted me in translating my own words into Italian for a research paper on epistolography. I am indebted to Maurizio Arfaioli for scrupulously reviewing all final translations from Italian. Needless to say, after so much expert assistance, all errors in this book are mine alone.

I owe a debt of gratitude to Laura Fortini and the other organizers of *Scrivere nel Cinquecento corrispondenze in prosa e versi* at the Università Roma Tre for inviting me to participate in an extraordinarily stimulating conference in May 2014. Many of the ideas that shaped this book sprang directly or indirectly from discussions with Ludovica Braida, Adriana Chemello, Monica Farnetti, Raffaele Morabito, and the others I met at that conference. The kindness and generosity of my Italian colleagues has been overwhelming, and I can never thank them enough.

I wish to thank the Medici Archive Project and the National Endowment for the Humanities for giving me the opportunity to spend three solid years reading letters in the Mediceo del Principato collection in the Florence State Archive. The experience of reading hundreds of sixteenth- and seventeenth-century letters has profoundly shaped my understanding of Renaissance epistolography. The time spent with the Medici Archive Project helped deepen my knowledge of the historical context of Renaissance correspondence and sharpen my paleographic abilities. I have learned much from my superb colleagues Maurizio Arfaioli, Alessio Assonitis, Sheila Barker, Elena Brizio, Marta Caroscio, Stefano

Dall'Aglio, Francesca Funis, Piergabriele Mancuso, Roberta Piccinelli, Mark Rosen, and Julia Vicioso.

In addition, during the early stages in the gestation of this book I had many discussions with friends and colleagues that helped shape its final form; among them were Cristelle Baskins, Virginia Cox, Tom Dandelet, Julia Hairston, and Sharon Strocchia. For their constant support, encouragement, and advice I am also indebted to Eve Borsook, Nick Brownlees, Ora Cipolla, Peggy Haines, Dale Kent, Maureen Miller, and Lino Pertile. And very special thanks go to Janet Robson, who deserves a prize for locating the lovely cover image for this book. I had asked many art historians for painted images of a Renaissance woman with pen in hand, and she was the one who suggested Pinturicchio's *Eritrean Sibyl* from the vault of the Baglioni Chapel in the Church of Santa Maria Maggiore in Spello.

To my dear friend Nicholas Hassitt I owe a warm debt of gratitude for reading over every word of the manuscript during the final phases of its completion and helping me with his excellent editorial advice. With their careful readings of the introduction and many thoughtful comments, both Francie Starn and Randy Starn provided essential help at a critical juncture. Marissa Moss, as always, has inspired me with her ideas and insights, as well as by example, showing me how to write in an engaging style. Lively conversations about Renaissance women's lives during long meanders through the Tuscan hills with Manuela Guerrera have energized me; with her constant friendship and jars of homemade *sugo* she sustained me throughout the research and writing process. I thank my children, Sacha, Danya, and Lena for their understanding and support, especially during the last stages of the writing of this book, when they stayed beside me, even though the seaside was beckoning.

And finally, for Gene Brucker, to whom this book is dedicated, the word *"grazie"* is insufficient to express the depth of my gratitude for his patience, kindness, and unstinting generosity toward me. During all the years of my graduate studies, week after week he taught me paleography, preparing lessons, correcting my transcriptions, explaining nuances of historical context, all this even though he was already in retirement. For me it was hard work, but exciting and fun as well, to penetrate six-hundred-year-old documents alongside one of the century's foremost archival historians. What passersby made of the peals of laughter that frequently rang out in the corridors of Dwinelle Hall from the office where we studied is anyone's guess. Most importantly, he has shown how from archival evidence a historian can draw out individuals' stories and make the experiences of Renaissance people come to life. I recently told Gene how several of my undergraduate history students read *Giovanni and Lusanna* and mistook its author for a woman. Although we both laughed over it, the truth is that in his writings and in his teaching Gene Brucker has always brought to bear extraordinary sensitivity to the historical conditions of women during the Renaissance, and has always demonstrated an awareness of the vital place of women in the contemporary academic world. More than anyone, Gene has made it possible for me to write this book and is responsible for my formation as a historian. My deepest, warmest thanks will always go to him.

A NOTE ON CITATIONS

In the interests of keeping the text uncluttered, citations in footnotes and in sections of Suggested Readings at the end of each chapter have been abbreviated. Full references can be found at the end of the book in the Bibliography.

REVIEWERS

Megan Armstrong, McMaster University
Jane Couchman, Glendon College, York University, Toronto
John Hunt, Utah Valley University
Margaret L. King, CUNY Brooklyn College/Graduate Center
Alison Williams Lewin, Saint Joseph's University
Margaret Meserve, University of Notre Dame
Ann E. Moyer, University of Pennsylvania
Ada Palmer, Texas A & M University
Caroline Sherman, The Catholic University of America

About the Editor

L isa Kaborycha, a native of New York City, moved to California, where she studied at the University of California, Berkeley. There she received a B.A. in Comparative Literature, an M.A. in Italian Studies, and a Ph.D. in Medieval and Early Modern European History. Specializing in the cultural and social history of Renaissance Florence, Kaborycha spent three years as a National Endowment for the Humanities research fellow with the Medici Archive Project at the Florentine State Archive. She has published various articles on Renaissance women, including figures such as Brigida Baldinotti and Giovanna d'Austria, and is the author of *A Short History of Renaissance Italy* (Prentice Hall, 2010). Dr. Kaborycha has been the recipient of a Fulbright Fellowship, a Mellon Foundation grant, and a fellowship with Villa I Tatti, the Harvard University Center for Italian Renaissance Studies. Over the past fifteen years she has taught at the University of California, Berkeley; Menlo College; the University of Minnesota study abroad program; and the British Institute in Florence. She currently lives in Florence, Italy, where she teaches courses on Renaissance history at the University of California Florence Study Center and works as a Senior Research Fellow at the Medici Archive Project.

Plate I: *Ippolito Andreasi, Self-portrait with family, 1578–1580. This sketch depicts an everyday scene in the household of Mantuan artist Ippolito Andreasi (1548–1608). The artist at his drawing board turns toward his eldest son who is holding up a book. His wife is seated in the foreground teaching a daughter to read. One of a Renaissance woman's tasks was to teach the ABCs to her young children of both sexes.*

Plate II: Biscotti quaresimali, traditional Florentine Lenten alphabet cookies. *These cookies, eaten during the season of Lent in Florence, recall the Renaissance custom of making letters of the alphabet in the form of "fruits, candies and other childish foods" to teach children to read.*

Plate III: *Sofonisba Anguissola,* Old woman studying the alphabet with a laughing girl, *1550s. In a reversal of roles, an elderly bespectacled woman is learning to read, while a young girl, perhaps her grandchild—who is presumably already adept at reading—laughingly "helps" the older woman.*

Plate IV: Alphabet and drawing of a saint in female hand, fifteenth century. *Contemporaries often discussed the important role that mothers played in Renaissance Italy teaching their children to read; however, they also taught writing to their sons and daughters, as demonstrated here. On the final page of this Florentine manuscript dedicated to various texts concerning St. John the Baptist; a woman or girl has copied these letters of the alphabet, abbreviations, and phrases, which are reminiscent of a needlework sampler. On the left-hand side is a drawing of an unidentified saint and martyr and on the right is a sentence that reads: "Most merciful father, give me memory so that I will be able to remember the whole alphabet."*

Plate V: St. Bridget at her writing desk, fifteenth century. *This is the first page of a manuscript of the* Revelations *written by St. Bridget of Sweden (1303–1373). The manuscript was copied by a nun, and her drawing represents the saint sitting at an angled writing desk, as was common at the time, with pen in hand, most probably in the same position as the copyist herself. Although the saint is depicted taking dictation from a heavenly vision, her role as scribe is not unlike that of the nuns who transcribed the visions of S. Maria Maddalena de' Pazzi or S. Caterina de' Ricci.*

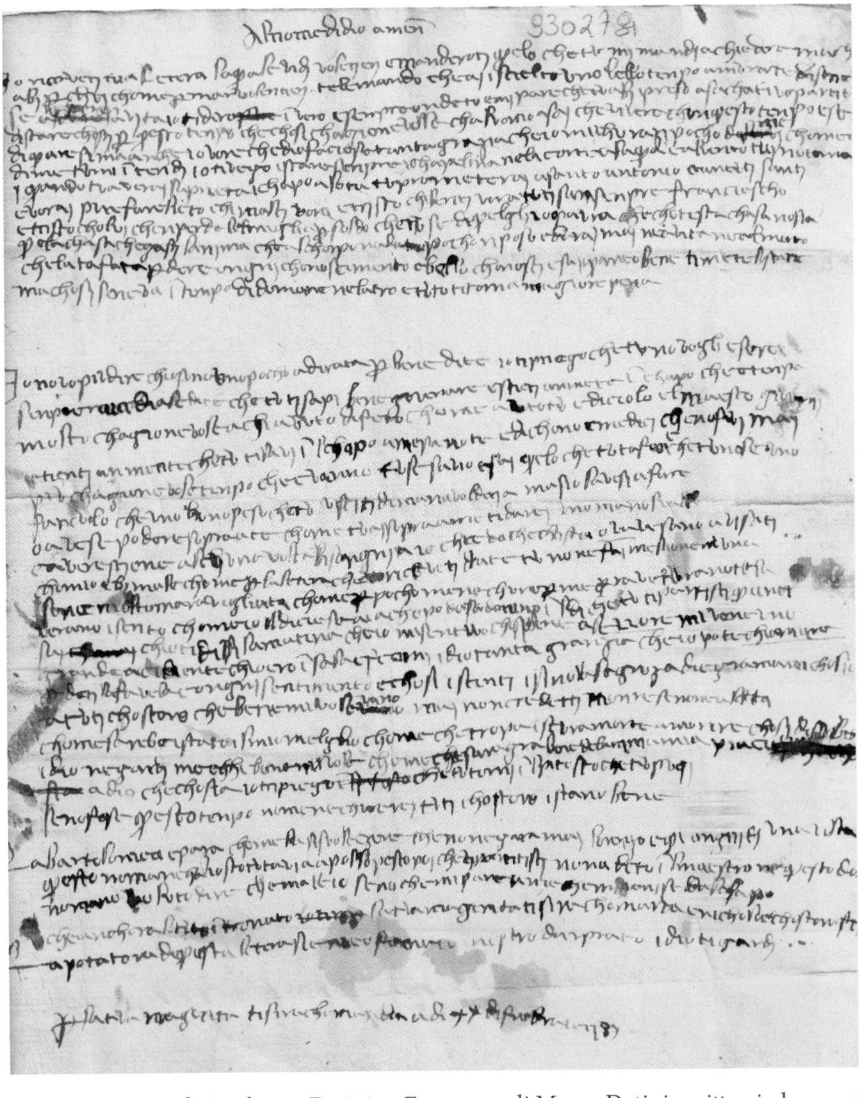

Plate VI: Letter of Margherita Datini to Francesco di Marco Datini, written in her own hand, February 19, 1399 [1398 Florentine dating]. *This is one of the first letters written by Margherita Datini to her husband, soon after she taught herself to write. It is signed "Per la tua Margerita in Firenze (From your Margherita in Florence)."*

Plate VII: Letter of Virginia Galilei (Suor Maria Celeste) to Galileo Galilei, October 29, [1623], written in her own hand. *This is a photo of a letter, showing how it was originally folded, sealed, and addressed, in order to be delivered; the reverse side of the page is visible through the paper. The spot left by the sealing wax is visible at the bottom; the seal was broken when Galileo opened the letter. In her elegant hand, Maria Celeste has written "To [my] magnificent, illustrious, and most beloved lord father, Signor Galileo Galilei in his home [in Villa]."*

Plate VIII: *Giuseppe de Gobbis,* The convent parlor, *c. 1760. Although painted more than a century after the latest letters in this volume, this image of a Venetian convent* parlatorio *(parlor) gives an idea of the socializing that was permitted at times to Renaissance nuns. Friends and family strut about, converse, and listen to a musician perform, while the nuns participate from behind an iron grating. One of the nuns lifts up a small girl—who is perhaps being kept in* serbanza—*to give her a better view of the scene.*

Plate IX: *Lavinia Fontana, Self-portrait in a study, 1579. This is the painting Fontana sent to Chacón in response to his request for a portrait of the artist. Fontana portrays herself in the setting of a* studiolo *(study). The artist has chosen to represent herself dressed as a gentlewoman posed in scholarly surroundings, with pen in hand.*

Armi che V. S. Eccellentis. desidera d'intēde-
re, appresso a che autore hò trouato ch' il famoso diluuio sia venuto per esser' sminuita la terra,
per causa della moltitudine e grandezza, e l'oro
viuere de gl' huomini. Alla qual dimanda rispondo, e gli dico non hauere appresso autore al-
cuno letto, ne credo che sia cosa lodeuole il scriuere l' opinione
d'altri autori come sua propria; non nego ch' io non legga di-
uersi autori speculando le diffinitioni loro, in quanto può passare il senso nostro, doue marauigliata de gl' ingegni e varie
opinioni loro, mi son posta a scriuere il parer mio. Ma
come mi sia posta a trattar di questa materia, e stato in vero il
conoscere con quanta ignoranza alla creatione nostra, e di più il conoscere che gl' elementi non ponno hauere quantità superiore
a la prima datagli da la natura, che cosi intendo di parlar hora
come e l' officio del Philosopho naturale, ne ancor può secondo
quelli longo tempo patir diminutione, che non ne appaia segno
manifestissimo, come per la sfera materiale si può ogn' vno me-
diocramente esercitato chiarire; che all' hora del famoso diluuio qual si dice esser stato vniuersale gl' huomini viuessero tante centenaia d'anni, benissimo si legge nel Genesis al quarto
cap.

f ij

ma fa sempre credere quello a che la materia e inclinata: et il
simile fa il core con il cerebro, quando lui e quieto, et il cerebro
turbato, ancor che lo faccia con maggior difficultà per esser' il
cerebro di più maninconica et humida natura, difficile da con-
sumare: però disse bene Marco Aurelio quando disse, chi vuol
hauere buoni pisseri, fa bisogno hauere le viscere sane, et il cer-
uello non contaminato, altrimente non farà opere buone. Qua-
to poi all' operationi de l' anima, e potere sio, non ve lo scriuo
bona si per esser l' bona tarda come per hauere lo scritto nel trattato ch' io faccio del peccato, ma di che materia se, quando, e con che virtù si genera l' anima nostra, voglio in vn' altra
mia farne ne capace, con vna bellissima e natural ragione, in
quanto può passare al senso nostro, ma bona non vi rispondo a
tutte l' allegationi che fate nella vostra, per hauerla hauuta tar-
di, et bona e l' bona tarda, per il corriero che si parte, ne hò io tē-
po d' hauerla potuta legere più d' vna volta, con poco tempo di
considerarla, ma dimani vi prometto di studiarla bene e daruc-
ne altra risposta. Quanto alla cosa del sole, io l' hò scritta, ma nō
hò rispo di copiarla, ne vorrei mandarla come faccio questa sen-
za tenerne copia e correggerla doue facesse bisogno, et ancomi
farete piacere se mi rimandarete questa in dietro, ouero portar-
la quando verrete a Padoa, accioche possa tener memoria di
quello ch' io hò scritto, non vi dico altro in questa materia per
bona, il Sig. la conserui sana e la feliciti. alli 9. di Nouembre.
1577.

Camilla Herculania Gregetta

Alma-

Plate X: Camilla Herculania Gregetta, Letters on natural philosophy, Cracow, 1584. An example of a printed sixteenth-century letterbook, this is a reproduction of a page of Erculiani's Letters on natural philosophy. A slender volume consisting of only 48 pages, this book is extremely rare; only two copies exist in all the public libraries in Italy.

Introduction

"I would like it if Your Lordship would send me some familiar letters as you once promised me . . ."

Sister Maria Celeste
in a letter to her father Galileo Galilei, March 14, 1630[1]

A nun in her cell writes a letter to her father. Amidst the lush flowering of culture, learning, and the arts, which took place roughly from the mid-fourteenth through the early seventeenth centuries, this is not an image that generally comes to mind when considering the Renaissance. Yet, enclosed within her convent, Sister Maria Celeste was participating in a quintessentially Renaissance activity, one that characterized the era as much as painting, sculpture, or humanist study. In addition to the many letters to her father (Color Plate VII), with her command of epistolary style and extremely elegant handwriting, Maria Celeste also wrote official letters for the abbess. In the letter cited above, she explains that "whenever it is necessary to write to persons of quality, such as our convent governor, the *operai*[2], and others, she [the abbess] charges me with that task, which is really not a small one, considering all my other occupations." Tired from her many chores, which include preparing medicines in the convent pharmacy, tending the sick, directing the choir, sewing, and cooking, Maria Celeste makes this request of her father: "[these duties] do not allow me the rest I need, so in order to lessen my burdens and to help guide me, I would like it if Your Lordship would send me some familiar letters . . ." These "familiar letters" she asks for were extremely popular printed personal letter collections that were read

---

1   Virginia Galilei to her father, March 14, 1629/30. Letter XLIV, A. Favaro, *Galileo Galilei e suor Maria Celeste*. Florence: G. Barbèra, 1891, 294. See pp. 258–259 on Suor Maria Celeste. This and all other translations are my own unless otherwise noted.

2   "*Opere*" were public works committees directed by laypersons called *operai*, who directed both civic and ecclesiastical projects.

not only for what they could teach of good writing style, but also as entertainment. Thus we see a large part of Sister Maria Celeste's energies concentrated on letters: She was at once writing personal letters to her father, composing official correspondence for the abbess, and reading printed collections of others' letters.

And she was not alone. Renaissance Italians of every profession and social class engaged in writing and reading letters. It was a practical necessity for everyday citizens, merchants, bankers, and statesmen to correspond with one another; without this written communication of news, business, and political information, the cultural achievements for which the Renaissance is so famous could not have taken place. Moreover, the art of letter writing—for in its highest form it was considered an art as exalted as poetry or painting—was considered a crucial skill that every gentleman and lady aspired to master. This book, then, considers the Renaissance through the practice of letter writing, or epistolography as it is also called. Moreover, by focusing exclusively on letters written by women, a new perspective on women's participation in Renaissance culture emerges. While women contributed to the creative innovations in the visual and performing arts and participated in humanist studies, their efforts have largely been marginalized because their production in those areas is overshadowed by that of their male contemporaries. However, Renaissance women made their most lasting impact in literature, specifically through letter writing. Women's letters are impressive for both the quantity and quality of writing—which matches and at times excels that of their male counterparts—and the extraordinary richness of their contents. Their letters express all the intellectual inquiry, energy, and self-awareness that is associated with the Renaissance spirit and reveal women's participation in a Renaissance that corresponds with the well-known male-dominated cultural movement, resulting in a "corresponding Renaissance."

A BRIEF HISTORY OF LETTER WRITING

> "Hi, wanna skype later? I'll be in around eight. Miss you!"
>
> *Twenty-first-century e-mail message*

Before discussing the phenomenon in the Renaissance, it is worth considering what it is to write a letter. We compose a message, handwriting or printing it on a piece of paper, slip it in an envelope on which we have written the addressee's name, and, attaching the correct amount of postage, bring it to the post office; from there it is taken by a mailman and delivered to its destination. Although we take the ability to do this for granted, even as these words go to print, the practice is dying out. The majority of our paper mail today consists of advertisements, so-called junk mail, and bills, although increasingly even those are disappearing as we are urged to "go paperless." As we seldom write or receive personal letters anymore, opening the mail is no longer an emotional experience: Many of us have never known the weeks or months of longing and anticipation, followed by the thrill of excitement or foreboding felt when tearing open a letter from a distant friend. Instead, we are increasingly relying on electronic communications, on an e-mail message exchange for instance, with which to set up a mutually convenient time for an online spoken conversation. Convenient, economical, and instantaneous, it is inevitable that these recent technologies will supersede paper and pen.

Thus, as a means of written communication that humans have practiced for over two thousand years stands on the brink of extinction, let us pause to consider: What is a letter?

The earliest letters from the Near East and ancient Egypt were inscribed on clay, wax, or ivory tablets, scratched on thin sheets of lead, painted on pottery shards, or written with ink on wood or papyrus. The Greeks and Romans wrote much of their correspondence on sheets of papyrus sewn together into rolls, and it is thanks to the dry Egyptian climate, favorable for preserving mummies, that many papyrus scrolls have come down to us today. We have for instance around seven hundred letters dating from the third century BCE belonging to a wealthy Greek landowner named Zenon, who lived in Egypt, where he cultivated vineyards, raised livestock, and loaned money.[3] As demonstrated in Zenon's letters, extensive networks of trade across the Mediterranean made long-distance communication essential. Along with its economic role in the ancient world, correspondence was equally vital to its political organization: Neither the highly efficient government bureaucracy of ancient Egypt nor the vast military conquests of the Roman Empire could have occurred without it.

In ancient Rome private letters, known as "familiar" letters (from the Latin *familiaris*, meaning "domestic, private, family"), addressed to a friend or family member were also common. These letters had their origins in the need to communicate information to a distant person when talking with him or her was impossible. In attempting to bridge the distance between friends, family members, or lovers who were separated, Latin familiar letters aimed at reproducing more of the natural cadence of speech. The most celebrated of these early familiar letters

---

3   Armando Petrucci, *Scrivere lettere,* 8–11. Much of this summary is derived from Petrucci, who gives the best account of the material and social context of the history of correspondence.

were written by the Roman orator and statesman Marcus Tullius Cicero (106–43 BCE), who composed over nine hundred of them. Many of his letters are highly informal, discussing domestic, business, or personal matters, while others are elaborately crafted analyses of political events that read like some of his senatorial speeches. Because Cicero was such a prominent figure, renowned for his eloquence, his familiar letters were copied and widely read, breaking down the barrier between private and public.

Recognized as a lively means of engaging with readers, the epistolary genre was frequently exploited by Roman authors who wrote letters with moral or didactic intentions, which were clearly meant to circulate to a wider public. These letters, which generally have a more stiff and formal tone and deal primarily with political, philosophical, or ethical issues, are often classified as "epistles."

SELECTIONS FROM TWO LETTERS BY CICERO AND SENECA

Believe me there is nothing at this moment of which I stand so much in need as a man with whom to share all that causes me anxiety: a man to love me; a man of sense to whom I can speak without affectation, reserve, or concealment. For my brother is away—that most open-hearted and affectionate of men. Metellus is not a human being, but "Mere sound and air, a howling wilderness." While you, who have so often lightened my anxiety and my anguish of soul by your conversation and advice, who are ever my ally in public affairs, my confidant in all private business, the sharer in all my conversations and projects—where are you? So entirely am I abandoned by all, that the only moments of repose left me are those which are spent with my wife, pet daughter, and sweet little Cicero. For as to those friendships with the great, and their artificial attractions, they have indeed a certain glitter in the outside world, but they bring no private satisfaction. And so, after a crowded morning levée, as I go down to the forum surrounded by troops of friends, I can find no one out of all that crowd with whom to jest freely, or into whose ear I can breathe a familiar sigh. Therefore I wait for you, I long for you, I even urge on you to come [. . .]

> Cicero to Atticus (in Epirus) Rome, 20 January 60 BCE
> trans. Evelyn S. Shuckburgh *The letters of Cicero*. London, G. Bell
> and sons, 1899–1900.

It is clear to you, I am sure, Lucilius, that no man can live a happy life, or even a supportable life, without the study of wisdom; you know also that a happy life is reached when our wisdom is brought to completion, but that life is at least endurable even when our wisdom is only begun. [. . .]

> Seneca to Lucilius, Epistle XVI c.62–64 CE
> trans. Richard Mott Gummere,
> Loeb Classical Library edition; vol 1, 1917

The most famous examples of these from the classical world are the *Moral Epistles* written by the philosopher Seneca (Lucius Annaeus Seneca, c. 4 BCE–65 CE).

Although Seneca's epistles are addressed to a certain Lucilius, the sustained serious tone and lack of practical day-to-day information belie their claim to being actual correspondence. The examples of Latin letters written by Cicero and Seneca would return to play an important role in the history of epistolography.[4] There was to be a long interim, however—over a thousand years would pass before their writings were rediscovered.

After the fall of the Western Roman Empire in the fifth century CE, the writing of letters became less common and literacy itself gradually dwindled. Although there are hundreds of letters written by Early Church Fathers such as Ambrose, Augustine, Jerome, and other Christian authors, notably Pope Gregory the Great (r. 590–604), who alone wrote 852 letters, that number drops sharply by the seventh century.[5] During the Early Middle Ages, from the seventh through the eleventh centuries, traditions of Latin learning were kept alive across Europe by members of the clergy, and especially in monastic communities, but few others were reading and writing. As a result, we have very little evidence of letters written by laymen during this period, and barely any by women. With incessant warfare and invasions, networks of trade and communications collapsed. Roads had deteriorated and travel was dangerous. Thus, even for those with the ability to write letters, the difficulties of delivering them were almost insuperable.

Things began to change around 1000 CE, when Europe gradually emerged from its political chaos and economic stagnation as population grew and cities began to be reestablished as thriving hubs of commerce. Education revived in urban centers, culminating in the founding of the great medieval universities of Bologna, Paris, and Oxford in the twelfth century. The courses, taught in Latin, covered a variety of subjects, including rhetoric. As there was a need for secretaries to write official letters on behalf of rulers and civil and ecclesiastical authorities, a branch of rhetoric known as *ars dictaminis* (the art of composition) was developed to teach epistolary style in Latin. One of the earliest manuals on the *ars dictaminis* was written by a Benedictine monk at Montecassino around 1087, and by the early twelfth century it was being taught as part of the curriculum at the University of Bologna. Within the medieval scholastic system, letter writing, like other subjects, was broken down into component parts and its rules were codified; thus, the elements of good epistolary style were divided into five parts.

---

4   See especially John Najemy, *Between friends*, 25–30.
5   Giles Constable, *Letters and letter collections*, 29–30.

THE FIVE PARTS OF A LETTER
according to the principles of *ars dictaminis*

SALUTATIO   The Salutation
(ex: "Most Highly Honored Holy Father")

EXORDIUM (CAPTATIO BENEVOLENTIAE)   The 'Capturing' of good will
(ex: "Knowing your reputation for fairness and clemency...")

NARRATIO   The Story
(ex: "Last year when I was in Rome I met with the cardinal who told me...")

PETITIO   The Request
(ex: "I humbly beg that you provide me with a salary...")

CONCLUSIO   The Conclusion
(ex: "With greatest respect...")

These basic principles of the *ars dictaminis* continued to be applied throughout much of the Renaissance in the composition of formal letters.[6]

The University of Bologna was renowned as Europe's premier school of law; the emphasis there on Latin composition reflected the practical necessities of the document-based urban society of northern and central Italian city-states, with their armies of secretaries, lawyers, and notaries who drafted not only letters but also contracts, wills, laws, and diplomatic correspondence in Latin. There were many career opportunities opening up for young scholars who flocked to these schools; however, for many of them, interest in these studies was more than just vocational. Whereas for much of the Middle Ages learning had been limited to members of the clergy, now a large number of secular students were bringing a fresh approach to study of the classical authors, giving birth to a vibrant new intellectual movement known as humanism. These scholars challenged standard interpretations of classical writings and began to explore the meanings of those writings within the historical context in which they had been created. In their own Latin compositions, the humanists broke away from the stiff, inelegant medieval writing style and tried to recapture the beauty of ancient Latin.

Of these, one man almost single-handedly changed the way Europeans wrote their private letters. Petrarch (Francesco Petrarch, 1304–1374), one of the earliest and most influential proponents of humanism, wrote over five hundred familiar letters in Latin. Petrarch rejected the rules of *ars dictaminis* and stilted medieval Latin in letter writing in favor of a more personal style. Although

---

6   On the *ars dictaminis* see Camargo, *Ars dictaminis* and for application of its principles during the Renaissance see Rice Henderson, "Erasmus on the art of letter writing," 333; and Grendler, *Schooling in Renaissance Italy* 114–115.

Petrarch modeled his letters on ancient authors, especially on the writings of his hero Cicero, he pioneered a brand-new style of writing, which he defined as "plain, domestic and friendly."[7]

PETRARCH TO GIOVANNI COLONNA
ON SEEING ROME FOR THE FIRST TIME

What can you expect from Rome after I sent you so many letters from the mountains? You must have supposed I would write something great when I arrived in Rome. And perhaps in the future I will write something great about this. For now, astonished by so many marvels and overcome with wonder, I do not even know where to begin. There is one thing, however, that I cannot be silent about—that my reactions were the opposite to what you had expected. I remember how you often used to advise me not to come here because you feared that, with its ruined appearance, the city could never compare with its fame and with impressions I had formed from books, and my ardor would weaken. And I too, even though burning with desire, willingly deferred my visit, afraid that everything I had imagined in my mind would seem inferior to my eyes when compared with the present, which is always the enemy of reputation. Instead, strange to say, reality diminished nothing, rather it increased everything. Rome was truly greater, and its ruins greater than I could have imagined. I do not marvel that the world was conquered by this city, only that I myself was conquered so late. Farewell.

Rome, the Ides of March on the Capitoline [15 March 1337]

Petrarch *Rerum familiarum* II, 14

Petrarch was the first humanist to gather his letters into a collection, which he edited and "published" himself.[8] Petrarch's collection, known as the *Rerum familiarum libri* or simply *Familiaris*, comprises 350 of his letters written to prominent individuals, friends, and family members, both alive and dead. Prompted by his discovery in 1345 of Cicero's letters to his brother Quintus and to his friend Atticus, Petrarch also wrote letters to the long-dead Roman statesman. Not twenty years after Petrarch's death, Cicero's vast collection of *Familiar letters* were rediscovered in 1392, inspiring generations of humanists to compose letters in Ciceronian Latin. Petrarch had started a trend, and throughout the fifteenth century it became common for humanists to write their own Latin letters and to circulate them.[9] Most tended, however, to adopt the manner of formal

---

7   "hoc mediocre domesticum et familiare dicendi," *Rerum familiarum*, I, 1, cited in Witt, *In the footsteps of the ancients*, 265. In Chapter 6 Witt describes Petrarch's contribution to humanist letter writing in detail. See also Najemy, *Between friends*, esp. 25–30.

8   The printing press was not introduced in Europe until the middle of the fifteenth century; however, Petrarch's works circulated widely in manuscript form during his lifetime. On Petrarch's editorial control of his own writings see Storey, *Transcription and visual poetics* esp. 201–224.

9   On humanist Latin letters see Clough, "The cult of antiquity." On anti-Ciceronian humanist letter writing see Rice Henderson, "Letter writing in the Ciceronian controversy." In *Ars Epistolica*, xiv–xvii.

epistles rather than the more relaxed style of the familiar letter. The humanist Latin letter was a vehicle for showing off linguistic bravura and communicating elevated philosophical or political concepts to other like-minded academics.

Writing letters was not merely an academic exercise, and humanists were not the only ones to be writing letters in Italy at the turn of the fifteenth century. There was an equally pressing practical need for writing in the vernacular or *volgare,* as the language spoken on the streets was known. The citizens of the Italian city-states in northern and central Italy needed to be able to communicate across long distances; the boom in trade and invention of international banking contributed to the widespread need for vernacular literacy and letter-writing skills in particular. Whether an epidemic or war broke out, a valuable shipment of goods was lost at sea, or a king defaulted on his debt, merchants' letters had to transmit all this. Over the course of the fourteenth century, public elementary schools opened all over the Italian Peninsula, and throughout this period vernacular literacy rates in Italian cities far outstripped those anywhere else in Europe, except perhaps the Netherlands. One scholar has defined Tuscany, in particular, as a region "stricken with a writing fever."[10]

This explosion of popular reading and writing was facilitated by the technology for making paper from rags, invented in China and introduced into Europe in the mid-twelfth century via the Islamic world. From the early Middle Ages, virtually all letters had been written on parchment, which is made of tanned animal hides, usually from cows or sheep.[11] Preparing sheets of parchment was time-consuming and the final product was expensive; moreover, it was not always easy to write on. Paper provided a cheap, practical alternative and came to replace parchment for the writing of manuscripts, letters, and other documents. However, during this period the use of paper was not widespread throughout Europe; only in Italy, where there were many water-powered paper mills, established as early as the thirteenth century, was paper a readily available commodity.[12] It is impossible to imagine, for instance, the 150,000 letters in the collection of Francesco Datini (1384–1410), the merchant from the Tuscan city of Prato, having been written without a cheap, plentiful supply of paper.[13]

---

10 Balestracci, *The Renaissance in the fields,* 1. See also Burke, "The uses of literacy."

11 Petrucci cites the last letter written on papyrus as that of Marginarius, abbot of the monastery of Saint-Denis, to Charlemagne, dated 788 CE. *Scrivere lettere,* 28.

12 In England, for instance, "the use of paper was very rare (but not entirely unknown) about the turn of the fifteenth century, that the proportion of all manuscripts written on paper rose to about 20 percent by about 1450, and that it reached 50 per cent or more by the final decades of the century." "Materials: the paper revolution," in Griffiths and Pearsall, *Book production,* 12.

13 See pp. 101–104 on Margherita Datini.

LETTER WRITING IN
SIXTEENTH-CENTURY ITALY

"These Italians are great printers of letters. I believe I have more than a hundred volumes of them."

Michel de Montaigne, 1588[14]

A fter paper, the technological innovation that most enhanced the spread of letter writing was the printing press with moveable type, invented by Johannes Gutenberg in 1450. Not long after, presses were established in the major cities of Europe, with Venice and Rome becoming two of the most important centers of printing activity.[15] Although the first book produced by the press in Mainz was the celebrated Gutenberg Bible, many types of works were soon being printed, and by the mid-sixteenth century one of the most popular genres in Italy was the familiar letter book. Even though people wrote their letters by hand, these printed letter books had an enormous influence on their correspondence. We cannot know which volume of letters Galileo had promised to give his daughter; it could have been one of literally hundreds in circulation by 1630. As indicated by French philosopher Michel de Montaigne (1533–1592), Italian letter books were a publishing phenomenon; numerous volumes were in circulation in his day. Between 1538 and 1627 the number of letter books published in Italy rose to 540, on average six books per year appearing. Within less than a century nearly 40,000 letters were printed.[16]

The man who is credited with kicking off this literary trend is Pietro Aretino (1492–1556), the first to come up with the idea of printing his own vernacular letters. The son of a cobbler, Aretino was born in the Tuscan city of Arezzo and became celebrated across Europe as a brilliant satirist and a prolific poet and playwright. He used his writing as a weapon to cut the mighty down to size, especially when they were unwise enough not to supply him with money and gifts. A mere suggestion that Aretino might pen (and print!) a critical letter was enough to extort large sums from powerful men. The "Scourge of princes, the divine Pietro Aretino," as he was dubbed by poet Ludovico Ariosto, was especially canny in his manipulation of print media and is often referred to as the first journalist. Aretino printed his first volume of letters in 1538; it was an

---

14 *Les Essays*, I, XXXIX, J. Balsamo et al., eds., Paris, 2007, p. 257.
15 Pettegree. *The book in the Renaissance.*
16 Quondam, *"'Le carte messaggiere'"*, 14, and Adriana Chemello, *Per lettera*, 31. Chemello provides further details on the phenomenon, specifying that of these letter collections, 85 percent contain single-authored works and the other 15 percent are anthologies, adding that the figure of 540 books includes reprints.

astounding success, to be reprinted twelve times in the next two years, and the author followed it with another five volumes by 1557. These vernacular letters—Aretino knew little Latin—are addressed to individuals across the social spectrum, from kings to prostitutes and cover a gamut of styles, subject matter, and emotions. The reading public delighted in letters that ranged from salacious gossip peppered with witty wordplay, to bold missives addressed to great artists and mighty rulers, to highly personal messages, such as the those expressing grief over the death of a beloved friend.

**PIETRO ARETINO TO FRANCESCO DEGLI ALBIZI
ON THE DEATH OF GIOVANNI DELLE BANDE NERE**

[*Mortally wounded in battle, Giovanni de' Medici had a gangrenous leg that was to be amputated. He died shortly thereafter in Aretino's presence*]

[. . .] Having been advised by his physicians, I went to him and said: "I would be wronging your mind if I tried to convince you with painted words that death heals all evils and ought not to be gravely feared, but because it is the height of happiness to do everything freely, let them remove that [leg] damaged by the artillery and in eight days you will be able to make Italy, now a servant, into a queen. And let the limp, which you will receive, take the place of the collar of a king; since you never wanted to wear one around your neck, let your injury—the loss of a limb—be the collar and medal of the familiars of Mars." "Let it be done quickly," he replied. At this, the doctors entered, and praising the bravery of his decision, arranged that evening to carry out what they needed to do. Having given him some medicine, they went to prepare the instruments [. . .] When the time came, these capable men appeared with the equipment suited to the task, saying that eight or ten people should be found to hold him down while the violence of the sawing lasted. "Not even twenty," he said, laughing, "could hold me." Raising himself with the most determined expression, he took the candle in his hand to shed light for the operation. I fled from there, stopping up my ears [. . .]

Mantua, 10 December 1526

By breaking with all the formal conventions of letter writing, Aretino demonstrated the suppleness and versatility of the vernacular letter. No subject was off limits to Aretino, and his style varied from earthy to exalted.

His letters also emphasized the aesthetic and expressive potential of the Italian language itself, reflecting ideas expressed by Pietro Bembo in his influential 1525 linguistic manifesto *Prose della volgar lingua*. Although the Tuscan vernacular had been the vehicle for literary masterpieces from the time of Dante's *Divine Comedy* (c. 1307–1321) and Boccaccio's *Decameron* (c. 1350), it was not until the early sixteenth century that the Florentine tongue was singled out among the many variants spoken on the peninsula as the official Italian language. The grammatical rules and spelling of Italian gradually came to be codified, and its utility and beauty were praised along with, and sometimes above, Latin. In 1542, only four years after the publication of Aretino's first volume of letters, Paolo Manuzio printed an anthology of vernacular letters written by a variety of authors entitled *Lettere volgari di diversi nobilissimi huomini*. In the dedicatory letter that opens the volume, Manuzio defends the use of the vernacular: "this language is beautiful, and noble, and it is ours, and this sort of writing is used every day."[17]

The son of famed printer Aldo Manuzio (1449–1515) and heir to his father's business, the Aldine Press, Paolo also promoted this volume of letters as a highly practical way to learn to write one's own letters. In the sentence following the one cited above, he writes that these examples "will inspire those who know how, and those who do not will be obliged to learn, as they can find in these examples the true form of good writing."[18] The ability to compose correspondence was a highly prized skill, and one of the best ways to learn good style in letter writing was to imitate recognized masters. Moreover, in addition to the examples provided in letter collections, a vast number of treatises on how to compose letters and handwriting manuals began to appear during this time.[19] Here, too, the new technology of printing, by providing resources to meet this need for instruction in epistolary style, promoted and spread the practice of letter writing in Italian.

"A profound anthropological shift" is how Adriana Chemello describes the literary revolution initiated by Aretino when he first published his private letters. She cites Aretino, who advises a friend to "put them away somewhere, so, like jewels, they can be taken out and from time to time displayed in all their glory and as a testament to your merit and talent [*ingegno*]."[20] Chemello underlines Aretino's achievement not only in "capitalizing" on his writings (like jewels, they could be sold) but also in establishing a new literary genre. The familiar letter became a showcase for creative genius, the private writings of one individual acquiring an authorial voice that had worth—both monetary as well as artistic

17 Ray, *Writing gender*, 36.
18 Ibid.
19 Stanley Morison describes the number of handwriting manuals produced between 1524 and 1530 as an "extraordinary flood of writing books," in *Early Italian writing-books*, 201. On writing manuals within the broader European context see Erdmann, Govi, and Govi, *Ars epistolica*.
20 "Pietro Aretino, l'iniziatore del nuovo genere «libro di lettere» in volgare, segnala la profonda alterazione antropologica dell'epistola in una sua lettera a Lodovico Dolce: Sì che riponetele [scil.: le lettere] in luogo che si possin mostrare di tempo in tempo, come gemme de la gloria loro e come corde del merito del istromento del vostro ingegno." "Il codice epistolare femminile. Lettere, «Libri di lettere» e letterate nel Cinquecento," Zarri, *Per lettera*, 31.

value—in the eyes of the general reading public.[21] Thus, by the beginning of the seventeenth century in Italy there was an explosion of printed collections of letters written by prominent Renaissance men and women from all walks of life— poets, scholars, religious reformers, actors, philosophers, countesses, and courtesans. These circulated as never before, read everywhere by lords and ladies in courts, by urban shopkeepers and village housewives, as well as by nuns behind their convent walls.

RENAISSANCE WOMEN'S WRITING AND READING

"The reason for writing this letter is that I have a new errand boy. He is the son of Ser Lapo and today I have had him start writing so that he can work in the shop [...]"

Margherita Datini to Francesco Datini, February 18, 1399

In 1538, the same year as Aretino's first volume, Vittoria Colonna's poems were published, and over the course of the 1540s writings by women began appearing in print in Venice. The first anthology of poetry by women authors to be published in Europe came out in 1559, Lodovico Dolce's *Rime diverse d'alcune nobilissime et virtuossissime donne,* comprising works by fifty-three Italian women. By the end of the century over two hundred women had their works published. An extraordinary cultural phenomenon, Italian women's literary production peaked between 1580 and 1630, when over sixty single-authored volumes written by women were published.[22] Italy in the sixteenth century, writes Virginia Cox, saw "the emergence of secular women as cultural protagonists in a quantity and with a prominence unprecedented in the ancient or medieval world" and unequaled anywhere else in Europe.[23] So great was the demand for female-authored

---

21   "La lettera, dentro il «nuovo genere», come indicano palesemente le scelte lessicali, assume uno spessore economico, viene assimilata alle gemme. Le lettere vengono riposte non per tutelarne la riservatezza, bensì per «mostrarle» al momento debito. Come le gemme, esse sono oggetti preziosi su cui è possibile investire e capitalizzare risorse per poi esibirle, spenderle acquistandone merito. La riproducibilità garantita dal mezzo tipografico trasforma il «luogo comunicativo» della lettera (riservato allo scambio tra un mittente ed un destinatario) in qualcosa di diverso. Il passaggio dalla epistola al liber realizza uno scarto segnalato, in primis, dalla sostituzione di un destinatario unico e ben identificato con un destinatario collettivo, il lettore del «libro di lettere». Il décalage dal manoscritto alla stampa consente all'autore di intervenire nei testi con correzioni, aggiunte, omissioni, censure, stravolgendo la fisionomia della lettera originaria. Questa operazione autoriale fa assumere al «libro di lettere» la fisionomia di vera e propria opera letteraria." *Per lettera,* 31.

22   Robin, *Publishing women,* xviii; Cox, *Prodigious muse,* xii.

23   Cox, *Women's writing,* xiv. Cox cites Erdmann's figures for the number of women's works published this period: two hundred in Italy, thirty in France, twenty in Germany, seventeen in England, thirteen in Spain and Portugal, three in the Netherlands. Erdmann, *My gracious silence,* 201–225.

texts that a number of popular sixteenth-century books were written by men posing as women, what Meredith K. Ray terms "female impersonations" such as Girolamo Parabosco's 1547 *Lettere amorose*, which included love letters written by the male author in a female voice, and Ortensio Lando's 1548 *Lettere di molte valorose donne*, composed by Lando; both of these volumes were extremely successful.[24]

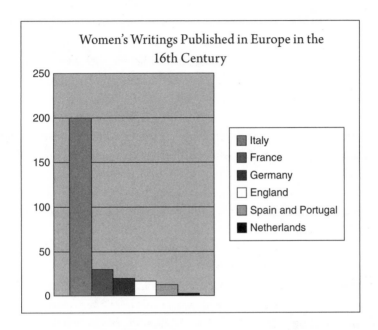

However, the emergence of women's printed literary writings in the 1500s is only the tip of the iceberg. As indicated by the above words of Margherita Datini, who was managing the business in her husband's absence, Italian women had been involved in vernacular written culture since at least the fourteenth century. In Tuscany, which has been the area most closely studied, literacy extended across both class and gender. Chronicler Giovanni Villani (d. 1348) estimated that in Florence in the 1330s between "8,000 to 10,000 boys and girls are learning to read." The overall literacy of Florentines is confirmed by the 1427 Catasto (income tax) records, which every head of household was required to file, and the majority of them wrote these themselves. Adult male literacy in Florence has been documented as between 69 and 83 percent in 1427, contrasted with overall adult elementary literacy rates throughout Europe at the time, which probably

---

24 See Ray, *Writing gender,* esp. Chapter 2, "Female impersonations." See also Chapter 5, p. 156, on Celia Romana and Emilia N., Fiorentina.

hovered around 5 percent.[25] Venice and Milan both had slightly lower although still comparable rates of literacy.[26] Women's vernacular literacy in many parts of Italy was nearly as high as that of men, although statistics are harder to come by; because of their subordinate social and legal status, women were rarely expected to write out documents such as the Catasto themselves.[27] For evidence of women's literacy we must look to other sources.

For one thing, it is known that mothers taught their young children to read at home (Color Plate I). Teaching within the household could take playful forms: Florentine humanist Matteo Palmieri (1406–1475) and merchant Giovanni Rucellai (1403–1481) both recommend forming letters for children out of "fruits, candies and other childish foods," to make the learning process more enjoyable[28] (Color Plate II). It has been generally assumed that women taught their children to read but not how to write; however, this is impossible to demonstrate. Indeed, manuscript evidence such as an alphabet copied in a fifteenth-century female hand like a written sampler, seems to indicate the exact opposite (Color Plate IV). Until the age of six or seven the education of both sexes was identical; however, from there it diverged. After learning to read in the vernacular, boys would traditionally study Latin at grammar schools and/or attend abacus schools to learn accounting practices, whereas girls would either remain at home or be sent to convents for their education. Although convents were often places where girls were held in safekeeping prior to marriage, in a practice known as *serbanza*, and education was sometimes little more than training in religion, manners, deportment, and domestic tasks such as needlework, girls were often instructed in reading and writing there as well.[29] This instruction would typically be in the vernacular, although there is at least one humanist, Laura Cereta, who described learning Latin from a nun (see pp. 91–92). For those who went on to take vows as nuns, tasks could include the copying of manuscripts (Color Plate V) or, in the case of at least one convent, working at a printing press.[30]

---

25 On literacy estimates for Florence see Black, *Education and society*, 42. For Europe see Graff, "On literacy in the Renaissance," 148–150.

26 Peter Burke, "Uses of literacy"

27 "Literacy in Florence not only extended to the majority of the male population but was widespread among women too. Social and legal expectations meant that women did not normally write their own portate; nevertheless, there are many instances in the 1427 Catasto of female autographs . . ." Black, *Education and society*, 36. On women's literacy see especially Miglio, *Governare l'alfabeto*.

28 Palmieri, *Vita civile*, I, 57, Gino Belloni, ed. Florence: Sansoni, 1982, p. 24; *Giovanni Rucellai ed il suo Zibaldone*, 14.

29 On the practice of *serbanza* see Strocchia, "Taken into custody."

30 For information on the prolific copying of the nuns at the convent of Le Murate in Florence, see Lowe, *Nuns' chronicles and convent culture*. On nuns' involvement in the early stages of printing see Gregori and Rocchi, eds., *Il "Paradiso" in Pian di Ripoli*.

Of course, not everyone approved of education for women. Certain fourteenth-century moralists, such as Francesco da Barberino (1264–1348) and Paolo da Certaldo (fl. 1347–1370), condemned the practice; however, the reality was that ever more Italian women were reading and writing.[31] By the sixteenth century an education in vernacular literature was considered an essential part of a well-brought-up girl's accomplishments. The Milanese pedagogue Fra Sabba da Castiglione (1480–1554) asks: "Do you not want this girl to know how to read and write well, so that by reading Dante, Petrarch, Boccaccio, and other authors, she is not held to be an ill-educated, rough peasant by other young women of our day who are noble, virtuous, well-born, and wise, and all greatly enjoy such refined delights?"[32] By 1581, Italian women's reputation for learning was known even in England, where Richard Mulcaster (1530–1611), wrote: "nay do we not see in our countrey, some of that sex so excellently well trained, and so rarely qualified, either for the tounges themselves or for the matter in the tounges: as they may be opposed by any of comparison . . . to the Italian ladies who dare write themselves, and deserve fame for so doing?"[33]

Moreover, even without a formal education, the plentiful supply of manuscripts and printed books in Renaissance Italy meant a woman could acquire the rudiments of literacy on her own, not only learning to read but, in one well-documented case, that of Margherita Datini, teaching herself to write.[34] For here it is important to note that literacy in the early modern world was in reality composed of two separate skills: reading and writing. While the ability to write implied knowing how to read, the reverse was not true: Many individuals could read but did not have the facility with pen and paper to do more than mark their names with an "x." Beyond a basic knowledge of the ABCs, writing involved a complex set of manual skills involving manipulating a goose quill, making sure that lines were parallel and well measured on the page, and managing to guide the ink smoothly from the nib onto the paper without blots,

---

31 As regards the Florentine context Sharon Strocchia has written: "Although Paolo da Certaldo's prohibitions on reading were reiterated and even embellished in the fifteenth century, his advice seems to have been more frequently ignored than followed in practice. Meeting the perceived moral dangers of female literacy head on was a set of competing practical and social pressures for the enlargement of women's reading skills in fifteenth-century Florence." "Learning the virtues," 45.

32 Fra Sabba da Castiglione, *Riccordi ovvero Ammaestramenti*, ed. Santa Cortesi, 286–287, cited by Grendler in *Schooling*, 88 and Strocchia, "Learning the virtues." Although Castiglione's overall intent is to deflect women from secular reading material, he is voicing a popularly held view of the accomplishments expected of young women of his day. For a thorough analysis of this passage see Baernstein, "'In my own hand',", esp. 132–133.

33 Stevenson, *Women Latin poets*, 142. Stevenson cites Shirley Nelson Kersey, *Classics in the education of girls and women*. Metuchen, NJ: Scarecrow Press, Inc., 1981, p. 54.

34 See Crabb, " 'If I could write',", 1193–1194; also James, "A woman's path to literacy," 43–56.

splotches, and scratches[35] (Color Plate VI). Writing was a messy and time-consuming activity and although it was common especially for merchants to have the "ink-stained fingers," described by Leon Battista Alberti, many people who either could not write or preferred not to made use of the services of a scribe or an acquaintance with professional writing skills.[36] The tendency of women, in particular, to have their letters copied for them has caused some misunderstandings about women's ability to write. Although it is true that an illiterate person (i.e., someone who could neither read nor write) would need to resort to use of a scribe, it does not follow that all who used scribes were illiterate. Renaissance princes who were too busy to sit down at a writing desk or nobles who did not want to soil their sleeves had secretaries who often copied out their letters for them from dictation; all they had to do was to add their signature at the bottom of the page. Not uncommonly, those whose hand-writing was serviceable but inelegant also chose to have others write for them. Galileo, for instance, often had his daughter write out his most important cor-respondence for him. For all of these reasons, women of means frequently made use of scribes. Thus, Margherita Datini, who took great pride in having taught herself to write, generally had one of her employees write for her. Margherita hurriedly finishes the message about the errand boy—who inci-dentally was probably the copyist of the actual letter—with the words: "Also send me that book on the Passion that is in Mona Margherita's room that is marked with an 'M' at the top and send me the little book. Send me some of these things. As I'm in a hurry, I have written no more." (Although she had no time for writing, Margherita makes it a point to send for books to read in her leisure time.) Alessandra Strozzi (pp. 131–132), too, preferred to have her let-ters copied for her by others. Although she wrote in a vigorous *mercantesca* (mercantile) hand, whenever she could she would ask her son Matteo to do this task, commenting on one occasion: "It's been inconvenient without him here because he writes all my letters for me."[37] Both of these women make it clear that it is because they are very busy and from considerations of convenience that they have someone else write for them.

---

35 In any case, there was no standard version of the Italian language until the sixteenth century. Lacking a unified grammar and stable orthography, the vernacular was not considered a legitimate language like Latin. The term "*letterato*" (literate) was used to define a person who knew Latin.

36 "It was a good sign if a merchant had ink-stained fingers." Alberti, *The family in Renaissance Florence*, Renée Neu Watkins, trans., 67.

37 *Selected letters of Alessandra Strozzi*, translated with an introduction and notes by Heather Gregory. Berkeley: University of California Press, 1997, 39.

Interestingly, Catherine of Siena's (Caterina Benincasa, pp. 33–34) use of scribes for the majority of her letters not only caused generations of scholars to believe she was illiterate, but also obscured her very authorship of the letters. It is well accepted now that Catherine was able to write; indeed, in one of her letters she describes the process by which she learned: "This letter, and another which I have sent you, I wrote in my own hand [. . .] as soon as [God] had left me, the glorious [John the] Evangelist and Thomas Aquinas appeared and while sleeping I began to learn [. . .]"[38] Whether she acquired writing skills through divine intervention or by more prosaic means, there is evidence that her confessor, Raymond of Capua, deliberately suppressed this letter, perhaps in order to perpetuate the image of Catherine as a kind of "idiot savant." Other holy women similarly chose not to put pen to paper; the learned Maria Maddalena de' Pazzi (pp. 56–57), for instance, would verbally describe her visions, allowing other nuns to transcribe them for her. Such use of intermediaries in the writing process raises the possibility of scribal intervention and weakening of the authorial voice; however, it is important to remember that women like Catherine and Maria Maddalena exercised editorial control, carefully reading over these transcriptions. Moreover, contemporaries considered dictating to be the same as composing (as indeed the term *ars dictaminis* indicated) and used the words interchangeably with the word "writing." "Writing," the relatively mechanical process of putting pen to paper, was not considered the essential part of the creative process.[39] Despite the collaborative nature of the transcription process, Margherita Datini, Maria Maddalena de' Pazzi, and Catherine of Siena ought to be considered authors in every sense of the word.

LETTER WRITING, A "NATURAL" FORM OF EXPRESSION FOR WOMEN?

While it is impossible to quantify exactly how many thousands of private letters were written by Renaissance women, published letter collections can be documented from the earliest years of printing.

---

38 My own translation. The original reads: "Questa lettera, e un'altra che io ve ne mandai, ò scritte di mia mano in su l'Isola della Rocca, con molti sospiri e abondanzia di lagrime [. . .] subito che fuste partito da me, col glorioso evangelista Joanni e Tomaso d'Aquino così dormendo cominciai a imparare [. . .]" Discussed at length by Jane Tylus, "Mystical literacy: writing and religious women in Late Medieval Italy," in *A companion to Catherine of Siena*, 155–183. Tylus also discusses this letter in *Reclaiming*, 11–12.

39 See Carolyn James' introduction to Margherita Datini, *Letters to Francesco Datini*, trans. Carolyn James and Antonio Pagliaro. Toronto: Iter Inc.: Centre for Reformation and Renaissance Studies, 2012, esp. the section on scribal mediation and "dictation and collaborative writing," 19–23. On dictation as composition see also Crabb, "If I could write," 1175–1178.

Italian Women's Single-authored Letter Collections Published 1450–1650*

1492 St. Catherine of Siena, *Epistole utile e divote*
      later expanded edition, reprints: 1500, 1548, 1562, 1584
1507 Osanna Andreasi da Mantova, *Libretto della vita [. . .]*
      second edition: 1524
1544 Vittoria Colonna, *Litere alla duchessa d'Amalfi*
1552 Lucrezia Gonzaga, *Lettere*
1558 Olimpia Morata *Orationes, Dialogi, Epistolae*
      later expanded editions: 1562, 1570, 1580
1562 Celia Romana, *Lettere amorose*
      reprints: 1563, 1565, 1572, 1584, 1594, 1600, 1607, 1612, 1624, 1628
1563 Paola Antonia Negri, *Lettere spirituali*
      reprint: 1576
1580 Veronica Franco *Lettere familiari a diversi*
1584 Camilla Erculiani, *Lettere di philosophia naturale*
1594 Emilia N. Fiorentina, *Lettere affettuose*
1595 Chiara Matraini, *Lettere*
      reprint: 1597
1602 Battistina Vernazza *Opere spirituali[. . .]lettere a diversi*
1607 Isabella Andreini, *Lettere*
      reprints: 1610, 1611, 1612, 1616
1636 Cassandra Fedele, *Epistolae et orationes*
1639 Margherita Costa, *Lettere amorose*
1650 Arcangela Tarabotti, *Lettere familiari e di complimento*

* sources include: Cox, *Women's Writing in Italy, 1400–1650*; Erdmann, Govi, *Ars epistolica*; Ray *Writing Gender*; Robin, *Publishing Women*

The term *incunabula*, from the Latin word for "cradle," refers to all books printed before the year 1501. Among the books that appeared during printing's infancy was a volume of the letters of Catherine of Siena, published in 1492.[40] It was a poor and incomplete edition but was followed in 1500 by a large folio edition with 353 of her letters, published by the prestigious Aldine Press. These letters remained popular reading and went through three more printings over the course of the century: in 1548, 1562, and 1584. Even before the advent of printing, however, Catherine's letters were widely read. From the end of the fourteenth century to the first decades of the fifteenth, fifty-five extant manuscripts of the *Letters* remain as testament to their broad circulation, establishing her as one of the most popular authors of the day.[41]

---

40 In the words of Adriano Prosperi: "Le sue lettere hanno accompagnato generazioni e generazioni di lettori e abitano da tempo ai piani alti del canone della nostra tradizione letteraria e linguistica. Il secolo della stampa si apre con le lettere di Santa Caterina da Siena." "Lettere spirituali," 228.
41 Zaggia, "Fortuna editoriale delle lettere di Caterina," 130. Maria Luisa Doglio writes: "Long before the impressive 1500 edition by the scholar-printer Aldus Manutius, which contained 353 of her letters, which heralded the great century of letters and letter collections, she exerted a strong influence on epistolary writing, and continued to do so in the Renaissance and Baroque periods." "Letter writing 1350–1650," in Panizza and Wood, eds., *A history of women's writing*, 15–16.

How can we account for the enduring appeal of Catherine's letters? Leaving aside their spiritual content, it is their orality, deriving from the dictation process referred to above, that gives the letters a fresh, vibrant quality, as if one were hearing Catherine's voice uttering the lines. This quality of orality, it will be recalled, was something Cicero strived for in his letters. A "dialogue with an absent friend" is how Cicero had defined the familiar letter, writing to his brother Quintus: "when I read your letter I hear your voice, and so, when I write to you I seem to be speaking with you."[42] To achieve this effect of "natural" speech, an author must use humble, everyday vocabulary and uncomplicated syntax rather than elaborate flights of rhetoric. The power of this kind of letter writing derives from the direct emotional impact on the reader of forcefully expressed ideas or feelings, highlighted by vivid depictions of actual people, places, and events. Like Pietro Aretino's account of the death of Giovanni delle Bande Nere, in her description of the execution of Niccolò di Toldo (pp. 33–37), Catherine makes the reader feel like a spectator at the grisly event.

Such letters have an immediacy that is almost journalistic. Aretino himself portrays the process of writing as merely recording what he witnesses in the world, writing in one letter: "I am secretary to Nature herself, who in her simplicity dictates to me that which I compose."[43] One must take care not to accept this statement at face value, however. As Aretino's contemporary Baldassarre Castiglione (1478–1529) wrote in his quintessential Renaissance guide to good taste, *The Courtier*: "One must avoid affectation and practice in all things a certain *sprezzatura*, disdain or carelessness, so as to conceal art, and make whatever is done or said appear to be without effort and almost without any thought about it."[44] The apparent ease and directness of Aretino's compositions, which are the antithesis of the studied formality of the humanist Latin epistle, nonetheless represent a deliberate set of literary choices on the part of the author. Before printing them, authors like Aretino often thoroughly revised or rewrote their letters, sometimes composing brand-new ones for the purpose of publication, years after their supposed dates. Although readers were aware of this, the idea of personal letters as a natural, "artless" form of writing was a belief held by many. Women's letters, in particular, were often seen as raw, unfiltered records of their experience. Unencumbered by a humanist education, most women had no choice but

---

42 "[...] cum tua lego, te audire, et quia, cum ad te scribo, tecum loqui videor." Cicero, *Epistulae Ad Quintum Fratrem*, ed. Bailey, I, i, 35. Chemello discusses the "amicorum colloquia absentium" and aspects of orality in Cicero in *Alla lettera*, ix.

43 "*La natura istessa de la cui semplicità son secretario mi detta ciò che compongo*" (Procaccioli I, 221) translated as "Nature herself, whose simple pleasures I record, dictates to me that which I compose" by Meredith K. Ray, in *Writing gender*, 30. Ray's chapter entitled "Women's vernacular letters in context," pp. 19–42, provides a masterful overview.

44 *The courtier*, Book I, Chapter 26, Charles S. Singleton, trans.

to write in the vernacular, and women were believed to write simply as they spoke, with no thought for rules of literary composition or rhetorical style. This view has persisted. When Catherine of Siena has not been viewed as merely mouthing words placed there by her confessor, she is typically seen as a naïf who poured out random mystic utterances. Under closer examination, however, the letters of Catherine of Siena reveal a rich and varied stylistic palette. In the words of Maria Luisa Doglio: "The distinctive expressive strength of her letters combines with a complex variety of tone. St. Catherine employs both the language of the Holy Scriptures and contemporary idiom. Metaphors drawn from Biblical language and the Epistles of St. Paul mingle with simple expressions about domestic matters and the minutiae of daily life, mystical terminology with popular Sienese dialect."[45]

Thus female authors often crafted their letters as carefully as men did so that they would *appear* natural. However, let us consider for a moment how "natural" it was for women to express their words in print at a time when they were discouraged even from public speech. In the words of Venetian humanist Francesco Barbaro (1390–1454): "the discourses of a woman should not be common, for the speech of such a woman is not less to be feared than the nakedness of the body."[46] A woman's proper sphere was within the home or convent, and in both places she was expected to remain chaste. For a woman to expose her writings to the world, taking part openly in a form of public discourse, was comparable to sexual promiscuity.[47] Although we have seen that many women were writing in Renaissance Italy, the decision to make those writings public was considered as transgressive, especially among certain upper-class circles. Thus both Veronica Gambara (p. 215) and Vittoria Colonna (pp. 168–169), respectable noblewomen, resisted having their individual poetry collections printed. An acquaintance who had unwisely permitted Colonna's *Rime spirituali* to be published complained to her brother Ascanio that "she turned against me because I handed it over to be printed or because I did not prevent it."[48] Colonna made a hand-copied manuscript of the same poems as a gift to her friend Michelangelo but was averse to public

---

45 "Letter writing, 1350–1650" in Panizza and Wood, *A history of women's writing in Italy*, 15. Catherine's possible motivations for choosing to distance herself from the writing process are persuasively argued by Marina Zancan, *Il doppio itinerario*, 114–116.

46 *De re uxoria* (*On wifely duties*), Book II, Chapter 3.

47 As Virginia Cox has pointed out, an exception was made in the case of delivering public orations: "While moral concerns certainly existed regarding women and speech, staged and officially sanctioned displays of female eloquence were socially and morally acceptable." *Women's writing*, 9. Examples of women who delivered public orations were Isotta Nogarola (pp. 67–68), Cassandra Fedele (pp. 45–46), Costanza Varano (pp. 70–71), Battista Sforza (p. 79), and Ippolita Maria Sforza (pp. 189–190).

48 Scarpati, *Le rime spirituali*, 693, n2.

exposure.[49] It is within the context of this taboo on women's participation in the public sphere that we must view the vitriolic slander aimed at Isotta Nogarola, accusing her of committing sexual transgressions, including incest, when she became well known through her writing (pp. 67–68). Margaret King has pointed out that eulogies of female humanists tended to emphasize their chastity over their learning as a way of containing the transgressive power given them through public displays of learning.[50] It is not a mere chance that so many of the Renaissance women who had their literary works printed were courtesans, actresses, and singers, such as Veronica Franco, Tullia d'Aragona, Isabella Andreini, Gaspara Stampa, and Margherita Costa, women who were either professional sex workers or at least accustomed to exhibiting themselves in the public eye.

Considering the social constraints on women's lives, with the strictly gendered division between private (female) and public (male) realms, the "profound anthropological shift" introduced by printed letters takes on even more startling significance. By asserting themselves as published authors, women not only claimed an authority traditionally reserved to men but many also began to speak out on behalf of women as a whole. The "woman question," the so-called *querelle des femmes* of women's rightful place in society, had been raised since antiquity and before the advent of print had found one of its most forceful exponents in Christine de Pizan (c. 1364–c. 1430), in her 1405 *Book of the City of Ladies*.[51] Now, through the medium of print, in their letters and in other writings, women were able to present feminist points of view to a broader audience. Some of the women who expressed these views in the form of familiar letters as well as formal epistles, in both the vernacular and Latin, were Laura Cereta (pp. 91–92), Isabella Andreini (pp. 149–150), Arcangela Tarabotti (pp. 205–206), and Veronica Franco (pp. 144–145).

There is a sense, however, in which women's letters from this period can be termed "natural" in the sense of "authentic" or "unstudied." While some Renaissance women used the written word to voice polemics and enter into the arena of public debate or, in the case of female rulers, to write letters of state, the vast majority had more common, everyday objectives in mind when they sat down to write a letter. Marriage customs in Italy at the time dictated that once a woman was married and left her parents' home for her husband's she belonged to her husband's household. This often led to a severing of ties with a woman's birth family, leaving her feeling isolated, regardless of the actual physical distance.

---

49 There may also have been an element of avoiding undue attention from religious authorities; see pp. 168–169 on Colonna's reformist ideology.

50 King, *Humanism, Venice, and women*, and King and Rabil, eds., *Her immaculate hand*, 12–13.

51 Pizan was born in Venice but moved while very young to France. Both her parents were humanists. The best summary of the history of the *querelle des femmes* debate is the editors' introduction to the series "The other voice in early modern Europe," to be found at the outset of each volume.

With the advent of the Italian Wars in the late fifteenth century and ensuing economic crises, the population throughout the peninsula was becoming more mobile, causing more women to be separated from their families, and for many the only way to maintain even a tenuous connection was through letters. Moreover, women were frequently separated from their husbands, who, whether fighting in these wars, traveling as merchants, or exiled for political reasons, were forced to spend long periods away from home. Information concerning the management of property, livestock, and businesses had to be communicated between husband and wife by means of writing. Women such as Pandolfina Baglioni (p. 129), Cassandra Chigi (pp. 141–142), Guglielmina Schianteschi (pp. 112–113), and Alessandra Strozzi (pp. 131–132), who otherwise would perhaps have had little need in their daily lives to put pen to paper, found themselves writing frequent letters to distant mothers, sons, and husbands. There is an unguarded quality to these letters, written by women under physical, emotional, and financial duress, who express themselves directly and "naturally." Unlike the women whose writings were published in the letter books mentioned above, none of these letters was composed with literary intent. Indeed, few of these day-to-day letters have found their way into print, and those few have been published only centuries later because of the interest of modern historians.[52] Armando Petrucci has described the "disturbing novelty" these women's everyday communications brought to letter writing. The content of their letters, with descriptions of illnesses, loneliness, and family problems, carried a strong "emotional charge," in Petrucci's words. Often with no thought for niceties of handwriting or stylistic concerns, these women used whatever language came to hand to best express their situation.[53]

A RENAISSANCE OF ONE'S OWN

" […] the dead poet who was Shakespeare's sister will put on the body which she has so often laid down […]"

Virginia Woolf, A Room of One's Own, *1929*

---

52 For instance, Alessandra Strozzi and Margherita Datini.
53 "Esse spesso riversano nella loro corrispondenza scritta una forte carica emotiva, che si manifesta nella narrazione minuta, e si direbbe compiaciuta, delle loro malattie e sofferenze fisiche e nervose, dovute alla solitudine, ai contrasti all'interno del nucleo familiare, alla necessità di cure […] esponendo ad altri, sia pure in modi turbati, la loro personale e sofferta esperienza […] Questa, in un certo senso, è la novità introdotta dalla corrispondenza scritta femminile nell'epistolografia 'ordinaria' dell'Europa moderna. Anche perché le donne scriventi irruppero in quel quadro, apparentemente ordinate da regole precise, grafiche e testuali, con sconvolgenti novità che investirono sia il contenuto e il linguaggio epistolare, sia le forme grafiche e materiali delle lettere da loro scritte." Armando Petrucci, *Scrivere lettere*, 101–102.

Who were the great women writers of the past? Virginia Woolf suggested that if Shakespeare had a sister, she might have been a brilliant poet yet she would have died unknown, like so many women whose social roles kept them from accomplishing great things. Along the same lines, in 1971 Linda Nochlin posed the hypothetical question: "Well, if women really are equal to men, why have there never been any great women artists (or composers, or mathematicians, or philosophers, or so few of the same)?" and provided a nuanced exploration of the various social factors that have kept women from achieving in these fields at the same level as men.[54] Focusing on the Renaissance, in 1977 Joan Kelly went even further, suggesting that during this period of extreme cultural flowering, women's agency and self-expression were actually curtailed compared to earlier eras, answering her own question "Did women have a Renaissance?" in the negative.[55] It is undeniable that the majority of women who lived in Italy during the period known as the Renaissance possessed neither the political nor economic power of their male counterparts, and that the fields of the arts, sciences, and humanist studies were overwhelmingly dominated by men. However, scholarship over the recent decades has revealed much about women's contributions to society and the arts during the Renaissance that had previously escaped notice, causing scholars to reevaluate Kelly's provocative statement.

For instance, we now know that the many women who became nuns—as much as half of the female population of sixteenth-century Florence[56]—made important contributions to Renaissance society and culture from behind convent walls. Beyond the devout writings of prominent holy women and the pervasive spiritual influence of so-called living saints,[57] we are continually learning more about nuns' roles in pharmacology, printing, theater, and a variety of art forms.[58] There has also been a wave of studies on notable female artists, musicians, and patrons, as well as numerous academic conferences and museum exhibits, such as the 1990 show *Italian women artists from Renaissance to Baroque: four centuries of women's art* at the National Museum of Women in the Arts in Washington.[59] Digital projects such as IDEA, the Isabella d'Este Archive, and

---

54 Nochlin. "Why have there been no great women artists?" 22–39, 67–71.
55 Kelly, "Did women have a Renaissance?" 19–50.
56 King, *Women of the Renaissance*, 82.
57 Zarri, "Living saints: a typology of female sanctity in the early sixteenth century," in Bornstein and Rusconi, eds., *Women and religion*, 219–303.
58 Strocchia, "The nun apothecaries of Renaissance Florence" and *Nuns and nunneries in Renaissance Florence*; Weaver, *Convent*; Lowe, *Nuns' chronicles*.
59 See for example the suggested readings for chapters concerning Artemisia Gentileschi, Lavinia Fonatana, Francesca Caccini, as well as Jonathan Nelson, ed., *Suor Plautilla Nelli (1523–1588): the first woman painter of Florence*. Florence: Cadmo, 2000; Reiss and Wilkins, eds., *Beyond Isabella*; and Strunck, ed., *Medici women as cultural mediators*.

the Medici Archive Project's Jane Fortune Research Program on Women Artists in the Age of the Medici promise to produce much material for future research on women's role as artists and patrons of the arts in the Renaissance.[60] All of this work has caused a reassessment of their cultural contributions and is constantly stimulating new research.

But it is especially in the area of literature that women emerge as major protagonists in Renaissance culture. With the many groundbreaking volumes produced by Margaret King and Albert Rabil for *The other voice in early modern Europe 1300–1700* series[61], we now possess works for the first time in English translation by authors such as Gaspara Stampa, Laura Terracina, Isabella Andreini, Veronica Gambara, Lucrezia Marinella, Vittoria Colonna, Antonia Pulci, Moderata Fonte, Veronica Franco, and dozens of other female writers. The irony is that over the centuries their works have fallen from the Renaissance literary canon; all these women in their day were celebrated authors whose poetry, plays, treatises, dialogues, and letters were published in numerous editions and widely read. If there is any area in which women most definitely "had a Renaissance" it was in the field of literature. Indeed, since nothing like this had ever taken place either in the ancient or medieval world, Virginia Cox has pointed out that rather than calling women's literary production a "Renaissance" or "rebirth," the phenomenon ought to be simply called a "*naissance*" or "birth."[62]

CRITERIA OF SELECTION FOR LETTERS AND EDITORIAL CONCERNS

W omen's letters in particular are fascinating to study not only because they are a testament to their active participation in a much-admired Renaissance literary genre, but also for what such documents can reveal of the lives of the letter writers themselves. My goal in this volume was not merely to create an anthology of fine letter writing but to choose letters whose contents provide snapshots of individual women's lives and illuminate aspects of Renaissance society and culture as experienced by women as a whole. I have tried to gather interesting samples of all the various types of letters described in the previous pages, from the most eloquent humanist epistles written in Latin to the humblest vernacular letters. In terms of social class, the majority of the letter writers come from decidedly

---

60 Isabella d'Este Project www. http://isabelladeste.ucsc.edu/; Medici Archive Project http://www.medici.org/.

61 Published by the University of Chicago Press; the Centre for Reformation and Renaissance Studies; and Iter: Gateway to the Middle Ages and the Renaissance.

62 Cox, *Women's writing*, xiii.

privileged backgrounds. I could have included letters written to persons of power by women lower down on the social ladder; there are hundreds of such petitions to the Medici and other courts to be found in the archives. However, these are highly repetitive and not particularly interesting to read, not nearly as interesting as personal letters. This is not to say that no personal letters were written by any but elite women, but to be preserved, letters had to be either printed or collected in a family or state archive. It is something of an exception for personal correspondence on a more humble level to survive. The letter of Cecilia Liconella to nobleman Nicolò de Lazara (pp. 164–165) is just such an exception, as are those of Cornelia Collonello (pp. 217–220) and Margherita Aratori (pp. 221–222).

As regards the period of time covered, I have set rather broad parameters for this Renaissance collection. The earliest letter, that of Catherine of Siena, written in 1375, is more or less in tune with what most historians would now agree was the beginning of the Italian Renaissance, an era of cultural resurgence following the devastation of the Black Death in 1348. However, several of the selections in this volume exceed by a century or more what is generally understood as the peak of High Renaissance culture in Italy. Michelangelo, who outlived almost every other Renaissance artist, died in 1564, after all. It is my belief that in examining women's history, traditional chronological limits may not always apply. As Joan Kelly rightly remarked, "events that further the historical development of men, liberating them from natural, social, or ideological constraints, have quite different, even opposite, effects upon women."[63] We see this, for example, in the case of the Counter-Reformation, a time generally accepted as inimical to free speech, in which plentiful writings were produced by Italian women, many of them advocating reform of the Catholic Church.[64] Carla Hesse, in *The Other Enlightenment: How French Women Became Modern* (Princeton University Press, 2001) approaches the issue as it relates to the period of the Enlightenment. Hesse's answer to the implicit question: "Did women have an Enlightenment?" is essentially yes—but not at the same time as the traditional Enlightenment, and played out in different terms. Thus, I expanded the traditional time limits of the Renaissance; I could not leave out the generation of outspoken and accomplished creative women whose lives spanned the first half of the seventeenth century, including Artemisia Gentileschi (pp. 227–228), Francesca Caccini (pp. 201–202), Margherita Costa (pp. 179–180), and Arcangela Tarabotti (pp. 205–206). With Tarabotti, especially, it seems that the Renaissance for women is brought full circle. Her powerful voice, used to hurl protest against a

---

63 Op. cit., Kelly, 19.
64 Cox, *The prodigious muse.*

society that kept her imprisoned in a convent, provides an interesting counter-point to a much earlier powerful voice, that of Catherine of Siena. The latest chronological selection in the volume is a letter by Elena Lucrezia Corner Piscopia from 1679. I hope I will be excused for stepping slightly outside the chronological boundaries I have set to celebrate her exceptional academic achievements and to indicate, as if in a coda, possibilities then opening up for women.

Nonetheless, the majority of letters in this volume fall within the central period of the sixteenth century, during the 1530s and 1540s, which Virginia Cox identifies as the peak of women's literary activity in Italy.[65] Moreover, to be as representative as possible, I have also attempted to include not only women from the large urban centers of Florence, Venice, Rome, Milan, and Naples, but also those from smaller cities and towns, the countryside, and courts, covering a broad geographical territory, with women from as many regions on the Italian Peninsula as possible. (See map following Table of Contents on page x.) In the interests of maintaining geographical, chronological, and thematic balance there are many women whose letters I had to leave out of this collection—women such as Ginevra Nogarola (fl. 1436), Tommasina Fieschi (c. 1448–1534), Eleonora Gonzaga della Rovere (1493–1550), Battistina Vernazza (1497–1587), Osanna Andreasi (1449–1505), Alfonsina Orsini de' Medici (1472–1520), Caterina Cibo Varano (1501–1557), Giovanna d'Aragona Colonna (1500–1577), Isabella Villamarini (1503–1559), Isabella Bresegna (1510–1567), Giulia Gonzaga (1513–1563), and Alfonsina Livia Vernazza (1590–1655), all of whom wrote letters, many of them fascinating, but there was simply no more room in this vol-ume.[66] Of the women whose letters did find their way into this collection, I had qualms about sometimes including short, relatively minor letters written by particularly accomplished authors. Taking as examples Vittoria Colonna and Veronica Gambara, among the hundreds of their letters to choose from, rather than exquisite examples of epistolary style, potent expressions of feeling, or descriptions of striking contemporary events, the two brief letters were chosen as illustrative of these women's interest in the visual arts, and especially to highlight Colonna's close relationship with Michelangelo. If short selections such as these whet the reader's appetite, the suggestions for further reading provide a brief bibliography of relevant primary sources, mostly in English whenever possible.

---

65 Cox, *Women's writing*, xiii–xiv.

66 On these women's letters see Mercati, "Lettere di Elisabetta e di Leonora Gonzaga"; Daniela Solfaroli Camillocci, "La monaca esemplare. Lettere spirituali di madre Battistina Vernazza (1497–1587)," in Zarri, ed., *Per lettera*, 235–261; Festa and Roncelli, eds., *Osanna Andreasi da Mantova*; Feliciangeli, *Notizie e docu-menti sulla vita di Caterina Cibo-Varano*; Chiomenti Vassalli, *Giovanna d'Aragona*; Cosentini, "Una dama napoletana del XVI secolo: Isabella Villamarino"; Mostaccio, *Osservanza vissuta, osservanza insegnata: la domenicana genovese Tommasina Fieschi*; Amante, *Giulia Gonzaga*; Dooley, *A mattress maker's daughter.*

When studying the history of Renaissance women one encounters problems that rarely come up with their male counterparts. One of these is names. Often in official documents such as a family's tax declarations the names of female members of the household were not reported. In the case of Lorenzo de' Medici this is not a problem as we know the identity of his mother—Lucrezia Tornabuoni. In the case of lesser-known figures the problem becomes more serious. The Pistoian nobleman Niccolò Baldinotti, for instance, in his 1427 Catasto declaration lists as a dependent merely "my wife who is pregnant," providing neither her name nor her age.[67] Brigida Baldinotti (pp. 38–39), who authored two of the most popular vernacular epistles in fifteenth-century Florence, is always identified as "the widow of Niccolò Baldinotti," yet frustratingly there is no positive documentation of her birthdate or of her death.

Another problem with women's names is that they usually do not appear in genealogies. Family trees by tradition have been constructed to show the male line of descent, usually indicating at most the year of marriage and sometimes the wife's name; rarely is her date of birth or death included. Likewise, with offspring, it is the male children who are carefully documented, with girls either sketchily indicated or completely left out. Careful archival research can sometimes turn up additional biographical information. It seems that like many other Florentines, Lorenzo de' Medici rounded out the age of his mother in official documents; thus, the birthdate of the most prominent female figure in Renaissance Florence, Lucrezia Tornabuoni, can be firmly established only by consulting her father's registration of the date of her birth in his investment for her in the dowry fund.[68] But even this type of documentation can be lacking for women in this time period. For Marietta Corsini, married to Niccolò Machiavelli, we have dates for her birth and marriage but not her death. After her famous husband's death, Marietta fades into obscurity, leaving no further trace in the historical record.

Furthermore, in the Renaissance, a woman's last name had a feminine ending, with the vowel "a"; thus, Veronica Franco was known in the sixteenth century as Veronica Franca. Although modern scholars have tended to change these endings to the standard masculine ending in most cases, some women's names have tended to retain the feminine ending, such as Laura Battiferra and Laura Cereta. Most Italian women, then as now, retain their maiden names, so

---

67 Archivio di Stato di Firenze, Catasto 226.
68 Salvadori, 3, n. 2. See also Kirshner, *Pursuing honor*. On misreporting women's ages in official documents see Molho, "Deception and marriage strategy"; on rounding of children's ages and gender imbalance of reporting children in the Catasto see Klapisch-Zuber, "Childhood in Tuscany," in *Women, family, and ritual*, esp. 100–103.

Lucrezia Tornabuoni and Maria Salviati, although both married to Medici men, are generally known by the names of their birth families. Once again, however, by scholarly usage, certain women, such as Alessandra Macinghi and Margherita Bandini, are better known by their married surnames as Alessandra Strozzi and Margherita Datini. Women's names also change when they become nuns; for instance, Maria Maddalena de' Pazzi, who was baptized Caterina but known as Lucrezia by her family, later took the monastic name Maria Maddalena. But what to call Galileo's daughter Virginia, whom he never legitimized? Her mother's name was Marina Gamba, so by all accounts she ought to be called Virginia Gamba. Her chosen religious name was Maria Celeste, with no surname. As she is best identified through her father, I have compromised by calling her Virginia Galilei for biographical references, but I often refer to her as Maria Celeste, the name she used when signing her letters. In the case of Caterina Benincasa, who since her canonization is generally known as St. Catherine or St. Catherine of Siena (to distinguish her from St. Catherine of Alexandria) or as Catherine of Siena (Caterina da Siena), I have likewise used her birth name for her biography but tend to refer to her as Catherine of Siena, which seems simpler. Whenever in doubt I have decided in this book to follow Virginia Cox's usage from *Women's Writing in Italy 1400–1650*.

Other concerns involve translation. For one thing, the conventions of Renaissance Italian epistolary style often have an elaborate, stilted feeling when translated into modern English. Take for example the salutations of three daughters to their mothers:

> *Magnifica ac generosa domina domina et mater amantissima post humiles comendationes etc. (Magnificent and Generous Lady and Most Beloved Mother, I Offer My Humble Esteem, etc.)*
>
> > *Pandolfina Baglioni (p. 129)*

> *Ill.ma princeps et Ex.ma domina d. mea et mater metuendissima (Most Illustrious Princess, Most Excellent and Esteemed Lady Mother)*
>
> > *Ippolita Sforza (p. 190)*

> *Madonna mia madre honoranda (My Honored Lady Mother)*
>
> > *Cassandra Chigi (p. 142)*

The content of all three of the above letters following the salutation is warm and decidedly less formal; however, each of the letter writers felt obliged to follow correct form in her salutation. Even today when we write letters we begin with formalities such as "Dear Sir or Madam" and end with words such as "Yours truly" or "Sincerely yours," forms of address that have little to do with actual spoken discourse. We merely accept that these are appropriate ways to begin and end a letter. Furthermore, it must be remembered that in the Renaissance, receiving a letter was a momentous event and depending on the circumstances of writer and recipient, letters were often read aloud before family members, guests, or members of a court, implying a certain performative element. Like the overture before the curtain goes up on an opera and its final crashing chords, a letter was meant to begin and end with a flourish. Thus, letters end with phrases such as "I kiss your hands" and "I am your humble servant." Parents are conventionally addressed as "Your Lordship" or "Your Ladyship," and in Italian the respectfully formal "voi" rather than the informal "tu" is generally used when addressing them.

Aside from the usual difficulties in translating archaic speech, given the broad range of geographical areas, there are regional dialect variations that complicate the translator's task. Women's lives often involved moving from one area of the peninsula to another, and their language reflects these geographical dislocations. Eleonora d'Aragona (pp. 109–110), for instance, writes an Italian that is inflected with both the Neapolitan she spoke as a girl and the Ferrarese dialect of her husband's court. Ippolita Maria Sforza's (pp. 189–191) writing, although not as linguistically complex as d'Aragona's, does reflect both her Milanese upbringing and her married life in the Kingdom of Naples. As previously mentioned, there was not one standardized form of Italian for most of the period covered in this book, so spelling and grammar tended to be rather free throughout the peninsula in any case, but the ad hoc approach to writing the vernacular is especially evident in the writing of women, who, as has been mentioned, often had much less formal education than men. Added to this is the difficulty of the subject matter of some women's letters; writers such as Cassandra Chigi (pp. 141–143) use idiomatic terms to describe daily life, mentioning everyday items such as clothing, household goods, and foods, many of which resist translation. The letters of Chigi to her mother, Gozzadini to her spiritual advisor, and Savorgnan to her lover are all examples of highly personal communications, in which the author employs certain forms of expression understandable perhaps only to the addressee.

Other challenges involve the accessibility of these texts. Because research on women's letter writing in the Italian Renaissance is relatively recent, it is not always easy to find the sources. While many of the letters in this collection are familiar to scholars and have been printed in modern editions in English translation—those of Catherine of Siena, Margherita Datini, Alessandra Strozzi, Laura Cereta, and Isotta Nogarola, to name just a few of the best-known examples—others are decidedly less familiar. Letters written by such women as Ceccarella Minutolo, Maria Savorgnan, Ginevra Gozzadini, Pandolfina Baglioni, Camilla Pisana, and Margherita Sarrocchi are available only in modern

Italian scholarly editions. But many of the letters I have gathered in this volume are virtually unknown today. Some were printed in Italian centuries ago and are extremely difficult to find, such as the letters of Isabella Andreini, Antonia Paola Negri, Margherita Costa, Emilia N. Fiorentina, and Celia Romana, while others have never been printed before at all. Letters in this last group I have had to locate in Italian archives and manuscript collections. Falling within this last category are the letters of Bartolomea degli Obizzi Alberti, Guglielmina Schianteschi, Cassandra Chigi, and Cecilia Liconella. Reading the handwriting of these letters was not always easy. In particular, the letters of Schianteschi and Chigi are in a poor state of conservation; in places the words are barely legible and involve a certain amount of scholarly guesswork to decipher.

Such are the challenges facing the historian, but they are more than compensated when, in reading a woman's letter, one can hear her speaking again after four centuries of silence. This silence, or rather the neglect of Renaissance women's writing, has been due to a number of factors. While not discounting misogyny as a motive behind the choices made by the predominantly male scholars who formed the literary canon, there are at least two reasons, I believe, that women's Renaissance writings have been marginalized. One of these is that, as has been demonstrated, a large part of women's literary production took the form of letter writing, itself a marginalized literary form. *The Cambridge History of Italian Literature*, for instance, has no section on epistolography, and the *Encyclopedia of the Renaissance* has only one page under "Letterbooks," mostly dealing with humanist letters in Latin. Another reason is the subject matter of many women's letters. Sixteenth-century writing as a whole, but in particular its religious writing, has been looked down upon. Literary critics since the nineteenth century have displayed, in the words of Virginia Cox, "an enduring unconcern with the literature of the later sixteenth century, especially the substantial proportion of that literature whose subject matter is religious."[69] I have tried to let these women speak for themselves, expressing their religious convictions, social views, and personal feelings, leaving the reader free to judge whether their writings are worthy to be read. If I have succeeded in restoring these women's voices and perhaps in stimulating further study, the labor will have been worthwhile.

---

69   Cox, *The prodigious muse*, xv.

Chapter One

The Active Versus
the Contemplative Life

The debate over which was preferable, the *vita contemplativa* or the *vita activa*, was central to Renaissance thought. Was it better to live a life immersed in contemplation, whether scholarly or spiritual, or should a person contribute to society, actively involved in business, politics, and other worldly matters? For most people, then as now, it was a matter of reaching a compromise between the two; finding a satisfactory balance between *otium/negotium* was a challenge faced by both men and women. Whereas men had a variety of careers open to them, as merchants, tradesmen, soldiers, artisans, or members of the clergy, women had more limited options, and the alternatives tended to be straightforward: marriage or the cloister. There was, however, room for women sometimes to carve out a compromise and lead satisfying lives that were both active and spiritual, as was the case for members of the tertiary or third orders. These were laypeople affiliated with a religious order such as the Dominicans or Franciscans; they did not take full vows, yet were allowed to wear the religious habit and performed acts of charity such as caring for the sick and needy in the community. Catherine of Siena, a Dominican tertiary, was extreme in her political and religious activism, while others, such as the Mantellate at Florence's Santa Maria Nuova hospital, described by Martin

Luther, who was a patient there, as the "noble women in veils," performed their chores quietly and efficiently. Otherwise, the religious life for a woman meant becoming a nun, taking vows of chastity and obedience, and living the rest of her life within convent walls. Throughout the Renaissance in Italy there was enormous growth in convent populations, due in part to intense dowry inflation, which made it difficult for families to arrange good marriages for all their daughters. Although forced claustration was forbidden, young girls, especially from large families, were often raised in the expectation that they would eventually take monastic vows and were encouraged in that direction, as Maria Maddalena de' Pazzi's letter indicates. Although some, particularly scholars and mystics, preferred life in the convent, many nuns struggled with the often harsh physical conditions and enforced isolation described by Virginia Galilei in her letters to her father (Chapter 8), but few responded as virulently as Arcangela Tarabotti (Chapter 6). A life of contemplation could also mean a secular life devoted to study, but this did not blend well with matrimony, and women who chose to marry usually abandoned their literary activities. Those who chose to pursue their studies while remaining unmarried were sometimes socially ostracized and, like Isotta Nogarola (Chapter 2), lived in the isolation of "book-lined cells."[1] Since a woman during this period was expected to have as many children as possible to offset high infant mortality, sometimes it was not marriage per se but the realities of motherhood that impeded her studies.[2] Olimpia Morata, for instance, continued writing throughout her married life, although there is no way of knowing if she would have done so if she had children. Thus, Cassandra Fedele's letter in response to Alessandra Scala, while it does not resolve the question, eloquently expresses the dilemma that learned women faced. Finally, there is a certain irony in Paola Antonia Negri's letter to Gaspara Stampa, in which the holy woman attempts to convince the singer/poet to turn away from worldly things; Negri herself was a tireless reformer who was actively involved in founding homes for wayward women.

---

1   King, "Book-lined cells".

2   "More than the fact of marriage, it was probably the size of a woman's family that determined the likelihood of her continuing her writing career after marriage. Of the most prominent Italian early modern women writers, many either were childless (Vittoria Colonna, Laura Battiferra, Maddalena Campiglia, Margherita Sarrocchi) or appear to have had just one or two children (Veronica Gambara, Chiara Matraini, Maddalena Salvetti, Lucchesia Sbarra, Lucrezia Marinella). Although women with larger families who continued to write are not unknown, they do appear to be exceptional. It is perhaps relevant to note that of the principal examples in the period examined here, Isabella Andreini, Moderata Fonte, and Veronica Franco (1546–91) all died in their thirties and forties, Andreini and Fonte in childbirth, while the mean age at death of the eleven writers listed above is, by contrast, somewhere in the mid-sixties." Cox, *Prodigious Muse*, 16.

1.

———

Caterina Benincasa describes the execution
of Niccolò di Toldo to Raymond of Capua

"I want no more words, but to find myself beside you on the battlefield, suffering and
fighting until death for truth, for the glory and praise of the name of the Lord, and for
the reform of the Holy Church," wrote Catherine of Siena (1347–1380) to Pope
Urban VI.[3] *The twenty-third child of cloth dyer Jacopo Benincasa and his wife Lapa*
Piacenti, from infancy Caterina Benincasa seemed marked with a special destiny.
Born on the eve of the Black Death, Caterina's twin sister was sent to a wet nurse and
died as a baby, but Caterina, breast-fed by her mother, survived. She experienced her
first mystical vision at the age of six and resolved to devote her life to God. Although
she was reluctant to marry, when she was twelve her parents began pressuring her and
sent Caterina to live with her married sister Bonaventura as an encouragement. When
her sister died in childbirth, Caterina became resolved never to marry; she did not,
however, choose the life of a cloistered nun. Instead she continued to live in prayer and
seclusion within her family's home in Siena; it was there, when she was in her early
twenties, that Caterina spent long periods in isolated meditation and experienced the
vision of her Mystical Marriage with Jesus. Around 1364 she became a Mantellata, *a*
Dominican tertiary, and actively engaged in acts of charity toward the poor and sick
in the community. She was a prominent figure in Siena, with her "physical and public
presence in abbeys, convents, churches, hospitals, piazzas, and council rooms, where
she is said, on various occasions, to have preached, sermonized, prophesied, prayed,
admonished, and taught."[4] *As her renown for holiness grew, Caterina was called upon*
to negotiate political treaties on behalf of her city; she also went as an emissary to the
pope in Avignon, urging him to return to Rome and to reform the Church. Her active
public role was matched by vigorous discipline in her private life, including the fre-
quent practice of fasting, which made it increasingly difficult for her to eat or sleep.
Weakened and emaciated, she died in 1380 at the age of 33 while she was in Rome,
where her body was buried in Santa Maria Sopra Minerva. Her remains were said to
work miracles and were venerated as relics; her head and thumb were transferred to

---

3   Caterina da Siena, *Lettere*, Tommaseo Vol. IV, 132.
4   Tylus, *Reclaiming*, 161.

the Basilica of San Domenico in Siena to be worshipped as relics there. In 1461 she
was canonized as Saint Catherine of Siena.

In this letter Caterina relates her impressions of the final days in the life of a con-
demned man whom she befriended and comforted up until the last moments of the
man's life, including his beheading, at which she was present. The man, who is un-
named in the letter, was most probably a young Perugian by the name of Niccolò di
Toldo, who was tried and found guilty of inciting political discord in Siena. She writes
to the Dominican friar Raymond of Capua (1330–1399), who was assigned to her as
confessor and spiritual guide in 1374. That same year he was by her side in Siena while
she cared for victims of the plague, and he was her companion on various diplomatic
missions, including the 1376 trip to Avignon to meet with the pope. Caterina dictated
many of her writings to Raymond, who wrote her biography and promoted her legacy.
This letter, the original of which has been lost, was probably dictated by Caterina to a
scribe sometime soon after June 13, 1375. The language is visionary and difficult to
render precisely, oscillating between the real ("I waited for him at the scaffold") and
the mystical ("There the sweet bride rests in her bed of fire and blood"), reflecting
the duality of Caterina's life itself.

In the name of Jesus Christ crucified and of sweet Mary.

My dearest and most beloved father and son in Christ,

I Catherine, servant and slave of the servants of God, write to you, recommending myself to you in the precious blood of the Son of God,
wishing to see you submerged and drowned in his sweet blood. This is
what my soul desires: to see you, Nanni, and Jacomo[5] in this blood,
ablaze with His most ardent charity. Son, I see no other remedy for
arriving at those basic virtues we need. Sweetest father, your soul could
not arrive there, this soul of yours on which I have nourished myself.
Not a day passes that I do not dine on that food at the table of the sweet
Lamb, drained of His blood through such ardent love.[6] I am saying that
without being drowned in that blood, you cannot achieve even the
small virtue of true humility, which is born of [self] hatred, and from
hatred turns into love. And thus the soul is born in perfect purity as iron
emerges purified from the furnace.

Thus, I want you to shut yourself within the open [wound in the]
side of the Son of God, which is an open shop, full of such perfume, that

---

5   Two followers of Catherine, perhaps Domincan friars.
6   This is a reference to Holy Communion, the moment during Mass when the worshipper eats the wafer
and drinks wine, partaking symbolically of Christ's body and blood. Raymond would give Catherine Communion often; she would sometimes subsist for long periods of time only on this, eating no other food.

sin itself becomes fragrant there.[7] There the sweet bride rests in her bed of fire and blood, there where the secret of the heart of God's Son is revealed. Oh uncorked barrel, which gives drink and fills every loving desire with drunkenness! You give joy and illuminate all our understanding. You fill our every memory as we weary ourselves, unable to hold or understand or love anything but this sweet, good Jesus, blood and fire, ineffable love! Once my soul has been blessed by seeing you drowned like this, I want you to do as someone who fills a pail with water and then pours it out elsewhere. And so you will spill the water of holy desire on the heads of your brothers and sisters, who are our limbs, bound together through the body of the sweet bride. And beware that that you never draw back, due to the devil's illusions—which I know have given you trouble and will continue to do so—or on account of any human words. Rather, even when you see the very coldest thing, always persevere, until we see blood spread all around with sweet and loving desires.

Get up, my sweetest father, let us sleep no longer, for I hear news that makes me wish for neither bed nor pillow! I have already begun by receiving into my own hands a head, which was sweeter to me than the heart can imagine, than the tongue can speak of, the eye see, or the ear hear. It went as God desired, along with the other mysteries that happened before, of which I do not speak, since it would take too long.

I went to visit the person you know, and he received such comfort and consolation that he confessed his sins and prepared himself very well. And he made me promise that for the love of God I would be with him at the moment of execution. And so I promised and did. In the morning before the bell rang, I went to him and he was greatly consoled. I took him to hear Mass and he received Holy Communion, which he would never again receive. His will was attuned to the will of God and submissive to it. His only remaining fear was that he would not be strong enough at that [final] moment. But the boundless, overflowing love of God tricked him, creating in him such affection and love in his desire for God that he did not know how to be without Him. He said, "Stay with me and do not abandon me; this way I will be alright and die content," as he stayed with his head on my breast. I then sensed boundless joy and a fragrance of his blood, which was not unmixed with the fragrance of my own, which I long to shed for my sweet spouse, Jesus.

---

7   The word *bottega* conjures images of a merchant's shop or storeroom filled with spices.

And as this desire grew within my soul, sensing his fear, I said: "Take comfort, my sweet brother, since we will soon arrive at the wedding celebration. You will go there bathed in the sweet blood of the Son of God, with the sweet name of Jesus, which I want never to leave your mind. And I will wait for you at the place of execution." Imagine now, father and son, that his heart lost all fear and his face transformed from sadness into joy. He was glad and rejoiced, saying: "How is it that there is so much grace for me, that my soul's sweetness will wait for me at the holy place of execution?" You see that he had arrived at a point of such illumination that he called the place of execution "holy"! And he said: "I will go entirely happy and strong; when I think that you will be waiting for me there, it seems like a thousand years until I can go to that place." And he said so many sweet words that one could burst with the goodness of God.

So I waited for him at the scaffold, in continual prayer, in the presence of Mary and Catherine[8], virgin and martyr. Before he arrived I kneeled down, stretching my neck out on the block, but the effect did not come to me there. I prayed and implored Mary that I wanted this favor: in that [final] moment that she would light his way and give peace to his heart, afterward watching over him as he returned to his destination. My soul was so full of the sweet promise made to me, that as I waited there amidst such a huge crowd of people, I could not see anyone.

Then he arrived, like a tame lamb, and seeing me, he began to laugh, and wanted me to make the sign of the cross over him. After he received the sign, I said: "Get down—off to the wedding, my sweet brother! Soon you will be in everlasting life." He lowered himself with great meekness and I stretched his neck out there, kneeling below, reminding him of the blood of the Lamb. From his mouth came only the words "Jesus" and "Catherine," and while saying this, I received his head into my hands. With eyes fixed on divine goodness, I said: "I want it!"

Then was God-and-Man seen, just as one sees the brightness of the sun; and [His side] was open and received the blood into his blood, a fire of saintly desire, given and hidden in his soul through grace; he received the fire of divine charity. After receiving his blood and his desire, [God] received his soul, which he put in the open shop of His side, full of mercy. The first Truth was made manifest, that only through grace and mercy

---

8   St. Catherine of Alexandria was a fourth-century Christian martyr, who, refusing to worship pagan gods, was first tortured on a spiked wheel and then beheaded. Sharing the same name, she would have been Caterina's patron saint.

did he receive it, and not by any other means. Oh how sweet and price-less it was to see the goodness of God! What sweetness and love awaited that soul, departed from its body! The eye of mercy turned toward his soul, when it came to enter His side, bathed in his own blood, worthy of the blood of the Son of God. Thus received by God—who through His power made this powerful deed come to pass—and the Son, Wisdom and Word incarnate gave him [Niccolò] the gift of participating in cru-cified love, with which He [Christ] received *His* painful and disgraceful death, out of the obedience to the Father in service of humankind and all human generations. And the hands of the Holy Spirit enfolded him [Niccolò].[9]

But he did something so sweet, which would win a thousand hearts. I do not marvel at this, since he was already tasting divine sweetness. He turned, as does the bride when she has reached her husband's doorstep; she turns her head and looks back, nodding toward the one who has accompanied her, and by that gesture expresses her thanks.

Now that he was safely put away, my soul rested in peace and quiet, in such a fragrance of blood that I could not bear to remove the blood that had washed over me from him. Alas, miserable wretch that I am! I do not want to say any more. I stayed here on earth feeling the greatest envy. And it seems to me the first stone has been laid. And yet, do not be surprised if I do not impose anything else on you but my wish to see you drowned in the blood and fire that pours from the side of the Son of God. No more negligence then, my sweetest children, as the blood begins to flow and to receive life!

Gentle Jesus! Jesus love!

---

9   Catherine here invokes the doctrine of the Trinity, consisting of Power (the Father), the Word (the Son), and Mercy (the Holy Spirit). Indeed, this passage in particular has the rhetorical cadence of preaching—for instance, the alliterative phrase: "*Così ricevuto da Dio per potenzia, (potente a poterlo fare)*."

2.

Brigida Baldinotti praises the women who serve at Florence's Santa Maria Nuova hospital[10]

Referred to as "the venerable Madonna Brigida, widow of Niccolò Baldinotti of Pistoia," Brigida Baldinotti's (c. 1412–c. 1491) letters were among the most frequently copied vernacular texts in mid-fifteenth-century Florence. She was the daughter of Piero di Benedetto di Messer Rinuccio, a wealthy landowner in Pistoia, who provided an immense dowry for her to marry Niccolò Baldinotti sometime around 1425 or 1426. The Baldinotti clan was noble and dated its lineage back to the tenth century. Extremely influential in local politics, the family featured prominently in Pistoian government, Niccolò serving as prior in 1430. Despite her husband's elevated status, however, Brigida and Niccolò experienced a number of hardships, including a fire in 1427 that destroyed their house and all their possessions, forcing them to move into his brother's home. Their financial situation continually worsened; by 1439 the couple was deeply in debt and forced to take in lodgers and used their connections to borrow money from the Medici. Sometime after 1439 Brigida's husband died, leaving her alone to care for their son Piero. Their daughter had become a nun several years earlier at the Dominican convent of Santa Lucia, an institution with which Brigida had close ties. When Piero eventually married in 1455, Brigida lived with his family, caring for his wife and child—named Niccolò after his grandfather—and tending to business matters for Piero while he was away traveling. Sometime in the 1470s Piero had a falling-out with Lorenzo de' Medici, and in the summer of 1478 both he and his son became involved in a plot to murder the ruler of Florence. The plot was discovered and the conspirators, including Piero, were put to death. Brigida's grandson was sentenced to life imprisonment but was pardoned by Lorenzo by 1481. In addition to the present letter, two other letters written by Brigida Baldinotti have come down to us. One is an epistle with advice to a young woman of the Bardi clan who was about to be married, the other a personal note to her son announcing the birth of his baby daughter.

In this letter Brigida celebrates the dedication of the lay sisters who nursed the sick at the Hospital of Santa Maria Nuova in Florence. The spirituality expressed by laypeople—everyday men and women who had not taken holy orders—and their

---

10   Reproduced with permission from *Speculum*.

important contribution to society was a theme that was very topical at this time in Italy. The two prominent women whom she holds up as examples are Dominican tertiary St. Catherine of Siena (see previous letter) and St. Elizabeth of Hungary (1207–1231), daughter of the king of Hungary, who although married was associated with the Franciscan order and renowned for her charitable deeds and sanctity. This letter, filled with learned quotations from the Bible and Church Fathers, was considered a model of eloquence by contemporaries and circulated in dozens of manuscripts in Florence throughout the fifteenth century, where it is usually described in the title as an "epistle."

Reverend Mothers and dearest Sisters in Christ,

May that divine grace, which makes our works acceptable in the eyes of God, be ever in your souls, and may they be worthy dwelling places for the Holy Spirit. May your souls be a gracious garden for God, for certainly the fresh garden in May adorned with a variety of flowers is never so pleasing to human eyes as is the gracious garden of the soul to eternal God, who is its true gardener. It is worked through sacred contrition, bathed by the supernal dew of devout tears, and bears the whitest roses of virginity as well as the reddest roses of charity, and many perfumed flowers of diverse virtues. How much this delights our heavenly king, hear from what he said with his own holy mouth: "My delights are to be with the sons of man".[11] And in contemplation [of those words], a soul that loved Jesus Christ cried out, saying: "Come, my darling, into his orchard, and eat of his fruits and apples".[12] He did not say "my garden," but "his," because he has worked it and ordered it, and adorned it so nobly with virtue that it is from him that we have all that is good within ourselves. Moreover, St. Paul says that we are not able to think of any good work on our own, but that our abilities derive from our Lord God. And though our earthly minds, weighed down by sins and worldly affections, are not capable of rising up to consider the order and magnificence of the blessed life, nonetheless, as St. Paul the apostle says: "When the creature considers and understands all these lower things, which are visible to us, created by God, by raising up the intellect to these things, one can come to meditate upon the invisible things of God".[13]

As we see in this life, when a great lord or temporal king loves one of his servants, he places that servant in a worthier post, so that he will be honored at court. Oh, most beloved of Jesus Christ, with most ardent love

---

11 Prov. 8.31.
12 Song of Sol. 4.16.
13 Rom. 1.20.

and inflamed affection raise up your mind's eye, giving thanks to God on high, the supreme king, who has chosen you for two of his worthiest offices, and the most honorable in all his court, so that the celestial *patria* may be fittingly honored. One, if I have considered correctly, is the office of holy virginity. How glorious and beloved of God is this virtue. My weak intellect and miserable tongue fail to express all its dignity; but such is its greatness that the Holy Scriptures marvelously exalt it. Heed St. Ambrose, who says: "Virginity takes precedence before all other human qualities for which men are likened to angels".[14] The victory of virgins is greater than that of the angels, because, being spirits, angels live without flesh, whereas virgins triumph over the flesh. Thus it is certain that where there is a greater battle, there is also the greater triumph; hence the humble virgin, she who is a true virgin in body and mind, is surely an angel on earth. But well does Augustine say that a humble wife is better than a proud virgin, as it is most displeasing to God that his own creature would exalt herself in pride for graces and gifts which she does not, in herself, possess, but which come from God; these are granted by him out of his goodness, not through our own merit. Oh, ineffable mercy of God, who in so many inscrutable ways provides for his elect! So that you may keep such a precious treasure whole and immaculate, he has given you continuous exercise, as leisure is the enemy of such a virtue. Thus we see many very delicate virgins, who, lacking exercise to weary them, mortify their delicate bodies with fasts, vigils, and other forms of abstinence in order to be able to preserve that immaculate treasure for God.

As for the second office, for which you have been elected through divine clemency, may it be grand and noble, as we may consider by its result: that on that terrible day of final judgment when we receive the ultimate reward for our works, in all the Holy Scripture there is not to be found anything else by which the highest judge shall examine us if not by our works of mercy, and most of all those done on behalf of the poor. By putting yourselves in the person of the pauper, surrounded by Christ's poor, by exerting yourselves, you shall receive the glorious reward not according to the amount of toil, but according to the greatness of the love that you bring to caring for their needs. Yet it is necessary that charity be mistress and ruler of such an office, so that it will be acceptable to God on high. In vain does a person tire herself out, even if she possesses all the laudable and gracious virtues, if she has no holy charity, without which

---

14 *De virgin.* 1.7.

none of our works can be pleasing to God. Such is its exalted nature that, lacking it, God's creature lacks every other virtue; only excellent charity lives and triumphs with souls in that eternal glory.

Rejoice, therefore, Oh beloved brides and ministers of Jesus Christ, and render him infinite thanks, that through his clemency he deigns to let grace dwell within you. And among yourselves be like the pauper, saying: "What you do unto the lowest beneath me, do unto me".[15] And it never has happened that he has appeared to one of his servants in this life in pomp or as a powerful king, but many a times as a *poverello*, as he appeared to St. Gregory and to St. Paul and to others. And this great favor and boundless love is demonstrated to us every year by the holy church when we sing, on the day of the glorious Nativity of Christ, "Born to us is the redeemer of the world, not as king of glory but as a poor, naked little child; and upon the straw between two animals." And he lived in distress as a poor man for our sins. And finally, for the sake of us miserable ones, we who are ungrateful for so many kindnesses, he from whom all treasures are created died naked upon the Cross. Oh, what agreeable joy your minds will feel, if you think that God eternal decided to leave behind celestial riches, and not out of obligation, but inflamed with love for our well-being, made himself poor and obedient to his creatures! Oh, what inestimable and peaceful jubilation you will savor if, while caring for the sordid wounds of the infirm, you think how Christ desired to be wounded for our sins! This gentle jubilation and most fragrant perfume was experienced by our St. Elizabeth, and so she always desired to care for the wounds of the sick with her own hands. This boundless sweetness was felt by Catherine of Siena, who, caring for a leprous woman, though it seemed to her that the sensuality was somewhat forbidden, assailed by the flame of celestial love, did not so much use her hands to wash it, but putting her mouth there, licked her [wounds clean]. Oh precious, oh pious transformation of lofty God, that, through the stinking wound of his creature, he desired her to put her lips to his most holy rib, to draw out such sweetness and such gentle aroma that never again did she take corporeal food![16]

This is that vast field from which, when sprinkled with pious tears, you will harvest joy, whereas this miserable life resembles winter, with its tempests and many tribulations. It is time to sow with plentiful tears and meritorious acts, so that in the next life, which resembles summer all

---

15 Matt. 25.40.
16 See biographical note on Catherine of Siena pp. 33–34.

serene and gracious, we can gather the fruits of our labors. And so glorious God says to one of his beloved souls: "Come to me, my beloved, winter has already passed, and summer has come".[17] May such contemplations be awakened in your minds, and your hearts be lit aflame in the furnaces of divine love, and living together, all in charity, you will do your work piously and joyously. And by so doing, you will fulfill the words of the prophet who says: "Serve the Lord with joy, because it is not out of fear, but out of love that he wishes to be served." Out of love he gave everything to us, even bitter death on the Cross, and from us he asks nothing but love, saying, "Son, give me your heart".[18] By this he meant not the heart of the flesh, but the effect of the heart, which is love. Thus, not through any corporeal action, but only loving with true love can his creature join with God on high, while in a mortal body; such is the force of this pure and holy love that it transforms the beloved into the lover. Thus one reads of many of God's servants, and I believe that they do still exist, who are so compelled and inflamed by that celestial love that their souls, by force of love, are lifted upwards, joining with that highest good that they love so much; and the body, as if it were dead, remains immobile.

But you must know that such heights cannot be reached if all God's creatures do not love each other out of love of the creator. And yet, beloved daughters and brides of God eternal, if you desire such a priceless gift with charity and love, with a single will, living all together, think how all of you are with God, in his house, selected for the same life and office, and for the same glorious end. Let your hearts and wills then be united in such unity of purpose, and with joy think upon your corporeal toil and its limits, for this life lasts but briefly; indeed, it is almost like a shadow, and the reward is eternal and without end. Rejoice in the saying of the apostle Paul, who says that these corruptible bodies, which shortly will return to ashes and food for the worms, will be clothed anew with the light of glory. Oh sweetest mothers and sisters in Christ, if you diligently carry out your pious office, committed to you by God, with what happiness you may expect to see, once and for always, yourselves all united in that blessed life. In youthfulness and with gracious appearance, dressed not in rough fabrics but in the light of glory, you will shine unbearably, more than the sun. No longer will you nourish the poor, but you shall be nourished by celestial God on a food of ineffable beauty; all

---

17 Song of Sol. 2.11–12.
18 Prov. 23.26.

of our beatitude is contained in that blessed vision. Oh how you will take joy together in the burdens that you have borne when you see yourselves in the company of angels and such multitudes of saints, and not just for a short time, but you will surely remain forever in that inestimable happiness and eternal repose.

You will feel the marvelous joy of beatitude all over again when you see, decked out in such great glory, that multitude of paupers, those you yourselves once cared for with such charitable hands. You once saw them vile and despised on earth, now by merciful God marvelously rewarded. You shall know that many who would have died like beasts, desperate, have attained the blessed life on account of your help and care. They pray for you who have been responsible for their welfare; among those I hope you will surely see your Maddalena[19], whose infirmities you so tenderly cared for. This woman, not wishing to be ungrateful for the favors she received from God and from you, persevered in her good purpose. Merciful God decreed that her desire be fulfilled; thus not only did he will her to give her virginity to her spouse, Jesus Christ, but now in this most holy Easter, by the grace of God, that she should give her whole self to that sweet God who was born for us on that glorious day, poor and full of humility. Stripping herself of worldly things and her own will, clothing herself anew in the holy faith and in humility, she will enter an excellent and devout convent of the rule of St. Dominic. There she will find venerable nuns who never are to be seen, nor ever eat meat, and live in great fear of God. As St. Paul says, "having nothing, they possess everything." Believing as you do, that Maddalena effectively prays to God for you, ah, to think that if she had not been cared for by you she could never have attained holy religion!

Now you see of how much good you were the cause. You must believe that such charity will not pass the sight of God unnoticed. I take the highest pleasure in this, and I feel within myself a most delicate joy at the thought of your spiritual and temporal deeds, to such a degree that I never tire of speaking of your charity and solicitude for the sick. I tell you this not in order that you raise yourselves in pride, but to praise God, as every good deed that is praised grows if it is well grounded in humility. But take care that ingratitude, that ruinous wind, which dries up the fountain of mercy, does not deprive you of such great eternal

19 The identity of this woman is unknown; she was presumably one of the patients at the Hospital of Santa Maria Nuova.

good. Think, my beloved ones, if you remain in true humility, of what vast gifts you will continuously receive from the highest donor, God. Think how many of God's creatures must sweat in the fields all day under great and terrible heat, and also in the greatest cold, badly dressed, and fed even worse; yet all this toil of theirs is worthless because they are not moved by love or fear of God, only by the desire to gather. Now, thinking about this, you will realize how much grace you have received from God eternal, and that if he has placed you in a situation of toil, you cannot take a step that is without great merit if you take it with saintly obedience and with right intentions. Let your souls be nourished by this food, never to be destroyed by thunderstorms, nor the fruit lost to hail. And as our merciful Father has abundantly seen to providing your bodies with the necessities, do not be ungrateful to the supreme giver, all you who are desirous, each according to your ability, to satisfy him and humbly thank him, praying him that he will keep you all together in his holy peace. Since wherever there is peace, there God abides; and whoever has true peace has the foretaste of paradise. Discord is the threshold of that miserable region where there will never be repose. The more one knows and is aware, the more that person must praise God's working and have compassion for those who do not know, while always recognizing indebtedness to God. To whom more is given, more is required. God created everyone, but differently and for different reasons that are evident only to him. Nevertheless, do as St. Paul says: let each one bear the burden of her companion, and thus you shall fulfill Christ's law, which God in his mercy has granted you.

I beg of you, most beloved [sisters] in Jesus Christ, that it please you to pray to God for my miserable little soul. I am always with you in true love, and I rejoice thinking of you, of the welfare of your souls as of my own. And, compelled by your love, I resolved that although my body could not be with you, at least I could meet with all of you by means of this letter so that you might remember me in your prayers. And pray God that, leaving every other thing, I may do his will. For now, nothing else occurs to me to relate. May Christ's peace and the profound emotion of the Holy Spirit be always within your souls.

3.
———

Cassandra Fedele responds to Alessandra Scala's request
for advice on whether to write or marry

After meeting her in 1491, humanist Angelo Poliziano proclaimed himself "amazed."
He described Cassandra Fedele (1465–1558) in a letter to Lorenzo the Magnificent,
saying "she is marvelous in both the vernacular and in Latin." Fedele was Venice's most
prominent female public intellectual; during her lifetime her reputation for humanist
learning overshadowed even that of Isotta Nogarola (pp. 67–68) and Laura Cereta
(pp. 91–92). She was born in Venice, to Barbara Leoni and Angelo Fedele, who be-
longed to the non-noble yet highly respected citizen class, which held most public offices
and produced some of the city's finest humanists. Cassandra was sent at an early age to
be educated in a convent where, in addition to sewing, vernacular reading, and writing,
she was taught the basics of Latin from a learned nun. An accomplished scholar himself,
Fedele's father had Cassandra study Greek, rhetoric, history, philosophy, and theology
with the learned Servite monk and astronomer Gasparino Borro. He also promoted her
career by sending copies of her writings to the humanist Tomaso of Milan. From her
early twenties, the young woman delivered public orations; her first was the Oratio pro
Bertucio Lamberto, *at the University of Padua in 1487. Although women were not*
allowed to study there, Fedele was chosen to address this group of male scholars on the
occasion of her cousin who was being awarded a degree in philosophy. The speech was
printed that same year and again in 1488 and 1489, winning Fedele recognition
throughout Italy. She delivered her second speech, De laudibus literarum *(In Praise of*
Letters), before the Doge and the Senate of Venice on the occasion of the visit of an offi-
cial delegation from Bergamo. So great was her reputation for eloquence that Queen
Isabella and King Ferdinand of Spain repeatedly offered her a position at the Spanish
court. Although she may have wanted to go to Spain, especially as she was in straitened
financial conditions without a stable patron, the Doge forbid her to accept. In 1500
Fedele married the physician Giammaria Mappelli and in 1515 the two went to live in
Crete, where Mappelli had a publicly funded salary. Five years later, on the return trip,
the couple nearly died in a shipwreck, in which all their belongings were lost. Soon after
their return to Venice in 1520, Fedele's husband died; unable to find work as a teacher
or writer she was once more plunged into financial difficulties. Finally, with the help of
Pope Paul III, Fedele found a position as director of the orphanage of San Domenico in
Castello, where she remained until the end of her life. During her widowhood, Fedele

may have worked on three writings that have not survived: Moral Reflections, On the Order of the Sciences, *and* Eulogies of Famous Men. *Two years before her death at age ninety-three, Fedele gave her last public speech on the occasion of the arrival in Venice of Bona Sforza, queen of Poland. Although her many letters and orations circulated widely in manuscript form during her lifetime, they were only published posthumously, nearly a century later (*Epistolae et orationes posthumae, *ed. G. F. Tommasini, Patavii 1636). At her death, Cassandra Fedele was honored by the Venetian Senate with a state funeral and a tomb with a funerary monument recognizing her exceptional cultural contributions.*

Fedele was at the height of her fame when she wrote this letter to Alessandra Scala (1475–1506). A poet and brilliant scholar of Greek, Alessandra was the daughter of the learned Florentine chancellor Bartolomeo Scala (1430–1497). Father and daughter were linked to the circle of intellectuals, poets, and artists who gathered around Lorenzo the Magnificent. Alessandra drew attention for her recitation in Greek of the part of Electra in Sophocles' tragedy, which Angelo Poliziano enthusiastically described in a letter to Cassandra Fedele. Only two works by Alessandra Scala survive, a Greek epigram written to Poliziano and a very brief Latin letter to Cassandra Fedele. The present letter is a response to a request for advice from the younger woman, who is at a crossroads in her life; however, Fedele refrains from pronouncing a judgment. Two years later Scala married Michele Marullo, a Greek poet. When he drowned in an accident several years later, Scala joined the convent of San Pier Maggiore in Florence, where she lived the rest of her life. Marriage made a serious impact on the intellectual productivity of both women; neither of them to our knowledge produced much writing after they were married.

> From your very elegant letter I saw clearly that you did not judge ours to be a commonplace friendship (a judgment which gave me great pleasure), since you wanted not only for me to know everything about you, but also to advise you on these same matters.
>
> And so, my Alessandra, you are uncertain whether to dedicate yourself to the Muses or to a Man? On this matter I think that you must choose that to which nature made you more disposed. For Plato maintains that any advice which is received is received according to the readiness of the receiver. For this reason, it will be very easy for you to make that choice, whereas no violently imposed decision lasts forever.
>
> Farewell.
>
> January 18, 1492

4.

———

Paola Antonia Negri urges Gaspara Stampa to choose
the life of the spirit over worldly life

Paola Antonia Negri (1508–1555), "one of the most controversial female figures with
a cult in the first half of the sixteenth century," [20] *was born Virginia Negri, the youngest*
child of a schoolteacher from a small town in Lombardy. Around 1520 she moved with
her family to Milan. Their home was near Santa Marta, a convent of Augustinian
nuns, who were known for their devoutly contemplative and mystical spirituality; the
abbess Arcangela Panigarola (1483–1525), was renowned for her prophetic visions.
Growing up under their influence profoundly shaped the young woman's spiritual for-
mation. Several years after the death of Panigarola, Virginia and two of her sisters
joined the noblewoman Ludovica Torelli (1500–1569) and a group of women who
formed a religious community known as the Angelic Sisters (le Angeliche) associated
with the male Barnabite Order. In 1536 Negri was one of the first to take her vows,
changing her name to Paola Antonia, and because of her charisma and spiritual vision
soon came to be revered as the leader of the Angelics. Not merely focused on contempla-
tion, under Negri's direction the order also founded a number of charitable institu-
tions, including hospitals and orphanages. They had a specific mission to reform and
care for "wayward women," and thus they went to the Veneto region, which was notori-
ous for prostitution (see p. 145 in Chapter 4, Veronica Franco) to open a number of
women's shelters. In 1537 Negri and the others established a home known as the Insti-
tute of the Converted Women of Saint Mary Magdalen (Istituto delle Convertite di S.
Maria Maddalena), and the following year they founded a hospital called the Derelitti
(the "derelict" or "abandoned") in Venice. Known by the names "Divine Mother" and
"Mother Mistress," by 1539 Negri's reputation for sanctity had grown, and large
crowds began gathering to hear her prophecies and interpretations of the Scriptures. In
the following decades of increasingly restrictive Tridentine [21] *control, Negri was accused*
of the heresy of Illuminism, promoting one's own version of divine enlightenment over
Church doctrine. In 1551 she and the entire order were ejected from Venetian terri-
tory. [22] *The following year members of the order were tried by the Inquisition and Negri*

———

20 Zarri, "Living saints," 231.
21 Council of Trent, 1545–1563.
22 It has been debated whether the Venetian ban on the order was motivated primarily on religious or political grounds, as the Angelics and the Barnabites were suspected of spying on behalf of Milan.

was condemned for "scandalous behavior." The Angelic sisters were forced into enclo-
sure and Negri was separated from them, taken to a Clarissan convent where she was
kept in strict isolation. She remained inside the convent until she became gravely ill;
when at last she was released, she died several months later. In the years following her
death, members of the order sought alternately to restore her reputation or to condemn
her, distancing themselves from the controversial founding figure.

Negri's letters were first published in 1564, but that printing had been halted
by the Inquisition; the collection was later censored, enlarged, and republished in
1576. That same year, a superior of the order, Giovanni Pietro Besozzi (1503–1584),
who had worked closely with Negri, wrote condemning her for abuse of her power, for
sexual misconduct, and for mystic visions that he asserted were inspired not by God
but by the devil. Besozzi furthermore claimed that he, not Negri, had written these
letters, although it is now believed that this correspondence was the product of col-
laboration between the two. The present letter is addressed to Gaspara Stampa
(1523–1554), a celebrated poet whose Petrarchan-style sonnets were first published
in 1553. Stampa was also well known as a virtuoso singer who performed at elegant
Venetian social gatherings, and it is believed she may have been a courtesan.

What marvel is there, oh dearest soul, most charming in the purest
blood of Jesus Christ, that I would love you as much as He loved you, He
who voluntarily delivered Himself to such a bitter and painful death out
of excessive love? If the creator loves you so much, why ought I not love
you, miserable creature that I am? If He was pleased to adorn you with
abundant graces, in order to make you pleasing to Him, why should
I too not be pleased by the wonderful works, which He has carried out in
you? If only in His goodness, He would make me worthy of perfecting
that lovely work, which He has begun in you. I am certain that He will,
if you wish it, and I hope you do wish it, because so many have spoken to
me of your noble spirit. I cannot believe that you would want to follow
the foolish ways of others who, gathering up gifts and graces bestowed
on them, become infatuated and so puffed up with pride that they make
idols out of those graces. They want to be adored, made much of, and
focus their every effort on pleasing the world and other men. And they
gratify themselves, their own senses, giving in to sensual pleasures and
other abominable desires, using the gifts God gave them to offend and
revile Him. If they could even more licentiously serve their own un-
bounded desires, ambitions, and other vices they would elect to do so, as
if neither God, nor the soul existed.

I pray that this never descends on your sweet soul, but that you are
always grateful for the graces bestowed on you, so that you are made

worthy for even greater graces. Remember, most beloved sister, that the graces you possess were given to you in order that you could more perfectly honor God, in order for you to become all spirit, an angel incarnate. Now, what evil it would be if, with such gifts and graces, you withdrew from God who created you and recreated you in the precious blood of His Son, and you gave yourself over to the illusive ambitions, vanities, and sensual pleasures of the world. Recognize, O recognize the beauty, the dignity, and excellence in your gentle spirit and seek to increase it by making it entirely divine through holy virtues. Remember that all these [worldly] goods are carried away with the wind and after death nothing remains but sorrow and cruel torment if you have not made good use of them. These virtues that the world honors give the soul nothing but a fleeting contentment that comes from admirers' praises, and once our eyes are closed in their final sleep, they are dead as well. But true virtues, holy, Christian virtues adorn the soul, they ennoble, enrich, embellish, and beatify it both in the present and in future life. Of what worth are those virtues, which when we die, die with us? How much worthier, more useful, and desirable is the virtue that always accompanies the soul and never abandons it, but always brings it new crowns, new palms, new triumphs! Oh God, can I believe that my loveable little Gaspara could be so unwise that she would not know how to make the correct choice, and would renounce heavenly goods for earthly ones? Oh, some will say to me that they want both and I reply, or rather it is our Lord who replies that no one can serve two masters.[23] Paul answers, saying that an unmarried woman who is a virgin thinks of those things that belong to the Lord, so that she will be holy in body and spirit. And the married woman thinks of worldly things and how to please her husband.[24] For pity's sake, dear soul, study how to be very chaste, very humble, very patient and full of the other saintly virtues, so that you may please your heavenly spouse, whose chaste embraces give more contentment to the soul than all the pleasure that are to be had outside of Him. And you, to whom He has given such graces, can you not with His help and grace make yourself fit to enjoy that [contentment] always? Would you then refuse such a blessing? Ah, for the love of God, no, blessed soul, redeemed at such a high price, no, rather leave all others behind and embrace Him. Do not let it

---

23 Matthew 6:24; Luke 16:13.
24 Corinthians 1, 7, 34.

bother you if you disappoint the world in its expectations of you. Whoever tries to convince you otherwise is no friend of yours, but feigns and flatters for some purpose of his own and out of evil intent. Open your eyes and look above you and do not believe the flatterers, those who love you in the way of the flesh. Do not let yourself be fooled, I pray you; cut yourself off from those behaviors and conversations, which alienate you from Christ. They place you in danger, possibly putting under suspicion that lovely decency, which in you outshines all other virtues, and for which I said that you ought not to marvel that I love you. I love you and will love you always. If you love Him, He who loves you so greatly, and not only with words, but with your blood, with your life and soul, I will be content. I will not draw away when it is within my ability to bring you help on the course of virtue. May He who has begun this in you, give you [the ability] to carry it through; through His grace make yourself familiar, by holy contemplation, with the torments and pains that He underwent for you. Withdraw for some time from other occupations in order to spend your time at the feet of your Savior—please do this so that you will be made worthy to receive the true light and real awareness of the will of God in you—train yourself in this way and pray for me. Greet both your mother and sister. Our Lady greets you; hail, spirit shaped in paradise, for you were familiar with that place until your pilgrimage here [on earth] and after [death] it will be your eternal dwelling. From the sacred place of San Paolo Apostolo in Milan on the 20th of August, 1544.

Yours entirely in Jesus Christ,
Antonia Paola Negri

5.

_____

Olimpia Fulvia Morata to Celio Secondo Curione
on "giving birth" to her writings

A brilliant humanist and an outspoken religious reformer, Olimpia Fulvia Morata
(1526–1555) was born in Ferrara, one of five children (four daughters and a son) of
Lucrezia Gozi and Fulvio Peregrino Morato. Her father was a university professor
who taught classical literature to the sons of Duke Alfonso d'Este. Recognizing that
from an early age Olimpia demonstrated an unusual gift for learning, her father taught
her Greek and Latin, so that by the age of twelve not only was she proficient in reading
and writing, but she could speak both ancient languages fluently. Between the ages of
twelve and thirteen Olimpia lived at court as the companion of Anne d'Este (1531–
1607), daughter of the Duke Ercole II[25] and Renée of France. The duchess engaged the
finest humanist tutors for her daughter, and as she pursued her studies at court along-
side Anne, Morata's intellectual life flourished. During this period she wrote a number
of declamations and poems in Latin and Greek, as well as a translation of the two first
stories of Boccaccio's Decameron *into Latin. In addition to classical learning, Morata*
also received thorough instruction in the Old and New Testament, with the aid of
many heterodox commentaries and interpretations. The atmosphere at the Ferrarese
court during that time was open-minded, the duchess herself tending toward Protest-
ant beliefs, and the young Morata had occasion there to meet and have discussions
with various reform-minded thinkers—John Calvin himself visited the court of
Ferrara. These experiences helped shape her religious convictions. In 1546 Morata left
the court to care for her father, who died in 1548, and she stayed for a time to care for
her younger siblings. When she finally returned to court, the atmosphere had changed;
the Inquisition was actively persecuting Protestants in Ferrara and many of the
reformers had fled. Morata herself fell from grace at court and was banished. In 1549
she met a young medical student and classical scholar from Bavaria named Andreas
Grunthler (1518–1555); the couple fell in love and the following year were married in
a Protestant ceremony. Toward the end of 1550 Morata left for Germany with
Grunthler, leaving behind her family but taking along her brother Emilio, who was
eight years old. By 1551 they were living in her husband's hometown of Schweinfurt,

_____

25 Eldest son of Alfonso d'Este and Lucrezia Borgia (pp. 116–117).

where Andreas practiced medicine and Olimpia wrote. During this time she composed a philosophical work entitled Dialogue of Theophila and Philotima, *a meditation on how Christian hope can aid in overcoming the sorrows of absence and the harsh choices one is forced to make in life, and she translated several Latin Psalms into Greek, which her husband was setting to music. She also maintained correspondence with friends and prominent Protestant theologians. Soon external events overturned their lives; Germany had been in violent turmoil since the death of Martin Luther in 1546 and battles between Protestants and Catholics raged. In April 1533 Schweinfurt was under siege for fourteen months; the family had to seek shelter in a wine cellar and Grunthler nearly died of plague. They almost took refuge in a church, but being warned to leave, they barely avoided being burned alive. Fleeing the town, they left on foot, traveling without shoes for days, only to be taken prisoner and sentenced to death. They were released and eventually found their way to Heidelberg, where Grunthler found a position teaching medicine at the university, but they had lost all their belongings, including most of Morata's books and her own writings. Morata became ill with tuberculosis, of which she died shortly before her twenty-ninth birthday. Within just a few months both her husband and brother were dead as well.*

Olimpia Morata wrote this letter soon after settling in her husband's native town of Schweinfurt. It is written in Latin to a close family friend, Celio Secondo Curione (1503–1570), a humanist scholar and reformer living in exile in Switzerland.[26] *In this letter Morata gives news of religious persecution in Italy and informs him of the unlikelihood that she and her husband will ever return there. She also updates him on some family matters, including a nearly fatal accident suffered by her eight-year-old brother when they first arrived in Germany. She requests that Curione send her certain books, and she sends him several poems. She promises to send him soon her most recent work, a "dialogue written in Latin," presumably the* Dialogue of Theophila and Philotima. *Curione treasured her letters and other writings; after her death he published everything he could find that she had written. There were three editions of Morata's works published by Curione, in 1558, 1562, and 1570.*

> Olimpia Morata Grunthler sends a greeting to Caelius Secundo Curio[27],
>   Most pleasing to me was your letter, from which I learned that such
> a great distance in time and space has done nothing to detract from

---

26 1503–1570. From a noble Piedmontese family, Curione studied classical literature and the law and became interested in the writings of Luther, Melanchthon, and Zwingli from an early age. The author of a number of books on religious reform, Curione was friends with Morata's father; in 1541 he was in Ferrara, where he met the young Olimpia Morata. He, too, was forced to leave Italy, going to live in Switzerland from 1542 through the end of his life. Morata kept up a regular correspondence with Curione over the years.

27 This is the Latinized form of Curione's name.

your kind feelings toward us. Such, of course, is how Christian friendships usually are. And so I offer thanks to my God who deems me worthy of such honor, that I am loved by His people. For I do not make much of impious persons, no matter how powerful, wealthy, noble, or even learned they are, whether they hate me or appear to love me. For that reason as well, your opinion of my poems was most pleasing to me. For since I hold you in the greatest esteem, if I had perceived that it had been otherwise, you would have deterred me from my zeal for writing. But now that I see that it is not condemned by pious men, and especially not condemned by you, to the extent that I am able, I will take pains to work on it.

Concerning your request, however, that if we ever return to Italy we go to visit you, it is not within my power to offer any positive affirmation that we will ever set out for that place; for we did not come here with the intention of traveling back to Italy. Surely it does not escape your notice, how dangerous it is for Christians to declare themselves openly where the Antichrist[28] has such great power; he already, as I have heard, rants so wildly against the saints and begins to rage so much that "you would say that the other one was mere play and pastime, compared with what the madness of this one causes."[29] He has sent his spies out to all the cities of Italy and, just like the other one, he is not able to be bent by any entreaties. For last year, I don't know if you heard, he ordered a certain Fanini[30], a pious man of the most steadfast faith, who had been imprisoned for about two years—for he never willed to deviate from the truth out of fear of death, nor out of love of his wife and children—to be strangled, then his body to be burned, and not content with that, his bones to be thrown into the Po. Thus, though I am possessed by an overwhelming desire to be with my family, I would go to the ends of the earth rather than return to where that man has power to rage so much. But if we had to depart from here, there is no other place I would more gladly wish to set out for than to you; for it would seem like being with my family if I could live near you. This is why, if my husband were able to find employment, either curing the sick or publicly teaching where you are, he would accept such an offer willingly for my sake. If that could happen, nothing

---

28 Morata is referring to Giovanni Maria Ciocchi del Monte (1487–1555), who had recently been elected Pope Julius III in February 1550. He replaced Paul III Farnese (r. 1534–1549), who initiated the Council of Trent and established the Jesuit Order and the Roman Inquisition.

29 Terrence, *Eunuchus*, Riley trans., line 301, p. 83.

30 Fanino Fanini was a baker from Faenza who was arrested by the Inquisition for his reform-minded beliefs. He was held in prison for eighteen months, tried, and finally executed on August 22, 1550.

would make me happier. Also, being closer to Italy, I would be able to write to and receive letters from my dearest mother and sisters, whom I imagine before my eyes day and night; for from here it is extremely difficult. I only just received one [letter] this month, after a very long interval.

And since I know that you wish us the best, it seems important to me that I keep you informed about all of us. My sisters were in service: one to Elena Rangoni Bentivoglio[31]; the other to her daughter, who was married in Milan, and whom, when I wrote to you, I believed to have come to Ferrara, but when she was being forced to go on her way, with everything prepared, a certain young man, an only son and rich enough, hearing this, did not let her depart, but married her without asking for a dowry. In May of this year, along with her husband, she visited her mother in Ferrara, staying with her for several days. As for my other sister, Lavinia della Rovere[32], the daughter-in-law of Camillo Orsini, took her away to Rome with her. There is no woman I know of in Italy more learned and, what is more important than anything else, more pious than she. In what wonderful ways does God treat His saints: even a little over a year ago, when we were in Würzburg with Sinapius[33], when we were in the greatest danger, He came to our aid. For my little brother, whom I have with me, fell from a very high window onto rough stones. We all believed he would die, or if he lived, to Sinapius and my husband it seemed an "impossibility"[34] that he would not suffer from epilepsy. And yet he was no more injured than if he had fallen onto the soft earth; and the place is so high that my soul still trembles to remember it. But on the topic of this protection with which God watched over us so closely, I have not dared to write to my mother. For no one could be brought to believe that he lives without seeing him. These are the things that I had to write about my family to you.

Yet I wish to ask one favor of you: when it is convenient for you, could you send me a copy of the book you wrote *On the Education of*

---

31 The Bentivoglio family were the de facto rulers of Bologna until 1506, when they were forced to leave the city by Pope Julius II, taking refuge in Ferrara under the protection of Alfonso d'Este.

32 Lavinia della Rovere (1521–1601) was a close friend of Morata's; the two had met at the court of Ferrara and shared scholarly interests as well as religious views. The two were regular correspondents.

33 Sinapius is the Latinized version of Senf, the family name of two German scholars Morata had studied with at the Ferrarese court: Kilian Senf (1506–1563), who tutored Morata in Greek, and his brother, the physician Johannes Senf (1505–1560), who was friends with Erasmus and Calvin. In October 1550 Morata and Grunthler stayed with Johannes Senf in Würzburg.

34 The word is quoted in Greek in the original.

Children[35], which I read at Sinapius' house? For I would like it to be read carefully by my sister, who is in Milan. If you also had the *Pasquillus*[36], which you wrote in Latin, we and several good men who are here would read it.

You have a fairly verbose letter before you. Of course, not that I am afraid of filling you up with writing, especially gathering as I do, that you do not despise my zeal for writing in this genre. Nevertheless I will write one more thing and then make an end. For I think I must respond to the question you ask me, whether I had produced any offspring. Those children, which I brought forth on the very day and hour I received your letter, that is to say those poems, I am sending you enclosed here. There is also a dialogue written in Latin, which I recently composed; when I have transcribed it I will send it to you. I have not given birth to any other children, nor thus far do I have hopes of it. I ask you, however, most learned Caelius, carefully to tell me how your wife is doing, how many children you have there, what they are learning. For everything that concerns you is of the greatest interest to me. But when you send a letter to me, send it to our friend Sinapius in Würzburg. The town where I am is only a day's journey from Würzburg. Farewell. My husband, as always sends great greetings to you all. Schweinfurt, 1 October, [1551], in haste.

---

35 *De liberis pie Christianeque educandis* (1542), a work on the Christian education of children dedicated to Morata's father.
36 *Pasquillus extaticus* (1544), a satire on Catholic beliefs and devotional practices.

6.

———

Maria Maddalena de' Pazzi sends Christmas nativity
scene decorations to her niece Maria

From her earliest childhood, Maria Maddalena de' Pazzi (Saint Mary Magdalen de'
Pazzi, 1566–1607) dreamed of entering a convent. The second of four children of
Florentine notables Maria Buondelmonti and Camillo di Geri de' Pazzi, the child
was baptized Caterina but was known as Lucrezia. When in her teens she professed
her vows as a nun she assumed the monastic name of Maria Maddalena. An unusu-
ally serious, contemplative child, she was educated in a convent administered by Jesu-
its; however, even as a child she sought a stricter discipline than that setting offered.
Although her family was not in favor of her religious vocation—as the only daughter
in an elite Florentine family she would have had the prospect of a brilliant marriage
ahead of her—she chose to join the Carmelite convent of Santa Maria degli Angeli in
1582, taking her vows two years later. In 1584, soon after her profession, the young
nun fell gravely ill; the sickness coincided with the onset of her mystical raptures, in
which she spoke to the Trinity and had conversations with Christ. Her earliest ecstatic
revelations were recorded by her fellow nuns in I quaranta giorni *(The Forty Days),*
which documents the experiences she underwent for forty days each morning after
Mass. Her visions later that year were transcribed by sisters Evangelista Del Giocondo
and Maria Maddalena Mori in Colloqui (Dialogues). *In June 1585, for eight days*
Maria Maddalena had a continuous series of mystical experiences, described in her
Revelatione e Intelligentie (Revelations and Knowledge). *While these and other*
records of her oral accounts of spiritual ecstasies were written down not by her but by
fellow nuns, in 1586, after a year in which she had no further visions, she wrote Ren-
ovatione della Chiesa (Renovation of the Church), *a series of epistles addressed to*
Pope Sixtus V; the archbishop of Florence Alessandro de' Medici; Caterina de' Ricci
(pp. 122–123), and other prominent figures within the Church. She wrote many let-
ters over the years, some with prophetic and reforming content, but mostly those did
not circulate beyond the walls of the convent.[37] *For many years, de' Pazzi's visions*
ceased and she underwent a spiritual crisis. Revered by her fellow nuns for her extreme

---

37 Specifically, the correspondence with Caterina de' Ricci was suppressed after her death for fear that the
emphasis on reform would impede her canonization.

austerity, fasting, and humility, she was regarded by many as a "living saint."[38] In 1600, before leaving Florence to marry the king of France, Maria de' Medici (1573–1642) visited the convent to meet de' Pazzi. Despite her spiritual raptures and reputation for holiness, the mystic participated fully in the life of the convent, holding various positions of authority; she was elected novice mistress in 1598 and sub-prioress in 1604. She was forced to resign this final position after eight months due to an illness, probably tuberculosis, of which she died, in extreme suffering, in 1607. She was beatified in 1626, nine years after her death. In 1660 she was canonized by Pope Clement XI after he reviewed the testimony of over fifty nuns and evidence of miracles said to have occurred to visitors at her tomb.

This letter, one of the most personal in her collection of letters, was written by the saint to her brother's daughter, Maria de' Pazzi (1586–1656). Her niece was only ten years old at the time this letter was written, but the girl seems already to have chosen to become a nun. Her aunt's sending of materials for the Christmas presepio (nativity scene or crèche) and discussion of the baby doll that would be placed there recalls the practice of giving girls destined for the convent holy dolls to play with.[39] Although it was common in the fourteenth century for a number of members of the same family to join the same Florentine convent, leading to the formation of close, almost maternal bonds between childless monastic women and their young relatives, this practice was frowned upon in the sixteenth century.[40] Nevertheless, the girl did join her aunt at Santa Maria degli Angeli in 1600, professing her vows several years later under the name Sister Maria Grazia. Maria Grazia would become prioress in 1625 and would go on to found the Carmelite Convent of the Barberine in Rome.

Darling, dearest Niece, greetings.

I am writing you these few lines, sending you supplies for the celebration of the Nativity of Jesus that I wish you to prepare for with fervor, so that preparing your heart you will be worthy on that holy night for the sweet tiny Baby to come and rest there with you. It is He whom I believe you have chosen for your husband and I do not believe I am mistaken. I would like you to pay close attention to the inspiration that He sends you and if you wish to show your gratitude, make sure that every hour the desire grows in you to serve Him and to become His bride.

I had heard from our honorable aunt that your brother Pierino was not feeling well and I would be very grateful if you could tell me how he's feeling and also give me news of your honorable father, mother, and

---

38 See Zarri, "Living saints."
39 See Klapisch-Zuber, "Holy dolls."
40 Strocchia, *Nuns and nunneries.*

your dear little sisters. I pray you to send me a few lines of your own, which would give me the greatest pleasure. For now, I have nothing else to say and thus will close, recommending myself to you a thousand times over. Send my greetings to your honorable father and dear mother, along with your sisters. May Brother Jesus fill you with his sweet love. From Florence, in our Convent of Santa Maria degli Angeli in Borgo San Frediano, 5 November, 1598.

Your most affectionate aunt,
Sister Maria Maddalena de' Pazzi

Suggestions for further reading

Letter 1, Catherine of Siena: Bynum, *Holy feast and holy fast*; Catherine of Siena, *Letters*, trans. Noffke; Del Pozzo, "The apotheosis of Niccolò Toldo"; Dupré Theseider, "Caterina da Siena, santa"; Luongo, *The saintly politics of Catherine of Siena*, esp. Chapter 3, "Niccolo di Toldio and the erotics of political engagement," 90–122; Muessig, Ferzoco, and Kienzle, *A companion to Catherine of Siena*; Noffke, *Catherine of Siena: an anthology*, Tempe: Arizona Center for Medieval and Renaissance Studies, 2011–2012; Karen Scott, "Io Catarina: ecclesiastical politics and oral culture in the letters of Catherine of Siena," In Cherewatuk and Wiethaus, *Dear sister: Medieval women and the epistolary genre*; Tylus, *Reclaiming Catherine of Siena*; Zancan, "Lettere di Caterina da Siena," In *Il doppio itinerario della scrittura*; Zarri, "Religious and devotional writing," In Panizza and Wood, *A history of women's writing in Italy*.

Letter 2, Brigida Baldinotti: Biscioni, *Lettere di Santi e Beati Fiorentini*; Gill, "Women and religious literature in the vernacular," In E. Ann Matter and John Coakley, eds., *Creative women in medieval and early modern Italy*; Henderson, *The Renaissance hospital: healing the body and healing the soul*; Kaborycha, "Brigida Baldinotti and her two epistles"; Lehmijoki-Gardner, *Dominican penitent women*.

Letter 3, Cassandra Fedele, Alessandra Scala: Brown, *Bartolomeo Scala*; Fedele, *Letters and Orations*, ed. and trans. by Diana Robin; Jardine, "'O Decus Italiae Virgo,'" esp. 801–811; King, "Book-lined cells"; King, "Thwarted ambitions: six learned women of the Italian Renaissance"; King and Rabil, *Her immaculate hand*; Robin, "Cassandra Fedele's *Epistolae*: biography as effacement."

Letter 4, Paula Antonia Negri, Gaspara Stampa: Baernstein, *A convent tale*; Bassanese, *Gaspara Stampa*; Stampa, *The complete poems*, Tower and Tylus, eds; Tylus, trans. Warnke, "Gaspara Stampa: Aphrodite's priestess, love's martyr," In Wilson, ed., *Women writers of the Renaissance and Reformation*; Zarri, "Living saints," In Borstein and Rusconi, eds., *Women and religion in medieval and Renaissance Italy*, esp. 231, 253–254.

Letter 5, Olimpia Fulvia Morata: Bainton, *Women of the Reformation in Germany and Italy*; Morata, *The complete writings of an Italian heretic*, Parker, ed. and trans.; Rabil, "Olympia Morata (1526–1555)," In Russell, ed., *Italian women writers: a bio-bibliographical sourcebook*, pp. 269–278; Smarr, *Joining the conversation: dialogues by Renaissance women*, esp. 72–81,

232–243; Smarr, "Olympia Morata: from classicist to reformer," In Looney and Shemek, eds., *Phaethon's children*; Stjerna, *Women and the Reformation*, 197–209.

Letter 6, Maria Maddalena de' Pazzi: Barzman, "Gender, religious representation and cultural production in Early Modern Italy," In Brown and Davis, eds. *Gender and society in Renaissance Italy*, pp. 213–233; De' Pazzi, *Selected revelations*, trans. and introd. Maggi; De' Pazzi, *L'epistolario completo*, Chiara Vasciaveo, ed.; Fabrini, *The life of St. Mary Magdalen De' Pazzi*; Klapisch-Zuber, "Holy dolls: play and piety in Florence in the Quattrocento," In *Women, family, and ritual*; Maggi, "The place of female mysticism in the Italian literary canon," In Benson and Kirkham, eds., *Strong voices, weak history: early women writers & canons in England, France, & Italy*, 199–215; Maggi, *Uttering the Word: the mystical performances of Maria Maddalena de' Pazzi*; Riccardi, "The mystic humanism of Maria Maddalena de' Pazzi," In Matter and Coakley, eds., *Creative women in medieval and Early Modern Italy*, esp. 212–236.

Chapter Two

Humanism and Its Discontents

S pringing from the Italian Peninsula in the fourteenth century in the wake of the Black Death, humanism stirred new generations to examine the culture and ideas of the classical world in order to understand the human condition. Beyond a Christian reward in the afterlife, they sought to be guided by ancient Greek and Roman thinkers such as Plato, Seneca, and Lucretius to seek guidance and inspiration for life here on earth. Both men and women were drawn to these new ideas, although since a classical education was required to read the ancient writers in the original, fewer women were able to participate in humanist studies. Renaissance women in Italy had higher literacy rates than women (or men) in most of the rest of Europe, although their reading and writing were limited usually to *volgare*, or the Italian vernacular. An education in the classical languages was considered unnecessary for women, and to participate in humanist discourse one had to know at least Latin, preferably also Greek. When she wanted to influence the learned Cardinal Bessarion, Nicolosa Sanuti, knowing neither Latin nor Greek, wrote a letter of protest in Italian and had a humanist scholar translate it into Latin for her. Interestingly, however, Sanuti's letter overflows with references to classical antiquity, citing many remarkable women, as does Isabella Andreini in her vernacular letter (Chapter 4). The names of the notable women cited by both Sanuti and Andreini were praised by Boccaccio in *De mulieribus claris (On Famous Women)* and recur often in humanist discourse on the *querelle des femmes* topic. Apparently, even without the privilege of a full humanist education, Renaissance women were familiar with the culture of ancient Greece and Rome. There were Italian women, however, who were lucky enough to be taught Latin and/or Greek as children, usually by humanist fathers who were proud of their accomplishments. A number of these women, such as Alessandra Scala (Chapter 1) and Isotta Nogarola, were widely praised as prodigies, and some played important political roles. Among these were Cassandra Fedele (Chapter 1), who delivered orations for the Doge of Venice; Ippolita Maria Sforza (Chapter 6), who recited her Latin before the pope; and Maddalena Scrovegni, who used her Latin skills to become spokesperson for her family to the duke of Milan. Olimpia Morata (Chapter 1), meanwhile, used her erudition to voice religious dissent. Drawing public attention to oneself as a woman in the Renaissance, however, could lead to disgrace; it was considered improper for a virtuous woman to display her learning too publicly, and a number of these brilliant women were silenced. Criticism was leveled at them by both men and by other women, as Isotta Nogarola laments. The women who were not silenced expressed a variety of outspoken opinions and were not always in agreement with one another, as Sanuti and Cereta demonstrate in their contrasting views on women's clothing. We must assume that then, as now, feminist debate could be contentious and at times hostile—although it is interesting to note that elsewhere Cereta praises Sanuti's learning. And while both Nogarola and Cereta complain of being ridiculed by other women, not all women were critical of them. Fellow humanist, Costanza Varano's letter overflows with admiration for Nogarola.

7.
———

Maddalena Scrovegni to Jacopo dal Verme in praise of Giangaleazzo Visconti[1]

"The first of the well-known learned women of the Quattrocento,"[2] *Maddalena Scrovegni (1356–1429) was born and raised in Padua. She came from a wealthy, noble family, daughter of Luisa di Pietro Rossi and Ugolino Scrovegni. The Scrovegni had originally made their fortune as moneylenders in the thirteenth century, enabling Maddalena's forebear Enrico Scrovegni to hire Giotto, the greatest painter of the day, to decorate the family's private place of worship, the Arena Chapel in Padua. Little is known about Maddalena Scrovegni's childhood, although through her writings and contemporaries' praise of her it is evident that she received an excellent education. Humanist scholars lauded her learning, virtue, and beauty: Antonio Loschi (1386–1441) wrote Latin epistles and poems in tribute to her and Petrarch's disciple Lombardo della Seta (d. 1390) dedicated a treatise (now lost) on the excellence of women to her. Maddalena married Francesco Manfredi in 1376 and left Padua, but after her husband died five years later, in 1381 she returned, although she never remarried. In 1390 Maddalena and others in the Scrovegni clan were forced to flee Padua, driven out by their enemies the Carrara. Maddalena lived the rest of her life in exile in Venice, leaving a provision in her will to establish a home for pious women there. Only four known writings of Maddalena Scrovegni exist, this and three other letters.*

Maddalena wrote the present letter in 1388, voicing her own and her family's support and admiration for the conquering forces of Giangaleazzo Visconti, who drove out the hated Carrara family that ruled Padua. The Carrara had come to power earlier in the century through intimidation, violence, and assassination. In establishing themselves as lords of Padua, the Carrara confiscated lands of their enemies and exiled many of them. Among those who suffered this way at the hands of the Carrara were the Scrovegni. Although Ugolino Scrovegni had made peace with Francesco Carrara, when the duke of Milan Giangaleazzo Visconti sent troops to conquer Padua, many members of the Scrovegni clan fought on the side of the Milanese. Less than two years later, in 1390, the Carrara returned to power and the Scrovegni were forced once

1   I am indebted to Jonathan Gnoza for his help translating this letter and the other Latin letters in this book. His many insightful editorial suggestions were greatly appreciated.
2   King and Rabil, *Her immaculate hand,* 33.

again into exile. Maddalena Scrovegni wrote this letter—more rightly termed an
"epistle" for its formal, celebratory tone—in Latin, yet it lacks the thorough command
of later humanist scholars such as Nogarola and Fedele, and unlike those humanists,
Scrovegni makes only Biblical references and no allusions to classical literature. In a
1405 letter to the learned Battista da Montefeltro Malatesta (1384–1448), humanist
Leonardo Bruni (1369–1444) would exhort a new generation of women scholars to
use classical Latin, rejecting Church Latin, with its "vulgar threadbare jargon which
satisfies those who devote themselves to Theology."[3]

A letter of lady Maddalena Scrovegni, daughter of lord Ugolino, of Padua to lord Jacopo dal Verme[4], joining in rejoicing over the acquisition of Padua by the Lord Count of Virtues[5], etc., which she wrote in her own hand.

To a man of famous excellence, the most glorious warrior Lord Jacopo dal Verme, an especially venerable lord.

Moved by the exhortation of an energetic man, my cousin Lord Ugolottto[6], though overly bold, I prepare to write to you, most glorious of heroes, worthy of honor for the renown of your character, having achieved your usual success. Accordingly, being of the weaker sex, these lines of David occur to me,

> "O sing unto the Lord a new song; for he hath done marvelous things.
> The Lord hath made known his salvation: his righteousness hath he
> openly shewed in the sight of the heathen."[7] "He heard my cry. He
> brought me up also out of an horrible pit, out of the miry clay, and set

---

3   Cited by King and Rabil, in *Her immaculate hand*, 13. From Bruni's *De studiis et literis* in *Vittorino da Feltre*, trans. Woodward, p. 123. See also Cox, "Leonardo Bruni on women and rhetoric."

4   Jacopo dal Verme (1350–1409) was a *condottiero* (mercenary captain) who served Giangaleazzo Visconti and conquered the city of Padua for him in December 1388.

5   Giangaleazzo Visconti (1347–1402) was also known as Il Conte di Virtù (the count of virtues) because through his wife, Isabelle de Valois, he had acquired the County of Vertus in Champagne. One of the most important political and military figures of the late fourteenth century, Giangaleazzo became ruler of Milan by overthrowing his uncle Bernabò Visconti in 1385, becoming the first duke of Milan in 1385. He conquered extensive territories in northern and central Italy; his forces were on the verge of attacking the Florentine republic when suddenly, in September 1402, Visconti died of a fever. Visconti was considered an enlightened prince and "Count of Virtue" to his supporters, an enemy of liberty and a tyrant to his enemies.

6   Ugolotto Biancardo, who was the governor of Vicenza for Giangaleazzo Visconti, duke of Milan; both Maddalena's brother and her father fought for Visconti under Biancardo.

7   Psalm 98:1, 2 KJV.

my feet upon a rock, and he hath put a new song in my mouth."[8] "Sing aloud unto God our strength."[9]

Most joyful and truly most fortunate citizens, the brightest light of the world, for which you have prayed, has just now shined on your most wretched city, as the divinity of the sky is serene, and the fog of our confused calamity has been lifted. To us an illustrious star appeared, sent by God from Heaven, delightful in clarity, luminous in justice and piety, the distinguished ornament of loftier experience, which I believe we ought to revere and worship on bent knees. By its venerable sign, by sure steering through this sea of life, the course of our pleasant prosperity must be directed so that, tossed along on so many very wicked waves of an adverse storm, at last we can arrive to dock safe on the shore. Thus, while the ship resists the storm, it may befall us to escape from so great a shipwreck, while clemency directs the rudder of Our Most Serene and Illustrious Lord Prince, who will put an end to arrogant men, and he will order the unjust to take their rewards, and the most cruel scepters to give forth tearful lamentations. For through his bright force, insolent tyrants have begun to stumble along their way, brought low, ready to suffer misfortunes and destruction. Rashly straying in the depravities of their crimes, they hastened to the sentence of divine judgment, heedless that the evil deeds committed by evil men must end in an evil way and must be trampled underfoot with bitter reproaches. They are sunk in the deep sleep of eternal darkness of their crimes, while they bring upon themselves the most thoroughly suitable punishments for their perfidy. Such perfidy, contrary to what is expected, often turns destruction upon itself, so that moreover, in its uncertainty it succumbs to its own guilt and adversely suffers awful punishment. Where iniquities originate, there of course they end, and unspeakable crimes return to their author. Therefore "I will rejoice in thy salvation", God, since "The heathen are sunk down in the pit that they made"[10] for "their works do follow them."[11] Thus praise, "honor and power belong to the Lord our God! For true and righteous are His judgments."[12] O true judgments of

---

8   Psalm 40:1–3 KJV.
9   Psalm 81:1 KJV.
10   Psalm 9:14–15 KJV.
11   Revelation 14:13 KJV.
12   Revelation 19:1–2 KJV.

God, weighed in the unerring balance and with grave heaviness! For what could be more miserable, calamitous, and unfortunate for a cruel tyrant than, with the applause of all, to be hurled down from his lofty peak and most arrogant throne to the depths of unhappy desolation so that he might realize that:

> "God shall likewise destroy thee forever, he shall take thee away, and pluck thee out of thy dwelling place, and root thee out of the land of the living . . . The righteous also shall see, and fear, and shall laugh at him: 'Lo, this is the man that made not God his strength; but trusted in the abundance of his riches, and strengthened himself in his wickedness.' "[13]

However, finally, while scepters fall and in a moment savage empires are swept away, their own private things are crushed in ruin by the hastened onrush of misfortunes, may God "Give them according to their deeds, and according to the wickedness of their endeavors: give them after the work of their hands; render to them their desert,"[14] saying: "Judgment also will I lay to the line, and righteousness to the plummet"[15] "And [the multitude of all the nations that fight] shall be as a dream of a night vision."[16] Thus truly do all the perverse magnates disappear into nothing and at last are handed over to their own wickedness to be punished. Obviously, he who prepares a place for injury also prepares the place of his own adverse defeat, because criminals, while avid for committing crime, work against themselves, and they do not take notice: nothing is more to be dreaded than the most wretched inflicting of terrible cruelties. Farewell, you who must be revered by me continuously, you to whose excellency I commend myself, a woman of the most uncultivated intelligence.

Maddalena degli Scrovegni

---

13 Psalm 52:5–7 KJV.
14 Psalm 28:4 KJV.
15 Isaiah 28:17 KJV.
16 Isaiah 29:7 KJV.

8.

Isotta Nogarola asks Guarino Guarini why he has not responded to her letter

When her letters, composed in flawless Ciceronian Latin, began to circulate among humanists in Venice in the late 1430s, they caused a sensation, and Isotta Nogarola (1418–1466), who was barely out of her teens, was hailed as a prodigy. She was born in Verona, one of ten children of nobles Leonardo Nogarola and Bianca Borromeo. Isotta's father died while she was young, and her mother, although herself illiterate, saw to it that all her children received fine humanist educations. There were four brothers: Ludovico, Antonio, Leonardo, and Jacopo; all except Jacopo, who died young, were prominent in political, academic, and clerical spheres. Isotta and her younger sister Ginevra (1417–1464)—and perhaps their other sisters Bartolommea, Laura, Samaritana, and Isabella—were educated at home by Veronese humanist Martino Rizzoni (1404–1488). Isotta and Ginevra, however, were the only two to become renowned for their classical studies, following in the footsteps of their aunt, Angela Nogarola (c. 1360–c. 1436),[17] a highly regarded author of poems in Latin. Both young women corresponded in Latin with preeminent humanists of the day and were highly praised for their erudition. Ginevra married in 1438 and gave up her humanist writing, whereas Isotta went on to write Latin poems and orations, some of which she delivered herself. In 1450 she traveled to Rome with an official delegation and recited one of her orations to Pope Nicholas V. She also composed dialogues, notably the philosophical work Dialogue on the Equal or Unequal Sin of Adam and Eve *(1451), which is considered a foundational text in the* querelle des femmes *debate. She also excelled at writing letters, twenty-six of which survive.*

It was after Jacopo Foscari, son of the Doge of Venice, passed one of her letters on to Guarino Guarini (Guarino Veronese, 1374–1460) that Nogarola's correspondence with the renowned humanist began. Isotta wrote an admiring letter to Guarino in Latin in October 1436; when, after six months, she still had received no response, she wrote him this letter, also in Latin, on April 10, 1487. Guarino wrote back immediately afterward, apologizing for his silence and praising the young woman's abilities

---

17 For Angela Nogarola see Parker, "Latin and Greek poetry by five Renaissance Italian women humanists." and Stevenson. *Women Latin poets,* 158–159, 510–512.

but exhorting her not to behave "so like a woman" but to have a more "manly soul."
Having moved to Venice, in 1438 Nogarola came under attack from an anonymous
Veronese pamphleteer, who accused her of various sexual crimes, including incest with
her brother and sister. Feeling her reputation and professional standing ruined, she
returned to Verona in 1441, leaving the public realm and dedicating herself primarily
to religious writing.

Isotta Nogarola sends very many greetings to the most learned man, Guarino Veronese,

As I oftentimes reflect[18] on women's worth, it occurs to me to lament my own fortune, since I have been born female and women are derided by men in deed, as well as in words. I voice this conclusion about myself in private, rather than publicly seek out you who have made me an object of ridicule. For I am afflicted with such great distress as never before, when I consider that you have been unfair to me in your writing. I certainly had forebodings that in writing to you I was writing in vain, but your humanity influenced me to do so, since those words of Cicero came to my mind where he teaches us that the higher we are placed, the more humbly we are obliged to act.[19] But, by Jove, I see your nature is unmoved and that you are at odds with that admonition. I was glad when I sent you that letter. Indeed, I judged it fitting to your praise of me, since I thought I had fully gained your good opinion. Now, however, grief outweighs gladness as I have come to know that things have turned out differently. I enjoyed your friendship in vain, and you had no more respect for me than if I had never been born. For throughout the city I am ridiculed; I am derided by my peers[20], and nowhere do I have a stable stable.[21] The asses rip me to pieces by biting me; bulls run at me with their horns. For even if I fully deserved this abuse, just the same it was unworthy of you. Why do you treat me with such contempt, father Guarino? Alas, how miserable I am! As before all this my spirit was

---

18 This phrase is an indirect quotation of the first words of Cicero's *De oratore*, an opening volley, in which the author demonstrates her erudition.

19 Reference to Cicero, *De officiis*, 1:90.

20 Margaret King translates *meus me ordo deridet* as "the women mock me," with the explanation of Nogarola's *ordo* or "rank" as being defined socially by her status as an unmarried woman. Nogarola, *Complete Writings*, 54.

21 As Margaret King indicates, this passage is a partial quotation and adaptation of the comedy *Aulularia* by Plautus (c. 254–184 BC), Act 2, Scene 2. Jonathen Gnoza points out that "A perfectly literal translation of Plautus' phrase *'stabile stabulum'* is 'a stable stable'; coincidentally this translation also brings out the alliterative wordplay of Plautus' phrase, which is matched in English by the different senses of 'stable' as an adjective and 'stable' as a noun." E-mail communication from Gnoza.

continuously alert in hope and fear, so after, with hope taken away, my wearied fear is benumbed and overwhelmed by despair. Since this is so, I beseech you by God, if you deem me worthy of your favor, to help me in my distress, and—to speak frankly—to come to my aid in this matter of my reputation, and not to suppose that this would be a criminal act unworthy of your deeds. You would help me, deficient in learning, since you will have conferred great dignity on me; [your words] would silence these wicked tongues, who call me a mountain of audacity and say I should be banished to the ends of the earth for my boldness. Nor do I know what cause I give them for such affirmations, but I acknowledge I must have erred and deserved blame. I come to beseech you to do something about this thing that troubles my spirit, and to carry out what I ask, and having obtained that, I will take my leave of you. Farewell.

9.
———

*Costanza Varano writes to Isotta Nogarola, expressing
admiration for her learning*

"*O honour and splendor of Latin-speaking girls,*" *begins humanist Guiniforte
Barzizza (1408–63), in a letter to Costanza Varano (1426–1447).*[22] *She was born
into the ruling family of Camerino, a remote mountainous territory in the region of the
Marche; her father Piergentile (1400–1433) married Elisabetta da Montefeltro
Malatesta (1407–1477) of the powerful ruling family from nearby Pesaro. The alliance
contributed to the envy and hostility of Piergentile's brothers, who murdered him in
1433. Elisabetta afterward fled with her children to Pesaro, taking refuge with her
mother Battista da Montefeltro Malatesta (1384–1448). Costanza's grandmother, to
whom humanist Leonardo Bruni had written* De studiis et litteris *(On the Study of
Literature), was a learned woman who wrote Latin prose and poetry*[23] *and was largely
responsible for the girl's education in Greek and Latin, studying the Church Fathers
and classical authors. In 1442, aged sixteen, Costanza Varano wrote and delivered the
"Oration to Bianca Maria Visconti,"*[24] *in which she asks the duchess of Milan to inter-
vene with her husband Francesco Sforza to restore the Varano as lords of Camerino.
This oration was widely praised, in particular by Guiniforte Barzizza. Varano followed up this oral performance by writing several political letters in Latin on the same
theme, two to Bianca Maria's father Filippo Visconti, duke of Milan, and another to
Alfonso VI, king of Aragon, along with poems in praise of his majesty; later that year
the young woman delivered a Latin oration before him. It was on the occasion of the
first oration that Varano met her future husband, Francesco Sforza's younger brother,
Alessandro, who, it is said, fell in love with her at first sight. The following year the
territory was restored to Costanza Varano's family, and in 1444 she and Alessandro—
who previously had no state to rule—were married. Their first child, Battista,*[25] *was
born in 1446; soon after giving birth to a second child in 1447, Varano died.*

---

22 Jane Stevenson, *Women Latin poets,* 167.
23 On Battista da Montefeltro Malatesta see King and Rabil, eds., *Her immaculate hand,* 16, 35–38, and
Cecil H. Clough, "Daughters and wives of the Montefeltro."
24 A translation of this oration is printed in *Her immaculate hand,* 39–41. On Bianca Maria Visconti see
pp. 138, 189.
25 In 1459, at the age of four, Battista was proclaimed a prodigy when she delivered a Latin oration to the
duke and duchess of Milan. On Battista see Clough, 40–41.

The present letter—the original is in Latin—was written by Varano in 1442, when Varano was sixteen and Nogarola twenty-four.[26] *Accompanied by a poem*[27] *in honor of Nogarola, this was not the only letter written by Varano to another woman scholar; in 1444 she wrote a similar letter to Cecilia Gonzaga.*[28] *The correspondence between Varano and Nogarola was apparently initiated by the latter, although no letters from Nogarola to Varano survive. This letter is the only one that has come down to us written by a woman to Nogarola.*

Costanza Varano sends very many greetings to Isotta Nogarola

Most erudite Isotta, as I read many times over your very elegant letters, which are redolent of that ancient dignity of the Romans, where the embellishments are fitting equally to both thoughts and words, I observed how your language shines with them. I was moved by the style of your speech to express in my letter what great love I have for you, although I do it in a style hardly harmonious, partly on account of the poverty of my intellect, and partly because I am very little trained in eloquence. Why do I say "trained," when I have scarcely crossed the first threshold? I myself express my joy for you, who with great glory and splendor of your name, have reached the highest peaks. For nothing could be more advantageous or fruitful for ladies than, neglecting bodily comforts, to take aim and strive for those highest things that Fortune cannot undermine. From your earliest years you had at your fingertips that maxim of Lactantius Firmianus, not the least among theologians, who says that they who neglect the good of the soul and long for that of the body dwell in darkness and death.[29] You had also observed what our Cicero wrote in *On Duties:* "For we are all attracted and drawn to a zeal for learning and knowing; and we think it beautiful to excel therein, while we count it bad and disgraceful to fall, to err, to be deceived, and to be ignorant."[30] This evident truth did not escape the famous orator Quintilian in his *Institutes of Oratory:* "just as birds are

---

26 On the possible dating of this letter to 1442 see Feliciangeli, 33.

27 The text of the poem as well as the other writings of Varano mentioned here are given in the original and in English translation by Holt Parker in "Costanza Varano (1426–1447): Latin as an instrument of state." In Churchill, Brown, and Jeffrey, *Women writing Latin: from Roman antiquity to Early Modern Europe,* 35–53.

28 Cecilia Gonzaga (1425–1451), daughter of the marchese of Mantua, studied Greek and Latin with Vitorino da Feltre (1378–1446) and joined a convent in 1445. A translation of the letter of Varano to Gonzaga is printed in *Her immaculate hand,* 53–54.

29 Lucius Caecilius Firmianus Lactantius, an early Christian author (c. 240–c. 320) and advisor to the Emperor Constantine. This passage refers to his *Divinae institutiones* 2:2. King and Rabil, *Her immaculate hand,* 136.

30 Cicero, *De officiis* I, 6, 18. King and Rabil, *Her immaculate hand,* 136.

born for flight, horses for running, and beasts for ferocity, so a certain activity and quickness of mind is our particular property."[31] All these maxims you yourself have gathered in your heart and always carefully kept there. The result is that you must be judged as an equal to those most learned women of older times, of whom there were so many in that age. Such were Aspasia[32], Cornelia the daughter of Scipio[33], Elphe[34], and too many others to name here. Indeed, you yourself know these things far better than I, since you have been vigorous in studies for no small length of time. I am able to hold these thoughts in my mind far better than to express in words how greatly I value you. And I would like you to be assured that I promise you that to add to the sum of your worthy reputation, there is nothing I would not willingly undertake with all my strength.

Farewell.

---

31   Quintilian, *Institutio oratoria*, I, 1, 1. King and Rabil, *Her immaculate hand*, 136.

32   Aspasia (c. 470 BCE–c. 400 BCE), a learned woman who was mistress to Pericles, ruler of Athens.

33   Cornelia Scipionis Africana (c. 190 BCE–c. 100 BCE), daughter of Scipio the Elder, hero of the Punic War. After her husband's death Cornelia refused to remarry, concentrating on educating her three children instead. She is one of the few women from Roman antiquity whose letters survive today, although the authenticity of her letters has been questioned.

34   King and Rabil suggest that Elphe is Elpinice (fl. 450 BCE). The sister of Cimon, who was accused of not having adequately defended Athens against the enemy, Elpinice saved her brother's life through her eloquent arguments. Cox suggests this might be a scribal error and the third name ought to be Sappho. *Women's writing*, 275.

10.
———

Nicolosa Castellani Sanuti to Cardinal Bessarion
challenging sumptuary laws

Nicolosa Castellani (d. 1505) was the daughter of a wealthy notary in Bologna who provided her with a large dowry, enabling her to marry the nobleman Nicolò Sanuti (c. 1407–1482) in 1446. In 1447 her husband became count of Porretta, site of a fashionable spa, where Nicolosa became renowned for her beauty and elegance. She is described by Giovanni Sabadino degli Arienti (1445–1510) as one of the narrators of the fictional tales in his Le porretane *(1468) as "Madonna Nicolosa Sanuti, magnificent countess of the Porretan baths, a woman most beautiful, moral, gracious, and charming as you could hope to find in Bologna." He goes on to describe her as dressed in a sumptuous purple silk gown and wearing a pink cloak trimmed with finest ermine.*[35] *In 1445 the young nobleman Sante Bentivoglio (1424–1463) became governor of Bologna, and sometime in the mid-1440s the two became lovers, revealed in a number of poems and letters they exchanged, which have survived. Whether the relations between the couple were generally known is unclear; nevertheless, Antonio Sanuti, son of Nicolò by a former marriage, publicly declared Bentivoglio the family's enemy. However, no bloody Renaissance revenge was carried out; instead, when in 1454 his wife's lover was married to Ginevra Sforza, it was Nicolò Sanuti's official duty to go to Milan to conduct the bride to Bologna. Of her learning, the only reference we have is from humanist Laura Cereta, who compares Sanuti with Isotta Nogarola and Cassandra Fedele. Cereta writes: "I will not mention here Cicero's daughter Tulliola or Terentia or Cornelia, Roman women who reached the pinnacle of fame for their learning; and accompanying them in the shimmering light of silence will be Nicolosa of Bologna, Isotta of Verona, and Cassandra of Venice."*[36]

---

35 "Madonna Nicolosa Sanuta, del bagno porretano, magnifica contessa, donna bellissima, morale, graziosa e venusta quanto altra bolognese donna a questi tempi se trovi . . . avendo de sopra una camura di purpurea seta, una turca roxata, foderata de bellissimi ermellini," 109. I am grateful to Mary Bulgarella Westerman and Roberta Orsi Landini for their help translating clothing terminology in this passage and others in Sanuti's letter.

36 Cereta, *Collected letters,* Robin, ed. and trans. 78.

Perhaps more properly termed a "treatise" (Kovesi), an "oration" (Frati), or a "little book" (Bosso) [37] because of its length and didactic content, the present work was a reaction to a sumptuary law promulgated on May 24, 1453, by the papal legate to Bologna Cardinal Bessarion (1403–1472). This legislation, which limited the types of clothing, jewelry, and other ornaments women of various classes of society could wear, was not unusual; various types of sumptuary regulations had existed since the Middle Ages, with penalties for violation ranging from a fine to excommunication. Although individual women had objected to such laws, Sanuti is the first to have stood up for women in general and to present a well-argued defense. [38] The letter appeared later in 1453 and sparked a heated public debate; the law, however, was not repealed. Sanuti composed this writing [39] in the vernacular but, to increase its force, had it translated into Latin by someone else, as she herself explains in a letter to Bentivoglio. There Sanuti describes how she "was moved to speak in the name of other women of this city and to place my own name on it. It was a work conceived of and carried out by myself alone. It came about that a man of great excellence and virtue translated it accurately into Latin so that its description would carry more dignity." [40] In this same letter Sanuti denounces that composition, declaring "those sentiments I now confess to have been false, the arguments of no value, everything in our defense and help was sophistically argued and untrue." It is a decidedly private letter blazing with jealousy and self-recrimination, written by Sanuti after learning of Bentivoglio's upcoming marriage. Elsewhere in this letter she tells her unfaithful lover that "the clothing, gold, pearls, and the lovely ornaments along with all the other precious things gave me pleasure only because by making myself more magnificent and attractive they made me prettier in your eyes." [41]

---

37 Matteo Bosso, who wrote a harsh reply to the original document, refers to it in his response as a "libellus." Lombardi, Traduzione, imitazione, plagio, 109.

38 Interestingly, Sanuti's argument would be picked up by Arcangela Tarabotti (pp. 205–206), who in 1644 "wrote a defence of female luxury insisting that beautification was the proprietà, the right of a woman. A woman is sacred and godly; she should embellish her feminine beauty with the most luminous, lovely, and precious accessories, so that her divine splendor might shine forth." Labalme, "Women's roles in Venice," in Beyond their sex, 135. Labalme cites Zanette, Suor Arcangela, 23.

39 Sanuti's part in the authorship of this letter has been called into question by a number of scholars. Virginia Cox writes: "The attribution to Sanuti is somewhat misleading, in that Sanuti herself acknowledges her use of a ghostwriter, in the form of a 'man of great excellence and talent' who 'dignified' her ideas by translating them into Latin; she was not Latin-literate herself," Women's writing, 261. Giuseppe Lombardi goes further, asserting that the author was in fact a man and Nicolosa Sanuti merely suggested the theme. Op. cit. 111.

40 Frati, Lettere amorose, 335. No consensus has been reached on the identity of this translator.

41 Ibid. 334. One scholar doubts Nicolosa's authorship even of this letter, suggesting that a certain Bedro de' Preti wrote it in her name. Comelli "Di Nicolò Sanuti," 121, n.1.

Nicolosa Sanuti, Bolognese matron to the Most Reverend Lord Father in Christ, the legate to Bologna, on restoring women's ornaments:

Though some call fortune omnipotent, it hardly seemed fitting to blame the condition of matrons on fortune, for others hold that Your Lordship is most likely to be influenced by the dignity of the religious life and sanctity. Particularly as Homer, considered by many to be a philosopher second to none, never mentions fortune, (and on account of this people believe that he thought that no such thing existed), I deem it more fitting to render perpetual and undying thanks to God the best and highest. He has offered such a case against us in order to prevent the female sex from a seeming degeneration from the customs of our ancestors; it is most difficult, especially for a woman, even to attempt to contest so great a thing. Nevertheless, Most Reverend Lord, those who approach your high office with some case are accustomed first to extol it with the most exquisite praises that they can muster in words issuing from their mouths. I generally call them flatterers and find their efforts laughable, for there is no one in his right mind who can consider himself able to worthily praise one who has superhuman authority and power. In consideration of this, I decided to pass over it in silence, rather than express myself in a shabby and unworthy manner.

But perhaps you will be surprised that I, a woman, deterred neither by modesty nor by your authority, plead a case in favor of matrons before your most righteous Lordship under the present circumstances, but I was emboldened by other women from earlier times, who we hear pleaded frequently before praetors and the other magistrates. It is clear that Hortensia, daughter of Quintus Hortensius, not only pleaded cases before the triumvirs[42], but also successfully petitioned that the greater part of the tax, which those very same triumvirs had imposed on women be lifted. Then I was also not a little moved by the unfailing, instinctive urge of men who, regardless of their rank and social position, wanted the law to forbid [women] that which their own avarice was prevented from doing.

Moreover, I was not a little persuaded of this by your immense kindness and incredible humanity, which is accustomed to hear not only great and excellent men, but also women and any other humble and unlearned people and indeed to listen reasonably with an

---

42 In 42 BCE, the Roman Republic was ruled by a council of three men called triumvirs; this period is called the Second Triumvirate. This episode is recounted by Valerius Maximus.

undisturbed ear. Finally, who could be so dull and slothful, what woman so unlearned, what female so lacking in spirit that she would not undertake the cause of restoring, defending and keeping her ornaments? Whose notice did it escape that gold and such insignia and ornamentation are testaments to virtue and the herald of a well-instructed mind? Our ancestors would not have actually decorated us with such great ornamentation, or permitted us to wear them if we had not merited them by our deeds or by some virtue. And so on behalf of all Bolognese women I have come before you, most humane Lord, to entreat you to repeal and thoroughly deplore the law, which was repeatedly brought against us once by Marcus Oppius, tribune of the plebians under the consuls Quintus Fabius and Titus Sempronius, against the honor and dignity of all Roman women, and was repealed twenty years later by Marcus Porcius Cato, that 'no woman would have more than half an ounce of gold or wear colorful clothing' or as we would say, that no woman should use 'clothing embroidered or woven with gold,' even when arranged appropriately.[43]

Nor do I doubt that once we have demonstrated that it is safe and decent that the law must be abolished, I will easily obtain Your Lordship's agreement. There are many in particular who believe that it must rather be done because, as it was introduced in accordance with the counsel and prayers of those people who care more for money than for honor, repealing this law poses opposition to their avarice. Who would not really judge it more convenient to defer to almost the entire populace rather than to the unfairness of a minority? We all take a stand, we urge our husbands daily with constant prayers to understand that they are men, and not only to maintain peace in the household, but also their own honor, by indulging their wives and members of their households. But how much inconvenience this causes our city is especially evident in the home, where now there are always disputes and quarrels, and where usually there is one spirit, one mind, one intention, now there is the greatest discord and disagreement of all wills; however, we did not cause this outrage. For throughout the ages, to every individual it has been permitted to protect personal dignity, and if that could not be achieved by words, no one was prohibited from wresting it or seizing it by force. Indeed,

---

43 Katherine Kovesi notes: "Cajo Oppius, Roman tribune, during the Second Punic War (215), after the defeat at the Battle of Cannae in 216 B.C., promulgated a sumptuary law that prohibited women from wearing more than fourteen grams of gold in their clothing, and from using purple and multicoloured fabrics in their clothes. It was abolished by C. Valerius Fundanius, not by Marcus Porcius Cato, in 195." *Heralds*, 273.

unreasonable and insane is the one who despises those things which will seem to be conducive to his own glory. Nor can I believe that there was ever anyone with such humility that he was not affected, at least in part, by the love of glory. We read in the works of the most noble ancients that though some men wrote much about despising glory, they nevertheless signed their names to those works and let it be publicly known that they were the authors, in order that they might attain recognition, nobility, and glory for despising glory. Who will accuse us then, if asking, entreating, insisting, at times asserting ourselves, we are eager to be allowed to use our marks of honor? Contentions will cease and concord will be at hand, most prudent Lord, if this law, which was unjustly introduced and spread about, is abolished, and the avarice of certain men is limited. And not only will these things cease, but—and I would like Your Lordship to consider this closely—Your Lordship will win the greatest goodwill among this community, esteem, praise, and outstanding authority among all those of whose interests, honor, and safety Your Lordship has been mindful.

But what is more unjust than to deprive us of that which was permitted by our ancestors, approved by most long-standing custom, sanctioned and guaranteed by law? For it is a fact all the way back to the time of Marcus Oppius that women adorned themselves and used abundant gold, jewels, and purple, not only to maintain their husbands' authority, but also to make themselves more beautiful. Then the Oppian Law was issued when the Roman people were in the greatest crisis, when they feared that Hannibal was about to set up camp right outside the city! When allies, soldiers, ships, provisions, and money were lacking: these were all the causes for passing this law, which was going to last just until the Roman populace was free from that calamity. When afterward the republic once again flourished, the consul Marcus Cato Portius, a man of utmost gravity and severity, by abolishing this law, restored to Roman matrons their ornaments, a situation that remained inviolate from that time up to this day by right. Have there been perchance any causes? Are there any crimes? Why does it seem to you that we must be deprived? Are there not to be found in the present day women similarly learned, modest, and endowed with every virtue, who also deserve greater things, as did the women of earlier times? Let us consider, if you please, the deeds in former times which pertain to the glory of our sex; thereupon we will most clearly demonstrate from the many very illustrious women who visibly flourish increasingly day by day.

To begin with, what greater or more excellent thing could be given to humankind than literature? Not that I will call to mind all the individual benefits, so I have always held that of all the things which have been given to men by nature herself or through industry, nothing more useful or excellent than the study of letters can be found. Through literature we are taught to pursue what is right, honest, holy, and sacred, and through literature we are instructed for both public and private affairs, and through literature we can be abundantly taught the things which concern the rites and ceremonies of holy religion. In fact, I would venture to say that a man cannot be considered wise in any way if he is wholly ignorant and lacking in experience of literature; he will fall in small things, and he will err in the most minuscule details and be deceived, and nothing could be more contrary to a wise man. For it is evident that wisdom is most bound together with the knowledge and understanding of things divine and human. So who revealed to mortals the use of this literature of such great utility and excellence? Who emerged as its originator? Women, surely. Do not the same men say that a woman, whether that daughter of Prometheus or else of Inachus, [Isis] introduced not only the cultivation of the soil and the working of cloth but also—a thing that is more excellent among the Egyptians—letters, which Nicostrata the daughter of Ion, the king of Arcadia, or the same woman as Evander's Carmenta not only gave to us Latins, but also thoroughly taught their combinations and sounds.[44]

But what will be said of the other arts? While Phoroneus reigned among the Argives and Ogyges among the Athenians, Minerva with her very keen intellect invented spinning and weaving and numerals and the figures of the same. They also say that this goddess or another—for we read there was more than one Minerva—stood out as the original inventor of olive trees, chariots, and wars. And what of Ceres who showed men, who had been subsisting on hard acorns like herds of animals, how to cultivate the earth and harvest its fruits? The result is that for these things, these two women are called goddesses, i.e. divine, among the pagans, and not undeservingly.

If we assess this fairly—pardon me men, but I speak the truth—we will find that women, if they did not surpass, at least equaled men in

---

44 Boccaccio, in *De mulieribus claris* XXVII, 3–8. recounts how Nicostrata became known as Carmenta because she made her prophesies in song (*carmen*). She guided her son Evander to the Palatine hill, where Rome would be founded. She helped the primitive settlers in becoming civilized, above all by giving them their own Latin alphabet, adapted from Greek.

every kind of virtue. I pass over Iphigenia, the untainted virgin daughter of Agamemnon; Cassandra, who refused even Apollo's advances; Vesta, daughter of Saturn, who was called a goddess on account of her extraordinary chastity; Penelope and Dido, who were each content with only one man, to whom the crown of modesty was usually given among the Romans. I pass over Lucretia and many other women, whom if I wanted to enumerate, the day would be over before the supply of them ended. Nevertheless, I will not pass over Hippo and Brictona[45], of whom the first, when she had been captured by the enemy fleet, was not afraid to cast herself overboard, in order to preserve her chastity by means of death. The other, whom Minos the king of Crete was pursuing, fled and flung herself headlong into the sea. What therefore, could purity not accomplish among us, if we were not only unwilling to spare our fortunes but even unwilling to shrink from our own death? However, since there is nothing that would render the female sex so remarkable, if it is pleasing, let us consider such an important matter a little more carefully.

For what else is serving husbands faithfully or waiting upon them with admirable love? What else is this other than upholding the laws of righteousness? Was not Aemilia extraordinarily faithful to Scipio the Elder, and Thuria to Quintus Lucretius[46]? When her spouse Lentulus was proscribed, in order to keep her faith intact, Sulpicia[47] did not hesitate to proscribe Scipio. Evadne loved her husband Capaneus so dearly that when his lightning-stricken and half-burned cadaver was placed on the funeral pyre, in her tremendous grief she hurled herself into the flames so that thus burned at the same time with him she would be laid to rest in the same urn, their ashes intermixed. Julia too, when she saw her husband Pompey's bloodied garments brought home from the Forum, suspecting what misfortune had befallen her spouse, was compelled by harsh pain both to eject the child that, conceived, was still in her womb

---

45 Brictona is mentioned by Boccaccio as a daughter of Mars in *Genealogia deorum gentilium*, Book IX, Chapter 3.

46 Tertia Aemilia was betrayed by her husband Scipio Africanus the Elder, who fell in love with a maidservant, but she forgave him. Thuria (or Curia) was married to Quintus Lucretius Vespillo, whose life was endangered by the proscriptions of 43 BCE. She protected her husband, hiding him in the rafters of their bedroom until he could be pardoned. Both these women are mentioned by first-century CE Roman writer Valerius Maximus in *Factorum er dictorum memorabilium*, 6.7.1–2, in a passage praising womanly virtue. Both are mentioned by Boccaccio in *De mulieribus claris*, Tertia Aemilia in LXXIV and Curia in LXXXIII.

47 Sulpicia was married to Lentulus Truscellio (or Cruscellio). When he was proscribed by the triumvirs in 43 BCE, Lentulus fled to Sicily, where despite her family's opposition Sulpicia followed him. Dressed as a slave she secretly left Rome. Valerius Maximus in *Factorum er dictorum memorabilium*, 6.7.3. *De mulieribus claris*, LXXXV.

and—what was more bitter still—to expire. What of [Artemisia] the queen of the Carian nation, who wanted to be the living, breathing grave of her husband?[48] Nor will I be silent about Hysicratea, who, by cutting her hair and transfiguring the exceptional splendor of her appearance into masculine form she would more easily be able to accompany her husband Mithridates; she followed that man, defeated by Pompey and fleeing with unwearied body and mind across many lands.[49] I would be unable to report, Most Reverend Lord, women's decency, innate to them from the beginning of the world, preserved and augmented up to our own day with the greatest diligence and self-restraint, without which there can hardly be any honor.

Cyrus's daughter, Calpurnia, the mother of Dionysius, Tanaquil, and the sibyls themselves, however, all equally attest with how much wisdom or rather divine excellence this sex of ours flourished. What else is fore-seeing the future in dreams or from portents, if not wisdom, and what is it to be set apart and to have been endowed with divinity? What could be more wise or divine than that in which our faith most consists—a concei-ving virgin, the advent, passion, death, and resurrection of omnipotent God—should be divined, foretold, and revealed in a multitude of words by all the sibyls? So great is the fortitude of our race and our sex that women are universally admired on account of these great ones and we are carried aloft to heaven with many praises. We have heard that Harpalyce of Thrace, by immediately gathering a multitude of people, freed her aged father Lycurgus, who was captured by the Getae, faster than could be hoped of any woman, with arms and her own strength. Moreover, where it is permitted, fortitude not less than piety can be found. I do not mention Semiramis, the queen of the Assyrians, who after her husband's death was accustomed to bear arms frequently and to do military service to defend the realm. Cloelia, however, given with others as a hostage to Porsena, the king of the Etruscans, having evaded the guards during the night, carried by the swift flow of the river, liberated her homeland. Now Portia had no mere womanly spirit, and when she learned of her husband Brutus's plan to murder Caesar, in order to find out how she would do away with herself calmly if her husband's intention failed, with a knife

---

48 Artemisia, widow of Mausolus, had her husband's remains cremated, then disolved the ashes in water and drank them.
49 Recounted in *De mulieribus claris*, LXXVIII, although the name is given as Hypsicratea by Boccaccio. See also Kovesi, *Heralds*, 275, n.85.

inflicted a profound wound on herself.[50] What follows is extraordinary, but much bolder: for this same woman, learning of Brutus's death at Philippi in the fields of Macedonia and having no sword, put burning coals into her mouth and swallowed them.[51]

If it is constancy we seek: Sempronia, the sister of the Gracchi and wife of Scipio Aemilianus, when she was being brought forward before the populace into the Forum by a tribune of the plebs, and the tribunician power was pressing on her with many threats, while the vague multitude of the crowd was making an uproar, with the utmost constancy she repelled the group of knights falsely wanting to usurp another's place with abominable audacity.

If it is generosity we are seeking, what is more generous than our sex? When Marius was judged an enemy of the Roman state by the Senate, Flavia took him into her house. A certain very wealthy Apulian woman named Busa with utmost generosity provided sustenance for some Roman citizens who were survivors of the battle of Cannae in her own home.[52] If filial piety is sought, we find that some in prison fed their fathers, others their mothers for many days on their own milk. Antigone, daughter of Oedipus, ceaselessly served as a guide for her blind, exiled father: a woman to be pitied. We read also that the daughters of Pelias, having compassion for the old age of their father, were never separated from him. When the vestal virgin Claudia put herself between her triumphing father and the tribune of the plebs dragging him from the chariot with a violent hand, she single-handedly deflected the tribune's force from her parent.

If skill in liberal arts is in question, there is first and foremost a contemporary of Alcaeus, Sappho from Lesbos, after whom they say that the Sapphic stanza was named. There is the woman who wrote the *Cento*, that I would term divine, as she drew so many verses from Virgil to [aid] the understanding of our God, though Jerome was of a different

---

50 Of this episode, Plutarch writes: "Porcia, being of an affectionate nature, fond of her husband, and full of sensible pride, did not try to question her husband about his secrets until she had put herself to the following test. She took a little knife, such as barbers use to cut the finger nails, and after banishing all her attendants from her chamber, made a deep gash in her thigh, so that there was a copious flow of blood." Loeb, ed., *The parallel lives*, 1918, VI, 113, 153.

51 "As for Porcia, the wife of Brutus, Nicolaüs the philosopher, as well as Valerius Maximus, relates that she now desired to die, but was opposed by all her friends, who kept strict watch upon her; whereupon she snatched up live coals from the fire, swallowed them, kept her mouth fast closed, and thus made away with herself." Ibid., 247.

52 This episode is described by Boccaccio in *De mulieribus claris*, LXIX.

opinion from us.[53] Nevertheless, because I cannot be faulted for this, I will call her a most learned woman. What of Maesia, whom they called Androgyne from the fact that beneath a feminine exterior she posses-sed a manly spirit? She pleaded her case before the magistrates amidst the greatest onslaught of the people, and with her first suit she was freed from almost all charges.[54] Gaia Afrania, wife of the senator Lucilius was also so good at [conducting] trials and lawsuits that she is said to have frequently delivered orations before various magistrates.[55] According to Macrobius, Augenona with her healing art, which they call medi-cine, is said to have served the men living near Lake Fucine, which she had previously occupied, to such an extent that they believed her to be a goddess. For this reason the Romans customarily celebrated her festival on December 21 at the shrine in Udapia.

But why continue? Am I so foolish as to believe that I could commemo-rate all the virtues and excellence of women? In our own age we saw the sister of Guidantonio, count of Urbino, Battista, for whom Leonardo Bruni, truly the most eloquent man of all in our time, wrote his *On Studies and Letters*;[56] we saw Elisabetta, wife of Carlo Malatesta, and another Elisabetta, the wife of Gentile of Camerino; and Costanza, wife of Alessandro Sforza, whose many letters, orations, and very graceful songs are still in the hands of many, some written for the Supreme Pontiff and others for a wide variety of other persons.[57] There is Paola[58], wife of the marchese of Mantua; and

---

53 Faltonia Betitia Proba was a fourth-century author who used verses of Virgil to create a Christian epic poem, the *Cento Vergilianus de laudibus Christi*. The work was criticized by St. Jerome.

54 Maesia of Sentinum is mentioned by Valerius Maximus, *Factorum et dictorum memorabilium*, 8.3.1 See also Anthony J. Marshall, "Roman ladies on trial: the case of Maesia of Sentinum." *Phoenix* 44(1) (Spring 1990), 46–59.

55 Gaia Afrania (d. 48 BCE), wife of Licinius Buccio, is mentioned by Valerius Maximus, who blames her as the cause for the passing of a law prohibiting women from pleading cases in court. *Factorum et dictorum memorabilium*, 8.3.2.

56 Battista da Montefeltro (1384–1448) was a learned woman and poet, married at the age of twenty-one to Galeazzo Malatesta, lord of Pesaro. Leonardo Bruni (1369–1444) writes in his dedication to *De studiis et liitteris*: "I am led to address this Tractate to you, Illustrious Lady, by the high repute which attaches to your name in the field of learning; and I offer it, partly as an expression of my homage to distinction already at-tained, partly as an encouragement to further effort. Were it necessary I might urge you by brilliant instances from antiquity: Cornelia, the daughter of Scipio, whose Epistles survived for centuries as models of style; Sappho, the poetess, held in so great honour for the exuberance of her poetic art; Aspasia, whose learning and eloquence made her not unworthy of the intimacy of Socrates. Upon these, the most distinguished of a long range of great names, I would have you fix your mind; for an intelligence such as your own can be satisfied with nothing less than the best. You yourself, indeed, may hope to win a fame higher even than theirs." Woodward, ed., *Vittorino da Feltre*, 123.

57 Elisabetta di Lodovico Gonzaga (1407–1477), first married to Carlo Malatesta, lord of Pesaro, then to Piergentile da Varano. She was mother of Costanza Varano Sforza (pp. 70–71).

58 Paola Malatesta (1393–1449).

Gentile[59], wife of another Malatesta; and the one who could easily surpass them all: Violante Colonna,[60] the wife of the illustrious and divine prince Novello Malatesta, who all excelled the women of old, I would say, not only in modesty, prudence, fortitude, constancy, generosity, piety and learning, but also in integrity and holiness.

But if we desire magnanimity, so great is this quality in Bianca[61], wife of the most illustrious duke of Milan, that with this one example our age can rival antiquity not only in magnanimity, but in every other kind of praise. I realize that the profusion of outstanding women who offered themselves of their own accord have presented an enormous amount of material for my discussion. Up to this point I have been carried away with a certain impetuosity and violence, without an opportunity for pausing, and I may perhaps have appeared to express myself carelessly, discussing some individuals, while passing over much more famous and illustrious ones. Thus we have observed Ricciarda of Saluzzo[62], wife of the divine and most illustrious prince Niccolò, marchese of Este, who was the last of his name to hold the principality of Ferrara, and her daughter Isotta[63]. Anyone who might wish to consider their appearance, grace, modesty, actions, voice, and face will conclude that they are no human women, but will assert that they, surpassing Venus herself in beauty, rather are goddesses. We read that these women were called happy: a Spartan who was daughter, wife, and mother of a king; a woman from the family of Curiones, in whose continuous line sprang up three orators; and one of the Fabii, from whom three consecutive leaders in the senate of the Romans issued: Marcus Fabius Ambustus, Fabius Rullianus, and Quintus Fabius Gurges. Not only could one add Ricciarda and Isotta to these, but it could be firmly asserted that they are far happier, since not only did they spring from a princely line, and great and excellent men were in their family, but also so great was their beauty, temperance, uprightness of character, and all the virtues, that they lacked nothing; it would be right for any goddess to choose to be a woman in our time.

But, in examining all these other women, are we neglecting our own? Who ever heard any immodesty of Bolognese matrons or that they were separated from virtue in any way? They are moderate,

---

59 Either Gentile Malatesta or her mother Gentile di Varano, married to Galeotto Malatesta.
60 Violante di Guidantonio da Montefeltro (b. 1439).
61 Bianca Maria Visconti (c. 1425–1468), married to Francesco Sforza, duke of Milan.
62 Ricciarda of Saluzzo (1410–1474) married Niccolò III d'Este, becoming marchesa of Ferrara.
63 Isotta (1425–1456) was the daughter of Niccolò d'Este and another woman, not of Ricciarda.

constant, generous, honest, pious, and chaste: it is scarcely believable that so many virtues could be collected by many cities in one age, or in many ages by one city. It has always been held that without virtue nothing can be the object of fervent striving; indeed, even if it were necessary, extreme tortures, pain, dangers, and even death itself would have to be tolerated for the sake of virtue by a strong spirit. But that is enough said of honor; now I will discuss necessity.

The human race is mortal and bound to perish; it is hidden from no one that one is born according to the law that one must die. Thus Pindar of Thebes, who easily excels all lyric poets, writes that man is a shadow and a kind of dream. Thus Theocritus[64] depicted two shepherds: when one had wanted to drive his cattle, he ran a little too carelessly across a certain hill, and a small thorn had been lodged in his ankle. Thoroughly terrified by the pain, he cried out to his companion, by the name of Coridon, to pluck out the thorn, and when Coridon had barely looked at it with intent eyes, and he had drawn it out with the tips of his fingernails, in the end he raised his voice in wonder, with the following words: 'How indeed does a tiny thorn master such a robust man?' It is for this reason that Homer wisely declared that the earth nurtures nothing more helpless than man.

Virgil also has Jupiter say the same thing eloquently, when he consoles Hercules for the future death of Pallas:

Then the Father consoled his offspring in loving words:

'Short bounds of life are set to mortal man.

'Tis virtue's work alone to stretch the narrow span.

So many sons of gods, in bloody fight,

Around the walls of Troy, have lost the light:

My own Sarpedon fell beneath his foe;

Nor I, his mighty sire, could ward the blow.

Ev'n Turnus shortly shall resign his breath,

And stands already on the verge of death.'[65]

---

64 Idyll IV, 50–55.
65 *Aeneid* X, 466–472, Dryden trans.

When the wise poet reminds us through the voice of Jupiter that even the children of the gods have fallen, we must believe that he means to show us nothing else, if not that this is common to the condition of such a race.

'Pale death beats her foot equally upon the taverns of the poor and the towers of the rich.'[66] No one, therefore, is allowed to extend his days. For we are driven by the fates and fate is inevitable. However, lest by chance my words be understood wrongly, I do not interpret fate in the sense of the Stoics, but by fate I mean the will of God. Therefore, by fate, i.e. by God's will, we all die and it is necessary that whatever is human must pass away. No one retains their outward appearance and nature changes one shape to another. Nor is it only men who give way, but everything that is born, as Crispus says: 'Everything that has risen falls, and everything that has waxed wanes.'[67] Nothing remains of Babylon, marvelous for its walls, its hanging gardens, its temple, and its citadel; nothing remains of Tyre, proud with its dye and purple; nothing remains of Corinth, noble for its bronzes; nothing remains of Athens, the inventor of all the good arts; nothing remains of [Crete] most celebrated for its one-hundred eight cities; nothing remains of Carthage, the rival of the Roman empire. All lie prostrate and shattered to pieces, and of some there are a few ruins, of others no vestige appears.

Well may the crow live for nine centuries, and the stag surpass it with four times the length of life, nevertheless both will know death. The poets represent Saturn, son of Uranus, devouring his own children so that with this image they may vividly show that time consumes everything. They mean that Saturn, in Greek, signifies nothing other than time, which being a celestial motion and measure, they declare arises from heaven. As Propertius[68] says, all things are overturned, as is forever this barbaric Memphis.[69] Virgil writes: "Time, the consumer of all things, and thou, hateful Old Age, together destroy all things; and, by degrees ye consume each thing, decayed by the teeth of age, with a slow death."[70]

All things surely perish, and after "on you Minos has made majestic judgment," as Horace said, "neither, Torquatus, shall family or eloquence

---

66 Horace, *Carmina*, Book 1, ode IV, 13–14.
67 Sallust, *Jugurtha*, II.
68 Book II, eleg. 8, v. 7.
69 Possibly a reference to Martial, Epigram XXXVI, "Regia pyramidum, Caesar, miracula ride; iam tacet Eoum barbara Memphis opus."
70 This is not Virgil, but Ovid, *Metamorphosis*, XV, 234–236, Riley trans.

or loyalty restore you."[71] As this is the case, it is easy to see that if it were not for this sex of ours, the human race would perish in a short time. Women are the ones who replenish families, republics, in fact, the entire human species, and what is greater still, they render it immortal. Knowing this, when the founder of Rome was lacking women, he did not hesitate to undertake a grievous war with the Sabines. For he was aware that such an empire would last only a very few days if women were not present. Thus, Most Eminent Lord, citing convenience, glory, and necessity, you have it in your power to judge most justly that the unfair law must be repealed and that our ornaments ought to be restored to us matrons. Besides, if the neighboring cities, the people of Rimini, Cesena, Forlì, Faenza, and all Flaminia, the people of Modena and Reggio and all Emilia and Liguria, the people of Mantua, Verona, Vicenza, Padua, and all Venice, and on the other side Tuscany and almost all the peoples who are less illustrious and dignified than we are enjoy these insignia of virtue, will it not be improper and unfair for the Bolognese, who deserve these ornaments most, to lack them, with which others are adorned, embellished, and ennobled? If we exceed others in virtue, ought we not at least to equal, if not surpass, others in this refinement that is proof of virtue? Thus patricians ought to be differentiated from plebeians, women of high rank from those who are low-born. Thus they say that the ancient Persian kings, having styles of dress varied for themselves and not worn by the vulgar, indulged themselves in much gold and many gems, so they might be distinguished from private citizens and ordinary subjects and so that the acts of veneration might be greater among them.

But certainly no one doubts that this city far outshines others? Listen, I beg you, Most Benign Lord, as I go through some proofs of her dignity and excellence, where, in order not to weary Your Lordship with an overly long recitation, I will not recount that, once called Felsina, it arose as a colony of Rome, and that after its overthrow, it was restored by a certain divine intervention. I shall not speak of the multitude of its population, the splendor of its buildings, the adornment of its churches, or the wonderful beauty of the city as a whole, which are by God evident and outstanding in its decorated elegance. I will narrate, rather, the thing in which praise and glory properly consists, about this city's industry, humanity, generosity, prudence, piety toward God, and religion. Taking everything into account, there is no city either in Italy or anywhere else in

---

71 Horace, *Carmina*, Book IV, 21–24.

the whole world which surpasses ours in matters either great or small, or in any kind of virtue. Leaving aside illiberal endeavors, where do the liberal arts thrive and seem to flower more than in Bologna? There is no one anywhere who knows anything of letters, who would not openly admit that he acquired it here, whether it is civil or canon law, whether philosophy or divine theology or the art of speaking itself; the mother and inventor of them all is Bologna. Not only the Tuscans, the Flaminians, the Venetians and the Emilians, but even Sicilians and inhabitants of the most distant reaches of Spain and almost all nations of the world flock here to the birthplace of all studies to lay hold of learning.

If we are looking for military prowess, which is by no means ignoble, we find even our deeds with those of others, and then we will realize what a difference there is between this city and the others. In particular, Bologna has waged many wars and resisted the mightiest enemies. She utterly defeated rising and formidable forces; nevertheless we have most firmly concluded that this was accomplished more through good judgment than by any other means. This is primarily because our citizens are so skilled that they sharply and quickly foresee favorable and unfavorable things, the future outcomes of things, almost as if they have been placed in a high position. On the other hand, in giving counsel, which requires the utmost wisdom, no one who received our advice ever failed to achieve what he desired.

Certainly how much the Bolognese excel in humanity can be easily ascertained by each man from the following: for it has always been the intention of this city that it should benefit the greatest number of people and that all should sense its generosity, especially those most in need. Therefore all who, either expelled by uprisings, or dispossessed by envy are driven as exiles from their homelands gather in Bologna, almost as if it were the sole place of refuge and protection of all. There is such attention to beneficence and humanity in this republic of ours that it appears to proclaim in a loud voice and publicly to affirm to all that no one should consider himself without a fatherland as long as this most noble city of ours exists. Not only are outsiders received with a joyful countenance and with the utmost favor and the utmost kindness of the residents, but if they have not seemed thoroughly undeserving they are assisted with resources and wealth. An almost infinite number of mortals are witnesses for me, that when mean circumstances were pressing on them and they had been unjustly exiled, they were helped by us with counsels and fortunes, and by the beneficence of our city they were restored to their homelands. I pass over the treaties arranged by our city between quarrelling peoples. I pass over delegations sent to reconcile opinions. Neither affection nor mercenary motives could ever persuade our city to consent to those wrongs by which some republic was being assailed. Nor did our city deem it fitting to be in tranquility or leisure while any city, whether ally or friend, or simply not an enemy, was in distress.

Moreover, that to this humanity and munificence was joined no less a sense of fidelity; we learn this from the fact that it was nowhere heard that this people of ours violated treaties or an oath due to partisanship, hatred, or self-interest. For this people of ours considered nothing more appropriate to honor than to preserve constancy in words and deeds, nothing further from it than betraying promises. Among other things, the greatest concern of our city has always been that one's own right might be most carefully rendered to each, otherwise it would not deserve to be called a city at all. Here no one can in any way suffer harm or loss of property unless he has wished it. The law courts and magistrates are pre-pared, the court and highest tribunal are accessible, and legal charges may be freely made against men of every rank. Who can adequately admire this honest and holy way of life? The youths themselves are so serious, restrained, honest, and religious as to have a certain divine quality and an almost prematurely aged wisdom, leading one easily to believe that all the virtues have made a fixed abode within the breasts of each one of us. If therefore this city wants for nothing that pertains to the highest praise and grandeur: not nobility of birth, as we arose from the Romans; not divine restoration; not ornament; not an abundance of all things; finally, not the entirety of dignity and excellence; shall we suffer this most distin-guished city to have its honor diminished in this one respect alone among other peoples? If, Most Reverend Lord, for women's renown, for their needs, or even for the greatness of our city you have no consideration, at least do not permit the men to be unpleasing to the women.

We know that when Romulus still ruled, it was women who brought a pause and an end to the harsh war between the Romans and the Sabines. And another time, when Coriolanus had pitched the camp of the Volsci within five miles of Rome and it seemed that the city would easily be overwhelmed by them, women turned away Coriolanus and the enemy troops. Likewise, when the city was captured by the Gauls, women brou-ght money into the public treasury to pay the ransom, and in many places, when there was need of Roman gold, Greek gold was added by them. Passing over other examples, when the Republic of the Romans was in the gravest danger, and they were summoning new gods to bring help, did not the women go all the way to the seashore to welcome the

Idean Mother? And when Fulvius desired Capua, were not two Capuan women such very good friends of Rome that one of them made incessant sacrifices daily for their army and the other, when the Roman troops were captured, supplied help out of necessity[72]? Women therefore settled the war with the Volsci, liberated their homeland, produced money to redeem it; they did not spare themselves labors, were assiduous in their prayers. Will the race of men be so ungrateful that in return for so many and such great benefits they will take away from us all our ornaments which are proofs of our very own virtue?

They say that Xenophon of Athens, the Socratic, in these books which he wrote about the education of Cyrus[73], reported that the Persians were very severe and vehement in their punishment of all crimes, and that they were accustomed to punish none with graver punishments than ingratitude, since in their opinion there was no greater vice, nor anything more foul, nor anything more pernicious to human society. If this law is not repealed, Most Righteous Lord, the whole sex will understand, the whole human race will understand that the thing was done not with that justice by which this populace has always achieved the highest praise, but with a very great iniquity. What indeed could be more unjust or iniquitous than to destroy the most just laws of the ancients and to corrupt customs approved over the longest period of time? For our ancestors were truly wise not to appear ungrateful, and they equipped the women with the most gracious decrees not only that they might use ancient insignia of the ears, purple robes, and glittering veils, but also what appeared worthier still, that men should yield to women in the street. Otherwise if it cannot be granted that this law against us be entirely abolished, then, I ask, demonstrate most openly that these insignia are fitting for women whose husbands use gold. These women, acting with similar authority to their husbands, ought to be subject to the same conditions, the same laws. For indeed, no one doubts that wives are made so illustrious in the human race through the nobility and glory of their lineage, and that the forum itself, which is suitable for their husbands, also pertains to them. And what renders our case more convincing is that when women marry a second time, choosing a man of lower rank, they are deprived of their earlier privileges by the later husband's social condition. Therefore, with good cause does Ulpian have it that only those women are known as most

---

72 Vestia Oppia and Pacula Clivia, described by Livy in *Ab urbe condita*, 26.23, 8.
73 *Cyropaedia*, I, 2, 7.

eminent who have been connected with the most eminent men. As long as daughters remain unmarried, their parents lend them rank and dignity. But when they are married to others, they are considered most eminent as long as they have remained with the most eminent men in marriage; otherwise, when separated from them they would not marry others of inferior rank. This right is ancient, not new, and to use the language of jurists, this right is recognized most clearly by the law. This case is demonstrated when Esther, on the recommendation of Mordecai, had approached her husband the Persian king Artaxerxes without invitation to intercede with him for the common sentencing of the Jews, and due to the very fact that she had not been invited, fear had seized her limbs (for there was a law that if anyone entered the king's presence without having been summoned he would be punished by death, unless the golden rod was immediately extended to him whom the king had wanted to be safe). The king drew his wife to his lap, caressed and kissed her, and persuaded her not to fear any harm from that approved law, adducing the fact that laws are declared for subjects, not for wives, who ought both to rule equally with their husbands and to have the same power. By this he seems to me to mean that whatever was permitted to men was suitable for their wives, and that women had been unjustly deprived of things which were allowed to their husbands.

But if you desire to be pleasing without considering convenience or the dignity of women or husbands, then keep faith, keep the laws, and at least keep the institutions of our ancestors. Be provident, and let not the avarice of some have more influence over you than the grandeur and glory of the whole city. Nor let the prayers of unjust men have more power than the most just petitions of the best. Allow virtue to attain her rewards. Permit the women who are worthy to use their insignia. Let not that which is permitted to inferior people be snatched from the more worthy through injustice. Public offices are not given to women, priesthoods, triumphs, the spoils of war, and they themselves do not contend; for such gifts by custom belong to men. But ornaments and their elegance, because they are the marks of our virtue, we will not allow to be taken from us, as far as we will be able.

Amen.

11.
———

*Laura Cereta to Agostino Emilio condemning women's
excessive luxury in dress*

*Writing mostly at night, when her household chores were done, Laura Cereta (1469–
1499) composed eloquent letters in Latin that blend both universal humanist themes
with a woman's more private, intimate concerns. Cereta was from Brescia, daughter of
the noblewoman Veronica di Leno and Silvestro Cereto, a well-to-do magistrate and
lawyer. The eldest of six children, Laura was sent to a convent at age six, where she
learned Latin from one of the nuns, whereas her brothers would be sent away to the
prestigious humanist school of Giovanni Olivieri. At nine years old she came home for
a time but then was sent back several months later for more Latin instruction. When
Cereta was eleven she was brought home to help take care of siblings, but she also
continued her studies with her father, with whom she remained close her whole life.
Relations with her mother appear to have been more problematic, although Cereta
recounts in her letters how from her earliest years she felt herself loved and treasured
above the other children. At age fifteen she married Pietro Serina, a Brescian merchant who had a shop on the Rialto in Venice. The marriage appears to have been
happy although short, as Serina died of the plague only eighteen months after the
couple was married. Cereta did not remarry, but throughout the following thirteen
years, until her death at age thirty, she continued her studies and writing. It is believed
that between 1486 and 1499 Cereta delivered public lectures in Brescia, but there is
no firm documentation for this. In addition to literature, her intellectual interests
spanned philosophy, mathematics, and astrology. Cereta's only work is a collection of*
Epistolae familiares *(Familiar Letters), comprising eighty-two of her Latin letters
preceded by a comic dialogue "Asinarium funus" ("On the Death of an Ass"). The only
woman's letter collection from this period to be deliberately assembled by the author in
order to create a literary autobiographical narrative, Cereta's volume circulated in a
number of bound manuscript copies from around 1488 but was not printed until
1640. These letters are written to learned men and women, including one to Cassandra Fedele (pp. 45–46). While many of Cereta's letters were written to real persons
whom she knew, such as her husband, her sister, female friends, colleagues of her
father, and her brothers' teacher, other addressees were fictional. She invented these
individuals as a device to frame more or less formal essays on humanist topics such as*

the true nature of pleasure, the active versus the contemplative life, how best to pursue virtue, and the power of Fortune over human life. In a number of Cereta's letters, she responds to critics who ridiculed her literary efforts or claimed that a man had penned her writings. The most interesting thing about her epistolary collection is the way Cereta mingles details of her personal life, marriage, and relations with family members with her elevated humanist discourse and succeeds in expressing a uniquely feminist perspective on Renaissance society.

Cereta wrote this letter around six months after her husband's death; its abrupt, almost cold description of his final days differs dramatically from the howling pain she expresses in other letters. We have no clue as to the identity of the Agostino Emilio to whom this letter is addressed, or indeed of determining whether he was an actual or fictive person. Apart from the opening, the focus of the letter is almost entirely a condemnation of women's frivolity and vanity, criticizing a misplaced concentration on the adornments of the body over those of the mind. The attitudes expressed by Cereta stand in sharp contrast to those of Nicolosa Castellani Sanuti (pp. 73–90), who defends the right to wear fine clothes and jewels as an outward sign of a woman's noble character.

Laura Cereta to Agostino Emilio

I was spending time alone in the country and delighting in humanist studies in the tranquility of leisure; however, you meanwhile were worried about my coming to my family's place, as if, insignificant as I am, you seemed much concerned about me.

I arrived just at the end, while my husband was feverish; feeling that I was myself dying, I found him half-dead. I comforted him when he seemed a little better, wept when he died, and fell lifeless over his dead body, and that fatal home, which was awaiting me for marriage, received me for mourning. Thus one unspeakable year saw me a maiden, a wife, a widow, and rendered destitute of all the goods of Fortune. This lot was drawn by her[74], not you; for the thing which occurred was demanded by your human condition.[75]

I am grateful to you for considering me of greater worth than I deserve and placing such honors on me, though I can hardly be ranked

---

74 *Fortuna* or Fortune—that is, the mythic figure from antiquity who was believed to control human destiny by turning her wheel.
75 There is some textual discrepancy here in the manuscripts; consequently this sentence is translated differently by King and Rabil in *Her immaculate hand,* 78, and Robin in *Collected letters,* 83. I have chosen to consider the "you" in this sentence as addressed to Cereta's deceased husband.

among Sarah[76], Esther[77], Zipporah[78], and Susanna[79], since [compared with them] I am like that glowworm shining at night among the blazing stars in the heavens. So I sufficiently fear that this high respect you have for me originates accidentally from some other source than your measured judgment. Imagine before you an insignificant woman, lowliest in appearance of both face and dress, as I prefer the study of literature over decoration. Naturally I bound myself thoroughly to that concern for virtue which can be useful to me not only in this life, but even after death. There are those who are captivated by beauty's allurements; I myself would rather have granted a greater reward to senatorial chastity, as especially in the attractive company of handsome youth, seductive passions often flare up. Nevertheless honor outshines beauty, the elaborately contrived arts of polish, and all pretty, little flowers of softness. Let Mark Antony delight in the bejeweled Cleopatra; I myself will imitate the chastity of Rebecca. Let Paris go off after the wandering Helen; I have chosen to imitate the modesty of Rachel. Wives are too beguiled by showiness; even more foolish are the men who through their appetite for those women destroy their patrimonies.

Nowadays the love for women has made our city a disciple, or rather a despoiler, of the East. In no other age has this luxury of vanity increased to such prodigality. Let those who do not believe me enter the public spaces of a church and observe a wedding, full of matrons in attendance; let them gaze upon these women, who in haughty majesty cut a path through crowds on the public streets. Among these, there will be this or that one who wears someone else's hair piled high like a tower and tied in a knot on top of her head; another has waves of curls tumbling down her forehead; another ties her strawberry blond hair up with a golden ribbon to bare her neck. This one drapes a necklace from her shoulder, another from her arm, another from her neck down to her breast. Others suffer their necks to be bound by a chain of pearls; as if, though born free, they glory in being held captive. And many display fingers sparkling

---

76 Sarah, wife of Abraham, known for her beauty and courage. Unable to bear children herself, Sarah offered her slave Hagar to her husband so he could have a child and continue the line of descent. Later Sarah was blessed by God as a "mother of nations," and at the age of ninety she bore a son, Isaac. Gen. 17:15–19.

77 Esther was a Jewish heroine who saved her people by intervening with her husband Xerxes, king of Persia, to prevent a genocide. Esther 2:7–22.

78 Zipporah (Sefora in Italian), wife of Moses. In Exodus 4:25 there is an episode in which she saves her husband from being killed God's wrath by snatching up a stone and herself circumcising their son.

79 Susanna was a Biblical character who successfully defended herself against the sexual advances of two Jewish elders and their unjust accusations in court. Dan. 13 RSVC.

with gems. One, desiring to take tinier steps, walks with a looser girdle, while another cinches hers tighter and has her breasts swelling outward. Some trail silken garments from their shoulders; others fragrant with perfume cover themselves in Arabian veils. There are also those who wear leather slippers with stilts under their feet[80], and it has become widely known that more fashionable women bind and cover their legs more softly with swathes of soft fine linens. Many press softened bread against their faces; many artificially enhance their skin which is covered with wrinkles. There are really very few who do not paint their ruddy faces with white lead pigments. Other women with other more exquisite refinements strive to be seen as more beautiful than the Creator of beauty allotted. The impudence of some women is shameful, reddening their milky-white cheeks with purple dye; with furtive glances and laughing mouths they pierce the poisoned hearts of their admirers. O, the polished aspect of ruined modesty! O the perverse weakness for luxury in our sex! What keeps us from resembling pagans when bracelets trembling with precious stones and emeralds drip from our ears? Is it for this perchance, that we are begotten, that with this shameless devotion we should adore the idol of our own visages in the mirror? Was it for this that when we were baptized we renounced showiness, so that Christian women should resemble Jews and barbarians?

Let ambition, greatly broken in this desire for superiority, blush with shame. Let the lustful dispositions of our frenzy be on guard against such great arrogance as this, and thinking of the ashes from which we come, let us curtail the errors being reborn from our desires. How will our lamentation be heard if heavenly anger and indignation should perhaps blaze against us miserable women? If those who revolt against the king ready their necks for the death blow, why should we women, rebels ourselves, or rather warriors against God, marvel if for our crime those multitudes of Turks rise up against the Cenomani?[81] Rome still deplores the arrival of the Gauls. A conquered Italy laments the swords of the Goths. Nor do the Greeks rejoice at Mahomed's tyranny. Not from our own violent force, but from on high these aggressive calamities come forth. Thus let each woman look after and heal the wound from which she, being wounded, languishes. Let us pursue

---

80 The footwear Cereta is describing is known as "chopines." Popular among Italian women in the sixteenth century, especially in Venice, the platforms of these shoes could be as high as 20 cm.
81 A tribe of Gauls who supported Rome but joined Hamilcar in an uprising against Rome in 200 BCE and were subsequently wiped from the historical record.

honorable decorations, not bawdy finery, and let us enjoy this life in such a way that we are always mindful of our mortality. For God the Father Himself has decided that it belongs to the good to die well.

I would therefore wish, Augustine, that as often as you have seen these inane glories of such great splendor among us, you would pardon the age or, at least, my sex. For our nature is not immune from this error; our mother [Eve] was produced not from earth nor from stone, but from Adam's humanity. However, humanity can always strive toward that which is beneficial or to that which is enticing. We are a rather imperfect animal, and our meager powers do not withstand mighty battles. You most eminent men, wielding such authority, who reach such heights of success, who rightly consider among your number so many modern-day Brutuses, so many Curiuses, Fabriciuses, Catos, and Aemiuliuses, look around more carefully: do not let yourselves be trapped in the snare of such well-arranged elegance. For where there is greater wisdom, there guilt weighs more heavily. Before the Ides of February.

Suggestions for further reading

Letter 7, Maddalena Scrovegni: King, "Goddess and Captive: Antonio Loschi's epistolary tribute to Maddalena Scrovegni (1389)," In *Humanism, Venice, and women*; King and Rabil, *Her immaculate hand*, 34–35; Kohl, *Padua under the Carrara, 1318–1405*, esp. 175–177, 261–262; Medin, "Maddalena degli Scrovegni e le discordie tra i Carraresi e gli Scrovegni"; Stevenson, "Women and classical education in the early modern period"; Stevenson, *Women Latin poets: language, gender, and authority*, esp. 157–158.

Letter 8, Isotta Nogarola: Fenster, "Strong voices, weak minds? The defenses of Eve by Isotta Nogarola and Christine de Pizan"; Jardine, "Isotta Nogarola: women humanists—education for what?"; King, "Book-lined cells"; King and Rabil, *Her immaculate hand*; Kristeller, "Learned women of Early Modern Italy: humanists and university scholars"; Nogarola, *Complete writings*, ed. and trans. King and Robin; Parker, "Angela Nogarola (c. 1400) and Isotta Nogarola (1418–1466): thieves of language," In Churchill, Brown, and Jeffrey, *Early modern women writing Latin*.

Letter 9, Costanza Varano: Clough, "Daughters and wives of the Montefeltro: outstanding bluestockings of the Quattrocento"; Feliciangeli "Notizie di Costanza Varano-Sforza"; Feliciangeli, Notizie e documenti sulla vita di Caterina Cibo-Varano; King and Rabil, *Her immaculate hand*, 18, 39–44, 53–56; Parker, "Costanza Varano (1426–1447): Latin as an instrument of state," In Churchill, Brown, and Jeffrey, *Early modern women writing Latin*, 31–53; Webb, "Hidden in plain sight: Varano and Sforza women of the Marche," In McIver, *Wives, widows, mistresses, and nuns in early modern Italy*.

Letter 10, Nicolosa Castellani Sanuti: Comelli, "Di Nicolò Sanuti primo conte della Porretta"; Frati, "Lettere amorose di Galeazzo Marescotti e di Sante Bentivoglio"; Frati, *La Vita privata in Bologna dal secolo XIII al XVII*; Kovesi, " 'Heralds of a well-instructed mind': Nicolosa Sanuti's defence of women and their clothes"; Kovesi, *Sumptuary law in Italy 1200–1500*; Lombardi, "Traduzione, imitazione, plagio (Nicolosa Sanuti, Albrecht von Eyb, Niclas von Wyle)"; Boccaccio, *Famous Women*; Hemelrijk, *Matrona docta: educated women in the Roman elite from Cornelia to Julia Domna*.

Letter 11, Laura Cereta: Cereta, *Collected letters,* ed. and trans. Robin; Gill, "Fraught relations in the letters of Laura Cereta: marriage, friendship, and humanist epistolarity"; King and Rabil, *Her immaculate hand*; Rabil, *Laura Cereta: Quattrocento humanist*; Robin, "Humanism and feminism in Laura Cereta's public letters"; Robin, "Woman, space, and Renaissance discourse," In Gold and Miller, *Sex and gender,* esp. 172–181.

Chapter Three

Governing the Household/
Governing the State

How much power did women wield in Renaissance Italy? If one is referring to political power, the answer is that it varied by region. The Italian penin-sula during this time was not a unified nation but was divided into a constellation of principalities, duchies, and republican city-states. In *The Prince*, Niccolò Machiavelli (1469–1527) describes the tactics employed by Renaissance kings, dukes, and despots such as Ferdinand of Aragon, Ludovico Sforza, and Cesare Borgia. All of Machiavelli's Renaissance "princes" were men; however, women also ruled, especially in duchies and smaller principalities. Women governed in place of their husbands, as did Isabella d'Este (Chapter 8) and her mother Eleonora d'Aragona, duchess of Ferrara, while their husbands were away at war, or ruled outright when widowed, as did Caterina Cibo Varano (1501–1557) in Camerino and Veronica Gambara in Correggio (Chapter 8). Few women defied the male hierarchy as openly as did Giovanna d'Aragona Colonna (1502–1575), who left her husband and went to rule as duchess of Tagliacozzo on her own, or Caterina Sforza (Chapter 4), who steadfastly defended her territories even as her children were held hostage. Even those who did not rule outright were deeply involved in decisions of state. Eleonora Gonzaga (1493–1550), duchess of Urbino, was her husband's valued confidante, and Lucrezia Borgia, in a letter written when she was only fourteen years old, demonstrates her political astuteness in her advice to her father, the pope. In contrast, women outside the court environment, for instance in the Venetian and Florentine republics, did not wield much political power, at least outwardly. Excluded from guilds and from participation in government, forbidden even to set foot in the Palazzo Vecchio (city hall), Florentine women sometimes influenced politics in other, indirect ways. Both Alessandra Strozzi (Chapter 4) and Lucrezia Tornabuoni took active roles in selecting spouses for their children, and in the case of Tornabuoni, her son Lorenzo de' Medici's marriage had a decisive impact on the future of the Medici dynasty. Similarly, Maria Salviati's steadfast refusal to her remarry after her husband's death made it possible to dedicate herself to helping her son govern as duke of Florence. Finally, the political arena is not the only one to be considered; power can also be exercised within the household or in control of a family business. Whereas humanist writers such as Leon Battista Alberti (1404–1472) in *I libri della famiglia* and Matteo Palmieri (1406–1475) in *Vita civile* portray a woman's role in society as extremely circumscribed, women such as Margherita Datini, Guglielmina Schianteschi, and Alessandra Strozzi emerge from their letters as forceful defenders of the family's economic and political interests. All three of these women were obliged to take control when separated from male members of their households who were either exiled or away on business. Even women who lived cloistered lives could be involved in influencing important family matters. From within the confines of her convent in Prato, young Saint Caterina de' Ricci gave her family members business and personal advice, even taking the time in the evening after one of her mystical visions to write a letter urging her father to resolve a family quarrel.

12.

___

Margherita Datini criticizes her husband Francesco Datini
for his handling of business matters

Margherita Bandini Datini (1360–1423) was the daughter of two Florentine nobles, Domenico Bandini and Dianora Gherardini. When Margherita was an infant her father, who along with other elites had been excluded from holding government offices, was involved in a plot to overthrow the Florentine Republic. The plot failed and Domenico was arrested and executed. Afterward, Dianora took Margherita and her other children and moved to Avignon, where she had relatives in the thriving Florentine merchant community that served the papal court. In Avignon Margherita met Francesco di Marco Datini (c. 1335–1410), a native of Prato whose parents had both died in the Black Death when he was thirteen or fourteen years old. Raised by relations, as a young man Francesco was apprenticed to a merchant, after which he set out on his own, becoming very wealthy selling weapons, cloth, and other commodities in Avignon. The couple was married in 1376; five years later they returned to Italy, dividing their time between two homes, one in Prato, the other in Florence. Francesco was frequently away on business and the two wrote constantly, mostly while one was in Florence and the other in Prato, about twenty-three kilometers away. Two hundred fifty-one letters from Margherita to Francesco and 181 letters from him to Margherita have survived. The letters were written between 1384 and 1410, dating from eight years after the couple's marriage until shortly before Francesco's death. While their correspondence also concerns business and political matters, it provides us with an unusually intimate view of the relationship between the Datinis. We learn from their letters, for instance, that Francesco fathered a number of illegitimate children; one, by a servant, was a son who died as a baby. Another was a girl named Ginevra, born in 1392, whose mother was a household slave. Margherita, who was often ill and unable to have children of her own, raised Ginevra as her daughter and in her letters demonstrates deep tenderness for the girl. Margherita often takes a harsh and reprimanding tone with her husband, scolding him for his bad habits, nagging him about his health, and giving advice on how to manage business affairs. Indeed, it emerges from the correspondence that during her husband's frequent absences Margherita not only supervised the household but also watched very closely over the business.

This letter is addressed to Francesco in Pisa, where he had a branch of his company. Margherita dictated this to a scribe; very few of the letters that have come down to us were written in her own hand.[1] Several years later Margherita would teach herself to write; however, even after learning to write, she preferred to dictate most of her letters. She is conscious not only of the scribe but of others who may have access to her correspondence with her husband. In several places she hints at sensitive material, which it is best not to put into writing. Indeed, at the end of her letter she tells Francesco that after reading it, he should destroy it. She also accuses him of being indiscreet in sharing too much personal information with business colleagues. Although her tone is brusque, Margherita is not all business in this letter; she also expresses a tender concern for her husband's health, both physical and mental, referring in particular to the condition of malinconia or "melancholy," a sadness or anxiety believed by doctors at the time to be caused by an imbalance of the bodily humors.[2] Margherita uses the word four times in regard to Francesco and once in referring to herself, describing how frightened she had been by a health crisis her husband had suffered. Perhaps it is not surprising that Francesco decided not to destroy this touching letter.

In the name of God, amen. On the 20th of January 1385 [1386]

Today I received your letter, written on the 19th of this month and I will respond here as necessary.

You say about one of the letters that I sent you that it was very nicely composed.[3] I don't know if you are saying that in jest, but if you meant it, I am pleased.

In my opinion it appears that Boninsegna and I have not advised you well, as you've never wanted to do what he tells you. I do not speak of myself, since I'm a woman and a man doesn't let himself be ruled by women's advice.

Concerning your arrival here, I am pleased. I ask you to make an effort and do me a big favor: I am begging you to avoid having gout this Carnival season. It would be very bad for you, with all you have to do right now. You should not always be having troubled thoughts, and don't go around saying that I make fun of all your suffering. I don't mind if you tell me face to face, but don't write these things.

You left a warehouse here to be managed by two people who might be said to be worth less than half a person. You know how your friend goes away as he pleases. One day the bell sounds at vespers; some days

---

1   Crabb writes that "only twenty-two of Margherita Datini's 285 letters are autograph" ("If I could write," 1174–1175), while James says that Margherita used "her own hand in less than ten of the surviving letters" (*Letters to Francesco*, 12).

2   Mellyn, *Mad Tuscans* 139–160 on the Renaissance medicalization of melancholy.

3   The Italian reads "*bene dettata*," literally "well dictated"; see introduction pp. 16–17 on collaborative writing. On dictation as composition see also Crabb "If I could write," 1175–1178.

it doesn't ring at all; and on Saturday when there is most need it doesn't ring. Think how your affairs are being managed! You send us letters constantly, and between having them carried over there where he is and having the others sent, the warehouse is closed half the time. A lot of people come looking for you and find the door shut; it seems like a business run by children. I would advise you if you have another leaky boat around, send him here, because you seem to like that. You can stay up late writing long letters of four or five pages, but it means nothing to the friend you send it to, since he has two lady-tutors who help him read: his mother and his daughter. They and all the other women at the warehouse read your letters. That's how much sense he has: this way you will never need to tell others about all your business. I don't know what need there is to write your friend telling him about all your cares [*maninchonie*] and every single matter. You might say to me: "What do you know about what I write to him?" I know nothing except what I can imagine, knowing what you are like. Simone tells me you write him letters that are three or four pages long; I can't believe these bibles you send day after day are all about business. This must be a way you have of unloading your soul of worries [*maninchonie*] that you have, but I would not trust him more than the others. The reason is that, aside from Boninsegna and Tieri, there is no one who doesn't cheat you a dozen times a day. You have seen it yourself and know whether or not I am speaking the truth and you ought to guard yourself against that one man most of all. He knows better how to do it than all the others, since he's had practice. I wish to God that these were outright lies about him, although it's rare that the things I tell you aren't true. If you were as highly honored as you have been disrespected it would be a good thing for you, since a hundred people wish you harm, although they didn't use to. I am telling you this because these things I hear people saying weigh on me and your shame seems like my own. I trust in God that you will recognize this one as you recognized the others. On this matter I will say no more. I pray you do not handle this like you do other matters; these are things that create too much hatred and could ruin your whole business. I pray you that you handle yourself calmly with him and with the others until you are somewhat relieved from these worries [*manichonie*] of yours and can deal with them as they deserve. For God's sake don't let yourself get carried away by this wickedness, since it would ruin you. Give them your word and many promises until you achieve what you want, as a man kisses the hand that he wishes to have chopped off.

I understood a lot of things from your other letter and it troubles me that it is written with much melancholy [*manichonia*] and that you are full of it. As you do not want to reveal anything to me, I believe it is for the best and I appreciate it. I wish you would do the same with others— you would be more praised than you are. It weighs on me that when you return, your health might be worse and this is the greatest worry [*maninchonia*] I have, since for so many reasons, you gave me the worst day of my life (even if perhaps I thought it was worse than it was). Think of living in a manner so that all your affairs will go well. They will succeed if you will it. I do not want to say any more about this. I am asking you to burn this letter after you read it; do this service for me, I pray you. Lapa and all the other women send a hundred thousand greetings. May God protect you always.

From your Margherita,
who commends herself to you, from Florence

13.
———

Lucrezia Tornabuoni reports her impressions of a prospective bride for their son to husband Piero de' Medici

When she died, Lorenzo de' Medici (the Magnificent, 1459–1492) wrote of Lucrezia Tornabuoni (1427⁴–1482) that he had lost "not only my mother, but an irreplaceable refuge from my troubles and relief in my labors." Born into an elite Florentine banking family (her father was Francesco Tornabuoni and her mother Nanna Guiciardini) and married at age seventeen to Piero di Cosimo de' Medici (1416–1469), until the end of her life Lucrezia Tornabuoni would be at the center of Florence's political, cultural, and religious life. Like most upper-class Florentine marriages, this was not a love match but a kind of business merger, consolidating the power of these influential clans. Nevertheless, the couple developed a close partnership, in which Piero came to rely on Lucrezia's wise judgment, as their son Lorenzo later admitted to doing. She handled many state matters, as her husband was frequently ill with gout, a disease that ran in the Medici family; she traveled to Rome, for instance, in 1467, where she discussed delicate diplomatic negotiations concerning Venice with the pope. She was also a shrewd businesswoman, who was responsible for renovating Bagni a Morba, a hot spring ten miles south of Volterra. There she supervised the installation of thermohydraulic equipment and the construction of a private estate for her family as well as an inn for paying guests. Although her own health was never strong—she suffered from a debilitating form of arthritis—Lucrezia gave birth at least six times, and raised five children who survived to adulthood. There were three daughters, Bianca, Lucrezia ("Nannina," pp. 136–137), and Maria⁵, and two sons, Lorenzo and Giuliano. When Piero died in 1469, Lucrezia was forty-two and her eldest son Lorenzo only twenty; she provided him with crucial guidance from behind the scenes during the perilous transition of power. During her widowhood Lucrezia Tornabuoni came into her own as both a writer and patron of literature. Lorenzo's tutor Gentile Becchi, in a letter to Lucrezia in 1473, mentions in passing: "You have always read so

---

4   Mario Martelli cites Lucrezia Tornabuoni's birthdate as June 22, 1427, from her father's registration of her Monte delle doti (dowry fund); later her age is rounded to 1425 by her husband and son in the family *catasto* (tax) declaration (see introduction p. 27). He credits Patrizia Salvadori with this discovery. *Les femmes* écrivains, 51.

5   Jane Tylus writes: "No birthdate is known for Maria, apparently the oldest of the five; it has been suggested that she was Piero's illegitimate daughter but raised within the Medici household." *Sacred narratives*, 31.

much that the study is full of books." It was probably during this period that she began writing a series of laudi *(sacred poems) and five* storie sacre, *or sacred narratives, extensive poems based on the biblical stories of Judith, Esther, Susannah, John the Baptist, and Tobias. She shared drafts with Florence's leading humanist, Angelo Poliziano, and the poet Luigi Pulci, who dedicated his epic poem* Morgante *to her. Lucrezia was devastated when her younger son, Giuliano was killed in the 1478 Pazzi Conspiracy; however, when in the aftermath of the assassination the rest of Lorenzo's family took refuge in Pistoia, she remained beside him in Florence during the crisis. Lucrezia Tornabuoni was known throughout her life for her religious devotion and extensive charitable works; the hundreds of letters to her in the Florentine State Archive are testimony to her dedication to helping the unfortunate.*

One of forty-nine surviving letters written by Lucrezia Tornabuoni, here she reports to Piero on a prospective bride for their son Lorenzo, Clarice Orsini (1453–1488). The Orsini were one of the most powerful noble Roman families, and in choosing a wife from outside the Florentine elite, it is clear that the Medici in their dynastic strategy were beginning to consider foreign alliances. The Orsini could establish connections with the papacy; indeed, it was a successful strategy, for Clarice's son, Lucrezia's grandson, would become Pope Leo X (Giovanni de' Medici, 1475–1521). In addition to the Roman family's connections and financial assets, however, in this letter Lucrezia focuses on the physical traits and comportment of her potential daughter-in-law, assessing her appearance and character in order to determine whether she will be a good match for the Medici and for her son Lorenzo. Piero trusted his wife's judgment in this very important family decision, and the couple was married in 1469.

Along the way I wrote to you often, telling you about the roads we took to get here. I arrived Thursday and was received by Giovanni[6] with great delight as you can imagine. I received your letter of the 21st, and it relieved me greatly to learn that you are no longer in pain. Nonetheless, every day seems like a year until I return, both for your consolation and for my own.

Thursday morning, going to St. Peter's I met Maddalena Orsini, the cardinal's sister; she had with her her daughter [Clarice], who is fifteen or sixteen years old. She was dressed in the Roman fashion, with a draped shawl, and dressed like that she seemed very lovely to me, fair and tall, but since the girl was covered up I could not see her as well as

---

6   Giovanni Tornabuoni, Lucrezia's brother, was manager of the Rome branch of the Medici bank and later became papal treasurer under Sixtus IV. Patrizia Salvadori identifies Giovanni as the copyist of this letter.

I would have liked. Yesterday, as it happened, I went to visit Monsignor Orsini, mentioned above, in his sister's home, which adjoins his. After I greeted him and paid my respects to his Lordship on your behalf, the sister unexpectedly appeared with the said girl, this time wearing a tight skirt in the Roman style, but without the shawl. We stayed quite a while talking together and I was able to study the girl closely. As I have said, she is of acceptable height and has fair skin; she has a sweet manner, but is not as well-bred as our girls; however, she displays great modesty and will soon learn our customs. She is not blond, because they are not like that here; her red hair, of which there is plenty, hangs loose. Her face is a little on the round side, but it does not displease me. Her neck is suitably slender, but seems to me a little thin, or rather delicate. We could not see her bust, because it is the custom here to go around all covered up, but it seems to be of good quality. She goes around with her head not held high like our girls, but she carries it a little forward, and this I believe is due to her embarrassment, for I see no reason for her posture other than that. Her hands are long and slender, and all in all, we judge her to be above average, although not to be compared with Maria, Lucrezia, and Bianca.[7] Lorenzo himself has seen her; you will learn yourself whether he is content. Whatever you and he decide will be fine and I will go along with it. May God guide you to make the best choice.

The girl's father is Jacopo Orsini of Monterotondo, and her mother is the sister of the cardinal. She has two brothers, one is a man of arms, who is held in high esteem by Signor Orso; the other is a subdeacon priest of the pope. They have one half of Monterotondo, the other half belongs to their uncle, who has two sons and three daughters. They have, in addition to this half of Monterotondo, three other castles, belonging to her brothers, and as far as I can learn they are well off, and doing ever better, for, besides being nephews of the cardinal, the archbishop, Napoleon, and the knight, through their mother, they are also cousins through their father's side since the girl's father is second cousin in direct line of the aforesaid lords, who love him dearly. And this is what I have been able to describe. If before setting the thing in motion you wanted to await our return, do as you see fit.

I am thinking of leaving here on Monday the 8th, taking the road that you know of and will be there at the arranged time. May God in His

---

7 These are Piero and Lucrezia's daughters.

Grace conduct us safely home and keep you in good health. I am not writing to Monna Contessina[8], since it does not seem necessary. Commend me to her and send the girls my greetings as well as Lorenzo and Giuliano. In Rome, on the 28th of March, 1467.

Your Lucrezia

---

8   Contessina de' Bardi (c. 1390–1473), Lucrezia's mother-in-law and widow of Cosimo the Elder.

14.
———

*Eleonora d'Aragona complains to husband Ercole d'Este about
his soldiers' unbridled violence*

*The daughter of Ferdinando I d'Aragona, king of Naples, and Isabella Chiaramonte,
princess of Taranto, Eleonora d'Aragona (1450–1493) outranked her husband the
duke of Ferrara not only in birth but in strength of character and judgment. Married
in 1473 to Ercole I d'Este (1431–1505), Eleonora gave birth to seven children in the
first eight years of the marriage. This rapid succession of children, five of whom were
male, guaranteed the continuance of the Este dynasty; her eldest child was a girl,
Isabella d'Este (pp. 213–214), her second was Beatrice d'Este (1475–1497), who
became duchess of Milan, and her eldest son was Alfonso I d'Este (1476–1534), who
would marry Lucrezia Borgia (pp. 116–117). While Ercole was away in 1476, two of
his cousins attempted a coup and Eleonora was forced to flee the palace with the three
small children, taking refuge in the fortified castle nearby. Her husband was often
away, either in the countryside hunting at one of his estates, or off on one of many
military campaigns, and on these occasions it was the Duchess Eleonora who governed
Ferrara. A contemporary chronicler wrote: "She holds audiences with the populace
and listens to their supplications and is well-regarded by the people of Ferrara, whereas
the duke is concerned with pleasures, playing [cards], and riding in the park." Known
as an extremely efficient administrator, she was frequently occupied with official duties,
which included traveling to other courts and attending ceremonies, even throughout
the years of continual childbearing. Her responsibilities as a ruler were always her foremost concern, as she advised her daughter Isabella in a letter: "Remember that you
must do whatever is necessary for your subjects and citizens according to their needs
and according to whatever situation may arise."[9] In 1482, at the time of the war between Venice and Ferrara, her husband was bedridden from a foot injury and uncon-
scious while Ferrara was under siege from enemy troops. Eleonora was called upon to
direct the city's defense; her courage and good judgment earned her the respect of her
subjects and rulers of other states. A treatise on governing well and a number of books*

---

9   Letter from Eleonora d'Aragona to Isabella d'Este, April 15, 1491, trans. Mazzocco, 288.

on the excellence of women were dedicated to her.[10] An important patron of the arts, Eleonora d'Aragona commissioned music and many works of art to decorate the Este palace in Ferrara; she was also the subject of a large fresco cycle there that unfortunately no longer exists. When she died of pneumonia at the age of forty-three, as Charles VIII was planning to invade Italy, Ferdinando I, king of Naples, is said to have exclaimed: "Now indeed has the staunchest bastion against the French fallen!"

This letter was written in early 1482 during the period immediately leading up to the War of Ferrara of 1482–1484 (also known as the Salt War), in which the Republic of Venice, Pope Sixtus IV, and his nephew Girolamo Riario, lord of Imola and Forlì, sought to conquer the territory of Ferrara. Aligned with Ferrara were the duke of Milan, the duke of Urbino, and the king of Naples. Renaissance military accounts are usually concerned with large-scale political conflict and details of battles but rarely focus on war's impact on civilian populations. In this letter Eleonora d'Aragona paints a vivid picture of the sufferings of the Ferrarese people, oppressed by the presence of a large military force. Ostensibly present to defend the city, paid soldiers of fortune were always on the lookout for plunder and if not reined in could give in to unbridled violence. She urges her husband to use his authority to halt the crimes committed by these "friendly" soldiers. By fall of 1482, when conditions worsened, with enemy troops surrounding the city, breaking into the game reserve, slaughtering animals, and preparing to besiege the city, Eleonora was forced to take control herself.

> If Your Lordship does not impose some kind of order on these soldiers who are staying here in the Barco[11], and see to it that they are punished for murdering, robbing, sacking, and mistreating your subjects, I see a very clear danger in this populace. I say this because of what happened after the murders carried out following Your Excellency's departure; yesterday they killed a respectable man here in Caldirolo after stealing a pig from him. Never were such pitiful sights seen: the tears and cries of brothers and parents of the dead, all bloody and discontent, who come before me demanding action. This morning around twenty men at arms with a good number of foot soldiers went to Baura[12] with good wagons and sacked the entire countryside, making off with wine, beds, linens, and everything those poor people had in their homes. And in the house of Alberto Francesco de Guarino they broke down the doors

---

10   Diomede Carafa, *Memoriale sui doveri del principe*, translated into Latin by Baptista Guarino as *De Regis et boni principis officio*; Bartolomeo Gogio, *De laudibus mulierum*; Jacopo Foresti da Bergamo, *De claris mulieribus*.

11   Created by Ercole I d'Este, the Barco of Belfiore was a large game reserve which extended from the northern wall of the city to the banks of the Po.

12   An area approximately 9 km outside the city of Ferrara.

and the locks and sacked everything. Besides the peasants' livestock they carried away from Baldissera fruit and some of his cows that he kept there, then took the whole herd and led it away. And they did these things to many other citizens, in such a way that not even an enemy with his army would have done a fraction of the harm, and it seems to me that because of poor discipline they have no fear and do want they want, feeling it is permitted since they have no superiors to punish them. [I am] reminding Your Lordship that these were not the troops of the Magnificent Messer Zohanne[13], but indeed Your Excellency's own men, because a manservant of Gregeto the crossbowman, along with some other troublemakers, was the one who killed the unfortunate man with the pig yesterday evening. And from what I was told, the ones with very little in their heads were the ones who carried out the sack of Baura today, because Bartolomeo was recognized as the head of the raid. Many others come every hour to lament similar extortions, wounds, and mistreatment in such a way that when I understand it and see that I cannot take care of them, not being in control of an army, poor woman that I am, I would wish to be found dead rather than alive, or so far from here that I would be unable to hear these diabolical things. The most Illustrious Messer Sigismondo cannot leave his house due to a foot injury he received during yesterday's raid. Messer Nicolò Corezo[14] has no authority and does not command obedience. I do not know where to turn to take care of so many insufficiencies, which unless God in His wrath refuses to tolerate it, I see this populace will need to throw off all restraint, and Heaven help us if they find the means to do so. So I beg and supplicate Your Excellency to deign to bring things to order as soon as possible, even if you need to come all the way here, so that those committing such atrocities are punished. What's more, it is up to Your Excellency to do it, not the citizens, who are in such obvious danger that they have no alternative but a popular uprising. I assure Your Lordship that from now on when you go away, you shall not leave me in such troubles and anxiety—even if I were forced to flee from here without giving any leave—because I find myself in such anguish that I could not withstand more. I commend myself to Your Lordship. Ferrara 29 May 1482.

---

13 Probably the renowned *condottiero* Gian Giacomo Trivulzio (1440–1518) who was employed by Ludovico Sforza of Milan in 1482.
14 Niccolò da Correggio (1450–1508), a poet, who also served as *condottiero* in the War of Ferrara, until he was captured by the Venetians.

15.

_____

Guglielmina Schianteschi informs her husband Luigi della Stufa
of her management of country property

Guglielmina Schianteschi, Contessa di Montedoglio (1463–1536), was a strong-willed
matriarch who managed her family's business and legal affairs largely single-handed, and
in a perilous political climate defended her husband and son against charges of treason by
the Florentine Republic. Descended from feudal nobility, Guglielmina Schianteschi's
father was Count Prinzivalle Schianteschi, her mother Niccola Chiavelli. Along with her
sister, Guglielmina was raised in the family castle in Montedoglio, a rural holding in Val
Tiberina near San Sepolcro. In 1483 Guglielmina married Florentine patrician Luigi
della Stufa (1453–1535) when she was twenty years old and he was thirty. Over the
course of their marriage, the couple had eleven children, nine of whom reached adulthood.
Luigi della Stufa was a Medici partisan; under Lorenzo the Magnificent he held impor-
tant government offices and traveled frequently on diplomatic missions. The overthrow of
the Medici and return of the Florentine Republic between 1494 and 1512 did not ad-
versely affect Luigi's career, but it did have a powerful impact on the family. After the
couple's eldest son Prinzivalle was involved in an attempted assassination of Piero
Soderini, the leader of the Florentine Republic, Prinzivalle fled Florence and Luigi was
also exiled to Bagnolo (near Empoli) in 1510. Most of the children went with their father
while Guglielmina was left to manage the family's various estates. The countess was forced
to handle the family's business, collecting rents, selling grain, and paying debts to the Flo-
rentine commune. Furthermore, she and her sister had inherited the land at Montedoglio
at the time of their father's death, and over the years she defended their legal interests
against three male cousins who sought to take possession of it. In addition to business and
legal matters the countess in her correspondence with her husband discusses her children's
education, expresses concerns about their unruly behavior, and pronounces moral judg-
ments. She was also a devout follower of Girolamo Savonarola, copying two of the friar's
1495 sermons in her letters. In addition to fourteen letters written to her husband, the
Florentine State Archive also contains Guglielmina's account book (ricordanze), with
minute records of all her business transactions. The humanist philosopher and friend of
Marsilio Ficino, Antonio Morali (Antonio Serafico di San Miniato),[15] dedicated a moral

_____

15 On Antonio Morali see Arthur Field, *The origins of the Platonic Academy of Florence*, Princeton, NJ:
Princeton University Press, 1988.

tract to "Madonna Guglielmina of Montedoglio." It is a treatise on marriage, on house-
hold management, and especially on the raising of children, in which the author praises
Guglielmina as an example among women, who have "moved boulders and oak trees,
subdued ignorance and malice."[16]

The present letter was written soon after Luigi went into exile. Guglielmina takes
care to inform him of all her business transactions and keeps him up to date on her
relations with local officials, describing preparations for a meal she has arranged for
the local officials such as the local provveditore, *(an administrator) and describing*
preparations for a meal she has arranged for and the wife of the podestà *of Arezzo*
and her retinue. She expresses concern over the education of their children and the
impact of this hardship on their characters. The overall tone of the letter is of worry
over lack of money. With Luigi caring for most of the children, gender roles have to
some extent been reversed, and Guglielmina has become the breadwinner in the
family. The burden of repairing the family's dire financial condition leads Guglielmina
to remind her husband repeatedly of the need to economize.

My Dearest Luigi,[17]

I am still here in Montedoglio where I will stay until Tuesday, which
will be the 25th, when, God willing, I will go to Calcione[18] to finish with
all the grain there. Perhaps I'll be able to earn some money from it for
what we need for the month of May, may God help us, He who can do
all. Between what I have sold here and what I will sell along the way I
estimate we will make 200 ducats; the amount earned until today will
be remitted through the *podestà* of Arezzo. You know that I am out here
truly to make money, as I have done and continue to do and I have sent
on all this money; of this I owe 206 ducats, plus 100 from Castiglione,
and 110 from here, which makes a total of 416 ducats. But this is [like
water flowing through] a pipe that never will be filled, so Luigi for love
of God, let's not spend any more until we are out of debt; I beg you, for
I see no way out of our situation unless God comes to our aid. As I said,
I have estimated that I will make another 100 ducats here and between
140 and 200 at Calcione, of which I want to give 200 to Santa Maria

---

16 "*Havete mosso e saxi et le querce, et domata la malitia et la ignorantia*" Biblioteca Med. Laur, MS Ashb.
1698, fol 1v.
17 I am indebted to Gabriella Battista for helping me decipher some of the more difficult words in this letter.
18 One of the family's farms in the teritory near Arezzo. Calcione is approximately seventy kilometers
southwest of Montedoglio. During this period Guglielmina was going back and forth managing both these
estates, as well as making trips to Florence to take care of matters there.

Nuova.[19] In any case, according to what you advise me to do, we must pay some of the fine for banishment, which is around 80 or 100. Therefore, if God wills it, I will be left without a penny; in short, I have done what I can to be of use, but until we cut expenses, we will always have these worries. Here around 700 bushels of grain have been given on credit and 400 of chicory, and the rest has been sold. The rest that has been given on credit we can easily sell for a price of 4 lire per bushel; here we won't get anything for it. Well, we will need God to help us all He can. Check to see if the supplies, the ten sides of dried meat and other foodstuffs, are on their way in the direction I sent them, since they were seized in Montevarchi—by smugglers it is said—and I still have not received [news] of them. On Sunday the *provveditore* is coming and we will see if we can find some way to recover the thousand florins, plus five. As I have said, on Sunday the wife of the *podestà* of Arezzo, that is [Girolamo] Capponi[20], is coming here and I have been told that there will be 14 horses and 20 people who are going to La Verna.[21] We will make an effort to honor them as well as we are able, considering this house is so small and I will try to manage as best I can with the stables here, making excuses for the village.

Having read your letters, one thing consoles me, that is, that you and the children are healthy and that God is watching over you. As you have seen, the matter of the teacher has been taken care of, the other one having been dismissed, so tell him to come with all haste to attend to our children. For I beg you; these boys of ours behave themselves fairly well, yet those who have been in want tend to think more of enjoying themselves than those who have not known hardship. May God give them the grace to recognize what is done for them; I have often had it explained to them that God through His gifts provides everything for the best. If to you it seems like a thousand years until I return, think how it must seem to me, as I am never in a good state of mind or body, though I do not want to cry out about this too. I have seen Dianora's[22] letter and

---

19   The largest hospital in Quattrocento Florence. Founded in 1288 by Folco Portinari, at the insistence of Mona Tessa Portinari, the Hospital of Santa Maria Nuova was an important object of charitable donations. See also Brigida Baldinotti's "Epistle to the women who serve at S. Maria Nuova," pp. 38–44

20   Lucrezia di Bongianni Gianfigliazzi was married to Girolamo Capponi. Lisabetta, Guglielmina's daughter, would marry their son Gino, three years later. De Luca, 81.

21   Said to be the site where Francis of Assisi received the stigmata, the Sanctuary of La Verna, a popular pilgrimage destination,is located in the hilly region of the Tuscan Apennines approximately thirty kilometers from Montedoglio.

22   The couple's eldest daughter, Dianora, was twenty-five years old in 1512.

also Gino's; in all I have two of yours: one from the 10th, and the other from the 11th. I must tell you that if you think only of keeping me informed, that is not enough, my Luigi. We need to eliminate all expenses, no matter how small, and make the best of it so we can help ourselves as best we can and pray God to assist us. Offending one another does no good and it makes me lose heart, so for love of God, don't keep telling me I am way out here to make money. Believe me, I have no need to be spurred on, because I am only too driven [to make money] and if God wills that you and our children want to get out of debt as much as I do, we will get out of it soon. I do not know what else to say; I feel I have already said too much, still it is necessary with someone one trusts: if a friend is removed from the breast, he cannot be left to go thirsty. You will see from a letter I have enclosed, although it is from the first [of the month] that with a little patience perhaps these times will give way to better ones; in short, I put all my faith in God, because I know my own character and that I have never thought of anything but doing my duty well for everyone. I know that this is very pleasing to God and everyone must place their hope and faith in Him. I recommend myself to you, in Montedoglio, on the 19th of May, 1512.

                                                  Your Guglielmina de la Stufa

16.

———

Lucrezia Borgia warns her father Pope Alexander VI Borgia to leave Rome

Lucrezia Borgia (1480–1519) was one of the most controversial figures of her time, and rumors of treachery, incest, and murder constantly surrounded her and her family. She was born in Subiaco, one of four children of Vannozza Cattanei and Cardinal Rodrigo Borgia. Her father, despite his reputation for immorality and corruption, went on to become Pope Alexander VI in 1492. The couple's only daughter, Lucrezia was by all accounts a lovely child with a sweet nature and the object of her father's intense affection. Nevertheless, he made use of her to forge political alliances by arranging a series of marriages for her, the first when she was thirteen years old to Giovanni Sforza of the ruling dynasty of Milan. When the tie with Milan was no longer politically expedient, in 1497 the pope annulled his daughter's marriage, marrying her the following year to Don Alfonso of Bisceglie of the house of Aragon, which ruled Naples. Lucrezia seems to have loved Don Alfonso and gave birth to their son, Rodrigo, in 1500. Several months before the birth, her brother Cesare's henchmen murdered her husband, who interfered with Cesare's political ambitions; in his place, her father and brother arranged for Lucrezia to marry Alfonso d'Este, son of the duke of Ferrara, in 1501. Lucrezia Borgia remained in the refined and cultured court of Ferrara until the end of her life, surrounded by musicians, poets, and intellectuals. Despite the immoral reputation attached to her through her birth family, she was well loved at the Ferrarese court, and even after the death of her father in 1503 and the subsequent fall from power of her brother Cesare, Lucrezia Borgia maintained her position of authority and respect in Ferrara. After her father-in-law died in 1505, as duchess of Ferrara she played an important political and diplomatic role, governing the territory and meeting with envoys during Alfonso's frequent absences. Although it was not a love match and the duchess of Ferrara had other romantic interests—she exchanged passionate love letters with the celebrated man of letters Pietro Bembo (see Maria Savorgnan, pp. 161–163) and later developed a romantic attachment to Francesco Gonzaga, marchese of Mantua, who was married to her sister-in-law Isabella d'Este (pp. 213–214)—with Alfonso she developed a close partnership. She was also nearly constantly pregnant throughout their marriage, having a number of miscarriages before giving birth to six children, and at the age of thirty-nine she died in childbirth.

In this letter, written during her first marriage, when Lucrezia Borgia was fourteen years old, she informs her father of the welcome she and her husband have received in the town of Pesaro. Also traveling with her were Lucrezia's cousin and tutor Adriana de Mila, her mother Vannozza, and the twenty-year-old Giulia Farnese, who was then the pope's mistress. At the time this letter was written in June 1494, the French invasion led by King Charles VIII to conquer Naples was imminent (his troops would enter Piedmont in September), and Lucrezia Borgia takes this opportunity to warn her father, urging him to leave Rome. Despite her youth, she has astutely grasped the danger the pope is in due to his close ties to the Aragonese in Naples.

Most Blessed Father, after kissing [your] blessed feet[23]

I want to inform Your Holiness that by the grace of Our Lord we arrived safe and sound here in Pesaro, where despite the rain, which disturbed us, we were greeted with great festivity and above all with the greatest demonstrations of love by the whole populace. We found ourselves lodged in a beautiful and comfortable house; descriptions of the furnishings and festivities that followed I will leave to Messer Francesco, who I am certain will inform Your Blessedness of everything.

We have learned that things are going very badly in Rome at the present moment, which causes us great distress and worry on account of Your Holiness's presence there. And so I entreat Your Blessedness as much as I am able, to get out of Rome, and if it is not convenient to leave, to be most vigilant and take great care. Your Blessedness ought not to impute this to presumption on my part, but to the greatest and most heartfelt love that I bear you, and Your Holiness should be assured that I will never have peace of mind unless I have frequent news of Your Blessedness.

I have nothing else to relate, but to implore Your Blessedness to remember both my lord and myself, who are everlasting servants of Your Holiness, whose feet we humbly kiss. Pesaro, 10 June, 1494.

Your Blessedness's unworthy slave

Lucrezia Borgia Sforza, with her own hand

---

23 This was a customary salutation when addressing a pope.

17.
_____

Maria Salviati tells Giovanni [?] of her determination not to remarry

Described as "un diablo del infierno" (a devil from Hell) by a Spanish envoy[24]*, Maria Salviati (1499–1543) was a forceful woman with a keen understanding of the political realities of her day. Although often overlooked by historians, she played a crucial role in firmly establishing the Medici as hereditary rulers of Florence, helping lay the foundation for a dynasty that would last two hundred years. Born in Florence, a descendent of the Medici on her mother's side—she was granddaughter of Lorenzo the Magnificent—and another elite Florentine banking family on her father's, Maria Salviati was the youngest of eleven children. In 1516 she was married at age seventeen to her cousin Giovanni de' Medici (1498–1526). While her husband was away fighting battles as a* condottiero[25], *Salviati raised their only son Cosimo (1519–1574) in relative obscurity and seclusion in the countryside. Widowed at age twenty-seven when Giovanni was struck by a cannonball and died from complications from an amputated leg,*[26] *Salviati never remarried but dedicated the rest of her life to her son. When in 1537 Duke Alessandro de' Medici was assassinated, Cosimo, not yet eighteen years old, became duke of Florence. Salviati was by his side throughout the difficult years of establishing his autocratic authority in a city accustomed to republican rule, when he brutally suppressed revolts by the* fuorusciti *rebels. She was also instrumental in arranging Cosimo's dynastic marriage with Eleonora di Toledo (1522–1562). Although she operated mostly from behind the scenes, we sometimes get a glimpse, as in this letter, of Maria Salviati's steely, determined character.*

This letter was written in 1531, when Salviati's family, led by her brother, Cardinal Giovanni Salviati (1490–1553), was pressuring the young widow to remarry. In this letter she appeals to a highly placed prelate in Rome, whose precise identity is unknown, to intercede with her uncle, Pope Clement VII (Giulio de' Medici, 1478–1534), to prevent this marriage. Salviati also shrewdly takes advantage of this contact with the pope to propose having a large debt incurred by her deceased husband canceled.

_____

24 Don Juan de Luna. Cited in Spini, *Cosimo I* 144. I am indebted to Niccolò Capponi for this reference.

25 A *condottiero* or *condottiere* was a mercenary soldier. The word derives from the *condotta* (contract), which secures the soldier's services.

26 See the introduction to Pietro Aretino's letter to Francesco degli Albizzi on the death of Giovanni delle Bande Nere, p. 10.

Revered, Magnificent, and as a Brother Honored[27],

Awaiting Your Lordship's letters for many days with longing, I have been pressured and overwhelmed by the arguments and persuasions of the most reverend Monsignor, my brother. Meanwhile, while his letters did not arrive as he had promised me; unable to wait any longer, I presented my case in that note, a copy of which Your Lordship will see enclosed with this one. After his letter of the 25th of April appeared, much later— it was presented to me at this very moment on the 3rd of May—I took no small pleasure in it for many reasons. Firstly, for having understood that Our Lord[28] is very fond of my son and myself (as I always considered him to be). Furthermore, because I know how Your Lordship handles our affairs with such affectionate care, mindful of the happy recollection of the lord father of my son and my lord consort,[29] and bearing fond affection toward what his memory left behind—that is, Cosimo, who wants to be the heir of this friendship, believing it to be among the most important things that remain to him [Cosimo].

But enough with words [to express these feelings], when the occasion for deeds presents itself. Thus it is necessary, our dear Messer Giovanni, that Your Lordship go to Our Lord and explain to him once again how as soon as the blessed soul of my lord consort left us, in that instant I determined to live with my son forever, for many reasons that would be too lengthy to relate in a letter. And for one very special consideration above all: that my son, born of those blessed bones, ought not to be abandoned by me. I can be so much more useful to him, standing by him than leaving him; I have been of this mind up until now and I hold fast. Seeing that at present His Holiness's convictions, the powerful arguments of my parents, and the terrible reasoning of His Reverence my brother are [for me] to do the opposite, feeling both doubtful and anxious, I wrote again to His Holiness and to all of my family, so that by now His Holiness will have had time to read it and even more, to have a change of heart for the above-mentioned reasons, as well as for what I will say next, to be repeated to His Holiness by Your Lordship.

---

27 It is unclear exactly to whom this letter is addressed. Twice in the text Maria addresses him as "Messer Giovanni nostro," but as the document in the ASF is a secretarial draft, not the final letter, there is no last name or address given.

28 Pope Clement VII (1478–1534), born Giulio di Giuliano de' Medici.

29 Giovanni de' Medici (1498–1526) was known popularly as "Giovanni delle Bande Nere" after the troops he commanded as part of the papal forces opposing the invading army of Charles V, which culminated in the sack of Rome in 1527.

They want to give me Signor Leonello[30] as a husband, a man fifty-eight years old, whose body is unpleasantly formed, whose breath seriously stinks, and who has the worst constitution imaginable. All this I have understood firsthand and have heard as much lately from Messer Gabriel Cesano, whose word I believe entirely because he has spoken and eaten many times with the aforesaid Signor Lionello; in truth, recalling it affrights me. And the family members I mentioned are blazing with anger over this, beyond all imagining, especially His Reverence my brother. He sends me many fiery letters, and from the two that I am sending with this one, you can see for yourself, and by showing them to His Holiness he can know what drove me to write the response I did; by no means would I be bound in marriage if possible, but I knew not what else to do or say on my own behalf. And so, our dear Messer Giovanni, I most deeply desire and pray Your Lordship to let our Lord see these two letters I mentioned, so that in some suitable way he could make His Reverence my brother and parents cease their efforts in that undertaking, that is, to have me married, as his Holiness will find a way, especially considering what I wrote earlier about signor Lionello's constitution. For if His Holiness does not accept this as his own special care, and does not throw them off this course, I don't know how I will be able to escape, knowing them to be so fired up about this. Above all I beg of Your Lordship to warn His Holiness not to disclose those letters or to mention having seen them, nor let it be known that they came from me, since I would not like to have to fight with the aforesaid Monsignor as well as my parents, and His Holiness can very well convince them if it is his will. If, however, His Holiness, against all my wishes, is pleased for me to do this[31] and it seems to him that I ought to go through with it, may he command me to do so, for I would throw myself into fire for him. Otherwise, I would like to be of use to Cosimo, remaining [single] as I am. As regards Cosimo's settlement, I am not displeased that the 30,000 ducats of my dowry will go to him and I know that His Holiness will want that as well. He will conclude that, by not binding me in marriage—for I do not have the slightest thought of it—he especially can carry this out, because if he wishes it to be so, signor Lionello will have to do as His Beatitude desires, provided that he urges him warmly. I pray Your Lordship speak and argue my case on Cosimo's

---

30 Guasti identifies this man as Lionello Pio da Carpi, who served as a *commissario papale*, a papal delegate, in the Romagna in 1530. *Giornale storico*, 28.
31 That is, to marry Lionello.

behalf before His Holiness, and repulse these maneuvers for my sake, with that prudence which is called for in matters of the utmost importance. By the by, encouraged by Your Lordship's offers [of help] and your good disposition towards us, I would like for you to manage a matter with His Holiness involving Alessandro del Caccia, to whom my dearly departed lord owed several hundred ducats. As this Alessandro owes the same amount to His Holiness, I say that Your Lordship ought to arrange for His Holiness to cancel this debt, doing this as a favor and benefit to Cosimo, as Alessandro is very forcefully demanding this of us at the moment. If Your Lordship might deign to trouble himself by putting this to His Holiness, I am nearly certain he will not fail to do us this favor, as His Holiness will not have to lay out a farthing. For this, we will be forever obliged to Your Lordship; along with me, Cosimo most heartily commends himself to you. Once again, I beg you to bring about a successful and happy resolution to this matter. May God grant you your every wish. From Florence, the 3rd day of May, 1531.

As a sister to Your Lordship,
Maria Salviati de' Medici

P.S. There is yet one more way [to do this] without bothering my family: namely, that Our Lord makes signor Lionello understand that he has other expectations[32], as His Holiness can do him much good.

I once again beg Your Lordship to entreat His Holiness not to discuss what I have written on this matter with anyone, not even you, on account of the many considerations involved, cautioning you that the two letters of His Reverence [Cardinal Giovanni Salviati] that are included with this letter ought not to be seen by a soul, and as soon as you have read them send them back to me immediately.

---

32 Indeed, Guasti points out that Lionello eventually married another Medici woman, Ippolita Comneno, widow of Zanobi Medici.

18.

———

*Caterina de' Ricci advises her father Pierfrancesco de' Ricci
to resolve a family quarrel*

*Caterina de' Ricci (Saint Catherine de' Ricci, 1522–1590) was born in Florence with
the name Alessandra Lucrezia Romola de' Ricci, known by the nickname of Sandrina.
She was from an elite banking family: her father was Pierfrancesco de' Ricci; her
mother, Caterina Ridolfi, died when the child was four years old. Her father remarried
soon after, having four sons and five daughters with his second wife. At around six
years old Sandrina was sent to school at a Florentine convent not far from the family
home, where her aunt, Luisa de' Ricci, was abbess. Later, at the age of fourteen she
joined the Convent of San Vincenzo in Prato, taking her vows under the name
Caterina, after Dominican tertiary Saint Catherine of Siena (pp. 33–34). Founded
in 1503 by women who were followers of the reforming Dominican friar Girolamo
Savonarola (1452–1498), this convent appealed to the young woman because of its
strict rituals and austerity. Nevertheless, Caterina had difficulties adapting at first;
she was slow to learn the convent rules and in 1538 developed a serious illness, which
was later interpreted as the precursor to her mystical experiences. It was believed that
Caterina was miraculously cured from this illness through the intervention of Savonarola, with whom she would be associated throughout her life. In February 1542
Caterina began to have weekly mystical ecstasies, which she referred to as "dreams."
These lasted for twelve years and were visions of the Passion of Christ and lasted, like
Jesus' ordeal, from Thursday at noon until 4 p.m. on Friday. In April 1542 she underwent a mystical marriage with Jesus and also began to show visible signs of the stigmata[33] on her body. These experiences were often witnessed by ecclesiastical authorities
and officials and ladies of the Medici court and were documented by the other sisters
in the convent, who also recorded cases of Caterina miraculously healing illnesses.
Although many began to venerate her as a saint, Caterina was not wholeheartedly
accepted by all the nuns; some regarded her with suspicion for her revelations or
prophecies that were closely linked to the tradition of the controversial friar. However,
she was supported by her uncle and confessor, the Dominican Timoteo de' Ricci, who*

---

33 "Stigmata," meaning "marks" or "signs" in Greek, refers to the phenomenon of bleeding at the points in
the hands, feet, side, and/or forehead where Christ was injured during the Passion. It is said that Saint
Francis of Assisi was the first to experience the stigmata.

was a devout Savonarolan. By 1548 the mystical ecstasies had ceased. This same year Caterina became subprioress; in 1552 she was elected prioress of the convent, a position she held many times. A century and a half after her death Caterina de' Ricci was canonized in 1746.

In many ways holding Catherine of Siena as her model, Caterina de' Ricci asserted her authority by writing letters to people of all kinds, including the wealthy and powerful, notably to the Medici grand duke, grand duchess, and members of their court and to religious figures, including Maria Maddalena de' Pazzi (pp. 56–57); in all, 1,064 letters of Caterina de' Ricci have come down to us. The present letter was written on a Friday, probably in the evening right after one of her spiritual raptures; indeed, in the letter she invokes the Passion and the wounds of Christ. Because she suffered from bleeding in her hands from the stigmata, many of her letters were copied out by one of the sisters. In addition to the "official" correspondence indicated above, over the years Caterina wrote numerous letters to her brother Vincenzo and other members of the family. She not only maintained close contact with them on a personal level but was often involved in their business and financial decisions. In this early letter, written when she was twenty-one years old, Caterina uses her spiritual authority to persuade her father to forgive her brother Ridolfo, whom he had cut off. Ridolfo, reduced to poverty, having squandered all his money on gambling and women, had visited his older sister several months earlier, asking for her help in approaching their father.

Jesus.

My honored and dearest father, greetings in [the name of] Our Lord,

I received a letter from you in which I learned that you are ill, and it grieved me very much. I say prayers for you and will continue to say them, asking God to give you back your health, if it pleases Him, as I know He desires nothing else. May it please Him in His goodness, to grant my prayer.

I still have not understood if you have made peace with Ridolfo, which troubles me greatly. I beg you, therefore, my good father, that for the Passion of my good Jesus and for love of the Holy Virgin as well, agree to do me this favor in any case, as I am telling you that so great is the sorrow I feel that it hurts me deeply. So I beg of you, my father, please relieve me of this pain. I wish that you would let everything go, not remember anything, and put the whole thing in the holy wounds of my good Jesus. And I wish that He would speak to you.

For pity's sake, father, don't say no to me! And if I am your daughter and you feel the affection that you show me, you have to do me this favor and remove this sorrow from my heart.

I am most certain that you will see to it that he lacks for nothing and you will provide him with everything. But only think: how can he be healed while he remains with that affliction in his heart, since you will not speak with him? I beg you that, as soon as you can, you let me know that you have done everything that I have said above.

I am as grateful as I can be for your kindnesses; may the Lord reward you for them. Nothing else occurs to me to write, except to recommend myself a thousand times to you and our mother. On the 23rd day of November 1543.

Your daughter,
Sister Caterina in San Vicentio

Suggestions for further reading

Letter 12, Margherita Datini: Cecchi, *Le lettere di Francesco Datini*; Crabb, "'If I could write':
Margherita Datini and letter writing, 1385–1410"; Datini, *Letters to Francesco Datini*, trans.
James and Pagliaro; James, "A woman's path to literacy: the letters of Margherita Datini,
1384–1410"; Nigro, *Francesco di Marco Datini: the man, the merchant*; Origo, *The merchant of
Prato*; Toccafondi and Tartaglione, "*Per la tua Margherita . . ." lettere di una donna del '300 al
marito mercante: Margherita Datini a Francesco di Marco, 1384–1401*; Rosati, *Le lettere di
Margherita Datini a Francesco di Marco, 1384–1410*.

Letter 13, Lucrezia Tornabuoni: Kent, "Sainted mother, magnificent son: Lucrezia Tornabuoni
and Lorenzo de' Medici"; Maguire, *The women of the Medici*, 60–126; Martelli, "Lucrezia
Tornabuoni", In Centre aixois de recherches italiennes. *Les femmes écrivains en Italie*; Milligan,
"*Unlikely heroines in Lucrezia Tornabuoni's Judith and Esther*"; Pernis and Schneider Adams,
Lucrezia Tornabuoni de' Medici and the Medici family in the fifteenth century; Ross, *Lives of the
early Medici as told in their correspondence*, 108–110; Salvadori, *Lucrezia Tornabuoni. Lettere*;
Tomas, *The Medici women: gender and power in Renaissance Florence*; Tylus, ed. & trans.
Lucrezia Tornabuoni de' Medici. Sacred narratives.

Letter 14, Eleonora d'Aragona: Chiappini, *Eleonora d'Aragona, prima duchessa di Ferrara*;
Bryant, "*Your obedient consort*"; Dean, "After the War of Ferrara: relations between Venice
and Ercole d'Este, 1484–1505," In *War, culture and society in Renaissance Venice*, 73–99;
Gardner, *Dukes & poets in Ferrara*; Gundesheimer, *Ferrara: The style of a Renaissance despo-
tism*; Gundesheimer, "Women, learning, and power: Eleonora of Aragon and the court of
Ferrara," In Labalme, *Beyond their Sex*, 43–65; Looney and Shemek, *Phaethon's children: the
Este court and its culture in early modern Ferrara*, Tempe: Arizona Center for Medieval and
Renaissance Studies, 2005; Mallett, "Venice and the War of Ferrara, 1482–4," In *War, culture and society in Renaissance Venice*, 57–72; Manca, "Isabella's mother: aspects of the art
patronage of Eleonora d'Aragona, Duchess of Ferrara"; Mazzocco, "Eleonora d'Este and the
heroines of Boiardo's *Orlando Innamorato*: challenging gender stereotypes at the Ferrara
court," In Altmann and Carroll, *The court reconvenes*, 284–293.

Letter 15, Guglielmina Schianteschi: Alberti, *The family in Renaissance Florence*, trans. by Neu Watkins, with an introd. by the translator; De Luca, *Guglielmina Schianteschi (1463–1536): A Tuscan countess and Florentine citizen*. Ph.D. diss., University of California, Riverside, 2004.

Letter 16, Lucrezia Borgia: Bellonci, *The life and times of Lucrezia Borgia*; Bembo, *The prettiest love letters in the world: letters between Lucrezia Borgia and Pietro Bembo, 1503–1519*, trans. and preface by Hugh Shankland; Bradford, *Lucrezia Borgia*; Fresu, "Alla ricerca delle varietà 'intermedie' della scrittura femminile tra XV e XVI secolo: lettere private di Lucrezia Borgia e Vannozza Cattanei"; Gregorovius, *Lucretia Borgia*; Gonzato, *Lux in Arcana*, 98–99; Mallett, *The Borgias*; Parker, *At the court of the Borgia*; Zarri, *La religione di Lucrezia Borgia: le lettere inedite del confessore*.

Letter 17, Maria Salviati: Brown and Benadusi, *Medici women*; Guasti, "Alcuni fatti della prima giovinezza di Cosimo I de' Medici"; Klapisch-Zuber, "The 'cruel mother': maternity, widowhood, and dowry in Florence in the fourteenth and fifteenth centuries," In *Women, family, and ritual in Renaissance Italy*; Langdon, *Medici women*, 23–58; Spini, *Cosimo I e l'indipendenza del principato mediceo*; Tomas, "Commemorating a mortal goddess: Maria Salviati de' Medici and the cultural politics of Duke Cosimo I," In *Practices of gender*, 261–278; Tomas, *The Medici women: gender and power in Renaissance Florence*.

Letter 18, Caterina de' Ricci: Capes, *St. Catherine de' Ricci: her life, her letters, her community*; Dall'Aglio, *Savonarola and Savonarolism*; Di Agresti, *Santa Caterina de' Ricci epistolario*; Di Agresti, *Prolegomeni alla spiritualtà di Santa Caterina de' Ricci*; Herzig, *Savonarola's women* esp. 186–188; Strocchia, Sharon. "Taken into custody: girls and convent guardianship in Renaissance Florence," *Renaissance Studies*, 77–200.

Chapter Four

Mothers and Children

During the Renaissance a woman, once married, belonged to her husband's clan; not only herself, her dowry, and any future children she might have but also her loyalties and affections were to be transferred to her husband's family. The move from her parents' home to that of her husband was both an actual as well as a symbolic rupture with her birth family. When her new home was physically distant, the separation could be painful for both mother and daughter, as seen in the deeply moving letters of Pandolfina Baglioni and Cassandra Chigi. At times, even when she lived nearby, a married daughter would express her frustrations to her mother by letter, as does Nannina de' Medici. Beyond biological motherhood, women also formed warm attachments to more distant female relations. Veronica Gambara (Chapter 7), for instance, who never had children of her own, was extremely close to her husband's daughter from a previous marriage. Holy women, too, formed "alternative families." The followers who gathered around Catherine of Siena were known as her "*famiglia*" and they addressed her as "*mamma*." The affection Maria Maddalena de' Pazzi exhibits in her letter to a young niece (Chapter 1) was not uncommon among nuns. Prevented from having children of their own, nuns often dedicated them-selves with maternal tenderness to younger members of the convent community. At times, however, Renaissance women reveal themselves to be tough when it comes to their children, both sons and daughters. When her sons were seized as hostages by rebellious subjects who threatened to kill them, Caterina Sforza held firm, defying her enemies' demands. A shrewd judge of political contingency rather than a callous mother, Caterina in her correspondence with her sons reveals herself to be a concerned parent and a source of thoughtful advice. Similarly, in her correspondence with her exiled son, Alessandra Strozzi is capable of dispassionately considering the possibility of her daughter's death in childbirth, and a seemingly cold-hearted mother approaches Veronica Franco seeking advice on how to train her daughter for the career of a courtesan. Women were often driven to such extremes by harsh economic realities of marriage, which depended on providing large dowries. Strozzi's daughter, for instance, would have lost her dowry—a huge sum of the family's money—if she died. If an honorable marriage could not be arranged, then a girl could be sent to a convent. Convents also required dowries (although smaller than that required for a secular marriage); if a convent was either not affordable or not acceptable, prostitution might be considered as an alternative. As Isabella Andreini's letter indicates, the birth of a daughter was often looked upon as a misfortune for a family, an attitude that is confirmed by the reality of the higher rate of abandonment of female babies in Renaissance orphanages.

19.

Pandolfina Baglioni expresses her desire
to see her mother, Pantasilea Salimbene

Pandolfina Baglioni (fl. 1463–1482) was the daughter of Pandolfo di Nello Baglioni and Pantasilea Salimbene of Siena. Her mother's family made their fortune as papal bankers, while the Baglioni were of ancient feudal nobility, many of whom, including her father, fought as condottieri. *Pandolfina and her sisters Andromaca and Atalanta grew up in the shadow of brutal internecine strife in Perugia during the second half of the fifteenth century. While aside from her name, next to nothing is known about the details of Pandolfina's life, much information has come down to us about her husband, who was a prominent participant in those violent struggles. She was married to Bernardino di Carlo Fortebracci, count of Montone (c. 1441–1532), who, like Pandolfina's father, was also descended from a line of* condottieri. *He and his father, Carlo Fortebracci, did not fight on the side of the papacy, which traditionally controlled Perugia, but for Florence; they were declared rebels of the Church by Sixtus IV, who seized Fortebracci lands in 1477, and thereafter Bernardino Fortebracci fought as a highly paid captain for the Venetian Republic. At his death, the Venetian Council of Ten granted his widow a pension of 300 ducats a year.*

In this letter, Pandolfina writes to Pantasilea, who had been widowed in 1460, expressing her great longing to be with her and informing her mother of her husband's health and upcoming visit. It is easy to forget, when reading this tender letter, that Pandolfina's husband is a mercenary captain fighting brutal battles in an especially tumultuous period of the history of the region.

Magnificent and Generous Lady and Most Beloved Mother, after humble recommendations, etc . . .[1]

From our man Ambruoscio I received your letters, from which I was as grateful as it is possible for a human tongue to express, having learned that you are recovering well and understanding from it your intense desire to see me, which shows the deep maternal love you bear me. I assure you that my desire to see you is no less than yours and so may God be pleased [to hear] our prayers, bring joy to our hearts, and give us

---

1   I am grateful to Maria Grazia Nico Ottaviani for her advice on translating portions of this letter.

this contentment, for at times I suffer deadly anguish that I can hardly describe.

Ambruoscio will be able to give you all the news of how we are doing, both myself and Count Bernardino, because I felt that I should send him to the count's camp with the letters you sent me, because his lordship will surely receive the greatest comfort from them, knowing the great love he bears you. He shows this to me, though he never feels he can do enough to please me in every possible way; his absence pains me so much that no one would believe it; however, the desire of seeing him soon in an improved state[2] counsels me [to wait] somewhat. His lordship writes you something about Salimbene; I pray you care for him well so that he can expect to be treated by you in the future as he has in the past. I am sure that you will do this, if for no other reason than for my love, which I know exceeds all else.

For now there is nothing else to tell you, save that I recommend myself to you always. Send my regards, comforts, and greetings to everyone there. From Villebelle[3], on the 5th day of December, 1482.

I have written to you many times, though from what you write it seems you did not receive my other letters.

Your Daughter,
Pandolfina Baglione de Fortebracci, etc.

2   In May 1482 Fortebracci led troops fighting on behalf of Venice against the duke of Ferrara, laying siege to an Este castle for forty days and destroying it. Although successful, Fortebracci fell seriously ill from both the strain of battle and the malarial air in the swampy areas around the Po River.
3   It is difficult to ascertain the precise location of this villa, although it must have been in the territory of Padua where Pandolfina and Bernardino were living at the time.

20.
───────

*Alessandra Macinghi Strozzi to her son Filippo Strozzi on taking
precautions against illness and death*

*Bringing with her with an immense 1,600-florin dowry, in 1422 the fourteen-year-old
Alessandra Macinghi (1408⁴–1471), who was born to a wealthy Florentine merchant
family of "new money," married into one of the largest, most highly respected Florentine
lineages, the Strozzi. Although there were no children for the first four years of their
marriage, between the years 1426 and 1436 Alessandra and her husband Matteo had
eight children, five of whom survived childhood. Because Matteo belonged to the
anti-Medicean political faction that in 1433 had exiled Cosimo de' Medici the Elder,
when Cosimo and his supporters returned to power the following year, Matteo and
other male members of the Strozzi clan were exiled to Pesaro, in the Marche. By
Florentine law, women family members were not included in a family's ban of exile;
nevertheless, Alessandra joined her husband there. In 1435 or early 1436 Matteo and
three of their children died in a plague epidemic, and Alessandra returned to Florence
with the other children. The twenty-seven-year-old widow could easily have remarried;
indeed, bringing with her such a large dowry, she would have been considered extremely
eligible for a second marriage.⁵ She chose instead to remain unmarried and devoted the
rest of her life to furthering her children's careers, arranging their marriages, managing
the family business concerns, and generally promoting the interests of the Strozzi clan.
When her sons came of age, with the ban of exile still in effect, they left Florence to join
Strozzi relations who ran a successful banking operation in Naples. Alessandra's presence in Florence was crucial to her children; she helped her two daughters arrange
marriages there and was able to keep her sons informed of the political climate in the
city dominated by the Medici family, always on the lookout for a favorable opportunity
for the Strozzi men to be repatriated. The seventy-three letters that have come down to
us were written by Alessandra between the years 1447 and 1470. These were not written with any literary pretensions but were meant exclusively as private communications to her exiled sons. Their content runs the gamut from highly practical business*

---

4   Heather Gregory questions Guasti's date of 1406, writing that there was no evidence of the 1427 *catasto
portata* that he references. Moreover, Alessandra's son Filippo wrote that his mother was 63 when she died in
1471, making her date of birth 1408.
5   On a Florentine widow's choices see Klapisch-Zuber, " 'The cruel mother': maternity, widowhood, and
dowry in the fourteenth and fifteenth centuries," in *Women, family, and ritual in Renaissance Italy.*

information, to gossipy physical descriptions of potential brides, to an extraordinary outpouring of grief at the death of her youngest son, Matteo; thus, these letters are some of the finest documentary evidence for private life we have from Renaissance Florence. Eventually her sons' exile was revoked in 1466, and when her son Filippo Strozzi ("the elder," 1428–1491) returned to Florence, he had become so rich that years later he was able to build the grandest Renaissance palazzo in the city, the Palazzo Strozzi. Alessandra did not live to see that, however; she died in her home in 1471.

In this letter Alessandra informs her son Filippo of a devastating plague epidemic that is sweeping Florence, which has killed a number of friends and many members of the extended family. Because of the disease, family members have taken refuge in their country homes, as was customary during such outbreaks. She tells him that she was sick with dysentery (itself a dangerous illness) and recounts the difficulty of being moved. Among information and advice on buying and selling merchandise and her intention to purchase a house, Alessandra discusses her intention to take out life insurance on her daughter Caterina, who is pregnant, in case she should die in childbirth. She ends the letter on a warn maternal note, trying to arrange for her sons to meet her in Rome and expressing her hesitancy to let her youngest son go to join the others in Naples, which would leave her alone to experience what we would define as empty nest syndrome.

In the name of God on the 26th day of December 1449

I have received several of your letters since August, but didn't answer any of them; the reason for this was first of all my illness, which began on the 9th of September. Then, on the 26th when the plague began to appear near us in Quaracchi, I sent Matteo to stay with Caterina and Marco in the Mugello, where he's been for more than two months.[6] So I didn't respond to your letters, because I couldn't, especially without Matteo. I will write to you myself in the future if it pleases God.[7]

Since I was sick with dysentery it was Marco who warned me that I ought to take refuge in his house in the Mugello, as the plague was nearing Quaracchi, but I was too sick to leave.[8] And while I was ill, people began dying of it [the plague] here, as I said above. And as I was not feeling any better, my brother Zanobi sent word to tell me to get out of here and to go stay with him in Antella where it was healthy and he had

---

6   Caterina was Alessandra's older daughter (b. 1431) and Marco Parenti was her husband. Matteo, named after Alessandra's husband, was her youngest son, born in 1436, soon after his father's death. Quaracchi is a small town on the western outskirts of Florence, about 10 km from the center of Florence. The Mugello is a rural, hilly region to the north of Florence where many Florentines had country homes, most notably the Medici family.

7   Alessandra preferred to have her son Matteo act as her scribe.

8   Dysentery, before the advent of antibiotics, was frequently fatal. It was an especially common cause of infant mortality.

a safe place.[9] So I went, although I was in such a state that it was very difficult getting me there, where by the grace of God I recovered. And finding myself well off there—being the beginning of winter and near Florence—I judged that things would improve, as they in fact did. And having also heard that Niccolò wanted to pass through here, I did not leave. I stayed there until the 16th of this month, as they returned to Florence for Niccolò's visit. I would have stayed two more months, until it was completely clear [of disease] that no one was dying anymore there with signs of plague, at a time when four or five, or even six a day were dying elsewhere. Indeed, in these eight days no more than one per day passed away. And because it's happened like this other times in the past, we cannot be sure [enough] about our family. May God free us completely from this pestilence.

I was told by you, and before that by Soldo degli Strozzi and Matteo di Giorgio[10] of the death of our Filippo, and I was very saddened by this, considering the damage it causes to us, in the first place, and then to our whole family. His virtue was such that he gave us all a good reputation. It is not possible to recover from such a death as this; we must bear it with patience and trust in God's will. F[rancesco] della Luna[11] also died, which was a great blow. And here Antonangiolo Macinghi died and many other of our Strozzi relations. And during these past days Margherita di Pippo Manetti[12] died, with her two children, so this time it touches us very close to home. May God in His mercy put an end to this. And regarding Filippo's death, I have letters from you and from Iacopo telling how he and Niccolò got together in Barcelona, may God grant them a good voyage. I have been informed that Niccolò[13] will be stopping by our house and I am to show him great hospitality, and that he will be taking Matteo to Barcelona, so I should be getting him ready. So I have done this and I await him gladly, as I have a great desire to see him. I will do my utmost to show him every possible honor. I know I am incapable of doing as much as he deserves, but I will be excused as long as I do everything I can and I do it willingly, just let God bring him here safely. Yesterday

---

9   Antella is a small town in the countryside, about 14 km south of Florence.

10   Heather Gregory: "Formerly a business partner of Alessandra's husband, he now worked for Niccolò Strozzi and his brothers." *Selected letters,* 225.

11   Heather Gregory: "Husband of Alessandra di Messer Filippo Strozzi, who was an aunt of the Filippo Strozzi whose death has just been mentioned." *Selected letters,* 225.

12   Heather Gregory: "A first cousin of Alessandra's husband." *Selected letters,* 225.

13   Niccolò di Lionardo Strozzi, first cousin to Matteo Strozzi, was a successful banker who helped Alessandra's sons by giving them work abroad. Unlike other male members of the Strozzi clan, Niccolò was not under the ban of exile and could come and go through Florence.

I heard he was in Rome; I guess he will leave there after the holidays are over, and he is expected here on the fourth or fifth of January.

I sent two large balls, a pair of penknives, and a dozen quills along with Soldo, seeing as Matteo wasn't going. I had ordered a pair of friar's clogs, some towels, and handkerchiefs sent to you, all for Matteo, now I must send for some more. Let me know if any wagoners arrive over there. I would also send you some fennel, if you want some. The cloth for the shirts is ready; up until now they had a lot of trouble spinning it because Alessandra was to have some for her shirts. It will be 110 or 112 *braccia*[14] in all; and when all's said and done, perhaps it will be too much for the shirts. For when it's finished and bleached and I am ready to sell it, I will have four *grossi* per *braccio* since this is how it is sold. You will not be able to have it until April or May, however, because of the bleaching. That linen you sent me turned a good profit: I sold 12½ pounds of it for 25 *grossi*. If you should come upon some more of this good material, or other of similar quality, get it for me and tell me the cost. If you need money I can send it. I will take up to 200 pounds of it. I believe this coming year here there will be very little of it. However, I am in no rush; I am just reminding you in case some good merchandise should fall into your hands.

I have been told that you would like me to send you a written list of all our debtors from Pesaro and how much each owes us, from the accounts that I have, and I will do this when I return to Florence. And once Niccolò has left here I will take down everything concerning him on paper in such a way that it will be understandable to you. I will also note down the guarantors of those debts I mentioned and send it all off to you.

Nothing at all is happening in the house of Donato Rucellai, on account of this plague, as he has not been in Florence. I want to let you know that it's mine to buy and that he can't have it without my permission.[15] I will not run out of time as I have many years in which to buy it; I am only waiting for the five hundred florins of Caterina's dowry to come to term, which as you know will be in April of 1450. Then I will be able to act on our behalf and they will see what I mean to do when I have the money in hand.

---

14 The Florentine *braccio* (meaning literally an "arm") was a common measurement equaling a little over 58 cm. A *grosso* was a silver coin.

15 In an earlier letter Alessandra had discussed wanting very much to purchase this house. By law, because it adjoined her own, she had the first right to buy it. She writes to Filippo on November 8, 1448: "I am not saying this for me, as I have only a short time to live, but for you, and your descendants, who will not always be in such hardship; as that house adjoins this one, it would make ours the most beautiful house in this neighborhood" (Guasti, 39). Years later, when Filippo returned from exile, one of the wealthiest men in Florence, he would indeed buy that adjoining house as his mother advised, then go on to build the Palazzo Strozzi, the most impressive private home in Renaissance Florence.

I believe Marco must have told you that Caterina is pregnant and is due to give birth in mid-February. It seems to me that given her state, we ought to take out insurance so that we do not lose the five hundred florins invested in the *Monte*[16]; we would lose the money and the person at the same time if God had other plans for her and we were to lose her before April. I have discussed this with Antonio Strozzi; in any case he thinks we could spend 12 florins in order to insure her those three months, namely: January, February, and March. I will wait to hear from Niccolò and I will do as he says, but then we must take swift action. Marco doesn't believe we should do it; he says she is in good health and he does not want to throw away so many florins. I think it's better to throw them away and be on the safe side. However, don't write to him, he might take it amiss, and it's our own business. I pray God that He does not take her away before her time—that she remains sound and healthy in both mind and body is my greatest wish.

I am thinking, God willing, to go to Rome for the Jubilee[17] in April; if there were any way you could come there, so I could see you before I die, it would be a great comfort to me. As you see, I have nothing else in this world besides you three sons of mine, and for your own good I have let you go, one by one, with no care for my own happiness and now I have so much sorrow at letting go of this last one[18] that I do not know how I will be able to live without him. The sorrow is too great and I love him too much, as he resembles his father. He has become a handsome boy during this time that he has been in the country, seeing him before and seeing him now, he has completely changed. May God grant that he gives me comfort. And so I pray you, since I will be left so dejected, to give me a little comfort when I go to Rome; may God give me enough life to see you all again as I desire.

I had letters in October from Lorenzo[19], who is well; write him often, as it is good for him. I received the power of attorney you sent me; when I need more documents I will let you know. Nothing else for now. God keep you safe from harm.

From your Alessandra, in Florence.

---

16 The Monte delle doti was a dowry investment fund initiated by the Florentine state in 1425. When a baby girl was born, parents invested money in the fund, which came to term when the girl reached marriage age. If the girl died, the money reverted to the state.

17 The Papal Jubilee began on Christmas Day in 1449.

18 Alessandra's youngest son, Matteo, was born in 1436. He went to join his brother in Naples the following year, when he was 14 years old. He died in August 1459, aged 23.

19 This is Filippo's younger brother Lorenzo (b. 1432). Heather Gregory notes that in 1453 he was in Bruges working for Jacopo Strozzi. *Selected letters*, 65.

21.

_____

Lucrezia (Nannina) de' Medici confides in her mother Lucrezia
Tornabuoni about a marital disagreement

Her parents must have been disappointed at first when Lucrezia de' Medici
(1447–1493) was born: Piero de' Medici and Lucrezia Tornabuoni (pp. 105–106)
needed a male child to ensure continuance of the family name. Nonetheless Nannina,
as everyone called her, grew up loved and pampered in the household of the most
powerful family in Florence, and the birth of her two brothers, Lorenzo and Giuliano,
guaranteed that the Medici line would continue. Nannina herself was destined to
provide heirs for another powerful elite Florentine clan: In her teens she was engaged
to Bernardo Rucellai (1448–1514), banker, ambassador, and man of letters, whose
gardens, the Orti Oricellari, would be a meeting place for notable Florentine intellec-
tuals, including Niccolò Machiavelli. Bernardo's father, Giovanni Rucellai, is best
known today as the fabulously wealthy merchant and patron of architecture who
commissioned Leon Battista Alberti to build the façade of Santa Maria Novella, the
family home Palazzo Rucellai, and its adjacent loggia. It was in the loggia that the
lavish wedding festivities between Nannina and Bernardo took place in June 1466;
the celebrations lasted three days. The couple had four sons and a daughter, also
named Lucrezia.

This letter was written from a villa in the country where Nannina and her family
had taken refuge from a severe outbreak of the plague. Judging their children's tutor to
be incompetent, her husband Bernardo had abruptly dismissed him. Nannina con-
cedes that the man was not expert enough to teach their ten-year-old son, who was at
an age to begin advanced instruction in Latin. However, she is against sending the
teacher away and asks for her mother's help in finding another position for him.
Mothers in elite Florentine families had a large measure of responsibility for the edu-
cation of their youngest children, often themselves teaching them to read and write in
vernacular. However, once the child acquired basic literacy, the task of finding tutors
and arranging for instruction would usually be taken out of her hands. Nannina
clearly chafes at not being allowed to retain this tutor and resents her husband's
heavy-handed treatment of an employee in their household. This letter, written in her
own hand, with accurate grammar and spelling and lovely handwriting, is the only
one that has come down to us from Nannina de' Medici Rucellai.

Dearest Mother,

I told you how Bernardo fired the [children's] tutor, which displeased me greatly, as I don't know where to send him, for at Figline where he's from there is a bad outbreak of the plague; indeed in his own house two of his brothers have died and his father is ill. He doesn't have a penny to his name; whatever he did have, he spent in our house to clothe himself and now we have paid him [only] with the words "Go with God", which could not have displeased me more. Whoever wants to do things as they wish ought to take care not to be born a woman. I would dearly appreciate it if you could ask Lorenzo[20] if it is not too much bother, to please find him a place where he would not be in the way for two or three months until the plague passes. I don't think he was capable of teaching Piero[21], but he can teach little ones and care for them. You couldn't possibly please me more because though it seems like I have someone who holds me in regard, this is not the case. As things stand, I would give him money of my own to help him out with clothing, as I believe he is very poorly off, but I can do nothing for him because up here I have no money. I would be glad if some small amount of money came into your hands—that could be a piece of luck for him or if you could help him by finding him some living, as I would not want to repay him with ingratitude. We are all well. I commend myself to you; send my regards to Lorenzo and kiss Giulio[22] for me. May Christ protect you. Take care of yourself. In the Casentino[23] on the 12th of July, 1479.

Your Nannina

20 Lorenzo the Magnificent, Nannina's younger brother.
21 Piero, their second son, was born in 1469 and would have been ten years old when this letter was written.
22 Giulio di Giuliano de' Medici (1478–1534), illegitimate son of Nannina's brother Giuliano, who was murdered in the Pazzi Conspiracy the year before. Giulio later became Pope Clement VII.
23 The Rucellai had a villa in Quaracchi in the Casentino Valley.

22.

_____

Caterina Sforza warns her son Ottaviano Riario to maintain
secrecy and beware of enemies

In an anecdote told by Niccolò Machiavelli, Caterina Sforza (1463–1509) is immortalized standing on the battlements of her castle, lifting her skirts and exposing her genitals, shouting in defiance of rebellious subjects who held her children hostage: "Go ahead and kill them; I still have the mold here for making more!"[24] *The illegitimate daughter of the Duke Galeazzo Maria Sforza of Milan and Lucrezia Landriani, Caterina was raised at court by the duke's mother, Bianca Maria Visconti, and by his second wife, Bona of Savoy. The two saw to it that the girl was given a good humanist education, and; it was at the Milanese court that she developed a taste for dancing, elegant clothes, and hunting. She also became interested in medicine and alchemy, later in life compiling a book on pharmacology called the* Experimenti. *She grew into a young woman reputed for both her beauty and her brilliant, witty conversation. When she was fourteen, in 1477 Caterina Sforza was married to Girolamo Riario, nephew of Pope Sixtus IV, to forge an alliance between Milan and Rome. The couple were given possession of the towns of Imola and Forlì in the troubled region of the Romagna, which over the centuries had fallen under control of the papacy. Sixtus was a corrupt pope despised for his nepotism, and when he died in 1484, Romans sacked the pontiff's apartments and destroyed all they could of the Riario family's property. Sforza then took control of the Castel Sant'Angelo in the Vatican, appearing before the populace seven months pregnant and brandishing a sword, in an effort to defend Riario interests. In 1488 her husband was murdered by subjects in Forlì and Caterina Sforza was taken prisoner, along with her six children. Caterina escaped, and with her children held as hostages, steadfastly managed to maintain possession of Forlì, giving rise to the legendary image invoked above. After Girolamo's death Sforza took a second husband, the young soldier Giacomo Feo. The marriage was held in secret so Caterina would not lose possession of her lands and regency of her son Ottaviano. However, Feo was unpopular and in 1495 was murdered in her presence. Throughout this period, but especially with the French invasion of 1494, Sforza's territories became of immense strategic importance to all the principal powers—France, Milan, Naples, the papacy, Florence—and she shrewdly played each off against another. In July 1499 Machiavelli was sent as a*

_____

24 For a nuanced interpretation of this anecdote see Hairston's "Skirting the issue."

diplomatic envoy to ascertain her position vis-à-vis the Florentine Republic and to secure her support; the future author of The Prince *was able to assess her character at first hand, gaining heightened respect for the "Madonna di Forlì," as he termed her, and her savvy maneuvering of the political situation.*[25] *In 1499, Cesare Borgia, son of Pope Alexander VI Borgia, was rampaging through the Romagna, conquering one town after another, and he managed to take Forlì in December, capturing Sforza and raping her. Eventually she was taken to Rome, but when she refused to cede her territories to the pope, she was thrown into a dungeon, where she remained for over a year, until 1501. When she was finally released, having renounced her lands and guardianship of her children, Sforza went to live in Florence. In 1497 she had married for the third and final time; her husband was Giovanni di Pierfrancesco de' Medici ("Giovanni il Popolano," 1467–1498). After her husband's death she had to fight the Medici for custody of their son, which she won, and she dedicated herself to raising the boy, inculcating in him the military values of the Italian nobility. Her son Giovanni de' Medici ("Giovanni delle Bande Nere", see pp. 118–119 Maria Salviati) went on to become a renowned* condottiero. *On her deathbed Caterina Sforza dictated a will, leaving a bequest for the cathedral of Florence and for the rebuilding of the city walls, money for Masses to be said at the Convent of Le Murate, and large dowries for two of her granddaughters.*

Throughout the tumultuous events of her adult life, Caterina Sforza was almost continually pregnant; from the age of sixteen until forty-five she gave birth to at least eight children who survived to adulthood. None of her children taken hostage in 1488 were actually harmed, and in spite of the famous legend of her behavior on the battlements of Forlì, there is no evidence that Sforza was not a caring mother. For a time she was regent over the territories in the Romagna for her eldest son, Ottaviano Riario (1479–1533), until he came of age; however, by the time the young man was twenty Cesare Borgia had already seized Imola and Forlì. The present letter (Frontispiece) *was written by Sforza not long after she settled in Florence. The death of Pope Alexander VI Borgia in August inspired Caterina with hope of reacquiring their lands in the Romagna and here she advises Ottaviano on strategy.*

My Most Illustrious and Dearest Son,

The money will be sent as I have promised; if Antenoro[26] were here or had returned as we thought he would, or if he would at least write about what has happened, we would already have sent the money, as I let you know in another letter. In any case, I will do all that I can to hurry matters and send it. Concerning the letter he sends you: I will do it, but it

---

25 See *Discourses*, III, 6, and *Florentine Histories*.
26 Antenore Giovannetti had been sent to Venice to negotiate with the Senate, offering Riario's complete loyalty if the Republic would support his reinstatement as lord of Forlì.

is to be wondered at that you permit yourself to be guided in such a manner [by others]; you should consider yourself subject to no one's criticism, nor be controlled by what they write you. What is being done, is done for your sake and for no other reason; however, make sure no one meddles in your affairs or watches what you do. Take care with the persons you trust and who advise you; you must realize that pernicious influences are everywhere and that if you let yourself be led by them, perhaps your cap will be pulled down over your eyes. Nevertheless, you ought to wake up and take notice of [matters in] Rome; I am informed of how things are being conducted there, so look out around you. You should know already, as I told you about it in another letter. You are an adult and have had plenty of time to become familiar with how people act in this world. There is no more [news]; I recommend myself to you and remind you that I am your mother and as far as the promise made, I will keep mine—you keep your word. As regards Ordelaffo[27], I am convinced that one ought to strike now while the iron is hot. Lose no time, as [popular] favor is an important factor in this undertaking and all you need to do is to get started—so rouse yourself. Friar Ciocha[28] passed through here, on his way to Rome; I believe the archbishop sent him, whether you know about this or not already, I am telling you. Nothing else, I recommend myself a thousand times over. In Florence, 28 October, 1503.

Caterina Sforza, with her own hand.

---

27 Antonio Maria Ordelaffi. The Ordelaffi clan had possession of Forlì since the end of the fourteenth century, until it was given to Riario, and unbeknownst to Sforza, with the aid of the duke of Ferrara and Bologna, Ordelaffi had already reentered and taken the town.

28 Luigi Ciocha, one of Caterina's supporters who at times served as her envoy.

23.

*Cassandra Chigi discusses household needs and shopping
with her mother Sulpizia Petrucci*

*Cassandra Chigi (1514–15??)²⁹ was the ninth of ten children of Sigismondo Chigi and
Sulpizia Petrucci; the marriage was a union of two of the most powerful families in
Siena. The Chigi were a prominent family of Sienese merchant bankers; her uncle was
Agostino Chigi, the fabulously wealthy banker to the pope. On her mother's side,
Cassandra's grandfather was Pandolfo Petrucci, the de facto lord of Siena. In 1531
Cassandra married Fabio di Aldello Placidi (1504–1552), a close associate of Pandolfo
Petrucci, Fabio also served in the Imperial Army at the siege of Florence in 1529/30.
Despite their prestigious origins, the couple had serious financial problems, dating at
least from 1536, when Fabio wrote to his mother-in-law lamenting his "ruin and bad
fortune." In 1539 Fabio was apprehended, along with other members of the Noveschi
faction, suspected of intrigues with Pier Luigi Farnese, and placed under house arrest.
Eventually the Placidi were banned from Siena. Throughout much of their marriage,
Cassandra Chigi appears to have been living in the Placidi country home of Poggio alle
Mura (today known as Banfi Castle), where she raised her children—seven sons: Fabio,
Tiberio, Aldello, Alcibiade, Aliprando, Ottavio, Ventura, and one daughter,
Filomena³⁰—in relative isolation. It is a rural area approximately 60 km south of Siena;
the closest town is Montalcino, which is 14 km away. It was common for members of elite
families to live in the country when under financial hardship. It was easier to economize
by living in the country, with less need for costly garments and showy display of wealth
that was customary in the Renaissance. Moreover, the family could "live off the land"
while closely managing the income from crops and livestock. Most of all, their penury
could be to some extent hidden in the rural setting. Since the death of Cassandra's father
in 1526, her mother, Sulpizia Petrucci, had assumed control of the family fortune, in her
widowhood becoming matriarch of the clan and power broker in her own right.*

---

29 I am indebted to Philippa Jackson for biographical information on Cassandra Chigi and her family.

30 The only record of this girl is the comment about her in this letter; although she is not identified posi-
tively as such, it seems safe to assume in context that she was Cassandra's daughter. There may have been
other girls; however, genealogical records from this period do not generally include female offspring, so they
are more difficult to locate than males. Fabio also had a sister named Filomena. She may have died by this
time, as it was common practice to "remake" a deceased loved one by giving his or her name to a child. See
Klapisch-Zuber, "The name 'remade'," in *Women, family, and ritual in Renaissance Italy*.

This is one of forty-one surviving letters written by Cassandra Chigi, in her own hand, to her mother and siblings during the years 1535–1556. Although it is written in an inexpert hand, which is difficult to decipher in places, and in a casual style showing little concern for grammar, the letter eloquently communicates Cassandra's sense of isolation and loneliness. Whereas in other letters she openly pleads with her mother for financial assistance, here she puts on a brave façade, asking only for a few articles of clothing and the loan of farm animals. She urges Sulpizia to come visit and suggests they meet in the nearby town of Montalcino to go shopping, if only she can find horses. What is unspoken in this letter, however, are the feelings of a young woman who had been raised in the wealthiest palazzo in Siena, once dressed in the finest silks and brocades, now relegated with her many children to a dusty life of rural drudgery.

My Honored Lady Mother[31],

    This morning Fabio received a letter from you, from which I see that you are well. Along with this I send for the serge fabric, *lanzino*[32], and slippers, as I am greatly in need of all these things. You do well to think that I am here in a light shirt. I feel as well as can be expected; nothing really hurts me[33], except for my outer dress and tunic. I'm starting to get a little chilly. Send me that little thing for Filomena, who has recovered; she is turning out to be a pretty girl. I pray you let me know when you want to come here, since I would like go to Montalcino to see the city if I can get horses; see if you can think how we can do it, as we are left on foot here and we do not have the means to buy any. I believe I will be forced to sell everything—the few clothes I have left—which truly grieves Fabio. God has even made harm come to our beasts: two buffaloes are dead, one through injuries, and the other died of cold. We must have patience. I beg you to write to Fabio and see if Mario[34] can send one of his worst creatures. Send my regards to him and please, if you yourself do not come this holiday, I pray as fervently as I can that Mario and Ortenzia do not fail to come. In any case I want to come with Fabio and spend a few days with you. We can go around and buy a pair of shoes for Aldello and some gloves. You could send the cap for Fabino, because his is small for him. I don't know what I'll make for Christmas; I've sent to buy some nuts, knick-knacks, and salted treats [. . .] The

---

31 This letter is in a very poor state of conservation, particularly along the right-hand margin, where the paper has decayed. I have had to guess at the meaning in places, but wherever the words are absolutely impossible to decipher I have placed ellipses.

32 I have been unable to identify this word.

33 Cassandra is probably referring to her need for maternity clothes.

34 Mario was Cassandra's brother; he was married to Ortensia Ghinucci.

hairnets that I sent for both times were not pretty, so I will need to go to select them myself. [. . .] Felice is coming for the holidays; I beg you don't come with him. I will try to have the sleeves spun in chestnut and walnut. It would be good [to have] those overcoats that belonged to the boys, which you mentioned. Could you have them cut and send them to me without sewing? I thought if I could prepare them the best I can they would sell well. I remind you to have Fabino's shirts well sewed [. . .] We could use a tub, a large one, if you can send it. I will say no more.

Please tell me if you want me to do anything for you. You see that without you here we can do nothing. I recommend myself to you; send my regards to everyone and do not fail to come here. It seems like a thousand years to me since I spent a few days over there. Mario promised me at firmly that he would come and bring Ortenzia, remember me to him and tell him not to fail; I want to go see Ortenzia. From Poggio on the 20th of December, 1538. I told this fellow to bring a token from here, remind him.

Your Daughter, Cassandra

24.

Veronica Franco reproves a woman who wants to train her daughter as a courtesan

Sixteenth-century Venice was famous for the elegance and cultural accomplishments of its most highly paid sex workers, the so-called honest courtesans, and the most renowned of all was the poet Veronica Franco (1546–1591). The daughter of a courtesan, both Veronica Franco and her mother Paola Fracassa were listed in the Catalogue of All the Principal and Most Honorable Courtesans of Venice, *a guide for potential clients, printed around 1565. Both her mother and father, Francesco Franco, belonged to the respected citizen class* (cittadini originarii) *of Venice that held most of the city's public offices; they had Veronica educated at home by private tutors alongside her three brothers. She was married while very young to a certain Paolo Panizza, a member of the medical profession; however, the two soon separated. It is unknown exactly when Veronica Franco began to practice the profession of courtesan, although it was certainly by 1564, when at the age of eighteen she was pregnant for the first time and drew up a will. In that document she names a man to whom she will leave the child in the case of her death; however, she states: "whether or not he is the father, all is known to the Lord God".[35] Through her contact with elite Venetian men Veronica Franco was able to share her poetry with writers in the most refined literary circles, for instance with the intellectuals who met at the home of her most important patron, Domenico Venier (1517–1582); by the time she was in her mid-twenties, Franco was a recognized, highly regarded poet. She wrote sonnets in the Petrarchan style, but in addition to writing tender love lyrics, she also knew how to upend the genre, with its idealizing tropes of feminine unattainability, and in her poems gamely celebrates her own sexual prowess. When insulted in verse by fellow poet Maffio Venier, she responded in kind, with lines of withering irony; when showered with admiring couplets, in her poetic responses she expressed sentiments of warm friendship and gratitude. Her peak of celebrity as a poet and as a courtesan coincided in 1574 when Henry III Valois was visiting Venice and the Venetian Republic selected Franco as the city's finest courtesan to entertain the French king. It was around this time that Franco's friend, the artist Tintoretto, painted her portrait (Worcester Art Museum, Worcester, MA). The following year, in 1575,*

---

35 *"Lasso a messer Iacomo de Baballi el figliolo over figliola che nasceranno de mi come a suo padre sia o non sia, il Signor Dio scia il tutto"* Rosenthal, *Honest courtesan,* 112.

a volume of Franco's poetry, Terze rime di Veronica Franca, *was published. During the years 1575–1577 plague raged in Venice, forcing Franco to take refuge outside the city, causing her difficulty in earning a living. Adding to her troubles, in 1580 Franco was accused of heresy and witchcraft[36] and tried by the Venetian Inquisition; although she was exonerated, this episode detracted from the aging courtesan's luster. Supporting a large household, including her children—she gave birth to six, two of whom survived to adulthood—as well as her brother's sons, their tutors, and servants, Franco slipped into poverty. By 1582, after the death of her protector Domenico Venier, Franco was living in reduced circumstances in one of the poorest neighborhoods of Venice. She died of a fever at the age of forty-five, leaving money in her will for "two prostitutes who might be found who want to leave their bad life either to become nuns or to marry."*

This letter is one of fifty that Franco published in 1580, under the title Lettere familiari a diversi. *Franco in her writings never tried to distance herself from the stigma of prostitution, as did the poet Tullia d'Aragona (see pp. 192–193); indeed, she appeared to use her poetry at times as a way of showcasing her charms and increasing her visibility among elite Venetian men. However, she was highly conscious of the risks to which women sex workers were exposed. In this letter, rather than considering the precarious life of prostitution, Franco urges the mother to send her daughter to a home for "at risk" young women. Renaissance Venice had a number of such institutions to handle the social consequences of its sex trade (see Paola Antonia Negri, pp. 47–48). Indeed, in 1577, three years before publishing this letter, Franco had written the Venetian authorities about founding a kind of halfway house for women, which she proposed to administer herself. Because existing institutions required either that women be unmarried or willing to accept severe religious discipline, Franco proposed an alternative: a home that welcomed repentant prostitutes as well as abandoned wives along with their children. Although she was not involved in running it, just such an institution, the Casa del Soccorso, was founded several years later in Venice.*

You go around complaining that I no longer want you coming to my house, which displeases me less—though I love you well—than your claim that my reason for it was frivolous. You have not stopped complaining about me and I want to reply to you in these pages, trying to deter you from your evil intention with a final attempt at making our friendship even closer than before, if you will obey the persuasive truth of my argument, and if not, to remove any hope of your ever speaking with me

---

36 The notorious witch-hunting in Western Europe took place during the mid-fifteenth through mid-eighteenth centuries. During this time an estimated 60,000 to 100,000 people, mostly women, were executed as witches. Prevalent mostly in the Germanic countries, France, Switzerland, and the Netherlands, there were occasional witchcraft trials in Italy. See also Skeeters, "Witchcraft, witches, and witch-hunting," in *Encyclopedia of women in the Renaissance, Italy, France, and England,* 390–394.

again. I do this not only to free myself from your imputation, but also to satisfy a humane obligation, by showing you an enormous hidden precipice, and shouting a loud warning, before you get there, so you may avoid it. And though this has to do primarily with your daughter's interests, I am speaking of you as well, for her ruin cannot be separated from your own, because as her mother, were she to become a courtesan, you would become her go-between. For this you would deserve to be harshly punished, whereas her fault would perhaps not be entirely inexcusable, as it was founded in your own guilt.

You know how many times I prayed and admonished you to protect her virginity. And since the world is so dangerous and so fragile and the houses of poor mothers are rarely safe against the snares of youthful amorous appetites, I showed you the way to free her from the danger and to have her adopt good customs in life and to have her decently married. I offered to help you in every possible way so that she would be accepted in the Casa delle Zitelle[37], what's more, to help you with the means at my disposal to accompany her there when the time came. At first you thanked me and made a show of listening to me and sharing my affectionate concerns. We came to the agreement that she ought to be taken in there and we were on the point of carrying it out, when I have no idea what spirit [suddenly] came over you. Where before you had your daughter go about plainly, adorned in a manner suitable to a girl with good morals, with veils covering her breast and other modest attire, you suddenly decked her out with all the signs of vanity—coloring her hair blond and having it preened so that all at once you had her appear with her hair in ringlets falling over her forehead and with her neck and chest all exposed and with all of her spilling from her garments, her forehead high and uncovered—with all the enhancements used to show off merchandise so that it quickly outshines the competition.

And I swear to you, on my faith, that when you first brought her to me disguised in this manner I barely recognized her. I told you what friendship and charity dictated, and you, taking offence at my words, as if I had said them maliciously out of some interest of my own, gave me reason to be displeased, which I have been since that moment on. Since then I have not taken pains to remain on familiar terms with you as before, but many times I have had them tell you I am not at home and other times I have given you a very cold welcome. I have complained about you for your own sake, to your family, and to persons with whom

---

37 This was a charitable home, which provided housing and marriage opportunities for unmarried women. See Chojnacka, 1998.

I thought my complaining might help, if news of it came to you. I thought that by repeating my words to you they would be able to take you to task seriously, and I heard that this indeed happened. I have carried out this duty with affection and out of a desire to be of use to you, but you remain hard and obstinate. On the one hand you go around preaching that your daughter is some kind of a saint, on the other you let it be known that she has little regard for her own honor, giving rise to gossip and scandal for you, who are her mother.

Now, finally, I did not want to fail to write you these few lines, urging and warning you once more about your situation. Do not, in a single blow, kill both your soul and your honor along with that of that of your daughter, who, just considering her physically, is so lacking in beauty—not to mention other traits, as my eyes do not deceive me— and possesses so little grace and spirit in conversation, that you would break her neck trying to make her successful in the profession of a cour- tesan. To succeed in this is very hard work for a woman who possesses beauty, style, and judgment, and who has cultivated many skills, let alone a young person who is completely lacking in many of these and little above mediocrity in the others. And as you obstinately persist in your error, you would say to me that it is a matter of luck, but first I must respond, saying that one cannot do worse in this world than give oneself over to the whims of fate, which can so easily administer evil as well as good. A person of good sense builds hope upon the solid foundation of what is within oneself and what one can do.

But I will add this: supposing fortune were to be favorable and be- nevolent to you in everything, this kind of life always results in misery. It leads to such wretchedness, going against the grain of human feeling, forcing both body and mind to such servitude that it is frightening only to think of it. To give oneself as prey to so many men, with the risk of being be stripped, robbed or killed, that in one single day everything you have acquired over so much time may be taken from you, with so many other perils of injuries and horrible contagious diseases; to drink with another's mouth, sleep with another's eyes, move according to another's desires, always running the clear risk of shipwreck of one's faculties and life, what could be a greater misery?[38] What riches, what

---

38 In Franco's *Capitolo*, 24, "To a man who has insulted a woman," she refers to the ritual disfigurement of courtesans known as *dare la sfregia* (to give the scar), writing "you threatened her mightily and swore that you would slash her face." Franco, *Poems and selected letters*, trans. Jones and Rosenthal, 245. Gang rape, known as "trentuno" (thirty-one), was a punishment meant to humiliate a courtesan. This was carried out, for in- stance, against Angela Zaffetta, who was raped by eighty men, instigated by an aggrieved former lover. The event was celebrated in verse by Lorenzo Venier in 1531. Rosenthal, *Honest courtesan*, 37–38.

comforts, what delights could be worth such a heavy price? Believe me, of all worldly misfortunes, this is the most extreme, and then if to the concerns of the world we add those of the soul, what could be more certain of perdition and damnation than this?

Pay attention to what is being said and in matters that pertain to life and salvation of the soul do not follow others' examples. Do not permit your wretched daughter's flesh to be cut to pieces and sold, you yourself acting as butcher. Consider how all this will end; and if you wish, look at all the examples: observe what you come across every day in the multitude of women who exercise this profession. But if reason, and all these worldly arguments ought to move you, even more so should those of Heaven replace them and draw you away from this grievously mistaken course. Turn your hopes to God and avail yourself of your friends' offers of help.

As for me, in addition to what I have promised, in which I will not fail you, let me know what else I can do and I will be eager to give you every kind of help. I urge you to avoid this most serious error, before it occurs, because once a stone is cast into the water, only with great difficulty can it be removed. If you do this, I will be your friend more than ever, just as if you do otherwise, you cannot blame me for disassociating myself from you, since if you follow through on your course of action you will be behaving like an enemy. Furthermore, you give others cause and opportunity to avoid you, even though they may love you, because they cannot stand by and watch you in this wretched business without being able to help you. Perhaps before long your daughter herself, realizing the enormous wrong you have done her, will shun you more than the rest, for as her mother, you who ought to have helped her, have oppressed and ruined her. This could be the beginning of a long agony for you; may Our Lord keep you from persisting in your evil intention, in which you show yourself willing to spoil and corrupt what you created from your own flesh and blood. I could never say so much on this matter that there would not remain much for me to say, yet I will go on no further and leave you to consider more deeply before coming to any decision.

25.

Isabella Andreini congratulates a man on the birth of a daughter

When she began her career, women who acted in the commedia dell'arte were consid-ered similar to prostitutes in social status, but Isabella Andreini (Isabella Canali, 1562–1604) earned respect and international acclaim not only for the artistry of her acting but also for her talents as a playwright, poet, and writer of letters.[39] Born in Padua of the Canali family, she became an actress when she was young, performing as prima donna in commedia dell'arte for many years with the Compagnia dei Gelosi, touring all of Europe. In 1578 she married Francesco Andreini, another member of the company. In 1588 Isabella's pastoral play Mirtilla *was published and reprinted many times throughout the sixteenth and seventeenth centuries. In 1589 the Gelosi were asked to perform at the Florentine court for the wedding of Ferdinando I de' Medici and Christine of Lorraine. There Isabella starred in a drama entitled* La Pazzia d'Isabella (The Madness of Isabella), *dazzling the audience with her mad scene. Her poetry, published in a volume of* Rime *in 1601, was highly praised by such renowned literary figures as Torquato Tasso and Giovan Battista Marino. She was honored as one of the first women to be admitted to the literary academy, the Accademia degli Intenti of Pavia. In 1599 and 1603 she performed at the royal court in France for Henry IV and Maria de' Medici. It was while returning from that tour that she died in 1604 in Lyon, at the age of forty-two, after having a miscarriage. She was survived by her husband and seven children. A work of hers entitled* Ragionamenti Piacevoli *and her volume of* Letters *were published posthumously by her husband in 1607. The letter book, in particular, was extremely popular and went on to be reprinted four more times over the course of the seventeenth century.*

It is unknown to whom this letter was written, or indeed if the intent of this letter was strictly polemical, with no actual addressee. In it, however, Andreini engages with a very real social issue, the preference for male children in Renaissance Italy. Nobles wanted to have male heirs to ensure the hereditary family line, and others preferred boys for the practical concern of passing on the family business. To this day, in Italy it is customary to wish a newlywed couple luck with the words: "Auguri e figli maschi!" ("Best wishes and male children") In addition, in the sixteenth and seventeenth centu-ries the prospect of having to pay an immense dowry when a girl reached marriageable

---

39 See especially Bosi, 77.

age could lead to a family's financial ruin; this meant that the birth of a daughter was often greeted with less than joyous celebration. Indeed, in Renaissance orphanages abandonment rates for girl infants greatly outnumbered that of boys. The arguments that Isabella Andreini employs and the examples she draws upon are familiar in feminist discourse from the time of Christine de Pizan (see introduction, p. 21) and also recall the arguments in Nicolosa Castellani Sanuti's letter to Cardinal Bessarion (Chapter 2) and those of humanists such as Cassandra Fedele, Laura Cereta, and Isotta Nogarola, although this letter was written in Italian, not Latin.

I learned with the greatest of pleasure that your wife, Signora N. gave birth to a most beautiful daughter, who as she grows in beauty (as is to be expected) will be perfect in both body and soul, as bodily beauty is a clear indicator of the beauty of the soul. Thus, as one kind of beauty leads us to infer the other, so both of them together lead to perfection. But as happy as I was for this birth, I was just as dismayed by your unjust sadness. I was told that you are greatly distressed at the birth of a female child, as if by being female she were not of your flesh, blood, and bones, as much as a male would have been. And is it possible that you, who are a man of such experience, do not choose to accept with a joyful spirit everything given by God, the wise Maker of all things? Are you not aware of the generally-held opinion of sages that in this world women outnumber men? A clear sign of feminine perfection is that eternal and infallible providence has seen fit always to adorn this world's lovely machine with its greatest and brightest splendor. There are already many pages praising the merits of women[40], ordered in writing in a more elevated, worthier style than I could ever do. However, though I could never describe with a pen, nor ever imagine such a thing, in order to lift this mad passion from your heart, I would contrive, like an inexperienced painter shading in [a picture], to sketch some praises of women in writing.

So then, your daughter is born, not only to increase this most perfect sex, but (who knows) to make you with time a most happy father, what should sadden you in this? What is the reason, against the will of heaven, which always acts for the best, to desire a male child? Oh how many fathers have there been, and still are, who are made desperately unhappy

---

40 For instance: Giovanni Boccaccio, *On famous women* (c. 1360); Christine de Pizan, *The book of the City of Ladies* (c. 1405); Henricus Cornelius Agrippa, *Declamation on the nobility and preeminence of the female sex* (1529); Moderata Fonte, *The worth of women* (1592); Lucrezia Marinella, *On the nobility and excellence of women* (1600). For more on this tradition of works in praise of women see Moderata Fonte, *The worth of women*, ed. Virginia Cox, esp. 12–17.

by their sons. Oh how many cases of families impoverished, disgraced, and devastated! Patient women content themselves with living in that subjection, in which they are born to a modest, regulated life. They content themselves with having the limited confines of the house as their sweet prison; they enjoy continual servitude; it does not weigh upon them to be subjected to another's stern will; they do not mind being in continual fear; and when, as the years go by, knowledge of the human condition[41] is permitted to them, they do not dare cast even a glance elsewhere, if not allowed by the person who takes care of them. How many [women] are there, who, in obedience to their parents' will, without raising any objection shut themselves forever within solitary [convent] walls, and how many are there who subject their necks to the marital yoke so as not to disappoint the wishes of others, taking a man who deserved to die before he was born? And with what patience they bear, for the most part, their husbands' unbearable defects? Males no sooner leave their teachers' supervision than they want to be their fathers' companions, then brothers, and then absolutely masters. Oh how many [men] there are, who yearning to have a male children, and obtaining them, then yearn for and achieve either their death or their ruin. The birth of Oedipus was the reason for the violent death of his father Laius, whom he killed with his own hand. With the birth of Paris, so too was born the conflagration of Troy and Hecuba; while she was pregnant with him, she dreamed of giving birth (as you know) to an immense flame.

There are infinite examples that I leave out, so as not to be longwinded; it is enough to say that women, all or at least most of them bring contentment and honor to their families. Doesn't it seem to you that they could call themselves entirely fortunate, those fathers to whom were born the ever famous Corinna, Sappho, Erinna[42], Aspasia[43], Diotima[44], Praxilla[45], Almathea[46], Manto[47], Arete[48], Carmenta[49], and numberless others, who not only rivaled, but surpassed men? Were they

---

41 That is, sexual knowledge, once they are married.
42 Three ancient Greek poets of the sixth century BCE: "Corinna of Thebes, who outshone Pindar in eloquence," Moderata Fonte, *The worth of women*, trans. Cox, 101.
43 Consort of the Athenian statesman Pericles, fifth century BCE.
44 Diotima of Mantinea, philosopher, character in Plato's *Symposium*.
45 Praxilla of Sicyon, Greek poet, fifth century BCE.
46 Cumaean Sybil mentioned by Boccaccio in *De mulieribus claris*, XXVI.
47 Prophetess, daughter of Tiresias, mentioned by Boccaccio in *De mulieribus claris*, XXX, and by Dante in *Inf.*, XX.
48 Daughter of Aristippus.
49 Also known as Nicostrata, learned woman, prophetess, mentioned by Boccaccio in *De mulieribus claris*, XXVII.

not most lucky, those from whose stock issued valorous Camilla[50], Hippolyta[51], Zenobia[52], Hypsicratea[53], Tamyris[54], Tiburna[55] and infinite others? Would we not call them the happiest of men, those who brought into the world the most chaste Penelope, Lucretia, Artemisia, and endless others? Certainly we would. How do you know that heaven will not grant you a daughter with Sappho's wisdom, Tamyris's valor, or Penelope's chastity? It could even be, that to make her more marvelous still, all these unique graces could be united in her, bringing your fatherland greater honor than Sappho brought to Lesbos, Tamyris to Scythia, and Penelope to Ithaca. Thus, console yourself, and celebrate with great festivity the birth of your daughter, who I hope will bring you infinite contentment. I also hope that at the peak of your joy, you will remember me as a fortune-teller. I kiss your hands and pray to God, that in His goodness he gives her long life so that we can enjoy the many marvelous deeds of your daughter.

---

50 Mythical virgin warrior princess mentioned by Virgil in *Aeneid*, 11.

51 In Greek mythology, queen of the Amazons, a tribe of women warriors.

52 Queen of Palmyra (r. 266–273 CE), warrior who battled the Romans.

53 Consort of Mithridates VI, king of Pontus (120–63 BCE).

54 Also spelled Tomyris (f. 530 BCE), queen of the Massagetae tribe of Scythia, said to have killed Cyrus the Great, emperor of Persia; mentioned by Boccaccio in *De mulieribus claris*, XLIX.

55 Wife of Murrus who roused her people to battle to avenge her husband's death; described by Silius Italicus in *Punica*, Book 2.

Suggestions for further reading

Letter 19, Pandolfina Baglioni: Black, "The Baglioni as tyrants of Perugia, 1488–1540"; Heywood, *History of Perugia*; Nico Ottaviani, "Nobile sorella mia honoranda," In Casagrande, *Donne tra Medioevo ed età moderna in Italia*; Nico Ottaviani, *"Me son missa a scriver questa letera,"* In *Lettere e altre scritture femminili tra Umbria, Toscana e Marche nei secoli XV–XVI*; Symonds, *The story of Perugia.*

Letter 20, Alessandra Macinghi Strozzi: Bullard, "Marriage politics and the family in Florence: the Strozzi–Medici alliance of 1508"; Crabb, "How to influence your children: persuasion and form in Alessandra Macigni Strozzi's letters to her sons," In Couchman and Crabb, *Women's letters across Europe, 1400–1700*; Crabb, *The Strozzi of Florence: widowhood and family solidarity in the Renaissance*; Gregory, "A Florentine family in crisis: the Strozzi in the fifteenth century" PhD Thesis, University of London, 1981; Guasti, *Lettere di una gentildonna fiorentina*; Klapisch-Zuber, " 'The cruel mother': maternity, widowhood, and dowry in the fourteenth and fifteenth Centuries," In *Women, family, and ritual in Renaissance Italy*; Phillips, *The memoir of Marco Parenti*; *Selected letters of Alessandra Strozzi*, trans. with an introduction and notes by Heather Gregory.

Letter 21, Lucrezia (Nannina) de' Medici: Gilbert, "Bernardo Rucellai and the Orti Oricellari"; Kent, *Household and lineage in Renaissance Florence: the family life of the Capponi, Ginori, and Rucellai*; Maguire, *The women of the Medici*, 115; Pernis and Schneider Adams, *Lucrezia Tornabuoni de' Medici and the Medici family in the fifteenth century*, 66–68; Ross, *Lives of the early Medici as told in their correspondence*; Tomas, *The Medici women: gender and power in Renaissance Florence.*

Letter 22, Caterina Sforza: Breisach, *Caterina Sforza, a Renaissance virago*; Hairston, "Skirting the issue: Machiavelli's Caterina Sforza"; Larner, *The lords of Romagna; Romagnol society and the origins of the signorie*; Lev, *The tigress of Forlì: Renaissance Italy's most courageous and notorious countess, Caterina Riario Sforza de' Medici*; Pasolini, *Catherine Sforza*, trans. and prepared with the assistance of the author by Paul Sylvester; Ray, "Caterina Sforza's Experiments with Alchemy," In *Daughters of Alchemy*; Ray, "Experiments with alchemy: Caterina Sforza in early modern scientific culture" In *Gender and scientific discourse in early modern culture*; De Vries, *Caterina Sforza and the art of appearances.*

Letter 23, Cassandra Chigi: Brizio, "In the shadow of the 'campo': Sienese women and their families (14th–16th centuries)," In Sperling and Wray, *Gender, kinship and property in the wider Mediterranean;* Eisenbichler, *The sword and the pen: women, politics, and poetry in sixteenth-century Siena;* Fantini, "Lettere alla madre di Cassandra Chigi," In Zarri, *Per lettera;* Hook, *Siena, a city and its history;* Jackson and Nevola, *Beyond the Palio: urbanism and ritual in Renaissance Siena.*

Letter 24, Veronica Franco: Adler, "Veronica Franco's Petrarchan Terze Rime: subverting the master's plan" *Italica;* Bassanese, "Private lives and public lies: texts by courtesans of the Italian Renaissance," *Texas Studies in Language and Literature;* Chojnacka, "Women, charity and community in Early Modern Venice: The Casa delle Zitelle," *Renaissance Quarterly;* Franco, *Poems and selected letters,* ed. and trans. by Jones and Rosenthal; Jones, *The currency of Eros: women's love lyric in Europe, 1540–1620;* Lawner, *Lives of the courtesans: portraits of the Renaissance;* Rosenthal, *The honest courtesan: Veronica Franco, citizen and writer in sixteenth-century Venice.*

Letter 25, Isabella Andreini: Andreini, *La Mirtilla,* trans. by Campbell; Andreini, *Lettere,* ed. by Francesco Andreini. Venice, 1607; Andreini, "The Madness of Isabella," *Scenarios of the Commedia dell'Arte,* trans. by Henry Salerno; Andreini, *Rime.* Milan, 1601; Paris, 1603; Milan, 1605; Andrews, "Isabella Andreini and others: women on stage in the late cinquecento," In Panizza, *Women in Italian Renaissance culture and society;* Bosi, "Accolades for an actress: on some literary and musical tributes for Isabella Andreini," *Recercare;* Clubb, "The state of the *arte* in the Andreini's time," In Biasin *Studies in the Italian Renaissance;* Macneil, *Music and women of the commedia dell'arte in the late sixteenth century;* Ray, "Between stage and page: the letters of Isabella Andreini," In *Writing gender in women's letter collections of the Italian Renaissance;* Tylus, "Women at the windows: commedia dell'arte and theatrical practice in Early Modern Italy," *Theatre Journal.*

Chapter Five

Love and Friendship

When Leon Battista Alberti inaugurated the *Certame coronario* poetry competition held in Florence's Duomo in 1441, the theme was *amicizia* (friendship). Renaissance poets and philosophers were obsessed with the topic, investigating every subtle shade of friendship and love. While Neoplatonists explored platonic love and poets composed erotic verse, one kind of emotional bond they overlooked was friendship between a man and a woman; the possibility of friendship between the sexes was rarely if ever considered. In her letters to a close male friend, the courtesan Camilla Pisana pours out her unhappiness about her lover's psychological cruelty, while Ginevra Gozzadini unburdens her heart to her spiritual father, recounting intimate details of her unhappy marriage. Both of these letters are expressions of warm friendship between men and women. Vittoria Colonna's correspondence with the artist Michelangelo, which included exchanges of poetry and drawing, reveals a friendship based on deep mutual admiration and respect. While women were generally the objects of men's love poetry, the voices of Renaissance women are not often heard discussing either love or friendship themselves. The passionate love letters written by Maria Savorgnan and Cecilia Liconella are very different from one another and serve to remind us of the social context in which they were written. From opposite ends of the social spectrum, Savorgnan writes an elegant letter full of literary allusions to her lover and social equal, Pietro Bembo, while the humbler Liconella pens a simple, adoring message to a nobleman she met while traveling. As opposed to these real-life letters, several selections in this chapter raise more complex questions of authorship and the male gaze. The letters purported to be written by a Roman woman named Celia were extraordinarily popular and went into many editions (p.18), while those ostensibly written by a Florentine woman named Emilia N. seem to be modeled directly on Savorgnan's correspondence. We do not know who these women were—if indeed they were actual women. If a man wrote these, we must ask ourselves what the content of these letters says about social perceptions of female desire and its expression. There was a precedent for this type of writing in Ovid's *Heroides*. A series of fictional love letters of famous women in antiquity written by the male author Ovid (Publius Ovidius Naso, 43 BCE–17 CE), this text was extremely popular in Italy from the time of the Middle Ages, when it circulated widely in manuscripts in both Latin and vernacular translation. In contrast to possibly male-authored letters, the "love letters" written by well-known courtesan Margherita Costa raise questions of their own. Costa's collection begins with letters very similar to the ones attributed to Celia and Emilia N., and indeed not dissimilar from Savorgnan's, but they become increasingly parodic, even grotesque, showing us that women knew not only how to write exquisite love letters, but how to mock them as well. On the other hand, Marietta Corsini Machiavelli's letter to her husband brings us back to reality, reminding us that even though most elite marriages at the time were not contracted out of love, very tender relationships could, and sometimes did, develop between a woman and her husband during the Renaissance.

26.

Camilla Pisana complains to Francesco del Nero about her lover, Filippo Strozzi

Around 1515 in Florence, Camilla Pisana and her friend Alessandra Fiorentina were the most glamorous and sought-after courtesans in Florence. Along with two others, they shared a house outside the Porta San Gallo, opulently furnished and decorated by the painter Rosso Fiorentino. This setup was paid for by the banker Filippo Strozzi (1489–1538)[1], one of the wealthiest men in Florence, as a place where he could entertain his male friends and associates. Strozzi's circle represented the very highest echelon of Florentine society—among Strozzi's guests was Lorenzo di Piero de' Medici (1493–1519), ruler of Florence—who came to enjoy themselves in the company of these alluring women. Reputed for her beauty, Camilla appears to have been the center of this group and Strozzi's "official" lover for some time. We do not know anything about Camilla's life before she met Strozzi, except that she was probably originally from Pisa, as it was common for sex workers, who often traveled from place to place, to assume the name of their city or country of origin. The last name of her friend Alessandra Fiorentina, for instance, means "Florentine." Camilla must have studied music and literature, for she was the most cultivated of the four women and often entertained company by singing and playing the lute. In one of her letters she mentions a book she had written, which might have been poetry; however, this has not survived.[2] It is unclear precisely how long this living arrangement lasted; however, by 1517 all four women had moved to Rome. Alessandra and the two others lived in a house near Camilla, who took an apartment off the via Giulia, where she entertained clients. Among those who frequented her Roman parties were the writers Agnolo Firenzuola (1493–1543) and Pietro Aretino (pp. 9–11), who celebrates Camilla's beauty in his 1525 comedy La Cortegiana *(The Courtesan).*

---

1   Filippo Strozzi, often known as "the younger," was the son of Filippo di Matteo Strozzi and grandson of Alessandra Macinghi Strozzi (pp. 131–132). His family and the governing Medici had relations that fluctuated between cautiously friendly and openly hostile. Strozzi maintained good relations with Lorenzo de' Medici and was married to his niece, Clarice, with whom he had ten children. He later fell out with Alessandro de' Medici and after 1530 became the most prominent figure of the anti-Medici faction of *fuorusciti,* leading a rebellion against the regime. Strozzi was captured and died in prison in 1538; either he committed suicide or was killed by order of Cosimo I de' Medici.
2   It has been suggested that the texts for three madrigals set by Costanzo Festa were written by Camilla Pisana. For these texts see Flosi, 137–141.

Francesco del Nero (1487–1563) was Filippo Strozzi's brother-in-law and close business associate as papal banker. The lover of Alessandra Fiorentina, del Nero was a frequent guest at the women's house and over time Francesco and Camilla developed a warm friendship, evidenced in their correspondence; of her thirty-three surviving letters, twenty-seven are addressed to Francesco. In this letter, Camilla expresses her deep sense of betrayal and humiliation caused by a "trick" played on her by Strozzi, which involved making her sexually available to various of his male friends. Although she was a paid sex worker and a "kept woman," she shares with her friend the depth of her love for Strozzi and asserts her dignity as a human being.

My Dear Favorite[3],

    Although for several weeks now I do not seem to have merited even a single line from you, nor any response to my last letter, nonetheless believing as I do that you hold me in the same affection and good will, I find within myself that same deep faith and indescribable love toward you as ever, which makes me feel I can rejoice or lament with you depending on my circumstances. I believe, indeed I am certain, that you are aware of the intrigues that Filippo and Giovanni have come up with; I leave you to be the judge of the praiseworthiness of their activity.

    I had thought with all I had suffered in the past I had tolerated enough, without every year some new outrage being renewed against me. And if he has had enough of me, as his evil nature will have it, not my meager merits—I am referring to all the love I bear for him and not to other qualities that I do not possess—let him leave me to my ruin, but not give me away or bestow me as a favor on others, for I believe I was born free, and no one's servant or slave. He knows very well how often I told him never to undertake to bring other men to me, nor leave me to fall prey to them; however, I believe he has done all this out of scorn for my love of him and that, in this way, he seeks to make me pay off my obligations toward him. I appreciate that he would defend me from the snares set by others; whoever thought he could come here to graze would be sent off to plow [elsewhere] in such a way that on the one hand they might laugh it off, on the other it would be no laughing matter, and they could not sneer at me as they wished. Since I well know that it is not love that induces him to such things, but the ability to chatter at our expense and to scoff at us to his heart's content, was it not enough for Filippo, what he had done with Dianora[4], wanting to come and end the

---

3   "Favorito" was Camilla's nickname for Francesco.

4   This is another courtesan; there is no further information about her, however.

party? If he does not take such things into consideration, *I* do; I feel love and am not a tiger like he is! I also believe that he recalls when he pulled another one on me with Alessandra; he said he was sorry for that, and I was heaped with contempt because of it, and yet every year he is back at it. The devil! He has so many women, youths, boys, and kids of every sort at his service that I would imagine his desire would be drawn away a thousand times over and that he would never think about matters over here. But he is like a flood that feels no love and washes over everyone alike; he keeps all of us women in the same corner and I believe, by God, that one could seek the whole world over and never find another man so lacking in affection. This makes me grieve for my unlucky fate, and I see nobody who treats his woman this way, nor who maintains her as an object of public contempt as he has always done with me. It would have been enough, once he conceived hatred for me, after fulfilling his desire, that he distanced himself in a gentlemanly manner, without wanting to give this woman, that woman, and me to other men. But I am not amazed that he would act this way toward me, knowing for certain that he treats every woman like this. And he never wants the one whom he has enjoyed to be left with a sweet taste in her mouth, but always a bitter one.

Never mind. I cannot help myself in complaining to you, where I always put away all my secrets, give vent to my passion, and then, I am certain that, although perhaps you may make a show of laughing about it in front of him, you have enough judgment in you that you can recognize when something has been done badly. Yet, paying him due respect and honor for his other qualities, you would not criticize the things he does. And though I know I do not need to prove that I am in the right, nor even less do I seek justly to avenge the wrongs he has done me, yet it is enough for me to know that you sympathize with me. Through this prudent silence of yours, I know that I cannot be found to be in the wrong. And since Giovanni writes, I believe at Filippo's instigation, that he will have the hospital taken away from Brother Giordano and that he is working on something else that will harm us, tell Filippo I take no notice of the hospital, as I have never been exposed to anything.[5] I had been under obligation for his kindness; nevertheless, if he believes he can harm me this way, he would be mistaken. Since I do not lack for means to live on, if he wishes for me to return the courtesies he gave me,

---

5   Giorgina Masson suggests a sinister interpretation of this phrase, writing of "Strozzi's despicable threat of having Camilla sent to the 'hospital', meaning that he would see that—like a common whore—she would be shut up with women suffering from venereal disease." *Courtesans of the Golden Age,* 63.

I would give them back to him as a present, so that he could see that this was not the reason that I fell in love with him and I would very much like to release myself from this obligation. Tell him, however, that I do not reproach him for such things and that I never thought to be tested this way, nor that our friendship would end so gracelessly, having loved him more than myself, and never having done anything that was not entirely pleasing, welcome, and of benefit to him. Have patience with me! I remind you, my Favorite, about the business of Messer Lionardo's land, since now that you have the power of attorney you can take care of this as quickly as possible, and both he and I will be most obliged to you. Nothing more on this.

Forgive me if I have made myself tiresome to you with my overly verbose letter, for it all comes from my certainty of your affection, generated by your infinite courtesies that I will never forget, nor can I fail to love you always, compelled not by one thing alone, but by infinite ones. I commend myself to you. Farewell.

27.

Maria Savorgnan to Pietro Bembo expressing the depth
of her love for him

"I am consumed in ardent flames of the sweet fire lit in my breast by your divine aspect, bright and serene," wrote Maria Savorgnan (fl. 1487–1511) in a sonnet to her lover.[6] Born in the town of Crema, near Milan, Maria Santagnolesca Grifoni was from a noble family and in 1487 married the Friulian condottiero Giacomo dei Savorgnan del Monte. She was widowed in 1498 and went to Venice to ask for support for herself and her four children in view of her husband's services to the Venetian Republic; in December she personally appeared before the Senate and Doge pleading for financial assistance and dowries for her two daughters. The Venetian government did not comply; nevertheless, Savorgnan remained in Venice, and it was there that in 1500 she met the celebrated man of letters Pietro Bembo (1470–1547; see introduction p. 10). Maria Savorgnan herself was an accomplished poet; however, she never appears to have circulated her writings publicly. Only six compositions in verse, which she included in her letters to Bembo, survive. Indeed, what little is known of her work as well as her life comes almost entirely from her correspondence with Bembo. The two became involved in a passionate love affair, which she was forced to keep secret because her husband's will required that Maria remain chaste and faithful to his memory. The husband's brother Tristano, head of the family after Giacomo's death, and a certain Bernardino, named as guardian, kept strict watch over her actions. From May 1500 through early 1501 when Tristano insisted she leave for Ferrara, she wrote seventy-seven letters to Bembo and he wrote eighty to her. He had a secretary write out his love letters to Savorgnan, and for fifty years Bembo kept copies of the letters, which he carefully arranged and edited, removing her name and referring to her as "that lady about whose name one remains silent." His letters were published in 1552, several years after his death. The identity of Savorgnan as his lover was not discovered until the 1940s, when the scholar Carlo Dionisotti identified the originals of her letters from a pile of documents in a private archive that were about to be destroyed. Her letters are now in the Vatican Library.

Having met in May 1500, Savorgnan and Bembo had become intimate by mid-July, meeting surreptitiously in her bedroom; sometimes she lowered a ladder from her

---

6 The entire poem, in Italian, is in Farnetti, *"Se mai fui vostra,"* 73.

window so he could climb up from a boat on the canal below. At the height of their affair, the couple often wrote several letters a day; the present letter was the third Savorgnan wrote on August 8. Intermingled with the breathlessly passionate tone of their letters are also practical concerns of hiding their affair from gossiping neighbors, reports of illnesses, and outbursts of jealousy. Savorgnan and Bembo also discuss poetry and make frequent literary references. For instance, here Savorgnan quotes a line from an unidentified barzeletta, *a form of verse. At times the two appear almost to collaborate on poetic compositions and discuss linguistic principles that Bembo would later codify in his foundational work on Italian grammar, the* Prose della volgar lingua (1525).[7] *"Let us go as equals toward love's torch," wrote the poet, recognizing their very similar social and intellectual footing.*

I know not what power you have over me, nor what I say or do when I am in your presence, but well I know this: that in thinking of you continuously I have forgotten my own self and this is certain.[8] I will say nothing else of this to you at present, but, if ever we should find ourselves together, we will speak of this more at length.

Be assured that, neither in truth, nor in jest do I say or chitchat about my desires and I will not "slip from your fingers." You have come up with an idea about coming to see me, which you do not want to express, fearing that your language might do you harm. Already you have forgotten what I have told you many times: do you not know that with me you can say everything you think and it will have been well said? Do I not tell you, without my language offending you, everything I wish to, that my hands miss you and a thousand other things? Yes, all but one phrase—the one that says "Go now, for it is time." And even the worst, I will in time say, because I tell you everything, and most of all you know my troubled state of mind, which needs to be kept under control all day long. And I dare to say so much, that any other woman than I would be lost in this desperate labyrinth. Now look and see me as I am; though when I find myself in your presence I seem to be light-hearted in appearance, nevertheless I can say, as in that verse: "inside, my heart flares up with worries."

Be content, until the stars indicate a happier path, to live according to my wishes, so that later, I will live according to yours. You will see

---

7   See for example Zancan, *Doppio itinerario*, 55, on mention of Bembo's *Asolani* and *Prose della volgar lingua* in the letters and Pozzi, "Andrem di pari," 89–94, on Savorgnan's Petrarchan style.

8   I am grateful to Monica Farnetti for her suggestions on the translation of several difficult passages in this letter.

whether I carry out what I promise. I wanted to write you these few lines you see above, but if I had the paper I would continue writing until tomorrow.[9] Yet, I will tell you this: that I love you and will love you still, even should you not want me to, and I want you to love [me]. If I can manage for you to come tomorrow I will send F. first and then the other one. I am yours.

I surely do not know what is meant on that sheet of paper. If I had been writing, I certainly would not have written that; I think you are making fun of me.

8 August, 1500

---

9   Indeed, her letter is contained on a single sheet of paper and at the bottom of the page she entirely runs out of space, squeezing this line in the very last bit of space.

28.

Cecilia Liconella expresses her love to Nicolò de Lazara,
a noble she met in Padua[10]

This love letter is the only trace that has come down to us of the life of Cecilia Liconella. Judging by her address in a working-class neighborhood of Venice, living in the home of an outsider from Friuli, across from a baker, she comes from decidedly more humble origins than the man to whom this letter is addressed. Nicolò de Lazara VIII (1553–1599) was from a noble Paduan family, son of Count Domenico de Lazara. When he was young Nicolò had a violent falling out with his father, who threw him out of the family home. A dashing military type, he went to fight as a condottiero *for King Henry III of France, who rewarded him by making him a knight of the Order of St. Michael, and in 1577 Lazara jousted in Innsbruck with Prince Karl in the presence of Archduke Ferdinand. In 1585 he went to Rome as part of a diplomatic mission to the pope with ambassadors of the Venetian Republic and served as ambassador himself in 1496 and 1498.*

This letter was written by Cecilia in her own hand, in a clear script, and apparently a short while after the couple met, probably in Padua. At the time of its writing, Nicolò was in Brescia, as is clear from the address on the reverse side, whereas Cecilia had returned to her place of residence in Venice. We do not know the circumstances of the couple's encounter, what Cecilia was doing in Padua, or the extent of their relationship. However, it is clear from her letter that Cecilia was entirely smitten with this young man—Nicolò was twenty-three years old at the time—who was far above her in social rank. Whether the affection was mutual or if the relationship continued is unknown; it is a fact that two years later, in 1578, Lazara, who inherited the title of count, married Arsilia Zabarella, a Paduan noblewoman, and the couple went on to have four children.

My Most Illustrious Lord, Salutations,

With this letter, Your Lordship will know that by the grace of the Lord, I have arrived here in Venice safe and sound, as I hope likewise is the case for Your Lordship, to whom I had already written before I left Padua, considering it my duty. Now, in this letter I am forced to give vent

---

10 I am grateful to Susy Marcon of the Biblioteca Nazionale Marciana for providing me with a photographic reproduction of this letter.

to my burning passion and the immense love I have, and will always have for Your Lordship; for I think of you day and night. I am continually awaiting the opportunity of seeing you again here in Venice, where Your Lordship will find me your most willing servant, as I am and will be as long as I live. I returned to stay in the *contrada*[11] of San Luca on the street of the pharmacy "Della Vecchia" in the house of Isabetta from Friuli across from the baker, where I was staying before I went to Padua. Yet Your Lordship should not fail to come visit me as soon as possible, as you would show me the most exceptional favor, and I would welcome you as willingly as I would a gentleman and patron, offering myself to serve Your Lordship in anything I am good for, and if you saw fit to command me it would be the greatest favor to me. I beg of you sometimes to remember me, wretched and unhappy as I am since the day that I saw you and knew that my heart would find no rest, tormented and afflicted on every side, so may Your Lordship give me some comfort soon, so that in some way I can be consoled. This you will do if you deign to visit me here in Venice. I humbly recommend myself to Your Lordship and kiss your hands. From Venice on the [ ] day of May, 1576.

Your Most Illustrious Lordship's good servant,

Cecilia Liconella

---

11 Venice is divided into 6 areas called *sestieri*; during the Renaissance period it was further divided into neighborhoods called *contrade*, centered around parishes.

29.

———

Marietta Corsini describes their newborn son
to her husband Niccolò Machiavelli

Married in August 1501 to one of the most famous writers of the Italian Renaissance, very little is known about Marietta Corsini Machiavelli (b. 1482[12]) herself. The daughter of Ginevra and Ludovico di Matteo Corsini, Marietta came from an old and respected Florentine lineage that was of a similar social status to the Machiavellis, and they lived nearby in the same neighborhood. The marriage, which was typical of the kind of marital arrangements worked out in patrician Florentine families, benefited both clans. Machiavelli, who was always in need of money, was able to make use of Marietta's dowry of almost 800 florins, and the Corsini family, excluded from civic participation because of their support of then exiled Medici, was able to take advantage of his connections within the government to improve their standing in Florence. It is unknown what Marietta's feelings about this marriage were, and it is unlikely that she was consulted beforehand. Over the course of their marriage, Marietta expressed dissatisfaction to her husband's friends about his many absences on diplomatic missions, the infrequency of his letters, and their chronic lack of money. Whether or not she knew about his liaisons with other women, such as the courtesan Lucrezia, known as La Riccia, whom he frequented from 1510 through 1520, or the singer and actress Barbera Raffacani Salutati, whom he met in 1524, there is no record of Marietta's opinion of her husband's fidelity or lack thereof. The couple had seven children. One daughter and four sons reached adulthood (Bartolomea [Baccina], Bernardo, Lodovico, Piero, and Guido), and two children died young (Primerana and Totto).

Written early in their marriage, this is the only surviving letter from Marietta Corsini to her husband; none of Niccolò's to her have come down to us. Machiavelli was in Rome in the fall of 1503, sending reports to the Florentine Republic on the struggle for power in the Vatican following the death of Pope Pius III on October 18. Marietta wrote this letter on November 24, sixteen days after the birth of the couple's first son, Bernardo, named after her husband's recently deceased father. Although it is impossible to judge a person's character from a single paragraph, Marietta displays a certain caustic sarcasm in this letter, as well as tender feeling for her husband.

---

12 Marietta Corsini's birthdate is known from the record of her father's investment in the Monte delle doti Kirshner and Molho, "Niccolò Machiavelli's marriage." See p. 135, n. 16 on the Monte.

To the notable Niccolò di Messer Bernardo Machiavelli in Rome
In the name of God, on the 24th day [November 1503]

My Dearest Niccolò,

You make fun of me, but it isn't right for you to do so, for I would thrive more if you were here. You who know well how happy I am when you aren't here, especially now as I have been told there is a dangerous disease over there [in Rome], think of how glad I must be, for there is no rest for me either by day or night. This is the joy I have with the baby. Nevertheless, I pray you to send letters a little more often than you have been doing, as I have had no more than three. Don't be surprised if I haven't written, because I haven't been able to, as I had a fever until now; I am not angry. For now, the baby is well and looks like you; he is white as snow, but he has a head that looks like black velvet, and he is hairy like you. Since he resembles you, to me he seems beautiful. He is alert and appears as if he's been in the world for a year. He had barely been born when he opened his eyes and let out a noise that filled the whole house. Our little girl[13] isn't feeling well, however. Remember to come back. Nothing else. God be with you and watch over you.

I am sending you a doublet, two shirts, two handkerchiefs, and a towel, these things that I am sewing for you here.

Your Marietta, in Florence

---

13 This was the couple's first child, Primerana, who died in early childhood.

30.
———

Vittoria Colonna explains to Michelangelo
Buonarroti why she has not written

The most published female poet of the Renaissance, the "Divine" Vittoria Colonna
(1490/92–1547) was celebrated throughout Italy for the beauty of her verse as well as
for her virtuous, noble character. Born near Rome in the family castle in Marino,
Vittoria was one of six children of renowned condottiero *Fabrizio Colonna and the*
cultivated Agnese di Montefeltro of Urbino. In 1509 she was married to Francesco
Ferrante d'Avalos, the marchese of Pescara (1490–1525), to whom she had been be-
trothed as a small child, to create a political alliance with the court of Ferdinand of
Aragon. Like Vittoria's father, d'Avalos was a professional soldier and for much of
their marriage was away leading armies into battle, while she lived mostly in their
palace on the island of Ischia, near Naples. There she took part in the brilliant court
held by her aunt, Costanza d'Avalos (1460–1541), and associated with intellectuals
and literary men such as Bernardo Tasso and Jacopo Sannazaro. In the early 1520s
Colonna was in Rome, where she met writers Baldassare Castiglione, Pietro Bembo,
and Iacopo Sadoleto. Although she had composed some poetry earlier, it was only after
her husband's death following the Battle of Pavia in 1525 that Colonna dedicated
herself to writing. The poems she composed during this period express bereavement
over d'Avalos, whom she portrays as idealized and heroic. In her early thirties, wealthy
and childless at the time she was widowed, Vittoria Colonna expressed a desire to join
a convent. Her family, hoping to arrange a second marriage for her, with the assistance
of Pope Clement VII prevented her from becoming a nun. She resisted their pressure to
remarry, however, and resided in various convents for the final two decades of her life.
Colonna surrounded herself with religious reformers influenced by the ideas of Martin
Luther and John Calvin; her later poetry reflects her deep spiritual concerns, turning
from love of her deceased husband to love of Christ. Her dedication to religious reform
and association with controversial figures such as Cardinal Reginald Pole, Juan de
Valdés, and Bernardino Ochino brought Colonna into conflict with the Church, and
her last years were troubled by investigations of the Inquisition. Over the course of her
life, Vittoria Colonna wrote nearly 400 poems, several printed in 1535 and 1536, but
not until 1538 was her volume of collected Rime *published. Over the next nine years,*
before her death in 1547, there were twelve more editions. She also wrote a number of
prose works on religious topics, and throughout her life she maintained a vast

correspondence with luminaries of her age, from Emperor Charles V to Pope Paul III, Pietro Aretino to Veronica Gambara. A selection of her letters was first published in 1544 under the title Letters of the Divine Vittoria Colonna, Marchioness of Pescara to the Duchess of Amalfi, on the Contemplative Life of St Catherine [of Alexandria] and on the Active Life of St Magdalen.

In Rome, sometime in 1536 or 1538 Colonna became acquainted with Michelangelo Buonarroti; by 1539, when she was living at the Convent of San Silvestro in Rome, the two had become close friends and met often. Of a much more elevated social status than the artist, renowned for her learning and her association with prominent advocates of religious reform, Colonna was highly respected by Michelangelo, who seems to have shared her ideas on spirituality and religious reform. Michelangelo treasured a volume of sonnets Colonna wrote for him and presented as a gift around 1540; he reciprocated by giving her several drawings, including the one referred to here, depicting Christ and the Samaritan Woman, which is now lost. The mutual admiration and affection lasted until the very end of Colonna's life, with Michelangelo present at her deathbed.

To the More than Magnificent and My More than Dearest Friend, Messer Michelangelo Buonarroti.

Magnificent Messer Michelangelo,

I did not reply earlier to your letter, since it was, one might say, a response to my own, thinking that if you and I continued writing according to my obligation and your courtesy, it would be necessary for me to leave the Chapel of Santa Caterina here, without being able to visit with these sisters during the ordained [visiting] hours and you would have to leave the Chapel of San Paolo[14], instead of being able to find yourself there before dawn and staying there all day in sweet conversation with your paintings, who with their natural accents speak to you no less than the real persons I have around me; so that we would both be remiss: I toward Christ's brides [the nuns], you toward His Vicar [the pope]. However, knowing the stability of our friendship, tied by the surest affection in a Christian knot, it does not seem to me that with my letters I need to procure proof of it from yours, but await with a ready spirit a substantial opportunity to serve you. I pray the Lord, of whom you spoke to me with such an ardent and humble heart, when last I saw you

---

14 After completing *The Last Judgment* in the Sistine Chapel, Michelangelo, over sixty years old, was commissioned by Pope Paul III to paint the walls of his private chapel, known as the Cappella Paolina. Michelangelo worked on these frescoes between 1542 and 1550.

in Rome, that I will find you when I return, with His image so renewed and alive through true faith in your soul, as you have so well depicted in my *Samaritan Woman*.[15]

I recommend myself to you always and also to your Urbino[16]. From the monastery of Viterbo on the 20th day of July [1543?],

At your command,
The Marchioness of Pescara

---

15 According to Vasari this was a work by Michelangelo made for Vittoria Colonna, now lost.
16 Francesco Amatore (d.1556) was the artist's trusted assistant for twenty-five years. Known as "Urbano" or "Urbino", he was married to Cornellia Collonello (pp. 217–218).

31.

Ginevra Gozzadini seeks marital advice from her spiritual advisor Leone Bartolini

"A woman broken by sorrows" are the words Ginevra Gozzadini (1520/27–1567) *used to describe herself as a result of her unhappy marriage.*[17] *Descended from the wealthy Bolognese governing class, the daughter of Sigismondo Gozzadini and Giulia Capoani, she was orphaned at an early age. Ginevra had no brothers or sisters, only a half-brother and a half-sister, her father's illegitimate children. After her parents' death, she became the ward of her father's brother Alberto, who arranged her marriage with another high-ranking Bolognese citizen, Giovanni Gaspare dall'Armi, in 1540. Ginevra's husband held many high political offices in Bologna, was elected senator in 1559, and was appointed ambassador to Rome in 1564 and 1566. While her husband enjoyed hunting, dining, and other entertainments with his noble friends, Ginevra was inclined to less worldly pursuits. Around 1550 she experienced a spiritual conversion after coming into contact with a holy woman named Giacoma Bartolini (d. 1565), a stigmatic she met when she was at the spa of Porretta for her health. Renouncing jewelry and luxurious clothing, Ginevra dressed simply, sometimes wore a hair shirt to punish herself, and spent much of her time in prayer. She formed around her a circle of devout noble Bolognese women, with whom she met frequently to discuss religion. The couple's differences were exacerbated by Ginevra's inability to have children and by Giovanni's infidelities. He had brought an illegitimate son, Gaspare, home to be raised by his wife; although she apparently loved the child, by 1556 Ginevra began to complain bitterly of her husband's repeated betrayals. Indeed, Giovanni went on to have at least two more illegitimate children. When Ginevra made out her will in 1562, she left nothing to her husband. Having no children, she chose to leave the majority of her inheritance to her friend Giulia Bonfigli. In her will she described Giulia as "my dearest sister in Christ, kin, the most faithful friend and exceptional companion."*

In 1549 Ginevra met the priest from Porretta, Don Leone Bartolini, a relation of holy woman Giacoma Bartolini. Leone Bartolini became Ginevra's spiritual advisor and confidant, with whom she shared the most intimate details of her married life, documented in around 350 letters she wrote him over the years. When she was concerned

---

17   *"Una donna rota neli dispiaceri."* Zarri, "Ginevra Gozzadini dall'Armi, gentildonna bolognese (1520/27–1567)."123.

over her inability to get pregnant, Ginevra wrote to him asking if she ought to visit doctors; Bartolini counseled against it, writing, "Don't get mixed up with Jewish doctors in order to have children."[18] *When she believed that she actually was pregnant, Ginevra shared that information with Bartolini as well. Troubled by her husband's extramarital sexual activities, Ginevra wrote asking Bartolini if she would be permitted to be excused from conjugal relations. Known as the "marriage debt," Catholic doctrine obliges both wife and husband to be available for sex when demanded by their spouse unless there are extenuating circumstances. Bartolini wrote back that she should refuse payment of the debt if Giovanni persisted in his "public adultery, grazing on Ginevra like a pig, not a Christian."*[19] *In this letter Ginevra provides a glimpse of her daily routine, describing mealtimes with her husband, and hints at the couple's tense sexual relations.*

Jesus, sweetest love[20]

I would not want my soul to be so overcome with joy and lightheartedness that I might not remember the words of the prophet: "Have mercy upon me, O God, after Thy great goodness"[21] I feel guilty that I have not only been lacking in praising the Lord myself, but that through me He has also been offended by three of His creatures: by a sister who caused bitterness and rage; by my nephew who showed ill will toward the priest, and a woman who responded two times with swearing. Truly, I am assured that it was not intentional on my part, but I reprove myself that I was the cause and the instrument, yet love comforts me. In my mind I had developed a strong suspicion concerning a young girl and a gentleman, but as always the [Holy] Spirit places an obstacle there, that ever keeps my conscience walking steadily and free from judgment.

I believe that Your Reverence knows that conversation between Messer Giovanni and myself occurs only at the hour of lunch and dinner, which is a singular blessing. And when Your Reverence has ordered me to say something to him, whether in asking to take my leave or something else, mysteriously obedience occurs, so that while we were washing our hands and sitting down to the table, I told him. Because it was his custom to leave the table while it was still set, I must tell you that now he behaves differently. I used to remain standing, withdrawn with Jesus while he prepared to eat; now he calls me to sit next to him. Plenty of occasions

---

18   "Del farli figliuoli non impazzate con hebrei." Zarri, "Ginevra Gozzadini dall'Armi, gentildonna bolognese (1520/27–1567)." 127.

19   "Se Messer Giovanni non crede lasciare 'il publico adulterio—scrive il Bartolini—e anco di pascersi di Ginevra come porco e non christiano', la donna deve rifiutarsi a lui." Zarri, "Ginevra Gozzadini dall'Armi, gentildonna bolognese (1520/27–1567)." 126.

20   I am grateful to Gabriella Zarri for help in interpreting some of the more difficult passages of this letter.

21   "Miserere mei, Deus: secundum magnam misericordiam tuam" is the first line of Psalm 50. Ginevra writes the line in Latin as "Miserere mei deus, secundan magnan misericordian tuan."

present themselves, though there is abundant aid to help keep me hidden away from the many opportunities to be caught up in sensuality[22]; I am not speaking of the caresses, or his dainty words, because fear—not fear but virtue—of the Holy Spirit comes to my aid showing itself clearly to him. I do not know if I am in error in this; from day to day my heart feels itself transported to its true abode.

And after eating, he remains at the table, while I rise to answer Jesus. In this new exercise I ask for new help. And, if in the past, allowing for my offenses, my intention said: "For your love, Lord," with a sure proof of my good will, now, dedicated to Jesus Christ, I intend and desire always to have Him before my heart as a clear mirror, since from these whiffs of earthly sensuality, even if they seem like small occurrences, even the tiniest breath can fog the glass. Yet I desire to receive everything he does to me counseled by the clear mirror of innocent chastity. However, I feel it rather exhausting and I am inexpert, though I am spurred on by great faith and [your] generous invitation, although I am wounded and do not know how to express to you the kind of blows I receive. You know better than I the importance of such a skirmish and what blows can be had; and I, with faith and obedience, seek always to be provided with the bandages and ointment of love, and without uncertainties, I go forward. Similarly, when I am instructed by Your Reverence in the praises and practice of love, sometimes I feel my heart hardened, but with the same firmness I put devotion into practice with my voice, my life, with my desire. For certainly, as to devotional sentiment, it could be false and hypocritical of me, but because this zeal is followed by outward effects, thus I wish to make use of it without fervor and like the hard earth, to have no choice but to produce flowers and fruits through the refreshing rainfall of the cool waters of divine praise.

And thus, as I know Him in the abundance of [His] spirit to be merciful, kind, loving, and compassionate, so then in the harshness and fragility of my continuous misfortunes from the great faith I possess in Him, just, merciful, [He is] benevolent in sustaining me. Sweet, loving, clement, and full of pity, He gives Himself to me, weighed down as I am by this wretchedness. It is now ringing 17 hours[23] and I end this letter though I have not ended [this topic]. Perhaps by mouth I will continue that which love wishes to follow. Give me your blessing.

---

22 Presumably Bartolini has urged Ginevra to refrain from retiring with her husband during the siesta hour after mealtime, in order to avoid sexual contact.

23 This letter was written late at night, seventeen hours after sunrise, which varies by season. As this letter is undated, it is impossible to calculate precisely.

32.
——————

Celia Romana describes amusements of Roman Carnival season
and expresses distress at her lover's neglect

The most popular woman's letter book of the Renaissance may possibly not have been
written by a woman. Nothing certain is known of the identity of Celia Romana,
whether she was indeed an actual person or merely a pseudonym for another writer,
possibly male. Ortensio Lando anonymously published the Lettere di molte valorose
donne *in 1548, with 253 letters by 181 different women. Purporting to be letters*
authored by women, it was the first female letter collection (aside from Colonna's
1544 small collection of spiritual letters) to be published after Aretino's. Girolamo
Parabosco, who wrote a volume of Lettere amorose *(Venice: Giolito, 1545), which*
included "some letters written by women," has been credited with being the author of
these letters.[24] However, there is a sonnet attributed to Celia Romana included in a
1568 collection of verse, so it is possible she was a real woman.[25] What is indubitable,
however, is the great popularity of this letter collection, entitled Lettere amorose di
Madonna Celia gentildonna romana scritte al suo amante *(Love Letters Written*
by Lady Celia, a Roman Gentlewoman to her Lover); it was first printed in 1562
and then went into ten more printings through 1628. These are sixty-eight letters,
among "thousands written to him over the course of twelve years," which the editor
dedicates to a certain "Magnificent and Illustrious Signora Lisa." Each letter is dated
and signed, the author sometimes signing herself as Celia and sometimes Zima, ad-
dressing her lover as Toso. The richness of detail concerning everyday life seems to in-
dicate an actual correspondence, and despite the sobriquet of "gentlewoman" applied
in the book's title, it seems likely Celia was a Roman courtesan, as she was identified
as Celia Romana in the 1568 poetry collection.[26]

The events described in this letter take place in Rome during Carnival, the period
of popular celebrations leading up to Lent, a time of abstinence and prayer, which
precedes Easter. It was typical during Carnival to dress in costume, wearing a mask,
and to take part in ritual games and general partying and afterward, during Lent, to

---

24 Ray, *Writing gender*, 231.
25 The collection is *Il tempio della divina signora donna Geronima Colonna d'Aragona*, Padova: Lorenzo Pas-
quati, 1568. Celia Romana's poem on fol. 31v is cited in Cox, *Women's writing*, 317.
26 See Camilla Pisana, p. 157, on prostitutes' names derived from their place of origin.

attend religious sermons. During the Counter-Reformation there was a crackdown on public morals and the appearance in public of prostitutes in Rome. In 1555 a city ordinance restricted prostitutes to certain areas of Rome, and in 1566 Pope Pius V decreed the enclosure of Roman prostitutes within walled areas, especially during the holy period of Lent.

Great and Secure Repose of My Travails,

I am glad that you are occupied with so many amusements during this Carnival season, which do not allow you to retain a memory of another's cares. I cannot say the same about myself, for neither pleasure nor any well-being do I feel, especially at the present moment, because it is a thousand years since I have had news of you. And yet in your last letter you promised [to see] me the following Saturday; I know not for what reason, nor can I imagine why [you didn't come] other than my own misfortune. Be assured that since Sunday I have been deeply distressed, knowing that I have been in no way to blame, because perhaps I am better at heart than others believe. Now that I haven't received a letter from you, neither on Saturday nor all the rest of the week, I can believe there is no other reason for this, as I have said, than that you are busy with delightful festivities in pleasant, light-hearted company, which have made you forgetful of everything else. During these past few days of general cheer I have had very little diversion, and if it were not that I pretend to want to see the masqueraders, I would not even dare to stand at the windows, where I stand willingly only in order to be able to enjoy the sight [of you], since for now you do not deign to grant me anything else. I do not know why several days ago N. sent a message to say that she had to speak with me of an important matter and then she never appeared, so that having received no letters from you this week makes me feel very depressed, worrying that some misfortune had occurred. I take enjoyment from the sight of you, infrequent as it is, which it pleases you to grant me so that you let me know you can act a little haughty with me. I saw you last Monday morning when I was inside a white coach[27] and as I raised the shade of the coach, once having passed our street, you did not even want to see me, going along as you were, in the comfort of that sweet company, so pleasing to you.

---

27 Laws were passed in Rome toward the end of the sixteenth century forbidding prostitutes from riding in carriages, presumably because they drew attention and were able to attract more clients this way, and also because the seclusion of a carriage also offered a place for them to ply their trade.

Then the other evening, after I had left my relative's house, you arrived there—Wednesday I think it was—and you didn't recognize me. Yet I could not help doing everything possible to see you leave after dinner; and I saw you there, wearing a fur, getting into a coach and going away without ever remembering even once to raise your eyes to your Celia. O unlucky Celia, certainly she doesn't know, why should she be treated this way? She does not believe that she offended you and yet she seems to have received a sign from your appearance, nevertheless she does not want to pass a rash judgment based on the company of that N. and several others, who cause her torment.

Yesterday I wrote to you from here at one in the morning[28] and this morning I received a letter from you, which amazed me because I seem to understand from this that you are angry with me, believing things about me that are entirely untrue. The tenor of that letter has so afflicted me that I do not know or perceive what I myself write, nor do I want do respond to you either with all that I could say, with good reason. I will only say to Your Lordship that I am sure that spending time with your companions and other gentlemen is enjoyable to you; however, I rejoice at your wellbeing and sorrow at my own misfortune, living as I do most of the time in pain and worry. But if you are truly enjoying yourself, I must tell you, my sweet hope, that you should not thus wound your unfortunate Celia, who never feels even a moment of contentment and knows for sure that in these past days the pleasures of her Toso[29] with his companions—between parties and other entertainments—are impediments that do not permit him either to write or do anything else. Even so, I am ever content as long as contentment is yours. I think I will go a number of times to hear the preaching; I will let you know if I can and when that will be. May Your Lordship remember that I am always yours, the same as I always was and will always be. Look for a good time [to come] and do not kill me with lack of sight of you, for I could never live without you. Thus I remain, making you reverence and kissing your hands. On the 18th of February, 1557. Just now I was invited to go see the hunt at the bridge[30], but I don't know if I can stand all the confusion, so if N. doesn't take me, I think I'll stay home.

---

28 Literally "at seven hours of the night," or seven hours after nightfall; thus, as the sun sets around 6 p.m. in February, seven hours after sunset would be 1 a.m.

29 Her lover's nickname.

30 As part of Roman Carnival festivities a "hunt" for bulls, a kind of bullfight, was held in the Rione (quarter) of the Sant'Angelo bridge. I am indebted to Giovanni Ciappelli for this information.

33.

Emilia N. Fiorentina, returns her lover's letters but asks him to publish his love poems

This is one of a collection of 105 letters published in Siena in 1594 under the title Lettere affettuose di madonna Emilia N. nobile fiorentina, scritte al caualier Bernardino N. *(Love letters of Madame Emilia N., a Noble Florentine Lady written to the knight Bernardino N.). There is no way of knowing if Emilia N. was an actual person or if these letters were composed by someone else, possibly a man. Virginia Cox has suggested that the letters may have been written in imitation of Pietro Bembo's correspondence with Maria Savorgnan, published in 1552 (pp. 161–163), especially as there are various poems and many literary references included.*[31] *In this tender yet entirely decorous parting letter, Emilia N. returns all her lover's gifts, including a portrait, and all his poems. By asking him to memorialize their love by publishing them in a volume, Emilia tacitly consents to sharing their correspondence with the world at large. This is either a recognition on the part of the woman of the literary value of the man's poetry or part of the clever fiction of this possibly male-authored letter collection.*

Here you have another of those pages, which you, in your benevolence, declare to hold so dear and so desire; and in this one I am letting you know that I have given orders that everything of yours should be returned to you. And since I will be deprived of your beloved image, as well as all of your writings that I possessed, please collect your lovely poems, which are so dear to me, into a volume and give them to me as a gift, for like the portrait they can serve no other purpose. For pity's sake, O, ultimate goal of my thoughts, give me such a present; and if it is true that you bear such great love for me as you show, let the sweet hope that I have for your return not be in vain, that we can shelter together under these skies, not only at the end of the time you have set, but sooner yet, and then I will be able to die happy and content. And clear from your breast that sinister belief that I do not love you entirely, as I do not want to offend God, nor break my vows. Consider, wise sir, what a grave error

---

31 *Women's writing*, 286–287.

I would be committing, if, being capable of tasting the sweetest fruits of virtue, I would rather come to know the bitter leaves of vice. Perhaps many women do that, not from lack of sound judgment, but because obsessed with sensual love, they do not see or recognize their duty and responsibilities. Thus, I am yours in everything that may please you and that my duty to honor permits; anything else, which might be unreasonable and against my will, I do not believe you would ever ask of me. I desire, My Lord, that just as this transient place has made us friends, the stable and permanent one will render us eternal companions, with the aid and grace of the One who is the giver of every grace. I am reading with delight the charming pastoral poem and I am infinitely pleased by the very modest [expression] of affection; in it love with honor, and honor with love are celebrated together. I have nothing else to tell you, but to repeat to you once again that I am yours, and without you I live in shadows.

34.
___

Margherita Costa, imagines a love letter written
by a beautiful woman to a dwarf

Margherita Costa (1600-1664),was a virtuoso singer and accomplished poet who has
been called "the most prolific female writer of the century."[32] *A native of Rome, after*
beginning her singing career there, Costa later was active at the Medici court in
Florence, the Savoy court in Turin, and the French royal court. Her writings span a
range of styles, from broad parodic humor to "serious" compositions; her early works
include: Il violino *and* La chitarra, *dedicated to the Grand Duke Ferdinando II de'*
Medici (1638); her 1639 poetry collection Lo stipo *(The Jewel Box) and her* Lettere
amorose *(one of which is translated here) of the same year. During the latter part of*
her career, Costa authored a variety of comedies and dramas, which she dedicated to
the most prominent crowned heads of Europe. Her last work was a theatrical piece,
Gli amori della Luna, *published in Venice in 1654. In a letter written toward the end*
of her life, Costa describes herself as a very poor widow burdened with two children.
She died in 1664.

Among the 325 pages of Costa's Lettere amorose *are a number of outrageously*
funny parodies of love letters. There is, for instance, a letter from a deaf woman to her
mute lover, a wall-eyed woman to her hunchbacked lover, a mangey woman to her
syphilitic lover. Each of these letters pokes fun at the hyperbole involved in amatory
correspondence and the absurdity involved in idealizing the physical attributes of the
beloved. This letter is one of three epistolary exchanges between a beautiful woman
and her lover, a dwarf; apparently Costa found the comic potential of this particularly
ill-matched pair of lovers too rich to resist exploiting several times. In this letter she
inflates the woman's size to grotesque proportions: her sighs are a "great burst of
breath" and the woman invites her tiny lover to enjoy the motion of her "great motor."
Not only does Costa invert the usual gendered tropes of the delicate, demure female
versus the strong, powerful male, but she packs the letter with erotic wordplay and
obscene double entendres.

___

32 Cox, *Women's writing*, 214.

Little vessel of my great sufferings,

Is it possible my handsome little charmer, that in your tiny breast such a little heart can make its nest? And how can you be so afraid? What makes you so frightened? Do you not see, my loving joke, that if fortune brought it about for my flames to be revealed and we were suddenly set upon by others, that your lovely petite body requires so little [space] for its security that in a snap I could keep you safely hidden; if there were no other place, I would hide you silently under my skirts. So my pretty Cupid (resembling him, your smallness I adore), I beg you, made bold by my ardent longing, can you take pleasure in exposing yourself to covert danger among my treasures, my smooth drop of ambrosia, and let your tiny vessel render less yearning, my yearning lips? Permit me, my beautiful nightingale, that to the sweet piping of your voice I add the great burst of breath from my sighs? Will you allow me to calm the flight of your lovely feathers within my capacious breast? Will you grant me that with your tiny motion I may be fortunate to enjoy the motion of my great motor? Abandon, O abandon your fears, mad fellow that you are, no woman ever had a less affected effect from you, for whom alone I wait.

Suggestions for further reading

Letter 26, Camilla Pisana: Bassanese, "Selling the self; or the epistolary production of Renaissance courtesans," In Maria Ornella Marotti, *Italian women writers from the Renaissance to the present: revising the canon*; Flosi, "On locating the courtesan in Italian lyric: distance and the madrigal texts of Costanzo Festa," In Feldman and Gordon, *The courtesan's arts: cross-cultural perspectives*; López, "The courtesan's gift: reciprocity and friendship in the letters of Camilla Pisana and Tullia D, Aragona," In Lochman, López, and Hutson, *Discourses and representations of friendship in early modern Europe, 1500–1700*; Masson, *Courtesans of the Italian Renaissance*; Pisana, *Lettere di cortigiane del Rinascimento*, ed. Romano.

Letter 27, Maria Savorgnan: Casella, *I Savorgnan. La famiglia e le opportunità del potere*; Kidwell, *Pietro Bembo: lover, linguist, cardinal*, esp. 24–70; Pozzi, " 'Andrem di pari all'amorosa face': Appunti sulle lettere di Maria Savorgnan," In Les femmes écrivains en Italie au Moyen Age et à la Renaissance, Centre aixois, 87–101; Savorgnan, *"Se mai fui vostra": lettere d'amore a Pietro Bembo*, ed. Farnetti; Savorgnan di Brazzà, Fabiana. Scrittura al femminile nel Friuli dal Cinquecento al Settecento; Bembo, *The prettiest love letters in the world: letters between Lucrezia Borgia and Pietro Bembo, 1503–1519*, trans. and preface by Shankland. Zancan, *Il doppio itinerario della scrittura: la donna nella tradizione letteraria italiana*, 55–58.

Letter 28, Cecilia Liconella: Plebani, Tiziana. *Il "genere" dei libri: storie e rappresentazioni della lettura al femminile e al maschile tra Medioevo ed età moderna*, 205–206; Ruggiero, Guido. *The boundaries of Eros: sex crime and sexuality in Renaissance Venice*.

Letter 29, Marietta Corsini: Atkinson and Sices, *Machiavelli and his friends: their personal correspondence*; Capponi, *An unlikely prince: the life and the times of Machiavelli*; Kirshner and Molho, "Niccolò Machiavelli's marriage"; Viroli, *Niccolò's smile: a biography of Machiavelli*.

Letter 30, Vittoria Colonna: Barnes, "The understanding of a woman: Vittoria Colonna and Michelangelo's Christ and the Samaritan Woman"; Brundin, *Vittoria Colonna and the spiritual poetics of the Italian Reformation*; Vittoria Colonna, *Selected letters*, ed. and trans. by Abigail Brundin; Vittoria Colonna, *Sonnets for Michelangelo*, ed. and trans. by Brundin; Cox, *Lyric poetry by women of the Italian Renaissance*; Cox, "Women writers and the canon in sixteenth-century Italy: the case of Vittoria Colonna," In Benson and Kirkham, *Strong voices, weak history*; D'Elia, "Drawing Christ's blood: Michelangelo, Vittoria Colonna and the aesthetics of reform"; Gibaldi, "Child, woman, and poet: Vittoria Colonna," In Wilson, *Women writers of the Renaissance and Reformation*; Jerrold, *Vittoria Colonna, with some account of her friends and her times*; Rabitti, "Vittoria Colonna as role model for cinquecento women poets," In Panizza, *Women in Italian Renaissance culture and society*; Robin, "The Salt War letters of Vittoria Colonna," In *Publishing women: salons, the presses, and the Counter-Reformation in sixteenth-century Italy*; Scarpati, *Le rime spirituali di Vittoria Colonna nel codice vaticano donato a Michelangelo*.

Letter 31, Ginevra Gozzadini: Guarnieri, " 'Nec domina nec ancilla, sed socia'. Tre casi di direzione spirituale tra Cinque e Seicento," In Schulte van Kessel, *Women and men in spiritual culture, XIV–XVII centuries: a meeting of South and North*; Hufton, "The window's mite and other strategies: funding the Catholic Reformation," *Transactions of the Royal Historical Society*; Zarri, "Il carteggio tra don Leone Bartolini e un gruppo di gentildonne bolognesi negli anni del Conciglio di Trento (1545–1563)," *Archivio italiano per la storia della pieta*; Zarri, "Ginevra Gozzadini dall'Armi, gentildonna bolognese (1520/27–1567)," In Niccoli, *Rinascimento al femminile*.

Letter 32, Celia Romana: Beebee, "The lettered woman as dialectical image," In *Epistolary fiction in Europe, 1500–1850*; Cohen, "Seen and known: prostitutes in the cityscape of late-sixteenth-century Rome"; Cox, Virginia. *Women's writing in Italy, 1400–1650*; Jensen, "Male models of feminine epistolarity, or, how to write like a woman in seventeenth-century France," In Goldsmith, *Writing the female voice: essays on epistolary literature*; Ray, *Writing gender in women's letter collections of the Italian Renaissance*, esp. Chapter 2, "Female impersonations: Ortensio Lando's *Lettere di molte valorose donne*," 45–80; Storey, *Carnal commerce in Counter-Reformation Rome*.

Letter 33, Emilia N. Fiorentina: Clarke, *The politics of early modern women's writing*, 4; Cox, *Women's writing in Italy, 1400–1650*, 240, 258, 286–287; De Jean, *Tender geographies: women and the origins of the novel in France*; Jensen, "Male models of feminine epistolarity, or, how to write like a woman in seventeenth-century France," In Goldsmith, *Writing the female voice: essays on epistolary literature*; North, *The anonymous Renaissance: cultures of discretion in Tudor-Stuart England*.

Letter 34, Margherita Costa: Bianchi, "Una cortigiana rimatrice del Seicento, Margherita Costa"; Costa, *The Buffoons*, Diaz and Goethals; Costa-Zalessow, *Scrittrici italiane dal 13. al 20. secolo*; Cox, *Women's writing in Italy, 1400–1650*, 212–216, 219–222, 225–226; Megale, "La commedia decifrata: metamorfosi e rispecchiamenti in Li Buffoni di Margherita Costa," *Il Castello di Elsinore*; Morandini, *Sospiri e palpiti: scrittrici italiane del Seicento*; Ray, *Writing gender in women's letter collections of the Italian Renaissance*, 181–183; Salvi, " 'Il solito è sempre quello, l'insolito è più nuovo': li buffoni e le prostitute di Margherita Costa fra tradizione e innovazione".

Chapter Six

Literature and Leisure

Women in Renaissance Italy were reading and writing in numbers unprecedented in European history. What were they reading and why? In the early Quattrocento, Bartolomea degli Obizzi Alberti discusses her approach to sacred reading in her letter to a female friend, detailing sophisticated theories concerning how to read such works; at the same time she provides insight into women's recreational reading, mentioning the reading of both chivalric tales and civic chronicles. Writing literature posed its own challenges and rewards for women. Poets Tullia d'Aragona and Laura Battiferra show us how, by the sixteenth century, women could assert their identity as authors, earning privileges and official protection. D'Aragona, a courtesan, obtains official exemption from wearing the humiliating yellow veil of the prostitute by virtue of her writing, and Battiferra dedicates a volume of poems to the duchess of Florence, thereby promoting not only her own career but that of her sculptor husband as well. Like their male counterparts, successful women authors like Battiferra also had to deal with the problem of others publishing pirated editions of their works, as she explains in her dedicatory letter. Whether writing as a career or reading for entertainment and/or edification, literature was only one of women's outlets during the Renaissance. Music was also an important occupation for women, who contributed to the art both as performers and spectators. However, for professional musicians such as Vittoria Archilei and Francesca Caccini, bravura was not enough; these women had to develop networks of patronage, often by exploiting their connections with powerful women. Both musicians display an ability to flatter, entreat, and cajole their social superiors; without these savvy social skills they could not have succeeded in their careers at court. Although some entertainments were limited to elite circles, theater was enjoyed by all, including cloistered nuns, who also composed and performed *sacre rappresentazioni* (sacred dramas). In her letter to a friar, cloistered nun Arcangela Tarabotti expresses her delight with a musical drama that he has written and sent to her. Neither were women humanists immune to amusement, as Ippolita Maria Sforza demonstrates in her letter to her mother detailing the charms of Renaissance courtly entertainment.

35.

Bartolomea degli Obizzi Alberti discusses theories
of reading with a female friend

*Bartolomea di Tommaso degli Obizzi (d. 1426) was from an ancient noble family in
Lucca, and although her first marriage ended when her husband died after only six
months, her life seemed perfect when in 1389 she married Florentine patrician
Antonio degli Alberti (c. 1363–1415). In fact, the Alberti villa outside Florence where
the lavish wedding festivities took place was called "Paradiso" (Paradise); it was the
idyllic setting for Giovanni Gherardi da Prato's tales in his* Paradiso degli Alberti.
*Her husband was a refined man of learning who frequented humanist circles and
wrote poetry. There is no reason to believe that the couple did not share intellectual
interests, for Bartolomea was highly educated, as demonstrated in her writing, where
she cites Church Fathers and in her own authoritative voice explains complex doctri-
nal matters.[1] Husband and wife also shared spiritual concerns: Antonio built a monastery for the Brigidine order on his land at Paradiso, while Bartolomea was an ardent
follower of the Dominican preacher Giovanni Dominici (1356–1419). Their lives
changed dramatically, however, when in November 1400 a conspiracy to overthrow
the Florentine Republic was discovered. Many members of the Alberti family were
implicated, leading to Antonio Alberti's arrest several months later. Forced to isssue a
confession under torture, all his assets were confiscated, he was threatened with death,
and in 1401 Antonio was sent into exile. His sentence was harsh: For thirty years he
was prohibited from coming within 300 miles of Florence. Under the law, women and
male family members under sixteen years of age did not have to leave, so Bartolomea
stayed in Florence, where she endured financial hardship, having no money left, not
even from her dowry of 1,400 gold florins. She petitioned for, and received, reimburse-
ment of 681 florins from the commune of Florence for another legal matter in 1401.
She also had her four children—Brigida, Bionda, Maria, and Francesco—to care for.
Born in 1400, Francesco, who was only a baby when his father left, was also sent into*

---

1   As Daniel Bornstein comments: "In these letters Bartolomea offers guidance on the spiritual life, teaching other devout women with calm assurance. She refers to the great figures of Christian spirituality, such as
Augustine, Jerome, Benedict, Bernard and Paul; she cites the canon of the mass [...] Bartolomea moves easily
through the technical terminology of contrition and compunction, *substantia* and *potentia* [...] But instead
of speaking as the disciple of her Dominican master (who is never mentioned), Bartolomea offers advice on
her own authority." Bornstein, "Spiritual kinship", 189.

exile, where he died while still young. Bartolomea's daughter Brigida separated from
her husband, who refused to give her back her dowry, and Bartolomea had to support
her. It was to help guide Bartolomea in raising her children that Dominici wrote his
Regola del governo di cura familiare *(On Raising a Family, 1401–1403); he also*
wrote Il Libro d'amor di carità *(Book of Love and Charity, 1402–1404) and*
Trattato delle dieci questioni *(Treatise on the Ten Questions, 1404) for her, as*
well as a number of letters, six of which are extant. The fortunes of the Alberti were
restored in 1428, but Bartolomea did not live to see it, as she died in 1426.

This letter is one of fifteen written by Bartolomea degli Obizzi Alberti to an un-
known female correspondent. No autograph copies of these letters exist; however, her
letters were copied in 1518, nearly a century after her death, by a nun at the convent of
Santa Lucia in Florence, who clearly felt they had value. The copyist was a certain
"Sister N.," who included the letters at the end of a manuscript containing writings of
Giovanni Dominici. Although she was devoted to Dominici's teachings, Bartolomea
degli Obizzi does not cite the influential preacher here but writes in an assured
first-person voice, giving advice on reading. She suggests what texts are best to read to
improve one's soul and outlines theories on how to use spiritual texts as a springboard
for meditation.

Every time that I speak or hear someone else speak about matters that
are not very well defined, I gather myself together and consider the material until it seems that I understand it better than when it was being
discussed. After you left,[2] going over in my memory our conversation
about reading, I seemed to comprehend that which, no matter how often
we discussed it, neither of us had grasped until then, each time going
over it from the beginning. I praise you for reading things that are useful;
[at the time] I did not know how to explain what I really meant by
"useful," nor am I entirely sure that I can tell you [now], though I will
try. What I call "useful reading" is that which causes the mind to collect
itself, drawing away from useless things, and suspends it among those
that are useful. And I do not say to concentrate on useful things, nor to
rejoice in them, for I think that each of these three actions is rather
distinct from the others, especially the first from the other two.[3] The
true and necessary act of the mind—that which I mean by "useful"—is

---

2   Although the name of the addressee is unknown, the phrase *"partita che tu fusti"* indicates that Bartolomea's interlocutor was a woman. Biblioteca Riccardiana, ms. Ricc. 1414 fol. 249r.
3   In three separate phases, the reader is first drawn from useless matters and "suspended" in the zone of the
useful; second she focuses on useful material; and finally, she comes to rejoice in its content. In the sentence
that follows Bartolomea defines what she means by "useful."

when it rises up in the presence of Divine Majesty with self-awareness and burning with desire for Him; from these two things it seems to me fervent and humble prayer will follow during that brief time that the mind has addressed itself to the Divine. And to me it appears that when we find a word in our reading that raises up our mind, we ought not immediately to go beyond it, but furthermore, we must first impose silence in that point in reading, so that the mind is not impeded by external distractions. I say that every time that we feel our mind fallen from that height it had risen to, we ought to undertake to raise it up again by rereading the aforesaid word that lifted it up in the first place, if indeed it can still be lifted up in that way. And so that we understand each other better, I declare that among all the Scriptures of the Old and New Testament, if I were to find one single word that had such power over me that every time I read it, it lifted my mind up in the manner described, I would never go beyond [that passage]. And if I did indeed go on [reading] there, I believe it would be out of harmful vanity, deserving of punishment. Because the books that you have heard me praise quite a bit not only show us the cure for purging us of vice, but rather, along with explaining the remedy, they actually apply this other effect: directing the mind to Him, who heals the infirm soul, which cannot help itself. Any other remedy scarcely helps, and thus I praise reading these things. And if they did not work this second effect that they appear to me to do, I would not say that there was a need to reread them so much. Now whoever has discovered both the first and second effects, not only in reading other books written and ordained by the saints, but in the *cantare* of Orlando[4] or chronicles of Florence[5], I would advise that they should concentrate on those since they do not find those effects in the books that are most adapted to it.[6]

And why do I say above that there is a distinction to be made when making the mind concentrate, rejoice, and suspend itself amidst useful things? I want to explain what I mean by "concentrating" and "rejoicing,"

---

4   *Cantari* were popular narrative poems, usually written in the verse form of *ottava rima*, which told stories from epics, mythology, or chivalric romance. The story of Orlando was one of the most frequently told; the best-known version is Ludovico Ariosto's sixteenth-century epic poem *Orlando Furioso*.

5   Various chronicles of Florence popularly circulated in manuscripts during Bartolomea's lifetime. These chronological accounts of events tended to emphasize God's intervention in determining outcomes of battles, ending famines, and so on. The best known today is the one written by Dante's contemporary Dino Compagni in 1310–1312.

6   This is an extremely complicated passage to interpret; however, the author seems to be suggesting that there are other worthy books, besides religious texts that can produce the effect of lifting up the reader's mind so that through them she may achieve a kind of enlightenment.

as I have discussed "suspending." To me it appears that it can be called concentration when the mind courses over the reading matter in accordance with the tongue or the eye as it passes over the book, not focusing on any one passage, but [the mind] pays attention to that and to nothing worse or less fruitful, otherwise I believe nothing would follow from such a reading. "Rejoicing" I hold to be when we find many useful things in our reading, which one after another lead us to understanding, and we dwell on none of them individually, out of the delight it causes the soul to feel. Then will the soul, filled with amazement feel a festive joy within herself, although I do not know if it will bear much fruit unless the necessary seed can bring forth worthy fruit in the thorny ground, as in the one who speaks to you. In writing, I realize that I ought to express a certain compunction rather than self-congratulation, because the one produces humility with pious entreaties, while the other seems to me to carry the danger of bestial repute and vanity.

Deo gratias. Amen

36.
―――――

*Ippolita Maria Sforza describes her impressions as a newlywed
at the Aragonese court to her mother Bianca Maria Visconti*

*The Latin style of one of Ippolita Maria Sforza's (1445–1488) orations was described
by humanist Pope Pius II Piccolomini as "so elegant that all present were transported
with admiration." Fourteen years old at the time she delivered the speech, the orator
was the daughter of Francesco Sforza, duke of Milan, and Bianca Maria Visconti.
Ippolita Maria's mother was a woman of learning who ensured that all her children,
male and female, received a fine classical education. Along with her brothers, Ippolita
studied Latin with Baldo Martorelli and Guiniforte Barzizza and Greek with
Costantino Lascaris. Before her marriage Ippolita Maria composed a number of Latin
works; in addition to the one cited above, notably she wrote an oration in honor of
Bianca Maria. Married in 1465 to Alfonso d'Aragona, duke of Calabria (1448–1495,
later Alfonso II, king of Naples), Ippolita Maria bore him three children: Fernandino in
1467, Isabella in 1470, and Piero in 1472. Although her husband was a condottiero,
he was also the brother of Eleonora d'Aragona (pp. 109–111) and, like her, raised with
a classical education and a taste for the arts. The court of the duke and duchess of
Calabria became renowned for the artists, musicians, and writers the two patronized.
Ippolita Maria, in particular, who appreciated ancient literature and philosophy, collected an impressive library, although she does not appear to have written anything of
a scholarly nature after her marriage. Ippolita Maria's cultural role as patron of the
arts and literature was at times curtailed by lack of financial resources, which drove
her to request loans from the Medici. Her close ties with Florence put her in opposition
to the official policy of the king of Naples, who was aligned with the papacy, yet she was
able to play a crucial role in facilitating the peace between Florence and Naples in
1479. As time went on, Ippolita Maria was placed in an ever more difficult political
situation as diplomatic relations between the courts of Milan and Naples broke down.
This culminated six years after her death, when her younger brother, the Duke of
Milan, Lodovico Sforza (1452–1508), "invited" the French to invade the Italian
peninsula to wrest control of Naples from the Aragonese.
    One of 312 of her surviving letters, Ippolita wrote this soon after her marriage
and arrival in Naples in September 1465, capturing for her mother the flavor of her
daily life at court. She describes her entertainments as a newlywed at the Aragonese
court, including reading a Spanish book on statecraft with her husband and her design*

of a studio *(study) for her own use. One of her first projects when she arrived in Naples, this* studio, *like the one designed by Isabella d'Este (pp. 213–214), was a personal space where she could read and write, surrounded by beautiful objects and portraits of family members, to whom she wrote many letters. She maintained close connections with her birth family, and her recommendation of various individuals for official positions at the Milanese court also reveals that she operated as a power broker in her own right. Overall, this letter shows Ippolita Maria representing a glowing picture of her new situation. Because of the intellectual interests she and her husband shared, in these early months Ippolita Maria may have expected a marriage that was to be a partnership of equals, based on mutual trust and respect; however, if she did, she was soon proved wrong. As in most Renaissance marriages, fidelity was demanded only of the woman, and Ippolita Maria became jealous of her husband's liaisons with other women, causing her to write only a year later to her mother that her heart was "broken in half by such great sorrow."*

Most Illustrious Princess, Most Excellent and Esteemed Lady Mother[7],

Your Most Illustrious Ladyship will be comforted to know that His Most Serene Majesty the King, as he informs me continually in his most pleasant letters, is very well. And so is my illustrious husband, who has returned from Puglia for this holiday and, what with hunting with falcons and kites, playing ball, as well as reading and translating for me a Spanish book of his on ruling the state and many other moral matters, he has given me the greatest pleasure and continues to do so.

Similarly the Most Illustrious Madonna Lionora (Eleonora d'Aragona, pp. 109–110) and my other brothers and sisters who are here are all most well, and all of them recommend themselves to Your Excellency.

Having finished the study that I use at times for reading and writing, I beg Your Most Illustrious Ladyship, as I have written, asking you at other times, to have made for me portraits from life of His Excellency my father and of Yourself, and of all my Illustrious brothers and sisters, for beyond the adornment of my study, seeing their images would give me continual consolation and pleasure.

His Sacred Majesty, the King gave me for Easter the present of a piece of thick crimson silk, saying that it was fabric like this that the Three Kings presented on that day long ago and thus His Majesty was doing the same. I answered him that his kindness led him to make too grand a comparison with myself, his humble servant and I thanked him countless times.

---

7   Bianca Maria Visconti (1425–1468), duchess of Milan.

My lady Pietra showed me a letter of Your Illustrious Ladyship in which, among many most prudent and sacred reminders, you remind her also to sleep with me. Concerning that matter, I am informing Your Ladyship that as soon as the Duke began to sleep with me, I had her lodged in a bedroom just outside of mine and had her given the key to watch over and to lock the door. And thus, when the Duke is absent, she always closes and locks it. But for certain good reasons I do not have her sleep with me.

I have sent off the letter about that business of Madonna Emilia's, and I added to it a letter of my own, with as much urging as I could, and I will do all in my power for her.

I have asked Madonna Antonia da Melia once again for a little of that civet[8] of Your Excellency's, but she has not answered. I received several containers and her granddaughter is sending the letter. And since the letter contains nothing else, I thank Your Ladyship and them for it.

Tomorrow my Most Illustrious consort will take me with him to Pozzuoli to go hunting, to see the baths and the antiquities there, along with the Solfatara crater that they call "the Mouth of Hell"; I am sure we will take great pleasure in it.

I thoroughly recommend to Your Excellency the wife of Donato Pistone as well as Francesco di Baiacchi and Catalina di Visconte his wife, father and mother to my man Galeazo Baiacca. Likewise, Zoanne Baptista, doctor in law from Cremona and all his brothers, who are also brothers of Gilio my head cook. I also recommend to Your Illustrious Ladyship the son of Madonna Margarita de Sanson, who as the greatest favor desires to enter the service of my Most Illustrious Father as an envoy.[9]

Everyone here is well, and once again we recommend ourselves to Your Excellency; similarly, I pray Your Excellency please tell my Magnificent Lady Grandmother that Messer Lupuo Spagnolo never tires of speaking of her and praising her to the skies. We also recommend all my Illustrious brothers and sister to you.

From the Castel Capuano on the sixth day of January 1466.

Your Most Illustrious Ladyship's

Most devoted daughter and faithful servant

Ippolita Maria Visconti of Aragon, etc.

Baldus M. [scribe][10]

---

8   Presumably for making perfume.

9   I am grateful to Roberto Bellosta for the translation of the term *fameglio cavalcante.*

10   Of the 312 letters of Ippolita that have come down to us, 63 are autograph (written in her own hand); the others she dictated to scribes. Castaldo, xiv.

37.

Tullia d'Aragona asks Benedetto Varchi's aid in drafting a letter
to Duke Cosimo I de' Medici and Duchess Eleonora

Writer and poet Tullia d'Aragona (1501/05–1556) was a courtesan born in Rome;
her mother Giulia[11] was also a courtesan. It is uncertain precisely who the girl's father
was, but it is likely that he was Cardinal Luigi d'Aragona, a highly placed member of
the Church. Like Venice, Rome was known for its many sex workers, from the lowliest
streetwalkers to the highest-paid courtesans. Renowned for her beauty, singing, genteel
manners, and eloquent speech, Tullia d'Aragona became wealthy and her richly
decorated home a gathering place for musical virtuosi and influential literati. Some-
time during the mid-1520s she began her long-term liaison with Florentine patrician
Filippo Strozzi (see Camilla Pisana, pp. 157–158), one of her most ardent clients. In
1535, a daughter, Penelope d'Aragona, was born; although she was declared to be her
mother Giulia's child, it is possible that she was actually Tullia's.[12] In Siena in 1544 she
married a man from Ferrara named Silvestro Giucciardini. During this period
d'Aragona had begun circulating some of her poetry in prestigious circles, notably
dedicating several sonnets to the duke of Florence and his mother Maria Salviati
(pp. 118–119). Being a married woman improved d'Aragona's social standing and
aided her desire for self-representation not as a courtesan but as a serious and virtuous
woman of letters comparable to the renowned writer Vittoria Colonna (pp. 168–169).
In 1547 she published Rime della Signora Tullia di Aragona e di diversi a lei (Poems
by Tullia d'Aragona and by Others to Her) *as well as a work in prose, the* Dialogo
della infinità di amore (Dialogue on the Infinity of Love); *these works were extra-*
ordinarily well received, and Tullia d'Aragona was indeed hailed by many as a succes-
sor to Colonna. During her final years, d'Aragona concentrated on writing an epic in
verse titled Il Meschino, altramente detto il Guerrino, *which was not published until*
after her death in 1560. She was survived by her son Celio, to whom she left the

---

11 Sometimes identified as Giulia Campana or Giulia Pendaglia, or simply as Giulia Ferrarese, after the
name of her hometown of Ferrara. For biographical information on d'Aragona see Hairston, 2014. On the
custom of referring to sex workers by their place of origin, see Camilla Pisana, p. 157–158.

12 In any case, Tullia appears to have developed a warm maternal relationship with Penelope (who was
twenty-five to thirty years younger) until the girl's death in 1549.

majority of her belongings; nothing else is known about the boy, either who his father was or what became of him.

Written in the spring of 1547, in this letter Tullia d'Aragona solicits help from Benedetto Varchi (1503–1565), the most prominent intellectual in Florence, to combat charges against her of violating Florence's sumptuary legislation.[13] She had been denounced for appearing in public without the yellow veil that prostitutes were required by law to wear. This was not the first time she had offended a city's sumptuary laws; several years earlier d'Aragona had fallen foul of Sienese regulations by wearing a luxurious cloak not permitted to sex workers. In Siena d'Aragona had defended herself successfully by declaring that she was a virtuous married woman, but in this letter she is looking for appropriate wording to defend herself on the basis not of her marital status but in virtue of her standing as a poet, appealing directly to the duchess of Florence as well as the duke. The strategy worked, and in May 1547 d'Aragona was officially exempted from wearing the yellow veil by reason of her "rare knowledge of poetry and philosophy."

My Most Respected Patron,

It is Don Pietro's[14] belief that I ought to present my sonnets to Her Ladyship the Duchess as soon as possible, accompanied by a petition entreating Her Excellency that with His Lordship the Duke, they might grant permission for me not be made to wear the yellow mark,[15] explaining briefly how I live quietly and that if I cannot obtain this favor from Their Excellencies I will be forced to leave Florence. Now that I am in such great need, I do not know where better to turn for help than to Your Lordship. And yet even if I knew of someone else, and could [have his help] I would not want it, because I have chosen Your Lordship for my protector and guide in every important matter, because your good judgment is needed, your reason and knowledge, your true kindness and the unshakeable faith that I have in the decency of your heart. So if Your Lordship has ever willingly troubled himself on my behalf—if you ever thought to assist me and to do something of benefit for me—help me now with your wisdom and come to my aid in the wording of this petition. For Your Lordship this will be just as easy as if you were

---

13 See Sanuti (pp. 73–90) on sumptuary legislation.

14 Don Pedro di Toledo was the brother of Duchess Eleonora and the youngest son of Pedro Álvarez de Toledo, Viceroy of Naples.

15 On October 19, 1546, Duke Cosimo I de' Medici passed sumptuary legislation concerning both men and women's dress, in which prostitutes in Florence were required to wear a yellow veil, shawl, or head covering; Biagi, 154–155. See also Calvi, "Abito, genere, cittadinanza nella Toscana moderna (secoli XVI–XVII)." *Quaderni storici.*

casually talking, and to me it would be such a favor that I could not hope for or desire anything greater, and since I am already obliged to you, I acknowledge that you do it out of kindness and the faith that I have in you. And the sooner you can do it, the greater will be the benefit that I receive. I remain your servant and kiss your hands. May Your Lordship make it known to me what I ought to say in response to Lord Don Pietro.

Your Lordship's Servant,

Tullia Aragona

38.

———

Laura Battiferra dedicates her book of poetry
to Eleonora di Toledo, duchess of Florence

Compared to the ancient Greek poet Sappho and called "the honor of Urbino," Laura Battiferra degli Ammannati (1523–1589) was the author of 400 poems, which circulated widely in many published editions during her lifetime. One of two illegitimate children born to Giovan'Antonio Battiferri, a high-ranking, richly paid cleric in the Vatican court, and his concubine Maddalena Coccapanni, Battiferra was later legitimized by her father in 1543. Although details of Battiferra's early education are unknown, it is likely that she was taught by her father, a man renowned for his humanist learning, well versed in Latin and Greek, and by her mother, who came from a literary family that boasted a number of intellectuals and poets. Battiferra was raised in Urbino, site of one of the most cultured and refined courts of Italy; her first husband, Vittorio Sereni, was the organist for Duke Guidobaldo II della Rovere (1514–1574). The couple was married sometime around 1543, but the marriage ended with Vittorio's death in 1549. However, it is to her husband's death that we owe Battiferra's first poetic efforts, nine sonnets dedicated to him. It was probably in Urbino that she met the sculptor Bartolomeo Ammannati (1511–1592), who was at work on a commission for the duke of Urbino; Ammannati would become her second husband in 1550. For the first five years they lived in Rome, where Ammannati had much work as a sculptor under Pope Julius III Ciocchi del Monte (r. 1550–1555). Battiferra enjoyed the rich cultural environment of Rome; through connections of her father she met many intellectuals who widened her literary horizons, and the majestic city inspired her poetry. When Julius III died in 1555 the couple moved to Florence, seeking the patronage of Duke Cosimo I de' Medici. Over the following five years Battiferra's poems began to circulate in various anthologies, and in 1560 she published the Primo libro delle opere toscane (First Book of Tuscan Works), *an entire volume of her own poems, along with poems written by a number of celebrated people to her. She was visited in her home by the most important literary and artistic figures of Florence, members of the Florentine Academy, including Benedetto Varchi, Annibale Caro, Bernardo Tasso, Anton Francesco Grazzini, Luca Martini, Benvenuto Cellini, and Agnolo Bronzino. During this time, Bronzino painted a striking portrait of Battiferra, which likens her to the two greatest poets of the Italian language: Dante and Petrarch. It was also in 1560 that Battiferra was invited to join the prestigious Academy of the Intronati* of Siena.[16] *In 1564 she published her second book, a free-verse translation of the Seven Penitential Psalms from Latin. Many of Battiferra's works are deeply religious, influenced by the Counter-Reformation values of the Council of Trent; both she and Ammannati were strong supporters of the Jesuit order. The couple, who never had children, by all accounts shared a creative partnership and a happy marriage.*

This is a dedicatory letter to the Duchess of Florence Eleonora di Toledo, published by Battiferra on the opening page of her 1560 collection of poems. It was customary at the time to address a work to an important or influential individual so that the book would be well received and perhaps make the author the recipient of gifts and other favors. Here Battiferra asks pardon for rushing to publish this volume, but as others have begun to publish her poems she wishes to exercise editorial control over her writings by printing this before anyone else, clear proof that her poems were already in wide circulation at this point. It is worthy of note that, while Battiferra appeals to the duchess on her own behalf, she also manages to insert her husband, Ammannati, into the dedication, along with Eleonora di Toledo's spouse, Duke Cosimo I. Having only recently reentered his native Florence, Ammannati was at the time completing his first major sculptural group for the duke, a fountain to be placed in the audience hall of the Palazzo Vecchio, and was competing with many artists for important state commissions. By bringing his name forward in the dedication and linking it to that of the duke, with this letter Battiferra is doing her part to promote not only her own career but that of her husband as well with the two most important patrons of the arts in Tuscany.[17]

> To the Most Illustrious and Most Excellent Lady Eleonora di Toledo, Duchess of Florence and of Siena, Her Most Revered Lady and Patron
>
> I would never have thought, Most Illustrious and Most Excellent Lady Duchess, that I would be obliged to print any of my compositions at this time; however, having learned from several trustworthy individuals that some persons have already gathered a good number of my works and are trying to gather some more, with the intention of publishing them, not only without my permission, but without my

---

16 *Accademie* (learned societies) flourished in Renaissance Italy, although membership was open primarily to men. It was a rare honor for a woman to be allowed to join an academy. Conor Fahy writes: "The most significant fact in the relationship between the Intronati and women is this: in the course of its chequered history (for the fortunes of the academy in the Cinquecento rose and fell with those of its parent city), it only admitted one woman member, the poetess Laura Battiferri, who figures in a list of members dated 1557." "Women and Italian Cinquecento literary academies," in Letizia Panizza, ed., *Women in Italian Renaissance culture and society.*

17 "It can hardly be coincidence that in the same year Battiferra brought out her *First Book*, dedicated to the Duchess Eleonora, Ammannati was appointed architect-in-chief for the renovation of the Pitti Palace, which Eleonora purchased in 1549." Kirkham, *Laura Battiferra and her literary circle*, 325.

knowledge, I was not a little disturbed. And so, not knowing what else to do, I decided as a lesser evil, with my husband's permission and on the advice of a number of friends, to print it myself, addressing it to the glorious name of Your Most Illustrious Excellency. This is not because I believed it worthy of such lofty regard, but to show you in this way, if not my entire gratitude, then at least to show myself as mindful, in part, of the enormous favors which you and the Most Illustrious Lord Duke have done and continue to do for me and for my husband Messer Bartolomeo [Ammannati]; neither he nor I desire anything but to be allowed to go on faithfully and worthily serving you. Taking into account our reverence and devotion to you, may Your Most Illustrious Excellency with your innate goodness and infinite generosity, deign to accept these labors of mine, such as they are and keep us in the good graces of yourself and of Your Most Illustrious and Excellent consort. May our Lord God preserve him as well as you and all your Most Excellent and Illustrious House in good health and happiness for the longest time to come.

Your Most Illustrious Excellency's

Most Humble and Devoted Servant

Laura Battiferra degli Ammannati

39.
———

*Vittoria Archilei laments her declining singing career and asks
the Grand Duchess Christine to assist her son*

*Making her entrance lowered from the heights of the Uffizi theater, as if descending on
a cloud, Vittoria Archilei (fl. 1582–1620) created a sensation singing at the 1589
wedding of Ferdinando I de' Medici and Christine of Lorraine.*[18] *Born Vittoria di
Francesco Concarini in Rome, in 1582 she married the musician Antonio Archilei,
with whom she may have been apprenticed as a singer. The marriage was probably
arranged by a patron to ensure the services of the two singers; over the years the couple
worked together and produced a family of five children, two boys and three girls. In
1584 they left Rome to perform at the wedding festivities of Eleonora de' Medici and
Vincenzo Gonzaga in Florence, and it was here that Vittoria Archilei's stunning
career as a virtuoso soprano took off. Vittoria and her husband worked in collaboration with impresario and composer Emilio de' Cavalieri (c. 1550–1602), who was
active in the Florentine Camerata, developing the emerging avant-garde style of solo
singing that would come to be used in the new art form of opera. The couple remained
in service at the Medici court, participating in the lavish celebrations for the 1589
Medici wedding festivities. In this production, Vittoria Archilei sang the role of
Harmony, in the words of one spectator "singing solo very, very excellently" as she descended to the stage. Throughout the 1590s she sang to great acclaim, dividing her
time between Rome, where she sang for the powerful Orsini family, and the Grand
Duchy of Tuscany for the Medici. The composer Jacopo Peri (1561–1633) referred to
Archilei as "that famous woman who may be hailed as the Euterpe*[19] *of our age [. . .] a
singer of great excellence as demonstrated by her wide renown [. . .] who, through her
singing, has always made my compositions seem worthy." Around 1600 the singer
began to have health problems and perhaps also vocal troubles. She recovered and
continued performing until around 1611, but after that there is no record of her
activities.*

*In this letter Archilei appeals directly to the Grand Duchess Christine (Christine
of Lorraine, 1565–1637) for financial help and assistance for one of her children. Of
Vittoria's three daughters, Cleria found a position in service at the Medici court*

———

18 See Treadwell: "She descended on a cloud 'from the highest spheres.'"
19 Euterpe was the muse of lyric poetry.

in 1607; Maria became a nun at the Convent of San Matteo in 1630; and the third,
Emilia, had died in 1597. Of two sons, it was the elder, Ottavio, who was constantly
getting in trouble (he would be arrested in 1608 for consorting with prostitutes), but
here it is the career of her other son, Ferdinando, that concerns her. Ferdinando was
studying to become a priest, and she asks the grand duchess for permission to remain
in Rome a little longer so that she can try to find him an appointment. Although she
had once been paid an extraordinarily high salary by the Medici, by this point the
former diva finds herself in financial difficulties. The pathos of the letter—the singer
recalls her past glory, acknowledging that with her fading vocal abilities all she has to
look forward to is poverty—underlines the precariousness of the career of a singer;
even the most brilliant was entirely dependent on her patron's will.

Most Serene Madame,

Today I find myself with the Most Illustrious Cardinal Montalto,
having thrust myself upon him in his home during the period that I must
be here in Rome. It seems as if I were serving the Most Serene Grand
Duke and Your Most Serene Highness yourselves, such a friend and
servant is his Most Illustrious Lordship of your Most Serene House.
And since I receive many favors every day from his Most Illustrious
Lordship, I wish to take this opportunity to hope that through Your
Serene Highness's grace and favor I might obtain some ecclesiastical be-
nefice for my son Ferdinando. He is a protégé of Your Most Serene
Highness, as you had him placed in the seminary, which he still attends.
He is progressing in his studies in order to be worthy in learning and
manners, as he desires to become a priest. I entreat you for love of God
to grant me the favor of remaining here serving His Most Illustrious
Lordship [the cardinal] for a short time still, as this way I can easily be
assured of obtaining that which I desire, for if he is recommended by
Your Serene Highness's benevolent hand, once he has finished his studies, my son will be able to serve Your Serene Highness as we do, and he
will know how to do everything good to serve you. Most Serene Lady,
I have spent all the years of my youth in the service of the greatest princes of Christendom and I do not believe I have been among the lowliest
of my profession. I find myself today in such straits that if by chance
I were to lose my husband, not only would I be unable to support my
family, but it would be very hard for me even to live myself. I can
truthfully say that I have nothing else in this world than that small bit of
dowry that my first patron, of blessed memory, gave me. I attribute this
to my ill fortune and not to any lack on the part of my Most Serene
patrons, for all others who served during the same time as I, from the

lowliest to the greatest, all have been in one manner or another rewarded, all except poor Vittoria. She who has exclaimed so much with her
poor voice that by now has become wearisome to everyone and is good
for little else, finding herself today old and impoverished. For this
reason, considering her situation while she still has a little breath in her,
and with Your Serene Highness's grace and favor, she [Vittoria] would
like to see if, in this favorable moment at least some small pension for her
son might be arranged, which would not be difficult, if, with your good
grace, she could stay on just a few more months here. During this time if
Your Serene Highness is pleased to continue paying her salary she would
be all the more greatly obliged to you; and even if you decide not to
grant this, in any case she will be satisfied and always remain most content that all should continue under the wholly good graces of the Most
Serene Grand Duke and of Your Most Serene Highness, to whom one
bows, kissing the hem of your garments with the greatest possible
humility, always praying to great and eternal God for your health. From
Rome, the 28th of January 1602.

Your Most Serene and Benevolent Highness's

Most Humble Servant,

Vittoria Archilei

40.
———

Francesca Caccini requests a libretto for her new composition
from Michelangelo Buonarroti the Younger

Born into the most celebrated musical family in Florence, which performed at the
court of the Medici grand dukes, Francesca Caccini (1587–c. 1645) grew up in a rich
cultural environment. From an early age, "La Cecchina," as she was known, and other
family members took part in court entertainments with her father, the renowned tenor
and composer Giulio Caccini (1545–1618), one of the innovators of opera with the
Florentine Camerata. Although Giulio fathered at least ten children by various
women, Francesca was the first legitimate child and eldest daughter, upon whom he
lavished a superb musical as well as literary education; throughout her life she wrote
poetry in Italian and Latin. In 1604–1605 the family troupe performed in Paris for
the recently married Maria de' Medici and King Henri IV. There, seventeen-year-old
Francesca Caccini's singing talent caught the attention of the king and she was offered
a musical position at the French court. Instead, she returned to Italy, where she per-
formed as a virtuoso singer and instrumentalist on a variety of string and keyboard in-
struments while teaching and composing music at various noble courts. It is, however,
with the Medici that Francesca Caccini's career is most closely associated; the period
of her greatest success at the Medici court coincided with the rule of two women,
Christine of Lorraine (1565–1637) and her daughter-in-law Maria Magdalena of
Austria (1587–1631). After the death of Grand Duke Ferdinando I in 1609 and
during the reign of his son Cosimo II, whose illness kept him from governing, his
mother and his wife ruled Tuscany as joint regents and continued to do so until his son
Ferdinando II came of age. Between 1607 and 1627 Francesca Caccini worked for the
Medici as the highest-paid musician in their court, composing and producing over a
dozen musical entertainments and publishing a collection of songs, Il primo libro
delle musiche, *in 1618. She composed her most famous theatrical work during this*
period, the opera La liberazione di Ruggiero dall'isola d'Alcina, *which was performed*
for the grand duchesses at the villa of Poggio Imperiale in 1625. Francesca Caccini
married twice, first to the singer Giovanni Battista Signorini, by whom she had a
daughter, Margherita. After Signorini's death she married Tomaso Raffaelli, a
wealthy music lover from Lucca, and the couple had a son, Tommaso. She continued
her musical activities in Lucca until her husband's death three years later. In 1633 she
moved back to Florence with Margherita, who was also a skilled musician, and for a

time the two were employed as court musicians by the Medici, this time for the young Grand Duchess Vittoria della Rovere (1622–1694). However, when her fifteen-year-old daughter was requested to perform onstage, Francesca refused, feeling that it would damage the girl's reputation, ruining chances for marriage or placement in a good convent. Eventually Margherita joined the convent of San Girolamo, where she took the name Suor Placida Maria and became renowned for her singing there. In 1641 Francesca Caccini left her service with the Medici court, with official letters praising her for "remarkable and fruitful virtuosity" over many years and promising her the continued support and protection of the Medici family.

This letter is to Michelangelo Buonarroti the Younger (1568–1646), who was nephew to the famous artist and well known in his day as a poet and man of letters. Because Buonarroti was out of town caring for a sick relation, Caccini was forced to put into writing many of the specific requirements of their new musical collaboration— Buonarroti wrote the libretti (texts) and Caccini composed the music. This letter provides a rare glimpse of the creative process. Although this message indicates how closely the two collaborated, throughout Caccini maintains a highly respectful tone with this man who was her social superior. Nevertheless, from this letter it also emerges that she is thoroughly familiar with the power dynamics at court, taking care to ensure that all elements of this new composition will please her patrons, and she swears Buonarroti to secrecy on the project, jealously protecting their creative project from possible competitors. Due to a combination of innate musical talent, superlative training, and a shrewd grasp of the workings of the Medici court in which she had been raised, Francesca Caccini's career soared. Just ten days before this letter was written, on December 17, 1614, Caccini's salary had been doubled, "making her one of the highest paid persons of the entire court."[20]

My Very Illustrious and Most Honored Lord,

Your Lordship's merits are so many and of such a nature that I would not attempt to describe them, because being ignorant myself, I would never be able to express even the smallest part of them, but would only succeed in clouding such merits; I well know how we ought always to hold in great regard the honors bestowed by great princes, and in particular by those who serve them.[21] And yet Your Lordship has never received from our Most Serene Ladies any favor or grace that was not proof of the truest of their good and kind inclinations toward Your Lordship. As for myself, I am certain that Your Lordship knows very

---

20 Kirkendale, 316.
21 Here Caccini is setting up a hierarchy of patronage: there are the Medici patrons at the top; below them are their servants (vassalli) such as Buonarroti; beneath that is Francesca herself.

well that I have been unable to do them any honor whatsoever, nor to their ladies who have had no need of my schooling, except to teach them some new compositions, which, moreover, they can very well do justice to on their own. However, because these are not the foremost obligations I owe Your Lordship, I do not take this for granted, but owe everything to your kindness.

I have felt the greatest pleasure and satisfaction to learn that your nephew is recovering his health: yet I have been sorrowed nonetheless both by the length of the illness and by the doubtful hope of Your Lordship's swift return. Signora Giralda[22] has learned your verses very well, but we are all still awaiting orders from the Grand Duke, who has not yet heard us; the reason I believe to be that he remains in those conditions in which Your Lordship left him, that is always in bed or on a divan[23], nor has he emerged from his bedroom; I leave it to Your Lordship's better judgment to determine how this may go and hope that Your Lordship might still come in time if Our Lord were to put an end to your nephew's fever.[24]

I do not have the least doubt that although Your Lordship is in a place far from the muses, among doctors and the sick, that you yourself being the very chamber and dwelling place of all Parnassus, no misfortune could chase them from their proper seat or alter their nature. Yet, if Your Lordship should happen to think of that comedy, of which I wrote you, I see no other difficulty, but that many things, which are usually discussed and agreed upon aloud on similar occasions, can hardly be dealt with and decided by letter. I have not made up my mind at all concerning the said comedy, because as I mentioned before, there are other worries besides music and comedies, but in order to satisfy what I know to be Your Lordship's taste, or to put it better, your need, I will tell you what has been discussed; however, I beg you that this remains between the two of us as a matter of utmost secrecy. Your Lordship ought to know then, that for the occasion of this little entertainment, it occurred to these court

---

22 Lisabetta Giraldi.

23 Being "*tra letto e lettuccio*" is a Florentine saying that refers to the period of convalescence in which an invalid is not yet fully recovered and can only get out of bed for short periods of time.

24 By urging Buonarroti that he might "still come in time," Caccini may be hinting that the grand duke's illness was considered quite grave indeed. In the secretarial minutes of his mother Christine of Lorraine, there is a letter dated November 16, 1614, in which she urgently writes to Cardinal del Monte in Rome asking him to send medicine; she refers to her son's condition as "very dangerous (*tanto pericoloso*)" (ASF Mediceo del Principato 6021, folio not numbered, Medici Archive Project Doc ID #24649). Despite these fears, Cosimo II did, however, recover from this illness.

ladies to ask Her Serene Highness the favor of being allowed to perform a comedy among themselves, because last year they had permission even though they had other impediments and did not do it. Continuing in order to satisfy you, the comedy ought to be of five acts, or else three, as Your Lordship judges best, and the *intermedi* should be *scherzi*, like those that Your Lordship made for us to sing ourselves; the quality of the comedy ought to be genteel, with foolish old lovers, mischievous servants, servant girls, and dwarfs.[25] In short, Your Lordship would not need to be subject to any specific requirements, but could make it with whatever characters that you wish; it's enough for it to be varied, cheerful and without overly long speeches. This is what I can tell you: it does not seem opportune to me that Your Lordship should lose any time on this until I know all the details with more certainty. What I have told Your Lordship on this matter I have done because I am most certain that, in our usual way, Her Most Serene Highness would call for Your Lordship in a rush and I did not want you to be taken by surprise, but rather that you may be able to think about this invention according to your own taste as you see fit, without having anything else to do but to put it down. Let Your Lordship receive my assurance that I have done all I can in good will to remove all bother for you; knowing how hectic our Carnival festivities can be I will try to learn more and I will inform you of everything. Indeed, if this business I am negotiating goes as planned I will tell you which part is proposed for each [of the ladies], inasmuch as none of them are little girls or babies, but only three young girls between eleven and twelve years of age. The rest of us are all older—it is enough for me to tell you that Signora Giralda will play a naughty boy and Signora Medici a servant and the comedy should turn on that—and we left it there. I will let you know of the rest as it develops. Pardon me if I tire Your Lordship overly by having you read such a huge bible; in order not to bother you, I bow to you, and both my husband and my father remind you that they are your servants, while I pray to Our Lord for every truly good thing for you. From Florence on the 27th of December 1614.

Of Your Very Illustrious Lordship, always most ready to serve you,

Francesca Caccini Signorini

---

25 Many of these are stock characters of the *commedia dell'arte* theater tradition. I am grateful to Kathryn Bosi for her assistance in interpreting these portions of this letter.

41.
—————

Arcangela Tarabotti thanks friar Giovanni Battista
Fusconi for sending her his musical drama

"My life is not a prison, but a hell, from which there is no hope of escape," wrote
Arcangela Tarabotti (1604–1652) in a letter to a friend. One of the roughly 6,500
cloistered nuns in Venice around midcentury[26]*, Tarabotti despised the convent and*
spent her entire life publishing works in which she railed against forced monacation
and other social constraints suffered by women. Born in Venice, Elena Cassandra
Tarabotti was one of eleven children of Maria Cardena and Stefano Tarabotti and the
eldest of six sisters. Very likely on account of an inherited defect of a misshapen spine
and leg, Elena was singled out from birth to become a nun. While two of her sisters
went on to marry and the three others would spend their whole lives at home unmar-
ried, at thirteen Tarabotti was placed in a convent as a boarding student at the
Venetian convent of Sant'Anna in Castello. Several years later she took her vows there,
changing her name to Sister Arcangela, but she never resigned herself to her fate. In-
stead, she wrote a series of polemical works, including L'inferno monacale *(Convent*
Hell, 1643, not printed until 1663); Paradiso monacale *(Convent Paradise, 1643);*
Antisatira (Antisatire Against Buoninsegni's Satire on Female Luxury, 1644);
Che le donne siano della spetie degli huomini (Women Belong to the Human
Race, 1651); La tirannia paterna *(Paternal Tyranny, 1654); and* Il purgatorio
delle mal maritate (The Purgatory of Unhappily Married Women); however, this
last work has not survived. Although as a cloistered nun Tarabotti could never leave
the convent, her writings traveled far; she published four books and circulated other
works in manuscript form. And even though she could only receive approved visitors
in the convent parlatorio *(parlor) from behind an iron grating (Color Plate VIII),*
Tarabotti communicated with prominent intellectual and literary figures throughout
northern Italy and France by writing letters, a collection of which she published in
1650. Her correspondents in the republic of letters included the French astronomer

---

26 Jutta Sperling writes concerning Renaissance Italian cities: "skyrocketing convent populations every-
where suggest that between 1550 and 1650, aristocratic girls were more likely to become nuns than wives
[. . .] On the basis of census data and various convent records, I have estimated that close to 54 percent of
Venice's patrician women lived in convents in 1581, with a rising tendency in the early seventeenth century."
Convents and the body politic, p. 18.

and follower of Copernicus Ismaël Boulliau (1605–1694); the French ambassador to Venice Nicolas Bretel de Grémonville (1608–1648); and Gabriel Naudé (1600–1653), French polymath and librarian to Cardinal Mazarin. Significantly, Tarabotti established a close connection with Venetian patrician Giovanni Francesco Loredan (1607–1661), founder of the prestigious literary academy the Accademia degli Incogniti. Active between roughly 1630 and 1660, the Incogniti was a gathering place for intellectuals and dissidents who resisted the restrictions on scientific inquiry and religious freedom imposed by the Counter-Reformation Church. Loredan provided Tarabotti with forbidden books and aided her in having her own works published. Tarabotti dedicated her familiar letter book to Loredan, with whose help it was printed. The two eventually had a bitter falling-out, and Tarabotti also quarreled with her brother-in-law and all those whom she perceived as trying to suppress or belittle her works. Suffering from serious respiratory illnesses during her final years, Arcangela Tarabotti died when she was forty-three, probably of complications from bronchitis.

This letter was written to Giovanni Battista Fusconi, a Genoese friar who was also a member of the Accademia degli Incogniti. He had sent Tarabotti a copy of Argiope, a musical drama written by him, published in Venice in 1649. The plot is based on a legend from Greek mythology and deals with Argiope, daughter of Teuthras, king of the Mysians, and her faithful love for Telephus, the son of Hercules and Auge. The plot involves the Trojan War, Argiope's discovery of her true identity as princess, and her plea for clemency on behalf of her father, which is granted by the queen, and all ends happily. Although virtually unknown today, this work reflects the innovations introduced by composer Claudio Monteverdi (1567–1643), especially in Venetian theater in the early 1640s—an exciting blend of heroic tales from classical antiquity, erotic love, and violence that would become hallmarks of the art form we know of as opera. Within her convent, Arcangela Tarabotti kept up with the latest artistic developments and here expresses enthusiasm for an exciting new secular drama, which she has been reading during the Easter season, meant to be a time for spiritual reflection.

To Father N.[27]

I do not know if Your Lordship has more satisfied the areas of my senses or damaged those of my soul by sending me your most beautiful *Argiope* during these holy days.

I well know that my mind, carried away to the paradise of Parnassus[28], departed from the contemplation of the Celestial, and that the mind in perusing it, infatuated by the perfection of those lines, though traced

---

27 The addressee is not otherwise identified in the printed collection of Tarabotti's letters.
28 The mountain from ancient mythology where the Muses, who inspired the arts, were said to dwell.

with black ink, averted its gaze from those that it ought to have been reading, etched in blood in the book of humanity of my God. I admired
the fine [*gentile*] invention, the smooth words, the sweet phrasing, the
marvelous verse, when I should have been considering the cruelest invention, the ghastly words, the bitter gall, and stupefying way that those
men delivered Him to death, [the one] who had given them life.
I sympathized with the passions and the hammerings suffered by those
earthly lovers, rather than weeping for the Passion of Christ and considering the hammer that crucified the Savior.

In short, I delighted more in a musical fable than in the funereal
tragedy of the Crucifix, and the fault is yours. I confess myself of this
before Your Most Illustrious Lordship, however; and while I await abso-
lution, I heartily thank you for the honor and I wish you a holy festival
full of spiritual joys. To see Christ resurrected, I accompany the Marys
and I go to the Holy Sepulcher, leaving you to go with the disciples to
Emmaus.[29]

With Reverence.

---

29 In the Bible there were three women by the name of Mary who were present at the crucifixion: the Virgin
Mary, Mary Magdalene, and Mary, wife of Cleophas. These women were also present at the tomb where
Christ was buried. After resurrection, Christ is said to have appeared to two of the male disciples while they
were walking to Emmaus. One of those disciples was Cleophas, so there is a parallel between men and
women in Tarabotti's Easter imagery.

Suggestions for further reading

Letter 35, Bartolomea degli Obizzi Alberti: Battista, *L'educazione dei figli nella Regola di Giovanni Dominici (1355/6–1419)*, esp. 90–94; Baxendale, "Exile in practice: the Alberti family in and out of Florence 1401–1428," *Renaissance Quarterly*; Bornstein, "Spiritual kinship and domestic devotions," In Brown and Davis, *Gender and society in Renaissance Italy*, 173–192; Debby, "Or' andiamo alla predicha, udiamo la parola d'Iddio: the stormy preaching of Giovanni Domenici in Renaissance Florence 1400–1406," 65–87; Gagliardi, *Sola con Dio: la missione di Domenica da Paradiso nella Firenze del primo Cinquecento*; Garfagnini and Picone, *Verso Savonarola: Misticismo, profezia empiti riformistici fra Medioevo ed Età moderna*, esp. 115–119.

Letter 36, Ippolita Maria Sforza: Bryce, "Between friends? Two letters of Ippolita Sforza to Lorenzo de' Medici"; Bryce, " 'Fa finire uno bello studio et dice volere studiare': Ippolita Sforza and her books"; Ilardi, "Towards the Tragedia d'Italia: Ferrante and Galeazzo Maria Sforza, friendly enemies and hostile allies," In Abulafia, *The French descent into Renaissance Italy, 1494–5*, 91–122; King and Rabil, *Her immaculate hand: selected works by and about the women humanists of Quattrocento Italy*, 20–21, 44–48; Lubkin, *A Renaissance court: Milan under Galeazzo Maria Sforza*; Sforza, Ippolita Maria, *Lettere*, Castaldo, ed; Welch, "Between Milan and Naples: Ippolita Maria Sforza, duchess of Calabria," In Abulafia, *The French descent into Renaissance Italy, 1494–5*.

Letter 37, Tullia d'Aragona: Allaire, "Tullia d'Aragona's *Il Meschino* as key to a reappraisal of her work"; Basile, "Fasseli gratia per poetessa: Duke Cosimo I de' Medici's role in the Florentine literary circle of Tullia d'Aragona," In Eisenbichler, *The cultural politics of Duke Cosimo I de' Medici*; Bassanese, "Selling the self; or the epistolary production of Renaissance courtesans," In Marotti, *Italian women writers from the Renaissance to the present: revising the canon*; Curtis-Wendlandt, "Conversing on love: text and subtext in Tullia d'Aragona's *Dialogo della infinità d'amore*"; d'Aragona, Tullia. *Dialogue on the infinity of love*, trans. by Russell and Merry; Hairston, trans. and ed. *The poems and letters of Tullia d'Aragona and others*; Jaffe, *Shining eyes, cruel fortune: the lives and loves of Italian Renaissance women poets*, 71–103; Jones, *The currency of Eros: women's love lyric in Europe, 1540–1620*; López, "The courtesan's gift: reciprocity and friendship in the letters of Camilla Pisana and Tullia d'Aragona," In

Lochman, López, and Hutson, *Discourses and representations of friendship in early modern Europe, 1500–1700*, 99–117; Smarr, "A dialogue of dialogues: Tullia d'Aragona and Sperone Speroni"; Biagi, "Un etera romana".

Letter 38, Laura Battiferra: Edelstein, "Bronzino in the service of Eleonora di Toledo and Cosimo I de' Medici: conjugal patronage and the painter-courtier," In Reiss and Wilkins, *Beyond Isabella: secular women patrons of art in Renaissance Italy*, 225–261; Fahy, "Women and Italian Cinquecento literary academies," In Panizza, *Women in Italian Renaissance culture and society*, 438–452; Jaffe, "Laura Battiferra (1523–1589) and Agnolo Bronzino (1503–1572): a poet, a painter, a portrait, and a poem," In *Shining eyes, cruel fortune*; Kiene, *Bartolomeo Ammannati*; Kirkham, "Creative partners: the marriage of Laura Battiferra and Bartolomeo Ammannati"; Kirkham, "Dante's fantom, Petrarch's specter: Bronzino's portrait of the poet Laura Battiferra"; Kirkham, *Laura Battiferra degli Ammannati and her literary circle: an anthology*; Kirkham, "Sappho on the Arno: the brief fame of Laura Battiferra degli Ammannati." In *Strong voices, weak history*; Veen, *Cosimo I de' Medici and his self-representation in Florentine art and culture.*

Letter 39, Vittoria Archilei: Carter, "Finding a voice: Vittoria Archilei and the Florentine 'New Music'," In Hutson, *Feminism and Renaissance studies*; Emerson, *Five centuries of women singers*; Kirkendale, *The court musicians in Florence during the principate of the Medici: with a reconstruction of the artistic establishment*; Newcomb, "Courtesans, musicians or muses? Professional women musicians in sixteenth-century Italy," In Bowers and Tick, *Women making music. The Western art tradition*; Treadwell, *Music and wonder at the Medici court: the 1589 interludes for La pellegrina*; Treadwell, "She descended on a cloud 'from the highest spheres': Florentine monody 'alla Romanina'".

Letter 40, Francesca Caccini: Bowers, "The emergence of women composers in Italy, 1566–1700," In Bowers and Tick, *Women making music: The Western art tradition*; Cole, *Music, spectacle and cultural brokerage in early modern Italy: Michelangelo Buonarroti il Giovane*; Cusick, *Francesca Caccini at the Medici court: music and the circulation of power*; Harness, *Echoes of women's voices: music, art, and female patronage in early modern Florence*; Kirkendale, *The court musicians in Florence during the principate of the Medici: with a reconstruction of the artistic establishment*; Raney, *Francesca Caccini, musician to the Medici, and her* Primo libro (1618).

Letter 41, Arcangela Tarabotti: Costa-Zalessow, "Tarabotti's *La semplicita` ingannata* and its twentieth-century interpreters, with unpublished documents regarding its condemnation to the Index"; Laven, *Virgins of Venice: broken vows and cloistered lives in the Renaissance convent*; Medioli, "Arcangela Tarabotti's reliability about herself: publication and self-representation (together with a small collection of previously unpublished letters)"; Muir, *The culture wars of the late Renaissance: skeptics, libertines, and opera*; Ray, "Letters from the cloister: defending the literary self in Arcangela Tarabotti's 'Lettere familiari e di compliment'"; Ray, "The pen for the sword: Arcangela Tarabotti's *Lettere familiari e di complimenti*," In *Writing gender in women's letter collections of the Italian Renaissance*; Sperling, *Convents and the body politic in late Renaissance Venice*; Tarabotti, "Letter to the Reader from *Paradiso monacale* and Ferrante Pallavicino's Letter 5, To an Ungrateful Woman, from *Corriero svaligiato*," In Panizza, *Paternal tyranny*; Tarabotti, *Women are not human. An anonymous treatise and responses*, trans. Kenney; Weaver, *Arcangela Tarabotti: a literary nun in Baroque Venice*; Westwater, "A cloistered nun abroad: Arcangela Tarabotti's international literary career," In Gilleir, Montoya, and van Dijk, *Women writing back/writing women back: transnational perspectives from the late Middle Ages to the dawn of the modern era*; Westwater, "A rediscovered friendship in the republic of letters: the unpublished correspondence of Arcangela Tarabotti and Ismaël Boulliau."

Chapter Seven

Art: Patrons and Painters

Excluded from guilds and academies, forbidden to study or paint male nudes, and often abused by male colleagues, female artists in the Renaissance faced overwhelming difficulties in their professional and personal lives. Most of the successful women artists of the period had fathers who were artists themselves or who appreciated art and promoted their daughters' artistic educations. Such women could encounter problems as well: Despite Orazio Gentileschi's (1563–1639) fostering of his daughter's talent, he could not protect her from being raped by a friend of his, a fellow artist. Nevertheless, Artemisia Gentileschi and other extraordinarily talented women were able to carve out successful artistic careers for themselves during this period, through a combination of hard work, careful image management, and a thorough understanding of their patrons' tastes. Painters Lavinia Fontana and Sofonisba Anguissola both crafted images of themselves as respectable noblewomen, which gained them entrée into circles of wealthy and powerful patrons. Fontana found ample clients among upper-class women of Bologna whose portraits she painted, and she received many commissions from clerics at the papal court, who found her sacred paintings completely in tune with Counter-Reformation ideology. Anguissola's talent was recognized by the king and queen of Spain, for whom she served as official portraitist and court lady. By painting a series of powerful canvases depicting heroic women triumphing over evil, Artemisia Gentileschi was able to turn her image around after the notorious rape trial and became one of the most famous painters of her day and, as her letter to a customer indicates, a shrewd business-woman. However, the putting of paint to canvas is only one part of the creative act involved in producing art. The role of the patron and the ideas expressed in the commissioning of a painting are also crucial to the final product, and it was only natural that Renaissance women were actively involved in this part of the creative process as well. As Margaret King puts it: "Wherever courts existed as centers of wealth, artistic activities, and discourse, opportunities abounded for intelligent women to perform in the role as patron of the arts and culture,"[1] as demonstrated in the correspondence of the marchesa of Mantua and the count-ess of Correggio. In their assessments of the work of contemporary painters, Isabella d'Este and Veronica Gambara demonstrate highly refined artistic sensi-bilities. As much as an artist needed to understand her patron, likewise an under-standing of the artistic temperament could be important to the potential patron. It is a measure of her deep respect for the artist that, in her letter to Leonardo, Isabella d'Este employs the most flattering language to propose a unique subject that she hopes will inspire him to paint for her, rather than haughtily ordering a work of art. Women's artistic patronage could also be more oblique, suggested by the warm bond that Caravaggio's patron Costanza Colonna had with the artist's aunt, the wet nurse of Colonna's children. Finally, Cornelia Collonello was no artist, and far from being a patron, was herself in need of patronage or protection from Michelangelo, who was named as one of her children's guardians in her husband's will.

---

1   *Women of the Renaissance,* 160.

42.

_____

Isabella d'Este proposes a subject
for a painting to Leonardo da Vinci

"The first lady of the world" are the words used by one contemporary to describe Isabella d'Este (1474–1539). The daughter of Duke Ercole I d'Este and Eleonora d'Aragona (pp. 109–110), Isabella d'Este was related by blood or marriage to many of the key figures of the Italian Renaissance: Her maternal grandfather was the king of Naples, her brother Alfonso married Lucrezia Borgia (pp. 116–117), and her sister Beatrice was the wife of Ludovico Sforza, duke of Milan. During her childhood at her parents' court in Ferrara, where she was surrounded by intellectuals and artists, Isabella received a humanist education, reading voraciously, and she was early recognized for her brilliant conversation. Immersed in the courtly entertainments of horseback riding, music, and dance and possessing a lifelong passion for art and antiquities, in a sense Isabella would become the female equivalent of the "Renaissance man," a central protagonist in the cultural history of the Renaissance. After marrying the condottiero Francesco Gonzaga in 1490, Isabella became marchesa of Mantua, presiding over a brilliant court there. Her husband was frequently away waging war, and during those times the marchesa ruled in his place. She successfully defended the territory against outsiders, in particular in 1509, after Francesco had been captured and was held prisoner for a year. However, it is primarily for her patronage of the arts that Isabella d'Este is famous. She turned the Palazzo Ducale in Mantua into a treasure box of exquisite works of art and precious objects, commissioning paintings on mythological and religious narrative schemes that she herself devised. The centerpiece of the palace was Isabella's studiolo or private study, the walls of which were decorated with works by Andrea Mantegna, Pietro Perugino, Antonio da Correggio, and others. The fame of her collection and the impeccable taste that had guided her selections were legendary among Renaissance courts, although unfortunately, after her death, the works of art and precious objects she collected were dispersed.

One painter whose works Isabella d'Este longed to add to her collection was Leonardo da Vinci. After being employed for years by Isabella's brother-in-law Ludovico Sforza, Leonardo was forced to flee Milan when his patron was ousted from power in 1500. The artist briefly stayed at the Mantuan court, where he drew a sketch of his hostess, presumably preliminary to a portrait, which he never painted. She was disappointed and tried for six years to obtain a work from this celebrated genius.

In this letter, one of over 16,000 letters sent by Isabella d'Este, the marchesa writes in a deliberately ingratiating tone to the illegitimate son of Ser Piero da Vinci, trying to persuade the artist to send her a painting, at any cost.

Lord Leonardo da Vinci, painter

Master Leonardo, having learned that you have stopped to stay in Florence[2], we have been begun to hope that the thing we so desired might come to pass—to have something made by your hand. When you were here you made a charcoal drawing of us[3] and you promised to do it one day in color. But as this would be practically impossible, as it is inconvenient for you to move here, we beg of you to satisfy that pledge that you made us, deigning to substitute our portrait with another figure that would be even more pleasing, that is, to make a boyish Christ, around twelve years old. He would be of the age when he disputed in the temple[4], and portrayed with that sweet and soft atmosphere[5] in which your artistry, in particular, excels. If you satisfy us in this, our supreme desire, know that beyond the payment that you yourself will set, we will be forever obliged to you and will think of nothing else than of doing agreeable things for you, and from this moment we put ourselves entirely at your convenience and pleasure. Expecting a favorable reply, we offer ourselves to do your pleasure.

Mantua, 14 May 1504

---

2   Leonardo stayed in Florence from April 1500 until mid-1508. During this time he worked for a time as an "architect and engineer" for Cesare Borgia, worked on the fresco of the *Battle of Anghiari* for the Florentine Republic, and also began work on a small portrait of Madonna Lisa, the wife of Francesco del Giocondo, today known as the *Mona Lisa*. In 1508 he returned to Milan to work for the French rulers there. He eventually accepted a position as "first painter and engineer" with François I, king of France, living in Amboise from 1517 until his death two years later.

3   Throughout this letter Isabella uses the royal "we," the majestic plural.

4   This is the only episode from Christ's childhood related in the Gospels. When visiting Jerusalem with his parents for Passover, the twelve-year-old Jesus went missing. "And it came to pass, that after three days they found him in the temple, sitting in the midst of the doctors, both hearing them, and asking them questions." Luke 2:46 KJV.

5   "Leonardo's *sfumato* (It.: 'smoked') manner, in which the contours are rendered elusive under a veil of intervening atmosphere." Martin Kemp, "Leonardo da Vinci," in *Grove Art Online*.

43.
———

*Veronica Gambara recommends a work
of the painter Correggio to Isabella d'Este*

Descended from a line of learned women—one of her aunts was the scholar Isotta Nogarola (pp. 67–68), another was Emilia Pio, one of the cultured protagonists of Castiglione's The Courtier—*Veronica Gambara (1485–1550) seemed destined for literary greatness. She was born in the castle of Pralboino, outside Brescia, to a noble family and received an excellent humanist education. From an early age she studied Latin, history, theology, philosophy, and literature, and she excelled especially in poetry. In 1509 she married her cousin, the* condottiero *Giberto (X), count of Correggio, a small state in the central Po Valley, and the couple had two sons. After her husband's death in 1518, when she was thirty-three years old, Gambara never remarried, ruling her territory on her own, defending it against attack, and successfully maneuvering amid the complex geopolitical diplomacy of the period. Veronica Gambara is best known, however, as a poet, whose writings were highly admired by her contemporaries and earned her admittance into a literary academy in Bologna (Accademia dei Sonnacchiosi). Her works circulated across Europe, both during her lifetime and after her death, appearing in over eighty printed poetry anthologies between 1505 and 1754. Gambara's poems were more often published than those of any other woman of the time, apart from Vittoria Colonna (pp. 168–169), a friend and correspondent of Gambara's. Along with Colonna and Gaspara Stampa (p. 48), today Veronica Gambara is recognized as one of the finest female poets of the Renaissance. Through her influence, the court at Correggio became a celebrated center of culture that attracted intellectuals, artists, writers, and musicians from everywhere in Italy.*

In this letter, written to Isabella d'Este, marchesa of Mantua (pp. 213–214), who was godmother to Veronica's older son Ippolito, the author describes a recent work by the painter Antonio Allegri da Correggio (1489–1534), known as Correggio, from the name of the town where he was born. Although not representative of the scope and eloquence of her vast correspondence—over 150 of her letters have survived—in this brief message Veronica Gambara shares her refined aesthetic judgment with another great female collector and patron of the arts.

Most Illustrious, Excellent, and My Most Highly Respected Lady,

Signor Don Lope has written to me expressly from Mirandola that Messer Tommaso Fornaro arrived there yesterday toward evening.[6] In response to his present instructions [from you], I am writing this letter to you straight away to let you know about it. At the same time I would feel myself greatly lacking in what I owe Your Excellency if I did not make an effort to give you some news concerning the painting that our Messer Antonio Allegri[7] has just now completed, knowing as I do how Your Excellency is most knowledgeable of such things and how much you delight in them. He represents Mary Magdalen in a horrible cave in penance; she is kneeling on the right side, with her clasped hands raised to heaven in the act of asking forgiveness for [her] sins. The beautiful pose and the noble, vivid pain that is expressed on her most lovely face are so wonderful, that they induce astonishment in the viewer. In this work he has expressed all that is sublime in art, of which he is a great master. I kiss your hands, and I recommend myself to you with all my heart. From Correggio, the 3rd of September, 1528

Veronica Gambara de Correggio

---

6   Literally "twenty-three hours," measuring time from sunset, this would be around 6:30 p.m.
7   This painting has not been identified.

44.

_____

Cornelia Collonello appeals to Michelangelo Buonarroti
in a legal dispute with her father

Born in Casteldurante in the Marches, Cornelia Collonello (fl. 1550–1559) was one
of four daughters of a local landowner. In 1550 she married Francesco di Bernardino
Amatore, known as Urbano, who was Michelangelo Buonarroti's assistant for
twenty-five years. The couple lived for four years in the artist's house in Rome; when
their first son, Michelangelo, was born, the artist probably stood as the child's god-
father. Cornelia was pregnant with the couple's second child when Francesco died in
1556. She left Rome later that year and returned to Casteldurante. She was still in
possession of a substantial dowry, and in 1559 she married again, this time to the
jurist Giulio Brunelli, who served as podestà.[8] *From the time of her first husband's*
death Cornelia wrote numerous letters to Michelangelo, who was designated one of
three guardians of her sons in her husband's will. Twenty-eight of these letters still
survive, in which Cornelia primarily discusses financial arrangements. Along with
the two other guardians, the artist controlled the administration of her husband's
estate and disbursement of funds for the raising of the children. In these letters she also
expresses deep affection, sends the aged maestro gifts of cheeses and handkerchiefs,
and requests that he come visit her and the children. There is only one extant draft of
a letter from Michelangelo to Cornelia; in that letter he asks her not to take offense
but not to waste money sending him gifts. Cornelia did not write the letters to
Michelangelo in her own hand but had them copied by various scribes, who were usu-
ally family members.

In this letter, written in 1558, Cornelia appeals for help to the eighty-four-year-
old Michelangelo. Her father had arranged a marriage for her that she considered
unsuitable, with the cousin of a local abbot. Cornelia presents herself as a dutiful
daughter although unable to accept her father's decision to give, in addition to her
dowry, a large amount of money to the groom that rightfully should have gone to her
sisters. Cornelia wants Michelangelo, who by this time was universally revered as the
greatest artist in Italy, highly respected and extremely wealthy, to use his authority to

_____

8 A *podestà* was a person with legal expertise who served as chief political magistrate of a city or town.

persuade her father to cancel the marriage. It is unknown whether Michelangelo inter-vened in this matter; nevertheless, the contract was annulled and Cornelia instead married Brunelli.

Most Magnificent and Like a Father Most Revered,

The gentle affection that Your Lordship has always shown to my chil-dren and to myself has been such that I can truly say that it is greater than that of my father, my mother, and any of my other relations, surpassing them all. Knowing this to be true, I have always loved, obeyed, and reve-red you as a father and as my most affectionate patron, and will always be most ready to obey you, serve you, and respect you; never would I think of doing anything without first knowing your wishes and your advice. If Your Lordship remembers, some days ago I wrote you a letter, telling about my father and mother's great desire to have me remarry; and that of all the matches, they very much liked a young man from Sant'Agnolo in Vado, the brother and first cousin of the local abbot. Although against my own inclinations, he was pleasing to the others, including my father and mother and since Your Lordship admonished and advised me to carry out their wishes, I wanted to obey them and do everything they commanded as befitted an obedient daughter. Thus I agreed to take him for my husband, even though it went against my will, as they liked this one so much. And it was my bad fortune that, as they say, I stumbled on a twig of straw and broke my neck thanks to my father, who made the worst mis-take that perhaps any man has ever made. He let himself be persuaded by persons—who bear little affection for him, for my sisters, my nephews, and for myself—to do something that he never ought to have even consi-dered, let alone do, persuaded by the abbot and the father of the man I was supposed to marry. As soon as [signing of] the dowry contract was celebrated, which was done publicly in the presence of all my sisters' husbands, other relatives, and close friends of ours, my father secretly, without my knowledge and against all reason, only to please the abbot, made me a gift of all his things, depriving all his other daughters and his grandchildren for no reason whatsoever. On account of this dishonest and irrational act, I have been so troubled and disturbed, that at this point I feel beside myself, to think that it did not occur to my father that he was denying his legitimate daughters, who are burdened with sixteen children, between boys and girls, by giving [his entire property] to me, I who already had a much larger dowry than the others—a thousand flo-rins, while my sisters only had two hundred each. After he had made me this gift, Your Lordship can imagine how much harm was done to my poor sisters, who are also my father's daughters, as legitimate and natural as myself. But God, who dislikes fraud and trickery, could not endure such iniquity. This donation,[9] which was revealed to me before my intended husband came to me, displeased me beyond all measure, so that out of affection for my dear sisters and my dear nephews, and to show the world that I was not an accomplice to such traps and deceptions, I sought to draw back from this evil deed in the best manner I knew how, with the consent of the father of the bridegroom and the abbot. I wanted to withdraw and to give my sisters back everything that my father had given me, contenting myself with my original dowry, and desiring that my sisters would have the same dowries as I, as is customary. But they [the father and the bridegroom's family], devoid of Christian charity, would not consent, indeed they more highly valued—and still do—material possessions over my own flesh. And I, with a more generous spirit, value my sisters, their husbands and children, over all my father's belongings, and I am firm in my intention to continue to do so. I am absolutely certain that if I did not do this I would forever be in animosity with my sisters, their husbands, and their children. So I decided right away to send for the father of the bridegroom, and in greatest anguish and discomfort to myself I told him what I thought was reasonable, begging him to be satisfied with my original dowry and not to wish me, along with his son, to be the cause of lasting hatred between [us], my sisters and their families. I received no resolution from that man; however, I sent my mother to the abbot, making him the same proposal that I had to the bridegroom's father. This one was also unreasonable, saying that he would not consent in any way to a reconveyance or a restitution of the donation. In fact, he let my mother know that if I was so unhappy and dissatisfied with the gift and if I was not content for it to proceed in this way, that I should mind my own business and they would mind theirs. Since these men made it clear they did not want to consent to my reasonable proposal, and having heard, besides, much sinister and evil news of him [the bridegroom], that he is full of the French disease[10], [and that] he is a rather dim-witted young man lacking in virtue, with many other personal faults, with few belongings, indeed hardly any, so I let it be publicly known that I in no way would be his son's wife. I let him know that he should mind his own

---

9   The *donatio inter vivos* was a legal bequest made while the donor was still alive. I am grateful to Elena Brizio for providing me with this information.

10   Because it appeared in Italy and began to spread around the time of the French invasions of 1494 and 1499, syphilis was known as *il mal francese*, or "the French disease."

business and I would take care of my own. Since this happened I find myself discontent and in a bad state, the more so because I see my father unaffectionate toward his other daughters and still remaining firm in his original purpose to have me pick that man as my husband, paying no heed to the grievous lamentations, cries, and distress of his daughters, sons-in-law, and grandchildren. All this I cannot bear, nor will I ever be able to tolerate that such serious harm and deliberate wrong is done to them, as they are all extremely poor.

Therefore, magnificent man, most honored as a father, I find myself in these troubles and travails, as you will understand. I do not know how I will get out of them, thanks to my stubborn father, who though he has been begged by many different good men, does not want to confess to having acted badly and [will not] repent for the deliberate wrong he has done his daughters. And if Your Lordship does not come to my aid with an affectionate letter, I will be given entirely to despair. I see no reason to go ahead with this bond between families, both on account of their rudeness, as well as his bad qualities, and also because after what has happened between us, with these bad feelings and rumors, I am absolutely certain that I would never have a moment of happiness [if I married him]. Thus I am resolved that it is for the best that this bond shall not go forward. In order to continue in this good purpose, I pray you as much as I know how and with all my abilities, that you give me assistance and counsel in order to move my father from his harsh obstinacy. I most firmly believe that with Your Lordship's influence he will give up, as he has great regard and reverence for you as his most revered superior. I will wait for Your Lordship to give me some advice and to persuade my father not to do such grave harm to his other daughters, giving me this unhappiness by being an unfairly biased, cruel man, with no pity what-soever. And if by this means I can [do] something for you, command me as a daughter and I will always be most ready to serve you; forgive me if I do not write more often, but my mind has been so occupied with wor-ries, that at times I am not in this world. Michelangelo and Francesco[11] commend themselves to Your Lordship, as do my father and mother; I kiss your hand. May Your Lordship deign to commend me to Laura and to everyone. From Casteldurante, the 4th of October, 1558.

As a loving daughter of Your Lordship,
Cornelia Amatori da Collonello

---

11 Cornelia's sons.

45.

Margherita Aratori expresses to Costanza
Colonna how she misses her

Although next to nothing is known about the details of the life of Margherita Aratori (fl. 1584–1601), the same cannot be said about the life and work of her celebrated nephew. The painter known to us today as Caravaggio (Michelangelo Merisi, 1571–1610) gets his artistic sobriquet from the place where he was born, as a subject of the marchese di Caravaggio, lord of the region. The ties between the artist's family and those of the ruling family were unusually close: His aunt Margherita Aratori and his sister Caterina Merisi both served as balie *(wet nurses or nursemaids) to the children of the marchesa. The women were well paid; indeed, Margherita's husband was able to purchase a field with the money his wife earned during the many years in service to the family. The land was purchased from the eldest son, Muzio Sforza, one of Margherita's former charges, demonstrating continued ties between the male head of the ruling family and his former nursemaid. His mother, the marchesa, Costanza Colonna (c. 1556–1626), was married when she was twelve years old, gave birth a dozen times in fifteen years, and certainly had need of assistance caring for her children. Her generosity to the Merisi family, however, went beyond mere remuneration for domestic servants and extended beyond the immediate household. Costanza Colonna was a patron of Lombard artists, in particular of Michelangelo Merisi da Caravaggio, to whom she often offered her protection. The artist was with her at times during her stay in Rome from June 1592 to June 1593, and in 1601. He was in her palazzo in Chiaia near Naples in 1610 just before he died.*

This brief letter exposes an intimate emotional bond between Aratori and her employer that lasted many years. It was written in 1601, eighteen years after Colonna was widowed, and her children were long past weaning. Wet nurses were the most highly paid domestic servants in the Renaissance; reliable ones were prized and highly rewarded.[12] Almost all Renaissance families of the middle to upper class employed

----

12   There is, for instance, a 1572 letter written by the Grand Duchess of Tuscany Giovanna of Austria (1547–1578) to Cosimo I de' Medici in which she asks a former grand-ducal wet nurse to be granted half a house, in view of her "vigilance, diligence, and greatest possible kindness" (ASF Mediceo del Principato 5926 fol. 117, Medici Archive Project Doc ID# 21760). See Klapisch-Zuber, "Blood parents and milk parents," in *Women, Family, and Ritual* for a detailed overview of the practice within the Florentine context.

lactating women to provide milk for their babies. A woman's nurturing of an infant with her breast milk often went beyond a mere job. Close bonds tended to be created not only between the wet nurse and child, but also between the "surrogate mother" and birth mother. Given the continuous pregnancies enforced on elite women, the wet nurse was a constant presence in the family's life. When she lived in the household (sometimes babies were sent away to the country to stay with the wet nurse), the nurse could be a source of advice and comfort for a young mother trying to rear multiple children. Costanza Colonna was particularly young and isolated at the time of her marriage, prompting an aunt to write in 1568: "there's no one there, the girl is all alone, without anyone of authority nor of counsel."[13] We must also assume that in a situation such as this the wet nurse could become a valued confidant and unusually close companion to the mother, and as a part of the extended family, the wet nurse's family was in a sense "related" to her employer's family. Thus, for example, in this letter, Margherita sends regards to the marchesa from herself and her niece Caterina, as well as from "my nephew the priest." This was Giovan Battista Merisi, the painter's brother, underlining the complex obligations and bonds of patronage that linked at least four members of the Merisi family with Costanza Colonna.

> Most Illustrious and Most Excellent Lady,
> To relieve a little of the pain that I felt at Your Excellency's departure, I wanted with these few lines to greet you and also to show you respect; begging Your Excellency to remember, even if you are far away, that I will always be your faithful servant. I hope to see you again in good health and this lightens my grief somewhat at not being able to see you before you left. Truly, not a night goes by that I don't speak to you in my dreams nor a day in which I feel like I ought to be serving you. With this I offer my respects to Your Excellency begging you to remember me from time to time in those most holy churches of Rome. May our Lord give you long life. My nephew the priest[14] likewise bows in perpetual obligation to Your Excellency. From Caravaggio the 28th of September, 1601.
> From your most affectionate servant the wet nurse Margherita
> The wet nurse Caterina[15] bows to you

---

13 Baerstein, "In My Own Hand," 144.
14 Giovan Battista Merisi, brother of the artist.
15 Caterina Merisi, the sister of the artist.

46.

---

*Sofonisba Anguissola asks Philip II of Spain
for a recommendation for her husband*

*Giorgio Vasari paid a visit to the childhood home of Sofonisba Anguissola (c. 1532–
1625) in Cremona to see some of her works and described several of her portraits
"which appear truly alive, lacking nothing but speech [. . .] executed so well that they
appear to be breathing and absolutely alive."[16] But by the time Vasari arrived at the
house in 1566, the artist was no longer there; she had moved to Spain, where she
painted for the king. Sofonisba was one of seven children of Bianca and Amilcare Anguissola, six girls and a boy, all educated in the classical literature of ancient Greece
and Rome and the sciences, music, and art. Their father, a Cremonese nobleman, recognized that from an early age Sofonisba had an unusual gift for art and arranged for
her to study painting, first with Bernardino Campi from 1545 to 1549 and then with
Bernardino Gatti. Amilcare also exchanged letters with Michelangelo about his
daughter's talent, sending samples of her work to the famous artist. Michelangelo encouraged the girl, sending letters with suggestions for subjects and advice on technique.
Sofonisba Anguissola eventually became a master in the refined mannerist style of
painting, but with a warm attention to human detail, evident especially in her portraits
of her family members and depictions of scenes from daily life (Color Plate III). Her
work came to the attention of Philip II, king of Spain, and in 1559 she was appointed
court portraitist, moving to Madrid. Anguissola remained at the Spanish court for the
next twenty years, earning 100 ducats a year, which enabled her to help her brother
financially. She also served as lady-in-waiting, and the king himself arranged her
marriage in 1572 to Fabrizio Moncada, brother to the Viceroy of Sicily; the queen
presented her with a dowry of 3,000 ducats. In 1580, after being widowed, she was
returning to Cremona when she met Orazio Lomellini, a nobleman from Genoa, and
married him. The couple lived in Genoa, where Anguissola received guests at her
salon. The last years of her life were spent in Palermo, where she lived on a lifetime
pension from the king of Spain. The Flemish painter Anthony van Dyck met her there*

---

16 "Che paiono veramente vive e che non manchi loro altro che la parola [. . .] paiono spirino e sono v250iviss-
imi." Vasari, "Life of Benvenuto Garofalo," in *Lives of the artists*, 2nd ed., 1568. This passage is discussed by
Jacobs, "Woman's capacity to create," 77–78.

when she was ninety years old and almost blind, yet he described her as still having a vivacious spirit and sharp mind.

In the present letter, the only one entirely in her own hand, the artist writes to the king of Spain. Here she reminds one of the most powerful men in Europe to send a recommendation for her second husband. It is unknown exactly for what purpose Orazio Lomellini needed this recommendation. The tone of Anguissola's letter to the king is humble but at the same time dignified, and she seems confident of a positive response.

Sacred Catholic Royal Majesty[17]

With Orazio Lomelino my husband I wrote to Your Majesty, begging that you grant me the favor of recommending him to you, not only on his own account, but also because he is my husband. Once again I write to remind Your Majesty to favor me with the aforesaid [recommendation] and to order that it be sent speedily. I entrust myself to Your Majesty's customary benevolence and generosity with members of his household[18], among whom I am one of the most affectionate. I cannot fail to expect other than good from the hands of Your Royal Majesty, on whom all my well-being depends, as from God, and I will put this obligation along with so many others that I have incurred with Your Majesty, whose hands I kiss with all the greatest reverence and humility. I pray to Our Lord God that the Most Catholic King, in the Person of Your Majesty remains in good health and happiness for many years. From Genoa, the 14th of October, 1583.

Your Majesty's most humble servant and faithful vassal,

Sofonisba Lomelina et Anguissola

---

17 The official title of the king of Spain was "the Catholic king."
18 Anguissola is alluding to the fact that she was a member of the Spanish royal household, tutor to the royal princesses and entitled to the king's protection.

47.
_____

Lavinia Fontana replies to Alfonso Ciacòn,
sending a self-portrait that he had requested

After having his portrait painted by Lavinia Fontana (1552–1614), Fra Francesco
Panigarola (1548–1592) wrote: "And it is true that, while in previous centuries
women have been able to compete in letters with men, in this century Lavinia does so
in the most noble art of Painting."[19] *Born in Bologna, the daughter of Antonia de*
Bonardis and the painter Prospero Fontana (c. 1508–1596), Lavinia Fontana was
provided with an elite education in letters and music and only later was trained in the
craft of painting by her father. In 1577 she married Gian Paolo Zappi, a minor noble-
man with little money. She gave birth eleven times, although only four of her children
survived infancy and just three outlived her. Fontana was one of the first female paint-
ers of the Renaissance to be widely recognized during her lifetime and professionally
successful. Fontana spent most of her life in Bologna, where she became renowned for
her many portraits of fashionable women of upper-class circles. She was equally cele-
brated for her sacred paintings, which captured Counter-Reformation sensibilities
and earned her many commissions from the pope. To be nearer the papal court, for
which she became official portraitist, during the last decade of her life she moved to
Rome. There she was honored by being accepted into the artistic Academy of San
Luca, normally closed to women.

In this letter to an influential patron who has requested the artist's self-portrait,
Fontana demonstrates her ability to craft an elegant letter that strikes the appropri-
ately self-deprecating tone, while the tone of the letter itself confirms her high social
standing. Alonso Chacón (Alfonso Ciacon or Ciacono, 1540–1599), of Spanish
origins, was a scholar and influential member of the clergy who owned a number of
portraits by Fontana.[20] *He also wanted portraits of famous men and women for his*
private collection and was eager to obtain a self-portrait of Fontana to hang there.
Chacón wrote that he was coming to Bologna specifically to see "such a rare thing as
your virtuosity, and a woman so famous and such an excellent artist that our times has
produced to accompany the beautiful and accomplished Sophonisba [Anguissola]."[21]

19 Caroline Murphy, *Lavinia Fontana: a painter and her patrons*, 78. Fontana's portait of Panigarola is on 69.
20 Caroline Murphy, *Lavinia Fontana: a painter and her patrons*, 49, 73–76.
21 Caroline Murphy, *Lavinia Fontana: a painter and her patrons*, 73.

In the self-portrait (Color Plate IX) that Fontana painted for her client she chose to represent herself in a room surrounded by decorously arranged antique models rather than the clutter and materials one would expect to see in an actual artist's studio. Indeed, rather than standing to paint, she sits at a desk in what more closely resembles a scholar's studiolo. The cubbyholes containing the models recall a cabinet of curiosities—the display area for treasured antiquities and unusual objects so fashionable in the homes of Renaissance intellectuals. Dressed not in an artist's work clothes but in the elaborately elegant attire of a noblewoman, Fontana wears a large crucifix; she holds a pen in her hand poised near a sheet of paper and gazes confidently at the viewer. The overall effect is of a dignified, accomplished, and prosperous woman, who is also very devout. All in all it is a very effective piece of image management calculated to advertise not only Fontana's artistic abilities but also the artist's social standing and religious credentials, presenting herself as worthy to enter the homes of nobles, cardinals, and the pope himself in order to paint for them.

I replied some time ago to Your Lordship's letter inviting me to send you my portrait, for you to hang alongside those of many illustrious individuals, and I am pained to hear that that letter went astray. Not wishing to repeat everything that I wrote then, and so that no more time would be lost, I chose to obey you promptly; the bearer will be Signor Paolo Emilio[22], who I hope will take my place with Your Lordship as I have urged him to do. I cannot help but tell you that you honor me too much with your overabundant praise, and in your intention of giving my portrait such an honored place, which I attribute both to your excessive kindness, as well as your desire to make the virtues and worth of Signora Sofonisba [Anguissola pp. 223–224] and other most excellent persons shine more brightly. These I know myself unworthy even to serve, much less to be considered their equal, but as good musicians sometimes put in discordant notes in order to make harmonies sound even sweeter, and as a few clouds can make the ornaments of the heavens more glittering, thus Your Lordship must have thought that my portrait, with in its shadowy imperfection, will make your most noble museum shine even more. Whatever the reason, I am satisfied just to obey you, and if I can do so again, Your Lordship will always know the readiness of my spirit towards you, whom I wish every happiness and I beg you to remember me in your prayers. From Bologna the 3rd of May 1579.

Your Most Reverend Lordship's [servant]

---

22 Paolo Emilio Luchini was "a lawyer, who had undertaken the initial shipment of portraits to Ciacón." Caroline Murphy, *Lavinia Fontana: a painter and her patrons*, 73.

48.

Artemisia Gentileschi discusses costs and terms of payment
for her paintings with Don Antonio Ruffo

In her lifetime, artist Artemisia Gentileschi (1593–1652/53) "was not merely success-
ful. She was famous."[23] *Born in Rome, Artemisia was one of four children of painter*
Orazio Gentileschi (1563–1639) and his wife Prudentia Montone. Although the
other children were sons, Artemisia's exceptional artistic talent singled her out from
an early age as the only one to be trained in her father's craft. She worked alongside
him, creating her first independent painting, Susanna and the Elders, *when she was*
seventeen years old. The following year, 1611, Orazio arranged for his daughter to
study perspective with his friend, the painter Agostino Tassi, who raped the young
woman. Tassi was tried in court and found guilty. Shortly afterward, Artemisia mar-
ried the Florentine artist Pietro Antonio di Vincenzo Stiattesi (b. 1584), and the
couple left Rome to live in Florence, where Artemisia was able to obtain a number of
important commissions thanks also to the presence of an uncle, the well-established
painter Aurelio Lomi (1556–1622). She became well known for her paintings of
female subjects, heroic figures such as her various portrayals of Judith Slaying
Holofernes, *painted in the dramatic style of Caravaggio*[24]*, and her sensitive, realistic*
treatment of female nudes. Gentileschi's painting earned her the protection and
patronage of the Medici, especially of Grand Duchess Christine of Lorraine and her
son Grand Duke Cosimo II, as well as the recognition of fellow artists and intellectu-
als. Among her acquaintances in Florence were Cristofano Allori, Michelangelo
Buonarroti the Younger (p. 227), and Galileo; in 1616 she was the first woman to be
admitted to Florence's Accademia del Disegno. Around 1620 she returned to Rome for
a time with her husband and the only surviving child of four she had given birth to in
Florence, her daughter Prudenzia (or Palmira), who would also be a painter.[25] *Aside*

---

23   Elizabeth Cropper, "Life on the edge: Artemisia Gentileschi, famous woman painter," in Christiansen, Keith, and Mann, eds., *Orazio* and Artemisia Gentileschi, 268.

24   Artemisia Gentileschi, like many painters of her generation, was influenced by the innovations introduced by Michelangelo Merisi di Caravaggio; these painters are known as Caravaggisti.

25   "There appears to have been a second daughter, born some years after Prudentia-Palmira, whose marriage to a knight of the Order of St. James on March 13, 1649, is mentioned by her mother in a letter on the day of the wedding [. . .] If, as seems probable, there were two daughters, it is noteworthy that both were painters." Garrard, *Artemisia Gentileschi*, 1989, 63.

from trips to Venice and notably to England, where she went to help her aging father in his painting of the ceiling decorations in the Queen's House in Greenwich, Artemisia spent the remainder of her life primarily in Naples, where she died in 1652 or 1653.

This is one of a series of thirteen letters written between 1649 and 1651 by Artemisia Gentileschi to her patron the Sicilian art collector Don Antonio Ruffo. The possessor of a sizeable collection, including works by Rembrandt, Ribera, Van Dyck, and Poussin, Ruffo commissioned half a dozen works from Gentileschi. The dense correspondence—twelve of these letters were written within one year, two of them on the same day—reveals the close interaction between artist and patron. In these messages Gentileschi discusses her setting of prices and means of payment; methods of shipment; behavior of untrustworthy customers; the costs of materials and of hiring models; and questions of artistic style and technique. In this letter, she acknowledges that her own criteria as an artist may differ from the expectations of her patron, yet she promises to produce a work "which will suit my taste and yours." Written when she was in Naples during the pinnacle of her career, Artemisia states her terms for producing a painting that he has commissioned, displaying professionalism, confidence in her abilities to satisfy her client, and sharp business acumen. She resists lowering the price of one of her paintings, slyly suggesting that by bargaining an artist down, the patron gets what he pays for.

My Most Illustrious Lord,

I would rather not discuss our business in this letter, if by chance that gentleman[26] might read it. So I say to your Most Illustrious Lordship, concerning your suggestion that I discount the price that I had originally given you for those paintings, [I can do] something, but let it not be less than four hundred ducats, and provided that you send me a deposit as all the other gentlemen do. However, I must say that the higher the price, the harder I will strive to make a painting pleasing to Your Most Illustrious Lordship and which will suit my taste and yours. In regard to the painting for Your Lordship that is already finished, I can't let it go for less than what I asked for because I cut back on everything in making you this final price. And I swear, your servant that I am, that the price I gave you I wouldn't have given even to my father. Signor Don Antonio, my lord, I pray you for the love of God not to make me go back on what I've said, as I'm sure that when you see it, you will say that I have not been impertinent, as your own nephew the duke can attest, I care deeply for Your Lordship. As for the price, I remind you only that there are

---

26   Refers to the person carrying the letter, whose identity is unknown.

eight [figures], two dogs, landscapes, and seascapes, so Your Lordship will see that the cost of models is unbearably great. I will not mention anything else, only this, which I have on my mind, that Your Illustrious Lordship will not lose [money] on me and you will find the spirit of Caesar in the soul of a woman. And with this I send you my most humble reverence. From Naples the 13th of November 1649.

Your Illustrious Lordship's most Humble servant,

Artemisia Gentileschi

Suggestions for further reading

Letter 42, Isabella d'Este: Ames-Lewis, *Isabella and Leonardo: the artistic relationship between Isabella d'Este and Leonardo da Vinci, 1500–1506*; Brown, *Per dare qualche splendore a la gloriosa cita di Mantua, Documents for the antiquarian collection of Isabella d'Este*; Campbell, *The cabinet of Eros: Renaissance mythological painting and the* studiolo *of Isabella d'Este*; Cartwright, *Isabella d'Este Marchioness of Mantua, 1474–1539: a study in the Renaissance*; Cockram, *Isabella d'Este and Francesco Gonzaga: power sharing at the Italian Renaissance court*; IDEA Isabella d'Este Project; Prizer, "Una 'virtù molto conveniente a madonne': Isabella d'Este as a musician"; San Juan, "The court lady's dilemma: Isabella d'Este and art collecting in the Renaissance"; Shemek, "Isabella d'Este and the properties of persuasion," In Couchman and Crabb, *Women's letters across Europe, 1400–1700: form and persuasion*; Shemek, "In continuous expectation: Isabella d'Este's epistolary desire," In Looney and Shemek, eds., *Phaethon's children: the Este court and its culture in early modern Italy*; Shemek, "Mendacious missives: Isabella d'Este's epistolary theater," In Shemek and Wyatt, *Writing relations: American scholars in Italian archives: essays for Franca Petrucci Nardelli and Armando Petrucci.*

Letter 43, Veronica Gambara: Fabbrici, Gabriele, and Giuseppe Adani, eds. *Il Correggio a Correggio: protagonisti e luoghi del Rinascimento*; Gambara, *Complete poems. A bilingual edition*, Martin and Ugolini, ed. and trans; Gambara, *Rime*, ed. Alan Bullock; Gambara, *Rime e lettere*; Gould, *The paintings of Correggio*; Jaffe, "Veronica Gambara (1485–1550)," In *Shining eyes, cruel fortune: the lives and loves of Italian Renaissance women poets*, 1–37; McIver, "Two Emilian noblewomen and patronage networks in the Cinquecento," In Reiss and Wilkins, *Beyond Isabella: secular women patrons of art in Renaissance Italy*; Poss, "Veronica Gambara: a Renaissance gentildonna," In Wilson, *Women writers of the Renaissance and Reformation*; Rabitti, "Lyric poetry, 1500–1650," In Panizza and Wood, eds., Brundin, trans., *A history of women's writing in Italy*, 37–42; Russell, "Veronica Gambara (1485–1550)," In *A bio-bibliographical sourcebook*, 145–153; Stortoni, *Women poets of the Italian Renaissance: courtly ladies and courtesans*, 23–27.

Letter 44, Cornelia Collonello: Barocchi and Ristori, *Il carteggio di Michelangelo*, 139–142; Buonarroti, Michelangelo, *Letters*, E. H. Ramsden, ed. and trans; Stott, "'I am the same

Cornelia I have always been': reading Cornelia Collonello's letters to Michelangelo," In Couchman and Crabb, *Women's letters across Europe, 1400–1700: form and persuasion,* 79–100.

Letter 45, Margherita Aratori: Baernstein, " 'In my own hand': Costanza Colonna and the art of the letter in sixteenth-century Italy"; Berra, *Il giovane Caravaggio in Lombardia: ricerche documentarie sui Merisi, gli Aratori e i marchesi di Caravaggio;* Calvesi, *Le realtà del Caravaggio;* Klapisch-Zuber, "Blood parents and milk parents: wet nursing in Florence, 1300–1530," In *Women, family, and ritual in Renaissance Italy.*

Letter 46, Sofonisba Anguissola: Garrard, "Here's looking at me: Sofonisba Anguissola and the problem of the woman artist"; Jacobs, *Defining the Renaissance virtuosa: women artists and the language of art history and criticism;* Jacobs, "Woman's capacity to create: the unusual case of Sofonisba Anguissola"; Low, *By her own hand: words and hands as personal iconography in the self-portraiture of Sofonisba Anguissola;* Murphy, *Lavinia Fontana: a painter and her patrons in sixteenth-century Bologna;* Pagden, *Sofonisba Anguissola: a Renaissance woman;* Perlingieri, Sofonisba Anguissola: the first great woman artist of the Renaissance; Pinessi, *Sofonisba Anguissola: un "pittore" alla corte di Filippo II.*

Letter 47, Lavinia Fontana: Cantaro, *Lavinia Fontana, bolognese: "pittora singolare," 1552–1614;* Cheney, "Lavinia Fontana, Boston *Holy Family*"; Galli, *Lavinia Fontana pittrice: 1552–1614;* Garrard, "Here's looking at me: Sofonisba Anguissola and the problem of the woman artist"; Jacobs, *Defining the Renaissance virtuosa: women artists and the language of art history and criticism;* Jacobs, "Woman's capacity to create: the unusual case of Sofonisba Anguissola"; Murphy, "Lavinia Fontana and *Le Dame della Città:* understanding female artistic patronage in late sixteenth-century Bologna"; Murphy, *Lavinia Fontana: a painter and her patrons in sixteenth-century Bologna;* Ragg, *The women artists of Bologna;* Schaefer, "A note on the iconography of a medal of Lavinia Fontana"; Wiesner, "Women and the creation of culture," In *Women and gender in early modern Europe,* 177–185.

Letter 48, Artemisia Gentileschi: Bal, *The Artemisia files: Artemisia Gentileschi for feminists and other thinking people;* Bissel, *Artemisia Gentileschi and the authority of art;* Bissel, "Artemisia Gentileschi: a new documented chronology"; Christiansen and Mann, *Orazio and Artemisia Gentileschi;* Cohen, "The trials of Artemisia Gentileschi: a rape as history," *Sixteenth Century Journal;* Garrard, *Artemisia Gentileschi around 1622: the shaping and reshaping of an artistic identity;* Garrard, *Artemisia Gentileschi: the image of the female hero in Italian Baroque art;* Harris, "Artemisia Gentileschi: the literate illiterate or learning from example," In *Docere, delectare, movere: affetti, devozione e retorica nel linguaggio artistico del primo barocco romano;* Longhi, "Gentileschi, padre e figlia"; Menzio, ed. *Lettere. Artemisia Gentileschi; precedute da Atti di un processo per stupro;* Pollock, "Review of Mary Garrard's *Artemisia Gentileschi,*" *Art Bulletin;* Solinas, ed. *Lettere di Artemisia: edizione critica e annotata con quarantatre documenti inediti;* Spear, "Artemisia Gentileschi: ten years of fact and fiction".

Chapter Eight

Inquiring Minds: Science and Philosophy

C uriosity, discovery, and scientific inquiry are all hallmarks of the Renaissance. Women as well as men were drawn to new fields of study and to reex-
amination of older ones. Although women did not have access to university
education, that did not stop many from examining the world around them and
forming theories about it. In her letter to a male friend, Ceccarella Minutolo develops an epistemological argument explaining how women can arrive at philosophical ideas without necessarily having access to the same learning as men.
This was a significant argument because when women did manage to overcome
social barriers and contribute original writings, they were often accused of bor-
rowing from men's works or indeed having men secretly author their writings;
this occurred in the fields of literature, philosophy, and science. The term
"science" was at the time evolving, having during the Renaissance a wider meaning than it has today. From the Latin *scientia* meaning "knowledge," science en-
compassed a broad range of intellectual investigation. Thus, in her subtly pacifist
argument, Chiara Matraini opposes so-called military science to the use of
reason, the highest of the human faculties, which it is meant to serve. She con-
curs with Aristotle that war only exists to guarantee the safety and peace required in society so that the pursuit of knowledge and philosophical reflection

can take place. Beyond the ideas of Aristotle, the so-called new philosophy, which was then emerging, involved the study of the natural world through observation and rational analysis, rather than merely accepting at face value ideas expressed by ancient or Christian authorities. This new approach came to be called "natural philosophy," an example of which is in the letter of Paduan apothecary Camilla Erculiani Greghetti. In this letter she examines the account of the Biblical Flood, expounding a theory of conservation of matter to explain where so much water came from and what happened to the receding floodwaters. The originality of her ideas brought Erculiani to the attention of the Church hierarchy, causing her to be called before the Inquisition. Another woman whose outspoken philosophical views were considered dangerous was Sara Copio Sullam, a prominent Jewish poet and intellectual in Venice. For her interpretations of the ancient philosophy of Aristotle and Plato, and the modern natural philosophy of Bernardino Telesio (1509–1588), Copio was publicly denounced by a Christian cleric for denying the immortality of the soul. It was dangerous in Counter-Reformation Italy to voice unconventional ideas that challenged religious doctrine: For their theories on the natural world Tommaso Campanella (1568–1639) was imprisoned for thirty years, and in 1600 Giordano Bruno (1548–1600) was burnt at the stake. Nevertheless, Margherita Sarrocchi, a brilliant polymath and hostess to an intellectual salon in Rome, was a passionate supporter of the discoveries of Galileo, promoting his career in the papal capital. In a 1611 letter she describes viewing the moons of Jupiter and the phases of Venus through Galileo's telescope, defending the scientist against his critics. Meanwhile, Galileo's own daughter Virginia was living quietly in a convent at the time her father's discoveries appeared, but that did not prevent her from participating in the excitement they aroused: In one of her letters she asks him to send his just-published work *The Assayer*. In contrast, rather than being enclosed in a convent, Elena Lucrezia Corner Piscopia was an active presence in the world. Renowned for her learning and rewarded with a university degree in philosophy, such was Corner Piscopia's authority that in her letter she uses her influence to see that her male mentor is awarded tenure.

49.

_____

Ceccarella Minutolo to Theophilo on how knowledge
is acquired and transmitted

"Publishing my little letters, it was to be feared that greater damage would be incurred to my honor than fame attached to my name, incited by friends' foolish entreaties, rather than by any expert skill."[1] With these words Neapolitan noblewoman Ceccarella Minutolo (fl. 1460–1470) opens her letter book. Almost everything that can be known about Minutolo's life must be surmised from her elegantly composed letters, which she "published" by circulating them in manuscripts among a select group of friends who were members of the Aragonese court in Naples. Little is known from other documents about her personal life, other than that she was the daughter of Francesco Minutolo, "il Monaco," Lord of Issico (a territory near Otranto), and Agnesella Filomarino, and that Ceccarella was married twice, first to Francesco Brancaccio and after his death to Camillo Piscicelli. About her own life, in the thirty-eight of her letters that have come down to us[2], Ceccarella provides some scattered clues. While many of the letters appear to be fictive or rhetorical in nature, others appear to be addressed to specific individuals and mention actual events. In her introduction, for instance, Minutolo dedicates the collection to Francesco Arcella, addressing him as "my affectionate brother." A learned man from the same elite circle of Neapolitan society as Ceccarella, he was praised by contemporaries as a man "dedicated to the sciences."[3] There is a letter to the Princess Eleonora d'Aragona (pp. 109–111) in which Ceccarella sends her the gift of a puppy named "Fidele" (Fido); one to the famous physician Giacomo Solimea (or Solimena) praising his abilities; another to Alfonso, duke of Calabria, exhorting him to pursue humanist studies; and one to King Ferdinand of Aragon asking him to find her a husband. Minutolo appears to have been renowned as a

_____

1   *"Dubitava de non incorrere maiore del mio honore damno che de fama celebrato nome acquistare, volendo alcune inepte, et più tosto [da] prieghe de amici che da incitata voglia et de perita arte, publicare mei licterule."* Lettere, Morabito, 34.
2   There were originally at least ninety letters in Minutolo's letter book, according to Olga Casale.
3   Benedetto Croce relates that the humanist Panormita (1394–1471) said of Arcella that he was "an ornament among the youths of his age" *("ornamento dei giovani suoi coetanei").* Croce, 64.

writer in her day, known to her contemporaries as the "Sybilla Parthenopea" (Neapolitan Sibyl, after the wise women from antiquity who wrote books of prophesies).[4]

The majority of the letters, however, are written to a man referred to only as "Theophilo," meaning "one who loves God." The letters to Theophilo are primarily although not exclusively about love, expressing jealousy, longing, and sorrow, but in them Minutolo also defends women, raising arguments from the querelle des femmes *debate, and discusses literary and philosophical issues. In the present letter Minutolo takes her friend to task for praising her too highly and claiming that her ideas derive from classical writers such as Cicero. Her response is that as a woman she has not had access to Cicero or the works of the philosophers, implying perhaps that it is because she has not studied Latin, although the letter itself is sprinkled with learned Latinisms. Moreover, she refers to Socrates, Aristotle, and Demosthenes, indicating that she is familiar with ancient history and philosophy; even without Latin she could have acquired this knowledge through the many vernacular texts that circulated in Quattrocento manuscripts. In any case, Minutolo demonstrates that she is well read. At the heart of her argument is her epistemological claim that the same knowledge can be attained by individuals coming from diametrically opposed philosophical positions; without being aware of the natural philosophy of the pagan Aristotle, many Christian writers arrived at similar ideas. Minutolo extends this reasoning to women, explaining that without access to the writings of Cicero and others, women can use their reasoning and "invention" as an alternative means of arriving at the same conclusions held by ancient philosophers.*

> "Letter to Her Theophilo, Who Highly Praised Women"[5]
>
> It seems as if our delightful enterprise has turned into regrettable quarreling[6], so it appears that I ought to make amends to your affectionate and kind will, particularly as it would be unjust of me to criticize you on any grounds except one: that you adorn me with so much extravagant praise. Certainly, in my judgment, which does not deceive me, I do not know one hundredth of all this. However, I am well aware of how your misguided opinion is counseled by the sincere love that produces it. Perhaps you are led to believe by vulgar and common experience that when some woman is granted praise she is never displeased no matter how excellent she may be, no matter how immoderate in its

---

4   Alfonso, duke of Calabria (Alfonso II of Aragon, 1448–1495) is said to have referred to Minutolo with this name. *Lettere*, Morabito, 11.

5   I am grateful to Raffaele Morabito for his assistance in clarifying some of the more complex passages of this letter.

6   The letter that precedes this one is entitled: "To Theophilo, defamer of women," in which Minutolo criticizes Theophilo for his negative opinion of women.

overabundance. O our miserable mortal condition! That we are not gods and that we desire to be praised as gods; we are not immortal yet we want to be, and absurdly believe that we are eternal. It is possible for me to lose my good sense. You well know, my exceptional and affectionate Theophilo, that Socrates, when asked in what way he was wise, answered prudently, even divinely, that he was wise in only one thing: that he was aware that he was not wise. Concerning the knowledge of oneself, you know that the foremost skill that is needed is not to be deceived in the evaluation of one's good qualities. Earning praise that pleases us obstructs our capacity for judgment and impedes our reason. It makes us disregard with false and presumptuous judgment every respect of others' qualities: Our own abilities ought to be seen clearly and not compared with those of others. You often argue to me of your "friend" Tullius—whose writings of course I've never seen—saying that I have borrowed from him.[7] Your background is good, but I certainly am not familiar with him; my intellect is merely that of a woman and my pen is nothing but a vile reed. So if my wild and unkempt writings might resemble those of some great author, [I say that] invention or rather, reasoning, is common to all women, nor are well-considered opinions attributed to one person in such a way that the use of them is forbidden to another. I believe I have heard that Demosthenes, that most eloquent Greek[8], had no equal in that mellifluous and persuasive art; all the same, Tullius, your friend and ally surpassed him in wealth of invention; in the art of quibbles and witty expressions; abundance of Latin discourse; and finally, in that which is most praised in a perfect and consummate orator, namely attractive and modulated pronunciation, in which he showed such skill that he seemed not a man, but a god, not a fountain but a river; he did not pronounce words but flash lightning. Similarly Aristotle said much of the state of secret things[9], as much of [earthly] nature as of the heavens, inspired by feeling, and others of our holy Christians have said the same from divine revelation, without one having heard or read

---

7   Marcus Tullius Cicero (106 BCE–43 BCE), Roman orator, statesman, philosopher. See the introduction pp. 4–6. Cicero writes: "the Pythian Apollo bids us 'learn to know ourselves'; but the sole road to self-knowledge is to know our powers of body and of mind, and to follow the path of life that gives us their full employment." *De finibus* Book 5, 16, 44, Loeb Classical Library, Harvard University Press, vol. XVII, second (revised) edition, 1931; trans. H. Harris Rackham.

8   Demosthenes (384–322 BC) was an ancient statesman and orator famous for his speeches.

9   Possibly a reference to the pseudo-Aristotelian text the *Secretum secretorum*, which circulated widely in vernacular translations in the Quattrocento. It is a translation of the Arabic "Kitab sirr al-asrar." This text has been identified in about five hundred medieval manuscripts. (M. A. Manzalaoui, ed., *Secretum secretorum, nine English versions*, vol. 1. Early English Text Society No. 276. Oxford University Press, 1977, p. ix.)

[the works of] the other. If I have been lazy in my writing or in the future might be, do not blame me, because my idle pen does not seem to be expansive and wonderful; and added to that my incurable, unknown illness, which makes me displeasing to myself, my intellect is clouded and pleasure leaves me, so that neither daring nor desired stylus [pen] suffice, by which I was often able to overcome the evils of idleness. Farewell.

50.

---

*Chiara Matraini to Maria Cardonia on the superiority
of philosophy to military "science"*

Chiara Matraini (1515–1604) was from a wealthy nonnoble family in Lucca that had originally made its living as weavers. The daughter of Agata Serantoni and Benedetto Matraini, she was orphaned at a young age and married Vincenzo Cantarini in 1530 when she was fifteen years old, giving birth to a son in 1533. Nearly everything else about her life was unconventional. A year after her marriage a number of members of her family were involved in a failed uprising to seize power from the elites in Lucca, ending in exile for some, imprisonment or death for others. Although disgraced, the Matraini family name was the one that the young woman chose to use throughout her career. In 1542 her husband died and by 1547 the young widow was involved in a scandalous affair with a married man, the poet Bartolomeo Graziani. The two lived openly together, entertaining intellectuals, including young men from the nearby University of Pisa, in a private academy in their home. At these gatherings, notorious for their extreme freedom of speech, Matraini recited poetry, played the keyboard, and sang. Several years later Graziani was murdered, perhaps out of revenge by members of his wife's family. In 1555 Matraini published her first literary work, Rime e prose *(Poems and Prose), which both celebrates her love for Graziani and laments his death. In 1556 she also published a translation from Latin of ancient Greek rhetorician Isocrates's (436–338 BCE)* Oration to Demonicus, *a work of advice to a young man. At the same time, she appears to have become estranged from her own son over control of her dowry, Matraini's means of economic independence. She wrote to her friend, the lawyer Cesare Coccapani, for advice on how to "resolve the lawsuit to wrest my dowry, my inheritance, and all my interests from the hands of my son who is so opposed to me." From this point on Matraini pursued a literary career, unusual for a woman, but especially for one of her class. Whereas other contemporary female poets were either courtesans like Veronica Franco (pp. 144–145) and Tullia d'Aragona (pp. 192–193) or noblewomen like Veronica Gambara (p. 215) and Vittoria Colonna (pp. 168–169), Matraini came from a respectable middle-class background. She was, however, a great admirer of Colonna, inspired by both the noblewoman's poetry and her reformist spirituality. In addition to secular poetry, Matraini wrote many devotional works, although she does not push for reform or challenge the authority of the Church in her writings. Instead, in her 1602* Dialoghi spirituali *(Spiritual Dialogues), the author* emerges as *"a combination of scholar-philosopher and Dantean poet-seer."*[10] *Matraini was eighty-seven years old when this last work was published. She died two years later and was buried in the Church of Santa Maria Forisportam in Lucca in a tomb she had designed years earlier. Above it was a painting commissioned by Matraini representing herself as the Tiburtine Sibyl, prophesying before the Emperor Augustus.*[11]

In 1555 Matraini published a collection of her poems along with letters on a variety of subjects, addressed to identifiable individuals such as Cangenna Lipomanni, Lodovico Domenichi, and her son Federigo Cantarini, as well as anonymous addressees indicated only by their initials or pseudonyms. Rather than the typical "familiar letters," with expressions of personal sentiment and descriptions of real-life events, Matraini's letters read more like short essays on moral or philosophical topics. In 1595, Matraini rewrote the work significantly, removing some poems and adding sixteen new letters. The present letter, added by Matraini in 1595, is the opening work in that volume.[12] *She would continue revising the volume, issuing a final edition in 1597, in which this letter appears second. In this letter she picks up on ideas expressed in her* Oration on the Art of War, *a prose work included in her 1555 collection, and elaborates on it. The impact of war on society, culture, and the arts in Renaissance Italy should not be underestimated. Known collectively as the Italian Wars, the series of invasions, sieges, and armed conflicts, which lasted from 1494 to 1559, affected everyone on the entire peninsula. Whereas Eleonora d'Aragona (pp. 110–111) in her letter provides an eyewitness account of the devastation of war, here Matraini theorizes on the intellectual skills required by military commanders and defines the objectives of war. War, she concludes, exists to provide the safety and tranquility that are necessary conditions for intellectual pursuits; she cites Marcus Aurelius as evidence that the active life of the soldier is subservient to the contemplative life of the philosopher.*

> To the Illustrious Lady Maria Cardonia[13], demonstrating that the sciences[14] are of greater excellence than arms
> I do not know for what merit of mine, valorous and illustrious Lady, that Your Ladyship has judged me to be of such a lofty mind and

---

10 Cox, *Women's writing*, 160.

11 Although the subject of this painting is often identified as the Cumaean Sibyl, Cox refers to the figure as the Tiburtine Sibyl (*Prodigious muse*, 91).

12 Matraini, *Lettere*, Rabiti, LXV, LXXVII.

13 "Cardonia" is an older form of the name "Cardona." Maria Cardona (1509–1563), marchesa of Padula and countess of Avellino, was a Neapolitan noblewoman celebrated by contemporaries for her intellectual acumen as well as her poetic and musical abilities. In 1552 Ortensio Lando published two works in praise of her. No literary works by Cardona have survived.

14 The word Matraini uses here and elsewhere in the letter is "*scienze*," which translates most appropriately as "knowledge" "learning", or "craft" rather than the modern term "sciences." The term was used quite differently in her day, encompassing study of the natural world, as well as a wide variety of philosophical inquiry, evidenced by Matraini's citing of authorities such as Aristotle and Marcus Aurelius in her argument.

profound intelligence, that I should be sufficient, armed with the force of my reason, to overcome those strong, valiant knights who in your presence these past days with such ornate words have argued, praising arms over the sciences. I am well aware that you are very generous and kind, desiring everything in my best interests and in my praise; nonetheless, taking into consideration that notable maxim of Chilon[15], a most famous sage renowned in all of Greece, who taught us most aptly that no one ought to attempt things beyond his strength, for some time I have held back over whether to respond to this subject matter or to remain silent, as more fitting to my feeble abilities. But mulling over how praiseworthy it is to yield obediently and promptly to the legitimate behests of one's betters. I put aside every excuse, no matter how correct and acceptable it might be, not wanting stubbornly to resist giving you (as best I can) a suitable answer. Whence, firstly I say to you that I believe that those valiant knights, whom Your Ladyship discussed with me in her letters, wanted for obvious reasons to show that the military arts were more noble and more excellent than the sciences, in order to make others aware of the vivacity of their sharp wits rather than because they felt there was any truth in those [arguments]. For who, with any familiarity with the human sciences, would not say, as Aristotle affirms, that the cause is always more noble and greater than its effect? And if one grants this, as indeed one rightly must, in what way then can one prove that the study of the sciences is not more worthy and by far to be praised than the profession of soldiering? Are not sciences the basic foundation and ruling principal of the entire military art? The truth of this can easily be demonstrated. For the fact is that even the strongest and most fortunate captain, victorious over his enemies, never receives complete and perfect praise, unless he has well obeyed all those rules through the use of wise cunning in order to obtain it [praise]. And though many may believe, without penetrating beneath the surface, that there is no difference between one victory and another, yet according to reliable judges the orders and the means that lead to victories are regarded more highly than the victories themselves. Since victories can often occur through small or unforeseen accidents even though the captain may be misguided and lack a true understanding of warfare, he may, at great peril, rashly carry the day. One can cite many manifest examples of this, only two of which I wish to recount at the present. The

---

15 Chilon of Sparta (sixth century BCE), to whom Diogenes Laertius attributed many wise sayings. Matraini also opened her 1555 *Oration* with this citation.

first is of Claudius Nero,[16] a most brave and forceful man, who finding himself on the borders of Puglia went up against the great captain Hannibal,[17] meeting Hasdrubal under extremely dangerous conditions in Metaurus, where by luck the longed-for victory was brought about. And although some authors praised his great spirit, nevertheless, considering the orders that he had to uphold and the enormous peril in which he placed himself through lack of intelligent reasoning, in the end they decided that he had been rash and acted without true prudence. Caesar too, did the same thing, when warring against the Pharaoh's soldiers; he engaged them in battle without due deliberation and was in great danger of losing his life. So that when he was overcome by the enemy, he was forced to throw himself into the sea, only escaping death because he knew how to swim well.[18] Thus it is necessary, in order to be an excellent warrior, to have understanding of the military art and to know well how to recognize the quality of the times; the nature of places; and the conditions of the enemy; to know with cunning how to interfere with their plans; and how to organize troops in such a way that the most intelligent in warfare would judge that nothing could be better arranged. And having done this, even if the captain, along with his whole camp, were to be routed by the enemy, he would not be reputed less worthy of praise than if he had enjoyed an honorable victory, which for many reasons can be taken from his hands. It cannot be denied that weapons bring the greatest advantages to civil life if they are employed to benefit the homeland and preserve political interests, since defending oneself from those who come there to attack and do harm is in complete accordance with true justice. However, although weapons may be instruments and means for serving the above-mentioned needs, they are not an end in themselves—that would be the more noble cause for which they are used, as those who have studied Aristotle's moral philosophy know.[19] And if someone were to say to me that just as deeds are superior to words, similarly weapons surpass the sciences, I would answer that

---

16 Gaius Claudius Nero was elected consul in 207 BCE along with Marcus Livius to lead Roman troops against the Carthaginians during the Second Punic War. The Battle of Metaurus was the decisive conflict that drove Hannibal, the Carthaginian general, from Italy. His brother, Hasdrubal, died in the battle.

17 Here Matraini's account of this episode in the Punic Wars differs from the standard sources, which relate that Claudius Nero never went up against Hannibal in battle, rather the exact opposite actually took place.

18 An episode described in Chapter 21 of Caesar's *The Alexandrian War*.

19 The reference seems to be to *Nichomachean Ethics*, X, 7, where Aristotle asserts that war cannot be considered an end in itself, and can only be considered a noble activity if it serves to promote the leisurely contemplative life of citizens.

the sciences belong to a class of activities of greater and of higher importance than that of weapons. Moreover, from the sciences one learns how
to govern and rule wisely, both republics and oneself, bringing much
praise in the active life and civil sphere. It is from these that men are
advised how their designs and endeavors can be brought to a good and
praiseworthy conclusion and that they ought to set out on high and
most honorable undertakings. I am not saying they should do this out of
greed for treasure like public thieves and the disturbers of others' peace
and repose, but to defend the homeland and to combat the unfaithful
and all diabolical persecutions. The good sciences are those that show a
person how he ought to cherish justice, in private as well as in public
matters, always giving each that which he duly deserves, without
making distinctions between great and small, but equally. Long ago the
sciences, through Solon's counsel, brought honor and usefulness to the
republic in the victory of Themistocles and the freedom of all Greece,
since the good counsel of wise men is the cause of all enterprises worthy
of good and valiant warriors and their fame.[20] But who better than
Alexander the Great demonstrated the excellence of writers to surpass
any warrior? Having arrived at the honored tomb of the brave and
mighty Achilles—so one writer[21] tells us—he said: "O fortunate man,
that you had the great Homer who sang so loftily of you, celebrating
your most worthy deeds!" Hence that great king rightly held that the
wondrous acts of prowess of that mighty captain would have soon been
cancelled from men's memories and cast into oblivion, if the talent of
such a great poet had not from the shadows of forgetfulness cast them in
the public light. Dionysius, the great prince of Syracuse recognized this
as well, when with such honor he went to meet Plato.[22] Pompey did likewise, lowering his grandeur when he went to visit the philosopher Posi-
donius.[23] And surely there is no one who does not know how we are
ennobled and separated from brute animals by means of the learned

---

20 Solon (c. 638–558 BCE) was a lawmaker and statesman in ancient Greece, and Themistocles (c. 524–
459 BCE), who lived a century later, was a general and Athenian politician who led the Greeks to victory
during the Persian Wars. Plutarch describes Themistocles' teacher, who was a disciple of Solon: "Mnesiphilus
received this *'sophia,'* and handed it down, as though it were the doctrine of a sect, in unbroken tradition from
Solon," who then passed it to Themistocles. *The Parallel Lives,* "Life of Themistocles," 2, 4. Loeb trans., 1914.
21 The 1595 edition has "Sallustio" (Sallust).
22 The text reads "Dionigio," not "Dionisio," but probably refers to Dionysius, tyrant of Syracuse. Plato lived
at the court of both Dionysius I and Dionysius II; it is unclear which of these men Matraini is referring to.
23 The Roman general Pompey the Great (106–48 BCE) visited the Greek polymath philosopher Posei-
donius (ca. 135–51 BCE) on a number of occasions, and it is noted that he lowered his *fasces,* the staff that was
symbolic of his power, as a sign of respect before crossing the threshold.

sciences, which are so necessary to hold the company of men together, for without them, they would be without manners, without laws, and without religion. Thus it was that the good Emperor Justinian[24] was used to saying that it was not only advantageous, but necessary that powerful kings and great emperors defend themselves more with sacred laws than with weapons, as they [laws] are the reason that peace is preserved in civil life. Indeed it is a fact that he was an emperor beyond compare, more illustrious and more glorious for the laws that he gave the world than the victories over the Vandals and other fierce peoples whom he subdued and made subject to the mighty Roman Empire. And the wise Marcus Aurelius[25], Roman emperor and valorous captain, experienced in great wars and immense victories, said: "I truly appreciate so greatly the wisdom of persons who know, that if there were warehouses of knowledge as there are of merchandise, I would give my entire state and all my treasure to have that; what one wise man can learn in a single day by reading and that which I learn in an hour I would not exchange for all the gold found on the earth, since books bring more glory than all the battles and all the kingdoms I have conquered by force of arms." Thus, the finest valiant warriors, worthy of true honor shall be those who, following the best [teachings of the] sciences, will strip themselves of ambition, of hatred, of greed for plunder, worldly vainglory, and all their immoderate affections and desires; they will arm themselves with faith, justice, charity, and all virtuous behavior and with these most powerful weapons they will overcome their internal and external enemies. Yet, with all this, I believe rarely are men such as these to be found, since if everyone acted this way, one would see only peace, wonderful calm, and a most happy union among men. But since it is nearly time to come to the end of this perhaps tedious argument of mine, with every gesture of reverence I lay at your feet all the weapons of my reason and recommend myself to you.

---

24 Justinian the Great (c. 482–565 CE) was Byzantine emperor from 527 to 565. He supervised the reform of the entire Roman legal system, instituting the *Corpus Juris Civilis*, also known as the Justinian Code.
25 Marcus Aurelius (121–March 17, 180 CE) was Roman emperor from 161 to 180, a Stoic philosopher, and the author of *Meditations*.

51.

Margherita Sarrocchi confirms Galileo's astronomical
observations to Guido Bettoli

"Most well-versed in philosophy, theology, geometry, logic, astrology, in many other most
noble sciences and belles-lettres" was how one contemporary described Margherita
Sarrocchi's (c. 1560–1617) accomplishments.[26] She was born to a well-off family in
Naples; after the death of her father, Giovanni Sarrocchi, care of her education was undertaken by his close friend Cardinal Guglielmo Sirleto, who placed her in the convent of
Santa Cecilia in Trastevere in Rome. There she received a humanist education in classical languages, as well as the sciences, from her teacher, the mathematician Luca Valerio
(1552–1618). By the age of fifteen Sarrocchi was known in Roman society as a prodigy
and was asked to contribute one of her poems to a literary anthology. By the late 1580s
she had married Carlo Biraghi and established a literary salon in their Roman home,
which was, in the words of one contemporary: "not only a hall of the greatest refinements, but of philosophy, theology, and all excellent disciplines."[27] Renowned for
her polymath abilities, Sarrocchi was invited to become a member of the scholarly society
the Accademia degli Umoristi. She joined the Academy around 1602—the first woman
to do so—and in the company of learned men she lectured and recited her poetry.
Sarrocchi was the author of Scanderbeide, an epic poem published posthumously in
1623. She also wrote many works that have not survived, including a commentary on
Giovanni della Casa's poetry; a theological treatise on predestination; a translation
from Greek of Hero and Leander by Musaeus Grammaticus; and an essay on Luca
Valerio's commentary on Euclid.[28] During this time Sarrocchi became acquainted with
a fellow Neapolitan, the poet Giovan Battista Marino (1569–1625), who attended
gatherings at her home. The two were initially close, but later the relationship ended in
acrimony and very public criticism of each other's literary work. She maintained close

---

26 "E non solo perita in queste lingue, e nella poesia, come l'Eroiche sue composizioni piena fede ne fanno,
ma anche nella Filosofia, Teologia, Geometria, Logica, Astrologia, & in tante altre nobilissime scienze, e
belle lettere versatissima." Cristofano Bronzini, *Dignità delle donne*, 130.
27 "Domum suam, non solum harum politissimarum atrium, sed philosphiae, theologiae, omnium
bonarum disciplinarum, denique virtutum omnium oraculum, haberi volebat." J.N. Erithreai cited in
Verdile, "Contributi alla biografia di Margherita Sarrocchi."
28 Sarrocchi, *Scanderbeide*, ed. Russell, p. 8.

friendships with other well-known figures in literature and the sciences and numbered among her correspondents poet Torquato Tasso (1544–1595) and Galileo Galilei.

Sarrocchi met Galileo in 1611 when he was elected to the Lincean Academy in Rome, the year after he published his discoveries with the telescope in the Sidereus Nuncius. *A correspondence began between the two, of which seven letters are extant, mostly concerning literature. Sarrocchi also corresponded with Guido Bettoli, a scholar at the University of Perugia, where there was some skepticism about Galileo's recent discoveries. In this letter, Sarrocchi confirms Galileo's discovery of the moons of Jupiter, based on her own observations using one of his telescopes.*

My Most Revered Illustrious Lord,

I received Your Lordship's letter of the 14th of June, though it seemed somewhat of a miracle to me that it took so much time to arrive, since I usually use the papal postal service and I didn't receive it before yesterday, and so do not wonder that I too am tardy in my response to you. It is true that two months ago I got a letter from a friar—which I didn't reply to, as I was sick in bed—and thus Signor Luca wrote to Your Lordship that in order to know my opinion he ought to ask Padre Innocentio[29] of the Augustinian Order who is over there in Santa Maria Novella about it. Now I will tell Your Lordship that everything that is being said about Signor Galileo's discovery of the stars is true, namely that near Jupiter there are four stars[30] wandering with their own motion always at an equal distance from Jupiter, but not from each other. I saw this with my own eyes using Signor Galileo's glass[31], and having shown them to various friends, the whole world knows about it. With Saturn there are two stars, one on one side, and another on the other side, which almost touch each other. Venus, when she is in alignment with the Sun can be seen to light up and to become crescent-shaped like the Moon, to such an extent that she can be seen to be entirely full and to appear gradually smaller, a clear sign, indeed a geometrical proof, that she revolves around the Sun. And when she is full, she is above it and from the great distance seems smaller; this, I say is proven by geometry, since she

---

29 Innocenzo Perugino, a Perugian friar and amateur astrologer. Favaro, *Amici,* vol. I, 28–31.

30 These are the four moons of Jupiter discovered by Galileo, which he named the "Medicean stars" in his 1610 *Sidereus nuncius* (*Starry messenger.*)

31 Improving on the Dutch spyglass, Galileo's invention was an instrument for viewing objects at a distance that was up to sixteen times as powerful. Originally he called it a "cannocchiale" (eyecane); fellow academicians at the Accademia dei Lincei coined the word *telescopio* (from the Greek for *tele* "from a distance" and *skopeo* "I see") for it in 1611. A copy of this letter was sent to Galileo, who wrote on the back of it this note: "Deals with the glass and new discoveries" (*"Tratta dell'occhiale e de nuovi scoprimenti"*).

cannot appear to be full if she is in opposition to the sun.[32] Many great mathematicians, in particular Father Claudio [sic] and Father Gambergere [sic] denied this at the outset and then they retracted, after attesting to it and they have given public lectures on it.[33] I do believe these gentlemen of the Studio and members of academies have written much against Signor Galileo and I will make it known to Signor Galileo, indeed I will send him Your Lordship's letter. In the meantime, Your Lordship should be assured that Signor Galileo, beyond the sublimity of his wondrous genius, is such a proper gentleman that even though they have written against him, he would be appeased with even a minimal apology from them, as he does not profess to do anything but to be of use to the world; if he were eager for fame he could have much more from the many exceptional writings that he has contributed in a variety of fields of learning.

This is all that I need to say in response to your question; besides that, I thank you for the kind affection that you show me and the praise you give me, which is greater than I deserve. And so I beg you to avail yourself of me whenever you have need, as you will find me most ready and obliged to your good will. May Our Lord protect you. From Rome, on the 21st of August 1611.

---

32 If Venus were in opposition to the sun, that is between the sun and earth, as according to the Ptolemaic conception of the solar system, Venus would be constantly in a crescent phase, rather than displaying a complete set of phases. This observation of Galileo's that Sarrocchi is reporting was the first empirical demonstration of the Copernican model.

33 Christopher Clavius (1537–1612) was a German Jesuit astronomer and mathematician largely responsible for creating the reformed Gregorian calendar; Christoph Grienberger (1561–1636) was his student. Both were initially skeptical of Galileo's discoveries with the telescope, but as Sarrocchi describes, by 1611 they were won over. Like many Italians, Sarrocchi had difficulty spelling these foreign names.

52.

Camilla Erculiani Greghetti explains her theory of the interaction of
physical elements at the time of the Biblical Flood to Márton Berzeviczy

Camilla Erculiani Greghetti (also Herculiana or Ercoliani Gregetta, c. 1540–1590?)
was one of six children of Paduan merchant Andrea Greghetti. In the early 1560s she
married the apothecary Alovisio Stella and the couple had at least one child. Alovisio
died sometime between 1568 and 1572 and Camilla was married a second time to
another apothecary, Giacomo Erculiani, with whom she had five children; Giacomo
died in 1605. Although she was not active in the apothecaries' guild, she is defined as
an apothecary (speciala) on the title page of her pamphlet, and in the letters she
mentions various medicinal concoctions, indicating a knowledge of pharmacology. In
these letters, Erculiani enters into a heated controversy concerning Biblical and
"scientific" truths, attempting to reconcile events described in Scripture with observed
phenomena in the real world. Published in Poland, probably in very few exemplars,
the letters bound in this slender volume (Color Plate X) came to the notice of the
Catholic Church. The atmosphere of the Counter-Reformation was not one tolerant of
divergent beliefs; the decrees of the Council of Trent (1545–1563) thoroughly codified
accepted doctrine and condemned the slightest heterodoxy. In 1585 Erculiani was
called before the Paduan Inquisition on charges of heresy based on the ideas expressed
in these published letters. The authorities were troubled by her assertion that being
made of earth, man was destined to die. Her argument seemed to imply that regardless
of tasting the forbidden fruit, man was from the moment of his creation condemned to
mortality, thereby denying the impact of original sin.[34] Her case was discussed by a
well-known jurist, Giacomo Menochio, who argued that the author was making a
distinction between philosophical and theological truths. Furthermore, concluded the
jurist, women, like children, are by nature too ignorant to be held accountable for their
beliefs and ought to be disregarded. It is unknown whether the case was dismissed or if
she was let off with a light punishment, as there is no further trace of Camilla Erculiani
Greghetti in the historical record.

The matter for scientific inquiry in this letter is where all the water of the Biblical
Flood came from and what happened to it after the Flood receded. The properties of

---

34 See Eleonora Carinci, "Una 'speziala' padovana."

earth (soil) and water and their relationship to one another had long been discussed in the Middle Ages, notably by Dante Alighieri in his 1320 Quaestio de aqua et terra (Inquiry Concerning Water and Earth). *During Erculiani's day, natural philosophers at the University of Padua were considering the many issues involving conservation of matter and the properties of the various elements raised by the Biblical narrative. This letter is addressed to Márton Berzeviczy (1538–1596 also known as Martin Berzevicze), who was the Chancellor of the king of Poland. He was present in Padua in 1568, when it is conceivable that Erculiani may have met him.*

To the Magnificent and Most Excellent Lord Knight, Signor Márton Berzeviczy, Chancellor of Transylvania for His Holy Majesty Stephen, Indomitable King of Poland, [35]

It appears to me that Your Most Excellent Lordship desires to know from what author I learned that the Great Flood was caused by the Earth being diminished, due to the multitude, great size, and longevity of men. To that question I respond by telling you that I have not read this anywhere else, nor do I consider it a praiseworthy thing to write down another author's opinions as if they were one's own. I do not deny that I read various authors, speculating on their conclusions to the best of my understanding; while amazed at their ingenuity and diverse opinions, I have offered up my own ideas in writing as well. But as I have set out to deal with this material, I have had to become truly familiar with the elements from which we are formed, and which have a share in the actual substance of our creation, and even more, to be aware that those elements cannot be of a quantity superior to that given in the beginning by nature—for thus I intend to speak now in the capacity of natural philosopher—nor can it suffer diminution over a long course of time, without a very clear sign appearing, as anyone with even mediocre knowledge of the material sphere can verify. That at the time of the Great Flood, which is said to have been universal, men lived many hundreds of years is easily discovered by reading Genesis, Chapter Four[36]; that during that same time giants existed is to be found in Chapter Six. That the Earth was submerged by the waters because it was diminished, speaking as a natural philosopher, is clear: The cause then of its diminution could not have been because it was changed into water, as its dryness resists that. Earth can be changed into mud by adding water, but it can never be made into water. Nor on

---

35 I am indebted to Paolo Galluzzi for his assistance with the translation of this text.
36 Genesis 5 lists the number of years that Adam lived and those of the generations that followed him.

account of its heaviness, density, and dryness can it be converted against its nature, indeed one sees that repelling it, water continually throws it [earth] off, away from itself, as is seen in springs. Neither could it be made into air, as it is in every one of its qualities opposed to that, as it [earth] is dense and heavy, while air is light and rarefied. That some of it was carried away elsewhere cannot be possible, for this is similarly against its nature, which, when reduced in the center, cannot be moved from there, and if some part is moved and transported by force, it can clearly be seen how with greatest furor of its own nature and of the other elements it recoils. If we wanted then to say that it [earth] was consumed by fire, neither can this be accepted by our intellect. Nor could it be that it was consumed by humidity, as fire cannot be lit where there is humidity and material; we see this in all things that burn, that once the humidity is extinguished, just the simple material remains. And where humidity is abundant, it [fire] has no power, just as a small quantity of humidity has no power over it. Thus, the Earth was incapable of having been diminished by any of these causes. The water could not have increased, on account of the inability of water to be made out of either earth or fire; nor can water be made out of air either, as it is impossible to make an infinite amount out of a finite quantity, as Alessandro Piccolomini[37] states clearly in the second part of the second book of his *Natural Philosophy*. Neither, as he demonstrates in the same book, can an infinite body be found, as indeed the air would be, if humidity fell during the night and springs and lakes derived from that. Rather the humidity that descends at night to the ground is drawn up high during the day by virtue of the Sun, from which later it is forced to descend, as is its nature when it is not sustained by the rays of the Sun. It is impossible to see air more clearly diminished and converted into water. And while it is true that some philosophers maintain that the elements convert themselves from one into another, it is impossible that fire can be converted into water, nor into earth, nor into air; neither can earth make itself into air, water or fire. And so it is for air; for the reasons produced, it is clear that without combining its qualities, one element cannot be turned into another, but assists it by means of destroying the mixtures, as did the water, assisting the earth, and similarly fire, although it was not universal, when it separated from those waters, leaving it in its dry state, as Ovid represents it as Phaethon driving his chariot.[38] It is true

---

37 Alessandro Piccolomini (1508–1578) was an astronomer, philosopher, and playwright. Part One of his *Natural philosophy* was first published in Rome in 1551.

38 The reference is to Ovid's *Metamorphoses*, Book Two, in which Apollo's mortal son Phaethon tries to drive the chariot pulling the sun through the sky but loses control, scorching vast portions of the earth.

that others say that air closed in the caverns underground converts into water and springs are created from it, not taking into account that springs and lakes are made by the passage of water through fissures in the earth; where they find an area that is soft and porous, they flow in great quantity, creating an opening, and they make a lake as deep as the material and base that they find, which, with strong density, resists. When it does not find it [the earth] soft, the water passes through more open and weaker paths, making springs. In short, I say, in order to keep this argument from becoming too lengthy, that if we wanted to make water from air, I do not know from what we will make air, since it is not of an infinite, but of a finite quantity. If it were infinite, it would follow that all other things would be destroyed. Being finite as it is, if it had to change itself into springs and lakes, the consequence would be its own destruction, a thing which cannot be affirmed as it has never been observed, and no evidence of this destruction of these elements can be found, nor can we investigate this with our senses. Thus, not being able for these probable reasons for one element to be destroyed, making the other more powerful than its original quantity and strength, I say there must be some natural cause and some mixed substance that is produced by it and the other elements, which had caused this universal phenomenon. Now, one is unable to find a compound of elements that could last longer than man, who can live eight hundred to nine hundred eighty years[39], a limit that cannot be achieved by any other animal, plant or edifice that is not made of stone, by which I do not mean that they are entirely transfigured, but that over time much is consumed, without restoring the original properties to each. So that it happened that it was diminished, as I have said in my writings, which I will demonstrate can be seen in the material sphere. There remains one aspect to tell you about—just finally to clarify for what reason it was not swallowed up either by flooding or by rain and was never later submerged as it was in the beginning of the year. To those words one can reply that the cause was already there, as the earth at that time was in parts spongy and muddy. All this had been foreseen by sages; it was expected then that with the planet Venus dominant, which in truth we can well believe that in that year she did dominate, since in the second month of the year, her predominance is toward the end of the month, Noah entered the Arc.[40] Shortly afterward Venus began to give a sign of her power, moving those [waters] from the depths to the heights, seeking

---

39 Genesis 5 recounts Adam's death at age 930; while Methuslah died at 969 years of age.
40 Genesis 7:11 states that the Flood began on the seventeenth day of the second month.

to reunite the waters with herself, as it comes from her; and this she could do, belonging to a more pure and perfect realm, and having power over water. Thus she was the cause of the moving and lifting up of water, so that the earth made partially spongy and muddy was reunited by her and returned to its own nature and center, providing an outlet for the power of those [waters], which was done and fulfilled through flooding, since the sources broke through from the abyss. As a consequence, it rained for forty days and water was lifted; then it ceased, thus allowing water to return to its own place. The substances and compounds were not consumed, but returning to the earth, replenished and increased it, reduced from its original quantity by their devastation. And at the same time, the dominion of Venus, the mistress of water ceased, and another planet, contrary to those [waters], took her place and thus finished the year of the influence of that planet. Yet one and a half months later, the other planet, using its power, caused the flooding to cease and the waters continued diminishing, as much as the substances, having converted into a diminished element, grew, so that every substance consumed and restored to its previous state, the flooding altogether ceased. Nor truly can a natural philosopher or an astrologer assign any other cause to this or to any other universal floods. It is true that the doctors of the Church and divine theologians have given other accounts and causes, but for me it is enough that God with that selfsame nature, does not work in opposition to those [causes], but makes use of them in His works, and as it is not fitting to the present work, I will leave these arguments for those others to deal with and decide with their celestial minds. Unable to find any other way to satisfy your request but with words, I wanted to give you my answer in writing, since I cannot speak to you in person, being indisposed for three months now with a tertian fever[41], nor for this reason did I want to fail to respond to you, explaining the cause that you asked me about. I will say no more about this, as perhaps I have already made myself tiresome to you with such a long discourse; however, if you desire clarification on any of the meaning of this work, you need only deign to inform me, for it is my desire for you to be satisfied. From home. 9 April, 1581.

Camilla Herculiana Gregetta

---

41   Malaria was known as "tertian fever" because the shivering and paroxysms would subside and then recur on the third day.

53.
———

*Sara Copio Sullam discusses philosophical and theological
views on human mortality with Baldassarre Bonifacio*

*Sara Copio Sullam (c. 1590–1640, also known as Sarra Copia Sulam), was born
into a prosperous family of Jewish merchants in the Ghetto in Venice. Her father,
Simone Copio, was a well-known and respected figure in the Jewish community who
corresponded with the celebrated rabbi and literary figure Leone Modena (1574–
1608). When her father died in 1606, her mother, Ricca Grassini, took over the
family's business affairs. One of three sisters, by the time Sara was fifteen, beside
Italian and Hebrew, she could read Latin, Greek, and Spanish and was an accomplished poet and musician. Reputed for her beauty, Sara married Jacob (Giacob)
Sullam, a banker, around 1613 or 1614; the couple had a daughter, who died at ten
months of age, and another pregnancy soon thereafter ended in miscarriage. Copio's
health was poor and there were no other children. By 1618 she was becoming known
as a poet, although only fourteen of her sonnets today survive. Sara Copio was also
renowned for a literary salon she held in her home in Venice; these gatherings were
attended by both Jews and Christians, some of whom were members of the
Accademia degli Incogniti (see Tarabotti, p. 206). When the poet Ansaldo Cebà
(1565–1623) published his sacred poem* Queen Esther *in 1615, with its positive
representation of a Jewish heroine, Copio was so impressed that she wrote to the
author. After that the two exchanged many letters; in 1623 Cebà published a collection of his fifty letters written to her. Although none of her replies has survived, it is
possible to glean aspects of Copio's personality even from this one-sided documentation. Above all, it is clear from his letters that she courteously but steadfastly resisted
all of Cebà's attempts to convert her to Christianity. Having become the most prominent female Jewish literary figure in Italy, Sara Copio attracted other attention as
well, with decidedly negative consequences. Baldassarre Bonifacio (1585–1659), a
prelate and man of letters who later became bishop of Capodistria, attended her
salon and exchanged letters with his hostess. In 1621 Bonifacio published this hith-
erto private correspondence, exposing Copio to charges of heresy not only from the
Christian Church, but condemnation by Jewish authorities as well. Copio responded by defending herself in her celebrated* Manifesto, *which she published that
same year. Adding to her troubles, in the mid-1620s she was the object of slander
and financial fraud perpetrated by two members of her literary circle. While others*

rose to her defense, it seems that Sara Copio had enough of public attention, and by the late 1620s she disappears from view; we have no further notice of her until her death in 1640.

The present letter is part of a correspondence that began in late 1619 with Baldassarre Bonifacio. In his previous letter of New Year's greeting, Bonifacio had opened by lamenting that whereas each year rejuvenates, we humans become old. After opening pleasantries, Copio begins her philosophical discussion, taking that remark as her starting point to explore questions of death and immortality. Well versed in ancient philosophy, she first provides a complex Aristotelian reading of the relationship between matter and form in the natural world; she then appears to embrace a more Platonic view, asserting that though matter decays, heavenly form endures. Next Copio turns to Creation, examining why God would have created humans as mortal matter if their essence was to be eternal and she questions indeed why biological generation and physical corruption would have been necessary in the divine scheme. She concludes with a metaphor drawn from Plato, comparing the human race with the ever-changing water in a stream; although individuals die, they are constantly being replaced by others and the species continues.

To the Very Illustrious Signor Baldassarre Bonifacio,

I could not expect anything but the most gracious effects from Your Lordship's gentlest mind, such were the happy greetings I received in your letter announcing the entry of the New Year. Moreover, the favor was tripled, accompanied by three sonnets in which you were pleased to honor the worthy portrait of my Signor Ansaldo[42] as I had entreated you to do. And although they were not entirely new to me, since they arrived I have, nevertheless, been contemplating their beauty with newfound admiration. For when you had recited them to me in passing, no sooner had they flashed before my weak mental faculties, than they immediately appeared as wondrous objects that leave our minds dazzled, just as the eyes tend to remain shaded when issuing out of a dark place into sudden light. So I offer Your Lordship those thanks, which at the time I let pass in devout and respectful silence, and I beg you to accompany these honors you do me with that of commanding me as well, as I will never fail to show deference to your merits on every occasion. I cannot refrain from adding that the loftiness of the ideas expressed in your

---

42 Ansaldo Cebà (1565–1623) was a Genoese poet, playwright, and academician with whom Sara had a long correspondence.

letter was very highly regarded and praised by Signor Paluzzi[43] who came here to my place to hear it read in the company of Signor Corniani[44], giving me an opportunity to have more than one discussion with them about it.

I cannot imagine how Your Lordship can display a certain envy toward the New Year, saying that it becomes rejuvenated, while we become older, since if you consider it as renewal when one year disappears with the succession of another one, this same happiness is enjoyed nore thoroughly by man. Inasmuch as man's duration does not end with one single turning of the solar sphere like the year—that now by means of the number 2, we know is no longer the same—and taking its essence from the number, it loses also its individual being, which appears in its numerical distinction. This seems so clear that it would be superfluous to provide proof. Thus if Your Lordship prides himself that the year keeps its character as a species and disappears in its numbers, you ought not to complain that men as they age do the same. Nor should you reply to me that the essence is only in the species and the individuals do not differ in anything except the accidents, because if this could be held to be true in some philosophical system then the essence of one man could not be distinguished from that of another.[45] It would follow that lacking the essence of Socrates, the essence of Plato would also be lacking, and so on, in such a way that in the death of one individual all would die. That the cause of all this corruptibility lies in matter is a commonly-held doctrine and a belief endorsed by the Peripatetics,[46] yet I believe it is easier to state this than to accept it. For if matter is the intrinsic and substantial part of the compound and it is eternal, how is it possible for a thing to take its corruptible being from that part, which in itself is

---

43 Numidio Paluzzi (1587–1625) was a Roman poet who was a friend and literary consultant to Copio. Along with the painter and poet Alessandro Berardelli, Paluzzi turned against her, and Copio reported the two to the authorities for fraudulently taking hundreds of ducats from her. Afterward Paluzzi published literary slanders against Copio Sullam entitled the *Sarraidi*; the work is now lost. Cox, *Women's writing*, 218–219.

44 Gianfrancesco Corniani (1582–1646) was Bonifacio's cousin, a Venetian poet. *Sarra Copia Sulam*, Harrán, 274.

45 The author is arguing along Aristotelian lines: "A substance—that which is called a substance most strictly, primarily, and most of all—is that which is neither said of a subject nor in a subject, e.g. the individual man or the individual horse. The species in which the things primarily called substances are called secondary substances, as also are the genera of these species. For example, the individual man belongs in a species, man, and animal is a genus of the species; so these—both man and animal—are called secondary substances" (Aristotle, *Categories* 2a13; J. L. Ackrill, *A new Aristotle reader*. Princeton, NJ: Princeton University Press, 1988, 7).

46 The Peripatetic school of philosophy refers to ideas of Aristotle and his followers.

eternal and incorruptible? And that matter is such can be seen explicitly, since when any compound dissolves and breaks down, what remains of matter are always only its primary sources, which are the elements. Thus, if of two component parts that we observe in natural things, I mean matter and form, one lasts eternally and the other vanishes, to which of them would it be reasonable to attribute corruptibility? Indeed heavenly matter, without having to resort to the sophistic doctrine of Telesio[47], shows us this truth very clearly, *pace* Aristotle, given that the incorruptibility of heaven derives from being incapable of receiving another form, and in consequence, it has one form and cannot receive corruptibility. Thus if that form were not eternal, it would be necessary in order to satisfy the eternity of matter that another would succeed it and if that were to be corrupted as well, another would, and so on, forever. Thus, the same power and infinite desire to assume form indicates the limited durability of these forms to satisfy such an appetite, which does not happen in heaven, where one sole form with its [infinite] duration fulfils every desire of matter. If matter were abandoned by form, and therefore needed to be remarried, it would be a sign that for its own part it cannot admit nonexistence. If the blame for the abandonment is in the form, why attribute it to matter?

It can well be supposed that in the loins of the first man the corruption of all human lineage had its beginnings, if indeed we want to upset Aristotelian doctrine, conceding beginning to generation. But why would the Creator not make man by nature immortal if He had the intention of preserving him as such? Or if He had not established that man were [immortal] why constitute his being miraculously, if it was not to last? I say "miraculously" as Your Lordship attributes to the virtue of supernatural grace the power of immortality that man enjoyed in his earliest state. If he had been preserved that way so that he could actually have continued being incorruptible, I would like to know if generation would have needed to continue as it did? And in that case, how would there have been a place for infinity, in a finite world? Or if indeed generation did not need to continue, it seems to me that the transmission of one's being would have ceased being the highest good. And forming a

---

47   Bernardino Telesio argued in his treatise *On the nature of things according to their own principles* (1565) that true knowledge of the world derives from the senses. Telesio advocated knowledge acquired through direct observation of nature rather than through the reading of Aristotle. His materialist ideas were condemned by the Catholic Church posthumously in 1593.

thing into being in any way that makes its survival impossible seems intolerable in men, let alone in God.

Thus let us grant, as we take it from these same propositions of Your Lordship, that man was always of mortal nature and that for that reason he did not pass from one species to another[48] in falling from his first state and it was granted in consequence that the waters are spread on the ground—*quasi acque dilabimur*—a truly remarkable passage in the Sacred Scriptures,[49] since like a flowing river it represents to us before our eyes waters that flow and pass in an instant, and yet it is always the same river and not always the same waters. Thus the human species shows us that individuals are changing every hour and are never the same, although the species is always the same.

And so, from the reasons indicated, we will clearly conclude that neither the year nor any other corruptible essence can undergo renovation or rebuilding. Such, indeed, is the example you yourself give of the bricklayer, who if he tries to rebuild a ruined house, will never be able to say that it is the same house, but only that it is fabricated from the same matter. Thus, my Lord, there remains nothing to be desired in these our individual beings, but duration, which is so brief that we can infallibly say that time is not the measurement of motion, as it appears to the philosophers, but that motion is the measurement of time, since with the movement of clocks the hours are measured; with the vigorous movement of the Sun the days are counted; and with the motion of the Moon the months are distinguished. As with the motion of the natural Sun the years are numbered, may it please Heaven with prosperous [astral] influences to make Your Lordship enjoy as many [years] as Nestor,[50] and may he please to excuse my boldness in having raised these weak objections, out of the desire to hear, in time, Your Lordship's clarification, and that of the Lord, who is always Supreme Deity. Venice, the 10th of January, 1620

> Your Very Illustrious Lordship's
> Most Affectionate and Obliged,
> Sara Copio Sullam

---

48 That is, man did not pass from the mortal condition to an immortal one.
49 The quote is from 2 Samuel 14:14: "For we must die, and are as water spilt on the ground, which can't be gathered up again." The Latin Vulgate reads "Omnes morimur et quasi aquae dilabimur."
50 Nestor, a mythical hero of antiquity, was described by Homer. He was said to have been 110 years old at the outset of the Trojan War.

54.

*Virginia Galilei sends for linens and requests a copy
of* The Assayer *from her father Galileo Galilei*

"A woman of exquisite mind" are the words used by Galileo to describe his daughter
Virginia (also known as Suor Maria Celeste, 1600–1634). Born in Padua, Virginia
was the eldest of three children of Galileo Galilei and Marina Gamba; the others were
Livia (b. 1601) and Vincenzio (b. 1606). All three were illegitimate, as Galileo never
married or lived with the children's mother. By 1610 Galileo had broken off with
Marina, and when he left Venice to return to Florence he left Vincenzio in Padua with
Marina, who had married, but took his daughters with him. In 1619 Galileo legiti-
mized his son so that he would become his heir; Vincenzio went on to study law at the
University of Pisa and in later years helped his father in his experiments. The daughters remained illegitimate, however, and their father decided they would become cloistered nuns in a convent just outside Florence. Virginia became a novice in the Clarissan
Convent of San Matteo in Arcetri in 1616, where she took the religious name Sister
Maria Celeste. Livia joined her the next year, taking the name Sister Arcangela. We
know next to nothing about her sister; from the little revealed in Virginia's letters, it
seems Livia was restless and resisted the discipline imposed by convent life. Apparently
resigned to her lot, the older daughter occupied herself in the convent apothecary
workshop, caring for the sick, conducting the choir, cooking, sewing, and writing letters for the abbess. After being condemned of heresy by the Roman Inquisition in 1633,
Galileo returned to live under house arrest in Arcetri not 300 meters away from his
daughters' convent. Ageing and emotionally shattered by the trial, Galileo was comforted to know that he would be living close to them; however, four months after he
arrived in 1634, Virginia, whose health had been declining, died of dysentery at the
age of 33.

This is one of 124 extant letters written between 1623 and 1633 to her father;
sadly, not a single letter of his to Maria Celeste has come down to us. At the time he
received this letter, the scientist was staying at the villa of Bellosguardo, about a forty-
five-minute walk from the Convent of San Matteo. In her letters Maria Celeste provides a glimpse of the hardships she endured within the austere Clarissan convent:
illness, cold, poor food, and lack of privacy. Her father sent her food, wine, linens, and
other necessary supplies, as well as books, and money, for instance to purchase a private room for herself. In return, Maria Celeste would prepare medicines, baked goods,

jams, and sweets for her father; sew clothing for him and other family members; and copy out many of her father's writings for him. They would also exchange literary compositions: On one occasion she mentions sending him a "small composition" of hers (October 20, 1623), and on another she tells him how she is enjoying reading a comedy he has written (October 31, 1633). She was deeply interested in Galileo's discoveries, as reflected perhaps in her choice of her religious name Celeste, meaning "celestial." She followed her father's research from her seclusion in the convent, reminding him in one letter to send her a telescope ("occhiale," November 2, 1630) and requesting, as in this letter, copies of his latest publications.

Very Illustrious Lord Father,

The infinite love that I bear Your Lordship and my fear that this sudden cold, generally so unfavorable to you, will cause a reoccurrence of your usual pains[51] and other indispositions, do not allow me to remain any longer without news of you. Thus I am writing both to learn something of how you are feeling, as well as to know when Your Lordship is thinking of leaving.[52] I have pressed ahead on making the linens and they are almost finished, but in attaching the fringes I find that there is not enough material for two of them, of which I am sending you a sample; altogether it comprises four *braccia*.[53] I would appreciate it if you could send it as soon as possible, so that I could send it to you before you leave; this is why I have taken such pains to finish them quickly.

Since I do not have a room to sleep in at night, Sister Diamante is kindly letting me stay in hers, depriving her own sister to keep me. But this room is very bad in this cold weather, and with my head so infected, I do not think I will be able to remain there, if Your Lordship does not come to my aid, lending me a canopy drapery, one of the white ones, which you are not using right now.[54] I would appreciate it if you could do me this service. In addition, I beg you to do me the favor of sending your book, which has just been printed[55], so that I can read it, having a great desire to see it.

---

51 Galileo suffered from arthritis. Virginia Galilei, *Lettere al padre*, Basile, 219.

52 Galileo was intending to go to Rome but delayed his trip until the following spring due to the extremely cold winter weather.

53 The *braccio* (meaning "arm") was a Florentine measurement used mostly for cloth, equivalent to 58.4 cm.

54 Maria Celeste would write asking for her father to send her 20 scudi to purchase a separate room of her own on July 8, 1629. Galileo sent the money.

55 The book in question is Galileo's *The Assayer*, in which he responds to critics of his hypotheses about comets and outlines the basics of scientific method. The work had just appeared in print in Rome in October and was dedicated by Galileo to his friend Maffeo Barberini (1568–1644), recently elected Pope Urban VIII.

These few pastries that I am sending you I made a few days ago to give you when you came to say goodbye to us. I see that as I feared, it will not be soon and I am sending them along so they will not get hard. Sister Arcangela still continues to purge herself and is not doing very well with the two cauterizations that they made in her thighs.[56] I am also not feeling too well, but being so accustomed to poor health I barely take notice, seeing that the Lord is pleased to visit me with a few troubles. I thank Him and pray Him to grant Your Lordship the greatest summit of happiness. And lastly, with all my heart I greet you in my name and for Sister Arcangela. From San Matteo, the 21st of November 1623.

Your Very Illustrious Lordship's
Most Affectionate Daughter,
Sister Maria Celeste Galilei

P.S. If Your Lordship has those collars to be bleached, you can send them to me.

---

56 Arcangela had been sick for some time; in a letter dated October 20, 1523, Maria Celeste informs her father that "Sister Arcangela is once again in the care of a physician." It is not clear from the description of the treatment precisely what Arcangela's malady was; along with bloodletting, purging and cauterization were standard medical procedures for treating a variety of illnesses during the Renaissance. Given the chronic nature of Arcangela's affliction, and her sister's reticence about a specific cause, it is possible that she was being treated for melancholy. David Gentilcore describes the following treatments used to cure melancholy: "The *curatio medica* of bleedings, cauterisations, fumigations, change of air and diet, baths, poultices and purgations was used in concert with the *curatio divina* of blessings and exorcisms [. . .] The most symbolically effective was no doubt the *purgatio*. Following the tradition of Hippocrates, vomiting was considered a purifying and liberating force against disease." *Healers and healing in Early Modern Italy,* 162. On melancholy among convent populations, see Strocchia, "The melancholic nun in Late Renaissance Italy," in Haskell, *Diseases* of the *imagination* and *imaginary disease* in the *early modern period.*

55.

Elena Lucrezia Corner Piscopia asks university director
Nicolò Venier to restore her mentor's tenure

The most accomplished intellectual woman of late Renaissance Venice, Elena Lucrezia Corner Piscopia (1646–1684) was born illegitimately, the fifth of seven children. Although her father, Giovanni Battista Corner Piscopia, was a Venetian nobleman, her mother, Zanetta Boni, whose family emigrated from the region of Brescia, was of much humbler origins and the two were not legally married until after Elena's birth. Because of their irregular social status, by law the children were denied the privileges of nobles in Venetian society until many years later their father paid a huge amount of money to have them recognized as nobility. From an early age Corner Piscopia was an extraordinarily gifted scholar and was given the finest education, learning Greek, Latin, Spanish, and French. Beyond the classical humanist curriculum, she was also trained in geography, mathematics, astronomy, natural philosophy, and music. Her father, who descended from a family of noted scholars, encouraged her studies, providing her with preeminent instructors. At the age of seven she began studying the classics with Giovanni Battista Fabris, and later she studied music with organist Maddalena Cappelli. She was also extremely devout, becoming a Benedictine Oblate (a third order of laypersons) at the age of nineteen, vowing perpetual chastity, against her parents' wishes that she marry. In 1667 Corner Piscopia met the renowned philosopher and mathematician Carlo Rinaldini, an admirer of Galileo who had taught for many years at the University of Pisa before taking a position at the University of Padua. The two met by chance in her father's library, where Rinaldini was impressed with the young woman's exposition of a geometrical theorem. After that, the professor took her under his wing, becoming her mentor in philosophical studies. Under Rinaldini's guidance, Corner Piscopia decided to pursue a doctorate in theology, something that no woman had done before her, in the process mastering Hebrew with instruction from Rabbi Shemuel Aboaf. By 1669 she was very well known and began to be inducted into a number of learned academies, which were normally exclusively male. She was visited by many heads of state, who quizzed her on various topics and came away dazzled with the extent of her learning. She was also called upon to demonstrate her erudition publicly, as in 1677, when Corner Piscopia participated in a philosophical debate with Giovanni Gradenigo, held in Greek and Latin before the entire college and a large part of the Venetian Senate. The next year Corner Piscopia, who was forbidden by religious authorities to earn a degree in theology, brilliantly defended theses on Aristotle before the College of Philosophers and Physicians (Collegio dei medici e dei filosofi) on June 25, 1678, and on July 9 she graduated as the first woman to earn a doctorate from the University of Padua.[57] *Although it was unanimously agreed by the examiners that Corner Piscopia had rightfully earned her degree*[58], *it was still highly controversial for a woman to be so honored. Indeed, the event set off a backlash and many decades would pass before another woman was granted a doctorate. Afterward, she returned home to live with her family, first in Venice and then in Padua, where she dedicated herself to her studies and writing. Corner's works include various academic discourses on moral, religious, and political themes, poetic works, letters, and a translation of a religious work from Spanish into Italian (Giovanni Lanspergio's Alloquium Iesu Christi ad animam fidelem), which was printed in five different editions between 1669 and 1706. She had been gravely ill for a number of years while pursuing her degree and her health continued to decline, until after a year of unbearable pain from a wasting disease that appears to have been cancer, Elena Lucrezia Corner Piscopia died at the age of thirty-eight.*[59]

My Most Illustrious, Most Excellent, and Most Honored Lord,

As the term of the contract has expired of the Most Illustrious Lord Carlo Rinaldini, Head Professor in Philosophy in this *studio*[60], a Lord with those talents very well known to all the Republic of Letters [*Republica Litteraria*], I appeal with my present humble petition at the feet of Your Excellency, so that with your usual humanity you may deign to console him with a renewal of his contract suitable to his unusual merit, as he is the ornament of this lyceum, not only with his most learned lectures, but also with his most erudite works, which are now

---

57 "Piscopia received a highly publicized degree in philosophy on 25 June 1678, after failing to receive permission for a theology degree. Therein lies her claim to be the first woman university graduate, and she is certainly the first that we can document in any detail, though wider research suggests that she was not an absolute first, since Costanza Calenda's medical degree of 1422 in Naples does seem to have been recorded in the city—unlike Bitisia Gozzadini's legendary degree of 1236 in canon law or any of the others that may have occurred in Bologna." Paula Findlen, *Elena Lucrezia Cornaro Piscopia (1646–1684): the first woman in the world to earn a university degree* [review]. *Renaissance Quarterly*, 61(3) (Fall 2008), 878–879.

58 The examiners pronounced that by common consent she be awarded the degree: "*communi consensu acclamatione et vivae vocis oraculo philosophiae magistra et doctrix acclamata fuit coram universo doctorum coetu.*" Maschietto, 122.

59 Maschietto provides a detailed description of her illness based on the available sources, in which her illness is defined as an "*incurabile cancrena,*" p. 201.

60 From the Latin *studium generale* the Italian word *studio* was often used to refer to an institution of higher learning such as a university. Founded in 1222, the University of Padua was during this period under the direction of the Republic of Venice, governed by a board of Venetian patricians known as the *Riformatori dello Studio di Padova*; Nicolò Venier was one of these.

going to press and will render the highest brilliance to this renowned university for all eternity. I entreat Your Excellency to tolerate my importunity, while the obligation that I have toward the aforesaid *virtuoso*[61], who ennobled my weaknesses with the degree in philosophy, spurs me to carry out such a proper duty toward him. The present circumstances also give me the boldness to remind Your Excellency's benevolence of the contract to be offered in the Most Excellent College to Lord Doctor Georgio Calafatti, whom I have recommended in other letters, so that you can be the special patron of the aforesaid, favoring him through your absolute authority. And affirming here my unchangeable devotion to the Most Excellent Lady Procurator your wife, I give myself over as long as I live. Padua, 16th of November, 1679.

The Most Humble, Most Devoted,
Most Obligated true servant,
Elena Lucrezia Corner Piscopia

---

61 Though this term is used in English primarily to refer to someone who excels in musical performance, in Italian it has a broader meaning, indicating an individual who excels in an artistic or scientific pursuits. In the Renaissance, *virtuoso* also implied a person of elevated cultural sensibilities possessing refined taste.

Suggestions for further reading

Letter 49, Ceccarella Minutolo: Astarita, *Between salt water and holy water: a history of Southern Italy*, 54–85; Bigelli, "Cecarella Minutolo," In *Dizionario biografico degli Italiani*; Casale, "L'epistolario quattrocentesco di Ceccarella Minutolo: fortuna critica e canone ecdotico," In *La critica del testo. Problemi di metodo e esperienze di lavoro*; Cox, *Women's writing in Italy 1400–1650*, 14–15; Croce, "Ceccarella Minutolo," In *Aneddoti di varia letteratura*; Minutolo, *Lettere*, Raffaele Morabito, ed; Morabito, *Lettere e letteratura. Studi sull'epistolografia volgare in Italia*, 87–98.

Letter 50, Chiara Matraini: Bellucci, *Maria de Cardona, contessa di Avellino, una nobildonna rinascimentale vissuta nella Napoli del Cinquecento*; Cox, *The prodigious muse: women's writing in Counter-Reformation Italy*, esp. 227–235; Jaffe, Irma, "The poet as sibyl: Chiara Matraini," In *Shining eyes, cruel fortune, the lives and loves of Italian Renaissance women poets*, 104–137; Marcheschi, *Chiara Matraini: poetessa lucchese e la letteratura delle donne nei nuovi fermenti religiosi del '500*; Matraini, *Selected poetry and prose*, Maclachlan, ed. and trans; Matraini, *Rime e lettere*, Rabitti, ed.; Rabitti, "Le lettere di Chiara Matraini tra pubblico e private," In Zarri, *Per lettera: la scrittura epistolare femminile tra archivio e tipografia: secoli XV-XVII*; Russell, "Chiara Matraini nella tradizione lirica femminile"; Smarr, *Joining the conversation: dialogues by Renaissance women*.

Letter 51, Margherita Sarrocchi: Favaro, *Amici e corrispondenti di Galileo*, ed. Galluzzi. Vol. 1, 29–30; Heilbron, *Galileo*; Pezzini, "Ideologia della conquista, ideologia dell'accoglienza: La Scanderbeide di Margherita Sarrocchi (1623)"; Ray, Chapter four, "Scientific Circles in Italy and Abroad: Camilla Erculiani and Margherita Sarrocchi," In *Daughters of Alchemy: Women and Scientific Culture in Early Modern Italy*; Sarrocchi, *Scanderbeide: the heroic deeds of George Scanderberg, King of Epirus*, Russell, ed. and trans; Verdile, "Contributi alla biografia di Margherita Sarrocchi," *Rendiconti dell'Accademia di Archeologia, Lettere e Belle Arti di Napoli*.

Letter 52, Camilla Erculiani: Carinci, "Una 'speziala' padovana: Lettere di philosophia naturale di Camilla Erculiani (1584)"; Erculiani, *Letters on natural philosophy*, ed. and trans. Carinci and Marcus; Ray, Chapter four, "Scientific Circles in Italy and Abroad: Camilla Erculiani and Margherita Sarrocchi," In *Daughters of Alchemy: Women and Scientific Culture in Early*

Modern Italy; White, "A Translation of the Quaestio De Aqua Et Terra," *Annual Reports of the Dante Society.*

Letter 53, Sara Copio Sullam: Adelman, "The literacy of Jewish women in early modern Italy," In Whitehead, *Women's education in Early Modern Europe: a history, 1500–1800;* Boccato, "Sara Copio Sullam: La poetessa del Ghetto di Venezia: Episodi della sua vita in un manoscritto del secolo 17"; Boccato, "Un episodio della vita di Sara Copio Sullam: Il *Manifesto sull'immortalità dell'anima*," *La Rassegna Mensile di Israel;* Copia Sulam, *Jewish poet and intellectual in seventeenth-century Venice: the works of Sarra Copia Sulam in verse and prose,* Don Harrán, ed. and trans; Cox, *Women's writing in Italy 1400–1650,* esp. 216–219; da Fonseca-Wollheim, "Faith and fame in the life and works of the Venetian Jewish poet Sara Copio Sullam (1592?–1641)," Ph.D. dissertation; Davis and Ravid, *The Jews of early modern Venice,* pp. 143–165, 276–279; Fortis, *La bella ebrea: Sara Copio Sullam, poetessa nel ghetto di Venezia del '600;* Harrán, "Sarra Copia Sulam: a seventeenth-century Jewish poet in search of immortality"; Sarot, "Ansaldo Cebà and Sara Copia Sullam"; Veltri, "Body of conversion and the immortality of the soul: the 'beautiful Jewess' Sara Copio Sullam," In Diemling and Veltri, *The Jewish body: corporeality, society, and identity in the Renaissance and early modern period;* Veltri, *Renaissance philosophy in Jewish garb: foundations and challenges in Judaism on the eve of modernity;* Westwater, "Sara Copio Sullam: life and family" and "Sara Copio Sullam: literary life and works," In "The disquieting voice: women's writing and antifeminism in seventeenth-century Venice," Ph.D. dissertation.

Letter 54, Virginia Galilei: Allan-Olney, *The private life of Galileo;* Galilei, *Lettere al padre,* ed. Bruno Basile; Sobel, *Galileo's daughter: a drama of science, faith, and love;* Sobel, trans. *Letters to father: Suor Maria Celeste to Galileo, 1623–1633;* Strocchia, "The nun apothecaries of Renaissance Florence: marketing medicines in the convent"; Strocchia, *Nuns and nunneries in Renaissance Florence.*

Letter 55, Elena Lucrezia Cornaro Piscopia: Derosas, "Corner, Elena Lucrezia," In *Dizionario Biografico degli Italiani;* Guernsey, *The Lady Cornaro: pride and prodigy of Venice;* Kristeller, "Learned women of early modern Italy: humanists and university scholars," In Labalme, *Beyond their sex: learned women of the European past;* Labalme, "Women's roles in Early Modern Venice: an exceptional case," In Labalme, *Beyond their sex: learned women of the European past;* Maschietto, *Elena Lucrezia Cornaro Piscopia (1646–1684): the first woman in the world to earn a university degree;* Pighetti, *Il vuoto e la quiete: scienza e mistica nel '600: Elena Cornaro e Carlo Rinaldini;* Revoltella, "Tre lettere di Elena Lucrezia Cornaro Piscopia a Nicolò Venier," In *Il Santo Rivista Antoniana di Storia Dottrina Arte;* Stevenson, *Women Latin poets: language, gender, and authority, from antiquity to the eighteenth century,* esp. 302–309; Tonzig, *Elena Lucrezia Cornaro Piscopia, prima donna laureata nel mondo. Terzo centenario del dottorato, 1678–1978.*

Bibliography

The following is a list of works mostly in English and Italian related to subject matter in this book. I have emphasized English-language resources in the "Suggestions for Further Reading" section in each chapter; however, it is important to point out that the pioneering research on Renaissance epistolography, which began in the 1980s is largely in Italian. Amedeo Quondam, Jeannine Basso, Adriana Chemello, Raffaele Morabito, Maria Luisa Doglio, Ludovica Braida, Gabriella Zarri, and Armando Petrucci are just a few of the most prominent scholars whose writings are fundamental to this field. Essential background reading for anyone interested in the field of women's writing in general during this period are *Women's writing in Italy 1400–1650* by Virginia Cox (Baltimore: Johns Hopkins University Press, 2008) and *Italian women writers: a bio-bibliographical sourcebook* by Rinaldina Russell (Westport, CT: Greenwood Press, 1994). For a broad overview of women's lives during this period, one cannot do better than Margaret King's superb *Women of the Renaissance* (Chicago & London: University of Chicago Press, 1991).

Adelman, Howard. "The literacy of Jewish women in early modern Italy." In Barbara J. Whitehead, ed., *Women's education in early modern Europe: a history, 1500–1800.* New York: Garland Pub., 1999.

Adler, Sara Maria. "Veronica Franco's Petrarchan Terze Rime: subverting the master's plan." *Italica,* 65 (1988), 213–233.

Alberti, Leon Battista. *The family in Renaissance Florence,* trans. by Renée Neu Watkins, with an introd. by the translator. Columbia: University of South Carolina Press, 1969.

Allaire, Gloria. "Tullia d'Aragona's *Il Meschino* as key to a reappraisal of her work." *Quaderni d'Italianistica,* 16(1) (1995), 33–50.

Allan-Olney, Mary. *The private life of Galileo,* compiled principally from his correspondence and that of his eldest daughter, Sister Maria Celeste. Boston: Nichols and Noyes, 1870.

Allen, Prudence. *The concept of woman: the early humanist reformation, 1250–1500,* Part 2. Grand Rapids, MI: W.B. Eerdmans Pub., 2002.

Amante, Bruto. *Giulia Gonzaga, contessa di Fondi, e il movimento religioso femminile nel secolo XVI.,* Bologna, Zanichelli, 1896, 421–482.

Ambrosini, F. "*Di mia man propria*, Donna, scrittura e prassi testementaria nella Venezia del Cinquecento." Iin '*Non uno itinere': studi storici offerti dagli allievi a Federico Seneca*. Venice: Stamperia di Venezia, 1993.

Ames-Lewis, Francis. *Isabella and Leonardo: the artistic relationship between Isabella d'Este and Leonardo da Vinci, 1500–1506*. New Haven, CT: Yale University Press, 2012.

Andreini, Isabella. *La Mirtilla: a pastoral*, transl. by Julie Campbell. Tempe: Arizona Center for Medieval and Renaissance Studies, 2002.

Andreini, Isabella. *Lettere*, ed. by Francesco Andreini. Venice, 1607.

Andreini, Isabella. "The Madness of Isabella." *Scenarios of the Commedia dell'Arte*, transl. by Henry Salerno. New York: Limelight Editions, 1996.

Andreini, Isabella. *Rime*. Milan, 1601; Paris, 1603; Milan, 1605.

Andrews, Richard. "Isabella Andreini and others: women on stage in the late cinquecento," In Letizia Panizza, ed. *Women in Italian Renaissance culture and society*. London: Legenda, 2005, 316–333.

Arcangeli. Letizia, and Susanna Peyronel, eds. *Donne di potere nel Rinascimento*. Rome: Viella, 2008.

Aretino, Pietro. *Lettere*. Paolo Procaccioli, ed. Milan: Rizzoli, 1990.

Astarita, Tommaso. *Between salt water and holy water: a history of Southern Italy*. New York: W.W. Norton & Co., 2005

Atkinson, James B., and David Sices, transl. and ed. *Machiavelli and his friends: their personal correspondence*. DeKalb: Northern Illinois University Press, 1996.

Backhouse, Denise, Philippa Maddern, and Natalie Tomas. *Women in medieval and Renaissance European history, c. 1100–1500: a bibliography*. Melbourne: Australian Historical Association, 1989.

Baernstein, P. Renee. *A convent tale: a century of sisterhood in Spanish Milan*. New York: Routledge, 2002.

Baernstein, P. Renée. " 'In my own hand': Costanza Colonna and the art of the letter in sixteenth-century Italy." *Renaissance Quarterly*, 66(1) (Spring 2013), 130–168.

Bainton, Roland H. *Women of the Reformation in Germany and Italy*. Minneapolis: Augsburg Publishing House, 1971, 253–268.

Bal, Mieke. *The Artemisia files: Artemisia Gentileschi for feminists and other thinking people*. Chicago: University of Chicago Press, 2005.

Balestracci, Duccio. *The Renaissance in the fields: family memoirs of a fifteenth-century Tuscan peasant*., University Park, Pa.: Pennsylvania State University Press, 1999.

Bandini Buti, Maria. *Enciclopedia biografica e bibliografica italiana: poetesse e scrittrici*. Rome: E. B. B. I., Istituto Editoriale Italiano B. C. Tosi, 1941.

Barnes, Bernadine. "The understanding of a woman: Vittoria Colonna and Michelangelo's Christ and the Samaritan Woman." *Renaissance Studies*, 27(5) (November 2013), 633–653.

Barocchi, Paola, and Renzo Ristori. *Il carteggio di Michelangelo*, edizione postuma di Giovanni Poggi. Firenze: Sansoni, [1965]-c1983. Vol. 5.

Barucci, Guglielmo. *Le solite scuse: un genere epistolare del Cinquecento*. Milan: FrancoAngeli, 2009.

Barzman, Karen-Edis. "Gender, religious representation and cultural production in Early Modern Italy." In Judith C. Brown and Robert C. Davis, eds., *Gender and society in Renaissance Italy*. London & New York: Longman, 1998, 213–233.

Basile, Deana. "Fasseli gratia per poetessa: Duke Cosimo I de' Medici's role in the Florentine literary circle of Tullia d'Aragona." In Konrad Eisenbichler, ed. *The cultural politics of Duke Cosimo I de' Medici*. Aldershot, England, & Burlington, VT: Ashgate, 2001.

Bassanese, Fiora. *Gaspara Stampa*. Boston: Twayne, 1983.

Bassanese, Fiora A. "Private lives and public lies: texts by courtesans of the Italian Renaissance." *Texas Studies in Language and Literature*, 30(3) (1988), 295–319.

Bassanese, Fiora A. "Selling the self; or the epistolary production of Renaissance courtesans." In Maria Ornella Marotti, ed., *Italian women writers from the Renaissance to the present: revising the canon.* University Park: Pennsylvania State University Press, 1996.

Basso, Jeannine. *Le genre épistolaire en langue italienne, 1538–1662: Répertoire chronologique et analytique.* 2 vols. Rome: Bulzoni, 1990.

Basso, Jeannine. "La lettera 'familiare' nella retorica epistolare del XVI e del XVII secolo in Italia." *Quaderni di retorica e poetica,* I (1985), 57–65.

Battista, Giuseppina. *L'educazione dei figli nella Regola di Giovanni Dominici (1355/6–1419).* Florence: Pagnini e Martinelli, 2002, esp. 90–94.

Baxendale, Susannah Foster. "Exile in practice: the Alberti family in and out of Florence 1401–1428." *Renaissance Quarterly,* 44(4) (Winter 1991), 720–756.

Beebee, Thomas O. "The lettered woman as dialectical image." In *Epistolary fiction in Europe, 1500–1850.* Cambridge, UK, & New York: Cambridge University Press, 1999, 103–136.

Bellonci, Maria. *The life and times of Lucrezia Borgia,* trans. by Bernard and Barbara Wall. New York: Harcourt Brace, 1939.

Bellucci, Marisa. *Maria de Cardona, contessa di Avellino, una nobildonna rinascimentale vissuta nella Napoli del Cinquecento,* Avellino: Il Terebinto edizioni, 2014.

Bembo, Pietro. *The prettiest love letters in the world: letters between Lucrezia Borgia and Pietro Bembo, 1503–1519,* trans. and preface by Hugh Shankland. Boston: D. R. Godine, 1987.

Benson, Pamela Joseph, and Victoria Kirkham, eds. *Strong voices, weak history: early women writers & canons in England, France, & Italy.* Ann Arbor: University of Michigan Press, 2005.

Berra, Giacomo. *Il giovane Caravaggio in Lombardia: ricerche documentarie sui Merisi, gli Aratori e i marchesi di Caravaggio.* Firenze: Fondazione di studi di storia dell'arte Roberto Longhi, 2005.

Biagi, Guido. "Un etera romana" *Nuova antologia* s.III, IV, 16, 1886, 655–711.

Bianchi, Dante. "Una cortigiana rimatrice del Seicento, Margherita Costa." *Rassegna critica della letteratura italiana,* XXIX (1924), 1–31, 187–203; XXX (1925), 158–211.

Bigelli, Ilaria. "Cecarella Minutolo." In *Dizionario biografico degli Italiani,* Vol. 74, 2010.

Biscioni, Antonio Maria. *Lettere di Santi e Beati Fiorentini.* Florence: Moücke, 1736.

Bissel, R. Ward. *Artemisia Gentileschi and the authority of art.* University Park: Pennsylvania State University Press, 1999.

Bissel, R. Ward. "Artemisia Gentileschi: a new documented chronology." *Art Bulletin,* 50(2) (1968), 153–168.

Black, C. F. "The Baglioni as tyrants of Perugia, 1488–1540." *The English Historical Review,* 85(335) (April 1970), 245–281.

Black, Robert. *Education and society in Florentine Tuscany.* Leiden & Boston: Brill, 2007.

Boccaccio, Giovanni, *Famous Women,* ed. and trans. Virginia Brown, The I Tatti Renaissance Library, Harvard Univ Press: Cambridge, Mass; London, 2001.

Boccato, Carla. "Sara Copio Sullam: La poetessa del Ghetto di Venezia: Episodi della sua vita in un manoscritto del secolo 17." *Italia,* 6 no 1-2, (1987), 104–218.

Boccato, Carla. "Un episodio della vita di Sara Copio Sullam: Il *Manifesto sull'immortalità dell'anima.*" *La Rassegna Mensile di Israel,* terza serie, 39(11) (November 1973), 633–646.

Bochi, Giulia. *L'educazione femminile dall'Umanesimo alla Controriforma.* Bologna: G. Malipiero, 1961.

Bornstein, Daniel. "Spiritual kinship and domestic devotions." In Judith C. Brown and Robert C. Davis, eds., *Gender and society in Renaissance Italy.* London & New York: Longman, 1998, 173–192.

Bornstein, Daniel and Roberto Rusconi, eds., *Women and religion in medieval and Renaissance Italy.* Chicago: University of Chicago Press, 1996.

Bosi, Kathryn. "Accolades for an actress: on some literary and musical tributes for Isabella Andreini." *Recercare,* 15 (2003), 73–117.

Bowers, Jane. "The emergence of women composers in Italy, 1566–1700." In Jane Bowers and Judith Tick, eds. *Women making music: The Western art tradition 1150–1950.* Urbana: University of Illinois Press, 1986, 116–67.

Bracke, Wouter. *Fare la epistola nella Roma del Quattrocento.* Rome: RR, 1992.

Bradford, Sarah. *Lucrezia Borgia: life, love and death in Renaissance Italy.* New York: Viking Penguin, 2004.

Braida, Lodovica. *Libri di lettere: le raccolte epistolari del Cinquecento tra inquietudini religiose e "buon volgare."* Rome: Laterza, 2009.

Breisach, Ernst. *Caterina Sforza, a Renaissance virago.* Chicago: University of Chicago Press, 1967.

Brizio, Elena. "In the shadow of the 'campo': Sienese women and their families (14th–16th centuries)." In J. Sperling and S. Wray, eds., *Gender, kinship and property in the wider Mediterranean: centers and peripheries (ca. 1200–1800).* New York: Routledge, 2010, 122–136.

Brown, Clifford M. *Per dare qualche splendore a la gloriosa cita di Mantua, Documents for the antiquarian collection of Isabella d'Este.* Rome: Bulzoni, 2002.

Brown, Judith C. "A woman's place was in the home: women's work in Renaissance Tuscany." In Margaret W. Ferguson, Maureen Quilligan, and Nancy J. Vickers, eds., *Rewriting the Renaissance: the discourses of sexual difference in early modern Europe.* Chicago: University of Chicago Press, 1986.

Brown, Alison. *Bartolomeo Scala, 1430–1497, Chancellor of Florence.* Princeton, NJ: Princeton University Press, 1979.

Brown, Judith C. and Giovanna Benadusi, eds. *Medici women: the making of a dynasty in gran ducal Tuscany.* Centre for Reformation and Renaissance Studies, Toronto, 2015.

Brundin, Abigail. *Vittoria Colonna and the spiritual poetics of the Italian Reformation.* Aldershot, England, & Burlington, VT: Ashgate, 2008.

Bryant, Diana Rowlands, ed. & trans. *"Your obedient consort": a selection of Eleonora d'Aragona's letters to Ercole d'Este (1477–1493).* Toronto: The Other Voice, forthcoming.

Bryce, Judith. "Between friends? Two letters of Ippolita Sforza to Lorenzo de' Medici." *Renaissance Studies,* 21(3) (2007), 340–365.

Bryce, Judith. " 'Fa finire uno bello studio et dice volere studiare': Ippolita Sforza and her books." *Bibliothèque d'Humanisme et Renaissance,* 64(I) (2002), 55–69.

Bryce, Judith. "Les livres des Florentines: reconsidering women's literacy in Quattrocento Florence." In Stephen Milner, ed. *At the margins: minority groups in premodern Italy.* Minneapolis: University of Minnesota Press, 2005.

Bullard, Melissa Meriam. "Marriage politics and the family in Florence: the Strozzi–Medici alliance of 1508." *The American Historical Review,* 84 (1979), 668–687.

Buonarroti, Michelangelo. *Letters,* E. H. Ramsden, ed. and trans. Stanford, CA: Stanford University Press, 1963.

Burke, Peter. "Uses of literacy in Early Modern Italy," in Peter Burke and Roy Porter, eds., *The social history of language.* Cambridge & New York: Cambridge University Press, 1987.

Butler, K. T., ed. *The gentlest art in Renaissance Italy: an anthology of Italian letters 1459–1600.* Cambridge: Cambridge University Press, 1954.

Bynum, Caroline Walker. *Holy feast and holy fast: the religious significance of food to medieval women.* Berkeley: University of California Press, 1987.

Caffiero, Marina, and Manola Ida Venzo, eds. *Scritture di donne. La memoria restituita.* Rome: Viella, 2007.

Calvesi, Maurizio. *Le realtà del Caravaggio.* Torino: G. Einaudi, 1990.

Calvi, Giulia, "Abito, genere, cittadinanza nella Toscana moderna (secoli XVI–XVII)." *Quaderni storici,* 37 (2002), 477–503.

Camargo, Martin. *Ars dictaminis, ars dictandi.* Turnhout, Belgium : Brill, 1991.

Campbell, Julie D., and Maria Galli Stampino. *In dialogue with the other voice in sixteenth-century Italy: literary and social contexts for women's writing.* Toronto: Iter Inc., 2011.

Campbell, Stephen. *The cabinet of Eros: Renaissance mythological painting and the* studiolo *of Isabella d'Este.* New Haven, CT, & London: Yale University Press, 2004.

Cantaro, Maria Teresa. *Lavinia Fontana, bolognese: "pittora singolare," 1552–1614.* Milan: Jandi Sapi, 1989.

Capes, Florence Mary. *St. Catherine de' Ricci: her life, her letters, her community.* London: Burns & Oates, 1905.

Capponi, Niccolò. *An unlikely prince: the life and the times of Machiavelli.* Cambridge, MA: Da Capo Press, 2010.

Carinci, Eleonora. "Una 'speziala' padovana: Lettere di philosophia naturale di Camilla Erculiani (1584)." *Italian Studies,* 68(2) (July 2013), 202–229.

Carter, Tim. "Finding a voice: Vittoria Archilei and the Florentine 'New Music'." In Lorna Hutson, ed., *Feminism and Renaissance studies.* Oxford & New York: Oxford University Press, 1999, 450–467.

Cartwright, Julia. *Isabella d'Este Marchioness of Mantua, 1474–1539: a study in the Renaissance.* London: John Murray, 1907.

Casale, Olga Silvana. "L'epistolario quattrocentesco di Ceccarella Minutolo: fortuna critica e canone ecdotico." In *La critica del testo. Problemi di metodo e esperienze di lavoro. Atti del Convegno, Lecce . . . 1984,* Rome: Salerno editrice, 1985, 505–517.

Casella, L. *I Savorgnan. La famiglia e le opportunità del potere (secc. XV–XVIII).* Rome: Bulzoni, 2003.

Cassidy-Welch, Megan and Peter Sherlock, eds., *Practices of gender in late medieval and early modern Europe.* Turnhout: Brepols; Abingdon: Marston, 2008.

Catherine of Siena. *The dialogue,* trans. and introd. by Suzanne Noffke; pref. by Giuliana Cavallini. New York: Paulist Press, 1980.

Catherine of Siena. *The letters of Catherine of Siena,* transl. with introd. and notes by Suzanne Noffke. Tempe: Arizona Center for Medieval and Renaissance Studies, 2000.

Cecchi, Elena, ed. *Le lettere di Francesco Datini alla moglie Margherita (1385–1410),* introduction by Franco Cardini. Prato: Società pratese di Storia Patria, 1990.

Centre aixois de recherches italiennes. *Les femmes écrivains en Italie au Moyen Age et à la Renaissance: actes du colloque international, Aix-en Provence, 12, 13, 14 novembre 1992.* Aix-en-Provence: Université de Provence, 1994.

Cereta, Laura. *Collected letters of a Renaissance feminist,* ed. and transl. by Diana Robin. Chicago: University of Chicago Press, 1997.

Chemello, Adriana, ed. *Alla lettera: Teorie e pratiche epistolari dai Greci al Novecento.* Milan: Guerini Studio, 1998.

Cheney, Liana. "Lavinia Fontana, Boston *Holy Family.*" *Woman's Art Journal,* 5(1) (1984), 12–15.

Chiappini, Luciano. *Eleonora d'Aragona, prima duchessa di Ferrara.* Rovigo: S.T.E.R., 1956.

Chiomenti Vassalli, Donata. *Giovanna d'Aragona: fra baroni, principi e sovrani del Rinascimento.,* Milano: Mursia, 1987.

Chojnacka, Monica. "Women, charity and community in Early Modern Venice: The Casa delle Zitelle." *Renaissance Quarterly,* 51(1) (Spring 1998), 68–91.

Chojnacka, Monica. *Working women of early modern Venice.* Baltimore: Johns Hopkins University Press, 2001.

Christiansen, Keith, and Judith W. Mann, eds. *Orazio and Artemisia Gentileschi.* New York: Metropolitan Museum of Art; New Haven: Yale University Press, 2001.

Churchill, Laurie J., Phyllis R. Brown, and Jane E. Jeffrey, eds. *Women writing Latin: from Roman antiquity to early modern Europe,* Vol. 3. Early modern women writing Latin. New York: Routledge, 2002.

Cicero, Marcus Tullius, *Epistulae Ad Quintum Fratrem*, ed. D. R. Shackleton Bailey, Cambridge: Cambridge University Press, 1980.

Clarke, Danielle. *The politics of early modern women's writing*. Harlow, England, & New York: Longman, 2001.

Clough, Cecil H. "The cult of antiquity: letters and letter collections." In *Cultural aspects of the Italian Renaissance: essays in honor of Paul Oskar Kristeller*. Manchester, UK: Manchester University Press, 1976, 33–67.

Clough, Cecil H. "Daughters and wives of the Montefeltro: outstanding bluestockings of the Quattrocento." *Renaissance Studies*, 10(1) (March 1996), 31–55.

Clubb, Louise George. "The state of the *arte* in the Andreini's time." In Gian Paolo Biasin et al., eds., *Studies in the Italian Renaissance: essays in memory of Arnolfo B. Ferruolo*. Naples: Societá editrice napoletana, 1985, 263–281.

Cockram, Sarah D. P. *Isabella d'Este and Francesco Gonzaga: power sharing at the Italian Renaissance court*. Farnham, Surrey, England; Burlington, Vermont: Ashgate, 2013.

Cohen, Elizabeth S. "Seen and known: prostitutes in the cityscape of late-sixteenth-century Rome." *Renaissance Studies*, 12(3) (September 1998), 392–409.

Cohen, Elizabeth S. "The trials of Artemisia Gentileschi: a rape as history." *Sixteenth Century Journal*, 31(1) (2000), 46–75.

Cole, Janie. *Music, spectacle and cultural brokerage in early modern Italy: Michelangelo Buonarroti il Giovane*. Florence: Olschki, 2011.

Collier Frick, Carole, Stefania Biancani, Elizabeth S. G. Nicholson et al. *Italian women artists: from Renaissance to Baroque*, Milan: Skira; New York: Rizzoli, 2007.

Colonna, Vittoria. *Selected letters*, ed. and transl. by Abigail Brundin. Toronto: The Other Voice, upcoming.

Colonna, Vittoria. *Sonnets for Michelangelo*, ed. and transl. by Abigail Brundin. Chicago: University of Chicago Press, 2005.

Comelli, G. B. "Di Nicolò Sanuti primo conte della Porretta." In *Atti e memorie della R. Deputazione di Storia Patria per le provincie di Romagna*, s. III, 17, 1899, 102–161.

Constable, Giles. *Letters and letter collections*. Turnhout: Ed. Brepols, 1976.

Copia Sulam, Sarra. *Jewish poet and intellectual in seventeenth-century Venice: the works of Sarra Copia Sulam in verse and prose, along with writings of her contemporaries in her praise, condemnation, or defense*, Don Harrán, ed. and trans. Chicago & London: University of Chicago Press, 2009.

Cosentini, Laura. "Una dama napoletana del XVI secolo: Isabella Villamarino, principessa di Salerno.," in *Rassegna pugliese di scienze, lettere ed arti*, 13 (1896), 89–95; 125–127, 179–180.

Costa, Margherita. *The Buffoons*, ed. and trans. by Sara Diaz and Jessica Goethals. Toronto: Centre for Renaissance and Reformation Studies, 2015.

Costa-Zalessow, Natalia. *Scrittrici italiane dal 13. al 20. secolo: testi e critica*. Ravenna: Longo, 1982, 146–152.

Costa-Zalessow, Natalia. "Tarabotti's *La semplicità ingannata* and its twentieth-century interpreters, with unpublished documents regarding its condemnation to the Index." *Italica*, 78(3) (2001), 314–335.

Couchman, Jane, and Ann Crabb, eds. *Women's letters across Europe, 1400–1700: form and persuasion*. Aldershot, England, & Burlington, VT: Ashgate, 2005.

Cox, Virginia. "Leonardo Bruni on women and rhetoric: *De studiis et litteris* revisited." *Rhetorica: A Journal of the History of Rhetoric*, 27(1) (Winter 2009), 47–75.

Cox, Virginia. *Lyric poetry by women of the Italian Renaissance*. Baltimore: Johns Hopkins University Press, 2013.

Cox, Virginia. *The prodigious muse: women's writing in Counter-Reformation Italy*. Baltimore: Johns Hopkins University Press, 2011.

Cox, Virginia. "Women writers and the canon in sixteenth-century Italy: the case of Vittoria Colonna." In Pamela Joseph Benson and Victoria Kirkham, eds. *Strong voices, weak history: early women writers & canons in England, France, & Italy.* Ann Arbor: University of Michigan Press, 2005, 14–31.

Cox, Virginia. *Women's writing in Italy 1400–1650.* Baltimore: Johns Hopkins University Press, 2008.

Crabb, Ann. "How to influence your children: persuasion and form in Alessandra Macigni Strozzi's letters to her sons." In Jane Couchman and Ann Crabb, eds., *Women's letters across Europe, 1400–1700.* Aldershot, UK: Ashgate, 2005, 21–41.

Crabb, Ann. " 'If I could write': Margherita Datini and letter writing, 1385–1410." *Renaissance Quarterly,* 40(4) (Winter 2007), 1193–1194.

Crabb, Ann. *The Strozzi of Florence: widowhood and family solidarity in the Renaissance,* Ann Arbor: University of Michigan Press, 2000.

Croce, Benedetto. "Ceccarella Minutolo." In *Aneddoti di varia letteratura. Seconda edizione, etc.* Bari: Laterza, 1953, 64–76.

Curtis-Wendlandt, Lisa. "Conversing on love: text and subtext in Tullia d'Aragona's *Dialogo della infinità d'amore.*" *Hypatia,* 19(4) (2004), 75–96.

Cusick, Suzanne G. *Francesca Caccini at the Medici court: music and the circulation of power,* with a foreword by Catharine R. Stimpson. Chicago: University of Chicago Press, 2009.

da Fonseca-Wollheim, Corinna. "Faith and fame in the life and works of the Venetian Jewish poet Sara Copio Sullam (1592?–1641)." Ph.D. dissertation, University of Cambridge, 2000.

Dall'Aglio, Stefano. *Savonarola and Savonarolism,* trans. by John Gagné. Toronto: Centre for Reformation and Renaissance Studies, 2010.

Datini, Margherita. *Letters to Francesco Datini,* translated by Carolyn James and Antonio Pagliaro. Toronto: Iter Inc., Centre for Reformation and Renaissance Studies, 2012.

D'Aragona, Tullia. *Dialogue on the infinity of love,* transl. by Rinaldina Russell and Bruce Merry. Chicago: University of Chicago Press, 1997.

Davis, Robert C., and Benjamin Ravid, eds., *The Jews of early modern Venice.* Baltimore: Johns Hopkins University Press, 2001, 143–165, 276–279.

Dean, Trevor. "After the War of Ferrara: relations between Venice and Ercole d'Este, 1484–1505." In *War, culture and society in Renaissance Venice: essays in honour of John Hale.* London & Rio Grande, Ohio: Hambledon Press, 1993, 73–99.

Debby, Nirit Ben-Aryeh. "'Or' andiamo alla predicha, udiamo la parola d'Iddio: the stormy preaching of Giovanni Domenici in Renaissance Florence 1400–1406." *Archivio italiano per la storia della pietà,* 12 (1999), 65–87.

D'Elia, Una Roman. "Drawing Christ's blood: Michelangelo, Vittoria Colonna and the aesthetics of reform." *Renaissance Quarterly,* 59(1) (2006), 90–129.

Del Pozzo, Joan. "The apotheosis of Niccolò Toldo: An execution 'love story'." *Modern Language Notes,* 110(1), Italian issue (January 1995), 164–177.

De Jean, Joan. *Tender geographies: women and the origins of the novel in France.* New York: Columbia University Press, 1991, 3–5, 98–101.

De Luca, Catherine. *Guglielmina Schianteschi (1463–1536): A Tuscan countess and Florentine citizen.* Ph.D. diss., University of California, Riverside, 2004.

De' Pazzi, Maria Maddalena. *Selected revelations,* transl. and introd. by Armando Maggi; preface by E. Ann Matter. New York: Paulist Press, 2000.

De' Pazzi, Maria Maddalena. *L'epistolario completo,* Chiara Vasciaveo, ed. Florence: Nerbini, 2009.

Derosas, Renzo. "Corner, Elena Lucrezia." In *Dizionario Biografico degli Italiani,* Vol. 29. Roma: Istituto dell'Enciclopedia Italiana, 1983.

Di Agresti, Domenico Guglielmo M., ed. *Santa Caterina de' Ricci epistolario.* Firenze: Olschki, 1973–1975.

Di Agresti, Domenico Guglielmo M., ed. *Prolegomeni alla spiritualtà di Santa Caterina de' Ricci.* Firenze: Olschki, 1975.

Doglio, Maria Luisa. *L'arte delle lettere: idea e pratica della scrittura epistolare tra Quattro e Seicento,* Bologna: Il Mulino, 2000.

Doglio, Maria Luisa. "Letter writing, 1350–1650." In Letizia Panizza and Sharon Wood, eds., *A history of women's writing in Italy.* New York: Cambridge University Press, 2000, 13–24.

Doglio, Maria Luisa. *Lettera e donna, Scrittura epistolare al femminile tra Quattro e cinquecento.* Rome: Bulzoni, 1993.

Dooley, Brendan. *A mattress maker's daughter: the Renaissance romance of Don Giovanni de' Medici and Livia Vernazza.,* Cambridge, MA: Harvard University Press, 2014.

Dupré Theseider, Eugenio. "Caterina da Siena, santa," In *Dizionario biografico degli italiani,* vol. 22. Rome: Istituto della Enciclopedia italiana, 1979.

Edelstein, Bruce. "Bronzino in the service of Eleonora di Toledo and Cosimo I de' Medici: conjugal patronage and the painter-courtier." In Sheryl E. Reiss and David G. Wilkins, eds., *Beyond Isabella: secular women patrons of art in Renaissance Italy.* Kirksville, MO: Truman State University Press, 2001, 225–261.

Eden, Kathy. *The Renaissance rediscovery of intimacy.* Chicago & London: University of Chicago Press, 2012.

Eisenbichler, Konrad. *The sword and the pen: women, politics, and poetry in sixteenth-century Siena.* Notre Dame, IN: University of Notre Dame Press, 2012.

Emerson, Isabelle Putnam. *Five centuries of women singers.* Westport, Connecticut; London: Praeger, 2005.

Erculiani, Camilla. *Letters on natural philosophy,* ed. and trans. Eleonora Carinci and Hannah Marcus, upcoming; The Other Voice series (Toronto).

Erdmann, Axel, Alberto Govi, and Fabrizio Govi. *Ars epistolica. Communication in sixteenth-century Western Europe: epistolaries, letter-writing manuals and model letter books 1501–1600.* Lucerne: Modena: Gilhofer & Ranschburg; Libreria Alberto Govi di Fabrizio Govi Sas, 2014.

Erdmann, Axel. *My gracious silence: women in the mirror of 16th-century printing in Western Europe.* Lucerne: Gilhofer & Ranschburg, 1999.

Fabbrici, Gabriele, and Giuseppe Adani, eds. *Il Correggio a Correggio: protagonisti e luoghi del Rinascimento.* Carpi, Modena: Nuovagrafica, 2008.

Fabrini, Placido. *The life of St. Mary Magdalen De' Pazzi, Florentine noble, sacred Carmelite virgin,* transl. from the Florentine edition of 1852 and published by Antonio Isoleri: Philadelphia, 1900.

Fahy, Conor. "Women and Italian Cinquecento literary academies." In Letizia Panizza, ed., *Women in Italian Renaissance culture and society.* Oxford: Legenda, University of Oxford, 2000, 438–452.

Fantini, Maria Pia. "Lettere alla madre di Cassandra Chigi." In Gabriella Zarri, ed., *Per lettera: la scrittura epistolare femminile tra archivio e tipografia: secoli XV-XVII.* Rome: Viella, 1999, 111–150.

Favaro, Antonio. *Amici e corrispondenti di Galileo,* ed. and with intro. by Paolo Galluzzi. Florence: Libreria editrice salimbeni, 1983, Vol. 1.

Fedele, Cassandra. *Letters and Orations,* ed. and transl. by Diana Robin. Chicago: University of Chicago Press, 2000.

Feliciangeli, Bernardino. *Notizie e documenti sulla vita di Caterina Cibo-Varano duchessa di Camerino.* Camerino: Tipografia Savini, 1891.

Feliciangeli, Bernardino. "Notizie di Costanza Varano-Sforza." *Giornale Storico* 23 (1894), 1–75.

Fenster, Thelma S. "Strong voices, weak minds? The defenses of Eve by Isotta Nogarola and Christine de Pizan, who found themselves in Simone de Beauvoir's situation." In Pamela Joseph Benson and Victoria Kirkham, eds., *Strong voices, weak history: early women writers & canons in England, France, & Italy.* Ann Arbor: University of Michigan Press, 2005, 58–77.

Festa, Gianni and Angelita Roncelli, eds., *Osanna Andreasi da Mantova, 1449-1-1505: la Santa dei Gongaza: lettere e colloqui spirituali.* Mantua: Casandreasi; Bologna: Studio domenicano, 2007.

Flosi, Justin. "On locating the courtesan in Italian lyric: distance and the madrigal texts of Costanzo Festa." In Martha Feldman and Bonnie Gordon, eds., *The courtesan's arts: cross-cultural perspectives.* New York: Oxford University Press, 2006, 133–143.

Fonte, Moderata. *The worth of women: wherein is clearly revealed their nobility and their superiority to men.* Ed. and trans. Virginia Cox, Chicago, Ill.: University of Chicago Press, 1997.

Fortis, Umberto. *La bella ebrea: Sara Copio Sullam, poetessa nel ghetto di Venezia del '600.* Turin: S. Zamorani, 2003.

Franco, Veronica. *Poems and selected letters,* ed. and transl. by A. R. Jones and M. F. Rosenthal. Chicago: University of Chicago Press, 1998.

Frati, Ludovico. "Lettere amorose di Galeazzo Marescotti e di Sante Bentivoglio." *Giornale storico della letteratura italiana,* 26 (1895), 319–335.

Frati, Ludovico. *La Vita privata in Bologna dal secolo XIII al XVII* 2. Ed. con aggiunte e nuove tavole illustrative. Bologna: Zanichelli, 1928.

Fresu, Rita. "Alla ricerca delle varietà 'intermedie' della scrittura femminile tra XV e XVI secolo: lettere private di Lucrezia Borgia e Vannozza Cattanei," *Contributi di filologia dell'Italia Mediana,* 18 (2004), 41–82.

Gagliardi, Isabella. *Sola con Dio: la missione di Domenica da Paradiso nella Firenze del primo Cinquecento* Tavarnuzze (Florence): SISMEL edizioni del Galluzzo. Florence: Fondazione Ezio Franceschini, 2007.

Galli, Romeo. *Lavinia Fontana pittrice: 1552-1614.* Imola: Tipografia Galeati, 1940.

Galilei, Virginia. *Lettere al padre,* ed. Bruno Basile. Rome: Salerno, 2002.

Gamba, Bartolomeo. *Lettere di donne italiane del secolo decimosesto.* Venice: Alvisopoli, 1832.

Gambara, Veronica. *Complete poems. A bilingual edition.* Critical introduction by Molly M. Martin. Molly M. Martin and Paola Ugolini, ed. and trans. Toronto: Centre for Reformation and Renaissance Studies, University of Toronto, 2014.

Gambara, Veronica. *Rime,* ed. Alan Bullock. Florence: Perth, 1995.

Gambara, Veronica. *Rime e lettere,* with a vita by B. C. Zamboni. Francesco Rizzardi, ed. Brescia: Rizzardi, 1759.

Gardner, Edmund G. *Dukes & poets in Ferrara: a study in the poetry, religion and politics of the fifteenth and early sixteenth centuries.* London: A. Constable, 1904.

Garfagnini, G. C., and G. Picone, eds. *Verso Savonarola: Misticismo, profezia empiti riformistici fra Medioevo ed Età moderna,* Florence: SISMEL edizioni del Galluzzo, 1999, esp. 115–119.

Garrard, Mary D. *Artemisia Gentileschi around 1622: the shaping and reshaping of an artistic identity.* Berkeley: University of California Press, 2001.

Garrard, Mary D. *Artemisia Gentileschi: the image of the female hero in Italian Baroque art.* Princeton, NJ: Princeton University Press, 1989.

Garrard, Mary D. "Here's looking at me: Sofonisba Anguissola and the problem of the woman artist." *Renaissance Quarterly,* 47(3) (Autumn 1994), 556–622.

Gentilcore, David. *Healers and healing in Early Modern Italy.* Manchester: Manchester University Press; New York: St. Martin's Press, 1998.

Giallongo, Angela, ed. *Donne di palazzo nelle corti europee: tracce e forme di potere dall'età moderna.* Milan: UNICOPLI, 2005.

Gibaldi, Joseph. "Child, woman, and poet: Vittoria Colonna." In Katharina Wilson, ed., *Women writers of the Renaissance and Reformation.* University of Georgia Press, 1987, 22–46.

Gilbert, Felix. "Bernardo Rucellai and the Orti Oricellari: A study on the origin of modern political thought." *Journal of the Warburg and Courtauld Institutes,* 12 (1949), 101–131.

Gill, Amyrose McCue. "Fraught relations in the letters of Laura Cereta: marriage, friendship, and humanist epistolarity." *Renaissance Quarterly,* 62(4) (Winter 2009), 1098–1129.

Gill, Katherine. "Women and religious literature in the vernacular." In E. Ann Matter and John Coakley, eds., *Creative women in medieval and early modern Italy: A religious and artistic Renaissance*. Philadelphia: University of Pennsylvania Press, 1994.

Goldsmith, Elizabeth C. "Authority, authenticity and the publication of letters by women." In *Writing the female voice: essays on epistolary literature*. Boston: Northeastern University Press, 1989.

Gonzato, Alessandra. *Lux in Arcana. The Vatican secret archives reveals itself*. Rome: Palombi Editori, 2012.

Gould, Cecil Hilton Monk. *The paintings of Correggio*. London: Faber, 1976.

Graff, Harvey. "On literacy in the Renaissance: review and reflections." In *The labyrinths of literacy: reflections on literacy past and present*. Pittsburgh: University of Pittsburgh Press revised and expanded, 1995.

Grafton, Anthony and Lisa Jardine. "Women humanists: education for what?" In *From humanism to the humanities: education and the liberal arts in fifteenth- and sixteenth-century Europe*. Cambridge, MA: Harvard University Press, 1986, 29–57.

Gregori, Mina and Giuseppe Rocchi, eds., *Il "Paradiso" in Pian di Ripoli: Studi e ricerche su un antico monastero*. Florence: Centro Di, 1985.

Gregory, Heather. "A Florentine family in crisis: the Strozzi in the fifteenth century" PhD Thesis, University of London, 1981.

Gregorovius, Ferdinand. *Lucretia Borgia: according to original documents and correspondence of her day*. Trans. from the third German edition by John Leslie Garner. New York: Appleton, 1903.

Grendler, Paul. *Schooling in Renaissance Italy: literacy and learning 1300–1600*. Baltimore: Johns Hopkins University Press, 1989.

Griffiths, Jeremy and Derek Pearsall, eds. *Book production and publishing in Britain, 1375–1475* Cambridge [England]; New York: Cambridge University Press, 1989.

Grössinger, Christa. *Picturing women in late Medieval and Renaissance art*. Manchester, UK: Manchester University Press, 1997.

Guarnieri, Romana. " 'Nec domina nec ancilla, sed socia'. Tre casi di direzione spirituale tra Cinque e Seicento." In Elisja Schulte van Kessel, ed., *Women and men in spiritual culture, XIV–XVII centuries: a meeting of South and North*. The Hague: Netherlands Govt. Pub. Office, 1986, 111–132.

Guasti, Cesare. "Alcuni fatti della prima giovinezza di Cosimo I de' Medici," *Giornale storico degli archivi toscani*, 2 (1858), 13–30.

Guasti, Cesare, ed. *Lettere di una gentildonna fiorentina*. Florence: G. C. Sansoni, 1877.

Guernsey, Jane Howard. *The Lady Cornaro: pride and prodigy of Venice*. Clinton Corners, NY: College Avenue Press, 1999.

Gundesheimer, Werner. *Ferrara. The style of a Renaissance despotism*. Princeton, NJ: Princeton University Press, 1973.

Gundesheimer, Werner. "Women, learning, and power: Eleonora of Aragon and the court of Ferrara" In Patricia H. Labalme, ed., *Beyond their Sex: learned women of the European past*. New York: New York University Press, 1980, 43–65.

Hairston, Julia, trans. and ed. *The poems and letters of Tullia d'Aragona and others*. Toronto: Centre for Reformation and Renaissance Studies and ITER, 2014.

Hairston, Julia L. "Skirting the issue: Machiavelli's Caterina Sforza." *Renaissance Quarterly*, 53(3) (2000), 686–712.

Harness, Kelley. *Echoes of women's voices: music, art, and female patronage in early modern Florence*. Chicago: University of Chicago Press, 2006.

Harrán, Don. "Sarra Copia Sulam: a seventeenth-century Jewish poet in search of immortality." *Nashim: A Journal of Jewish Women's Studies & Gender Issues*, 25 (Fall 2013), 30–50.

Harris, Ann Sutherland. "Artemisia Gentileschi: the literate illiterate or learning from example." In *Docere, delectare, movere: affetti, devozione e retorica nel linguaggio artistico del primo barocco romano*. Rome: Edizioni De Luca, 1998, 105–120.

Heilbron, J. L. *Galileo*. Oxford & New York: Oxford University Press, 2010.

Hemelrijk, Emily Ann. *Matrona docta: educated women in the Roman elite from Cornelia to Julia Domna*. London; New York: Routledge, 1999.

Henderson, John. *The Renaissance hospital: healing the body and healing the soul*. New Haven, CT, & London: Yale University Press, 2006.

Herzig, Tamar. *Savonarola's women: visions and reform in Renaissance Italy*. Chicago: University of Chicago Press, 2008.

Heywood, William. *History of Perugia*. New York: G.P. Putnam's Sons; London: Methuen, 1910.

Hook, Judith. *Siena, a city and its history*, London: H. Hamilton, 1979.

Hufton, Olwen. "The window's mite and other strategies: funding the Catholic Reformation." *Transactions of the Royal Historical Society*, Sixth Series, 8 (1998), 117–137, esp. 131–133.

IDEA Isabella d'Este Project. Online database with over 32,000 letters from Isabella d'Este's correspondence. www.http://isabelladeste.ucsc.edu

Ilardi, Vincent. "Towards the Tragedia d'Italia: Ferrante and Galeazzo Maria Sforza, friendly enemies and hostile allies." In David Abulafia, ed., *The French descent into Renaissance Italy, 1494–5: antecedents and effects*. Aldershot, Hampshire: Variorum: Brookfield, VT: Ashgate Pub. Co., 1995, 91–122.

Jackson, Philippa, and Fabrizio Nevola. *Beyond the Palio: urbanism and ritual in Renaissance Siena*. Malden, MA, Oxford: Blackwell Publishing on behalf of the Society for Renaissance Studies, 2006.

Jacobs, Fredrika. *Defining the Renaissance virtuosa: women artists and the language of art history and criticism*. Cambridge: Cambridge University Press, 1997.

Jacobs, Fredrika. "Woman's capacity to create: the unusual case of Sofonisba Anguissola." *Renaissance Quarterly*, 47(1) (1994), 74–101.

Jaffe, Irma. *Shining eyes, cruel fortune, the lives and loves of Italian Renaissance women poets*. New York: Fordham University Press, 2002.

James, Carolyn. "A woman's path to literacy: the letters of Margherita Datini, 1384–1410." In Megan Cassidy-Welch and Peter Sherlock, eds., *Practices of gender in late medieval and early modern Europe*. Turnhout: Brepols; Abingdon: Marston, 2008, 43–56.

Jardine, Lisa. "Isotta Nogarola: women humanists—education for what?" *History of Education*, XII (1983), 23, I–44.

Jardine, Lisa. " 'O decus italiae virgo', or the myth of the learned lady in the Renaissance." *Historical Journal*, 28(4) (December 1985), 799–819.

Jensen, Katherine Ann. "Male models of feminine epistolarity, or, how to write like a woman in seventeenth-century France." In Elizabeth C. Goldsmith, ed., *Writing the female voice: essays on epistolary literature*. London: Pinter, 1989, 25–45.

Jerrold, Maud F. *Vittoria Colonna, with some account of her friends and her times*. London: J.M. Dent & Co.; New York, E.P. Dutton & Company, 1906.

Johnson, Geraldine A., and Sara F. Matthews Grieco, eds. *Picturing women in Renaissance and Baroque Italy*. New York: Cambridge University Press, 1997.

Jones, Ann Rosalind. *The currency of Eros: women's love lyric in Europe, 1540–1620*. Bloomington: Indiana University Press, 1990.

Kaborycha, Lisa. "Brigida Baldinotti and her two epistles in Quattrocento Florentine manuscripts." *Speculum*, 87.3 (July 2012), 793–826.

Kelly, Joan. "Did women have a Renaissance?" In *Women, history, and theory: the essays of Joan Kelly*. Chicago: University of Chicago Press, 1984 (first printed 1977), 19–50.

Kent, Francis William. *Household and lineage in Renaissance Florence: the family life of the Capponi, Ginori, and Rucellai.* Princeton, NJ: Princeton University Press, 1977.

Kent, Francis William. "Sainted mother, magnificent son: Lucrezia Tornabuoni and Lorenzo de' Medici." *Italian History and Culture,* 3 (1997), 3–34.

Kidwell, Carol. *Pietro Bembo: lover, linguist, cardinal.* Montreal; Ithaca: McGill-Queen's University Press, 2004.

Kiene, Michael. *Bartolomeo Ammannati.* Milan: Electa, 1995.

King, Margaret L. "Book-lined cells: women and humanism in the early Italian Renaissance." In Patricia H. Labalme, ed., *Beyond their sex: learned women of the European past.* New York: NYU Press, 1980, 66–90.

King, Margaret L. *Humanism, Venice, and women: essays on the Italian Renaissance.* Aldershot, Hampshire, Great Britain, & Burlington, VT: Ashgate, 2005.

King, Margaret L., and Albert Rabil, Jr., eds., *Her immaculate hand: selected works by and about the women humanists of Quattrocento Italy.* Binghamton, NY: Center for Medieval & Early Renaissance Studies, 1983.

King, Margaret L., "Thwarted ambitions: six learned women of the Italian Renaissance." *Soundings,* 59 (1976), 295–299.

King, Margaret. *Women of the Renaissance.* Chicago & London: University of Chicago Press, 1991.

Kirkendale, Warren. *The court musicians in Florence during the principate of the Medici: with a reconstruction of the artistic establishment.* Firenze: L.S. Olschki, 1993.

Kirkham, Victoria. "Creative partners: the marriage of Laura Battiferra and Bartolomeo Ammannati." *Renaissance Quarterly,* 55 (2002), 498–558.

Kirkham, Victoria. "Dante's fantom, Petrarch's specter: Bronzino's portrait of the poet Laura Battiferra." In Deborah Parker, *"Visibile parlare": Dante and the art of the Italian Renaissance. Lectura Dantis 22–23* (1998), 63–139.

Kirkham, Victoria, ed. and transl. *Laura Battiferra degli Ammannati and her literary circle: an anthology.* Chicago: University of Chicago Press, 2006.

Kirkham, Victoria. "Sappho on the Arno: the brief fame of Laura Battiferra degli Ammannati." In *Strong voices, weak history: early women writers and canons in England, France and Italy.* Ann Arbor: University of Michigan Press, 2005, 174–196.

Kirshner, Julius. *Pursuing honor while avoiding sin: the "Monte delle doti" of Florence.,* Milan: A. Giuffrè, 1978.

Kirshner, Julius, and Antony Molho. "Niccolò Machiavelli's marriage." *Rinascimento,* 18 (1978), 293–295.

Klapisch-Zuber, Christiane. "Le chiavi fiorentine di Barbablù: L'apprendimento della lettura nel XV secolo." *Quaderni storici,* n.s. 57 (December 1984), 775.

Klapisch-Zuber, Christiane. *Women, family, and ritual in Renaissance Italy.* Chicago: University of Chicago Press, 1987.

Kohl, Benjamin G. *Padua under the Carrara, 1318–1405.* Baltimore: Johns Hopkins University Press, 1998.

Kovesi, Catherine. " 'Heralds of a well-instructed mind': Nicolosa Sanuti's defence of women and their clothes." *Renaissance Studies,* 13(3) (1999), 255–282.

Kovesi, Catherine. *Sumptuary law in Italy 1200–1500.* Oxford: Clarendon Press; New York: Oxford University Press, 2002.

Kristeller, P. O. "Learned women of early modern Italy: humanists and university scholars." In Patricia H. Labalme, ed., *Beyond their sex: learned women of the European past.* New York: NYU Press, 1980, 91–116.

Labalme, Patricia H. "Women's roles in Early Modern Venice: an exceptional case." In Patricia H. Labalme, ed., *Beyond their sex: learned women of the European past.* New York: New York University Press, 1980, 129–152.

Langdon, Gabrielle. *Medici women: portraits of power, love and betrayal from the court of Duke Cosimo I.* Toronto: University of Toronto Press, 2006.

Larner, John. *The lords of Romagna; Romagnol society and the origins of the signorie.* London, Macmillan; New York, St. Martin's Press, 1965.

Lawner, Lynn. *Lives of the courtesans: portraits of the Renaissance.* New York: Rizzoli, 1987.

Laven, Mary. *Virgins of Venice: broken vows and cloistered lives in the Renaissance convent.* New York: Viking, 2003.

Lehmijoki-Gardner, Maiju, ed., trans., & introd. *Dominican penitent women.* Mahwah, NJ: Paulist Press, 2005.

Lenzi, Maria Ludovica, ed. *Donne e madonne: l'educazione femminile nel primo Rinascimento italiano.* Torino: Loescher, 1982.

Lev, Elizabeth. *The tigress of Forlì: Renaissance Italy's most courageous and notorious countess, Caterina Riario Sforza de' Medici.* Boston: Houghton Mifflin Harcourt, 2011.

Levin, Carole, ed. *Extraordinary women of the medieval and Renaissance world: a biographical dictionary.* Westport, CT: Greenwood Press, 2000.

Lombardi, Giuseppe. "Traduzione, imitazione, plagio (Nicolosa Sanuti, Albrecht von Eyb, Niclas von Wyle)." In *Studi (e testi) italiani n. 1 – Furto e plagio nella letteratura del Classicismo,* a cura di Roberto Gigliucci, Rome: Bulzoni, (1998), 103–38.

Longhi, Roberto. "Gentileschi, padre e figlia." *L'Arte,* xix (1916), 245–314.

Looney, Dennis, and Deanna Shemek, eds. *Phaethon's children: the Este court and its culture in early modern Ferrara.* Tempe: Arizona Center for Medieval and Renaissance Studies, 2005.

López, Maritere. "The courtesan's gift: reciprocity and friendship in the letters of Camilla Pisana and Tullia d'Aragona." In Daniel T. Lochman, Maritere López, and Lorna Hutson, eds., *Discourses and representations of friendship in early modern Europe, 1500–1700.* Farnham, Surrey, & Burlington, VT: Ashgate, 2011.

Low, Megan Elizabeth McPherson. *By her own hand: words and hands as personal iconography in the self-portraiture of Sofonisba Anguissola,* A.B. Thesis, Honors in the History of Art and Architecture, Harvard University, 2004.

Lowe, Kate. *Nuns' chronicles and convent culture in Renaissance and Counter-Reformation Italy.* Cambridge, UK: Cambridge Universisty Press, 2003.

Lubkin, Gregory. *A Renaissance court: Milan under Galeazzo Maria Sforza.* Berkeley: University of California Press, 1994.

Luongo, F. Thomas. *The saintly politics of Catherine of Siena.* Ithaca, NY: Cornell University Press, 2006. Especially Chapter 3, "Niccolo di Toldio and the erotics of political engagement," 90–122.

Macneil, Anne. *Music and women of the commedia dell'arte in the late sixteenth century.* Oxford: Oxford University Press, 2003.

Maggi, Armando. "The place of female mysticism in the Italian literary canon." In Pamela Joseph Benson and Victoria Kirkham, eds., *Strong voices, weak history: early women writers & canons in England, France, & Italy.* Ann Arbor: University of Michigan Press, 2005, 199–215.

Maggi, Armando. *Uttering the Word: the mystical performances of Maria Maddalena de' Pazzi, a Renaissance visionary.* Albany: State University of New York Press, 1998.

Maguire, Yvonne. *The women of the Medici.* London: Routledge, 1927.

Mallett, Michael E. *The Borgias: the rise and fall of a Renaissance dynasty.* London: Bodley Head, 1969.

Mallett, Michael E. "Venice and the War of Ferrara, 1482–4." In *War, culture and society in Renaissance Venice: essays in honour of John Hale.* London & Rio Grande, Ohio: Hambledon Press, 1993, 57–72.

Manca, Joseph. "Isabella's mother: aspects of the art patronage of Eleonora d'Aragona, Duchess of Ferrara." *Aurora,* 4 (2003), 79–94.

Marcheschi, Daniela. *Chiara Matraini: poetessa lucchese e la letteratura delle donne nei nuovi fermenti religiosi del '500.* Lucca: M. Pacini Fazzi, 2008.

Marinella, Lucrezia, *The nobility and excellence of women, and the defects and vices of men*. Edited and translated by Anne Dunhill. Chicago: University of Chicago Press, 1999.

Martelli, Mario "Lucrezia Tornabuoni" In Centre aixois de recherches italiennes. *Les femmes écrivains en Italie au Moyen Age et à la Renaissance: actes du colloque international, Aix-en Provence, 12, 13, 14 novembre 1992*. Aix-en-Provence: Université de Provence, 1994, 51–86.

Maschietto, Francesco Ludovico. *Elena Lucrezia Cornaro Piscopia (1646–1684): the first woman in the world to earn a university degree*. Jan Vairo, William Crochetiere, and Catherine Marshall, trans. Philadelphia: Saint Joseph's University Press, 2007.

Masson, Georgina. *Courtesans of the Italian Renaissance*. London: Secker & Warburg, 1975, 60–64.

Matarrese, Tina. "Alle soglie della grammatica: imparare a leggere (e a scrivere) tra Medioevo e Rinascimento." *Studi di grammatica italiana*, 18 (1993), 233–256.

Matraini, Chiara. *Selected poetry and prose*, Elaine Maclachlan, ed. and trans.; intro. by Giovanna Rabitti. Chicago: University of Chicago Press, 2007.

Matraini, Chiara. *Rime e lettere*, Giovanna Rabitti, ed. Bologna: Commissione per i Testi di Lingua, 1989.

Matt, Luigi. *Teoria e prassi dell'epistolografia italiana tra Cinquecento e primo Seicento: ricerche linguistiche e retoriche (con particolare riguardo alle lettere di Giambattista Marino)*. Rome: Bonacci, 2005.

Matter, Ann E., and John Coakley, eds. *Creative women in medieval and early modern Italy: a religious and artistic Renaissance*. Philadelphia: University of Pennsylvania Press, 1994.

Matthews-Grieco, Sara F., ed. *Monaca, moglie, serva, cortigiana: vita e immagine delle donne tra Rinascimento e Controriforma*. Florence: Morgana, 2001.

Mayer, Thomas F., and D. R. Woolf, eds. *The rhetorics of life-writing in early modern Europe: forms of biography from Cassandra Fedele to Louis XIV*. Ann Arbor: University of Michigan Press, 1995.

Mazzocco, Elizabeth. "Eleonora d'Este and the heroines of Boiardo's *Orlando Innamorato*: challenging gender stereotypes at the Ferrara court." In B. Altmann and C. Carroll, eds., *The court reconvenes: courtly literature across the disciplines*. Rochester: Boydell and Brewer, 2003, 284–293.

McIver, Katherine A. "Two Emilian noblewomen and patronage networks in the Cinquecento." In Sheryl E. Reiss and David G. Wilkins, eds., *Beyond Isabella: secular women patrons of art in Renaissance Italy*. Kirksville, MO: Truman State University Press, 2001, 225–261.

McIver, Katherine, ed. *Wives, widows, mistresses, and nuns in early modern Italy: making the invisible visible through art and patronage*. Farnham, Surrey, England; Burlington, VT: Ashgate, 2012.

McIver, Katherine. *Women, art, and architecture in northern Italy, 1520–1580: negotiating power*. Aldershot, England, & Burlington, VT: Ashgate, 2006.

Medin, A. "Maddalena degli Scrovegni e le discordie tra i Carraresi e gli Scrovegni." *Atti e Memorie della Regia Accademia di scienze, lettere ed arti in Padova*, 12 (1896), appendix, 260–262.

Medioli, Francesca. "Arcangela Tarabotti's reliability about herself: publication and self-representation (together with a small collection of previously unpublished letters)." *Italianist*, 23 (2003), 54–101.

Megale, Teresa. "La commedia decifrata: metamorfosi e rispecchiamenti in Li Buffoni di Margherita Costa." *Il Castello di Elsinore*, 1,2 (1988), 64–76.

Mellyn, Elizabeth W. *Mad Tuscans and their families: a history of mental disorder in early modern Italy*. Philadelphia: University of Pennsylvania Press, 2014.

Menzio, Eva, ed. *Lettere. Artemisia Gentileschi; precedute da Atti di un processo per stupro*. Milan: Abscondita, 2004.

Mercati, Angelo "Lettere di Elisabetta e di Leonora Gonzaga a Francesco Maria della Rovere . . . (1521–1522)." *Atti e memorie della R. Accademia Virgiliana*, n.s. XXVI (1943), 3–77.

Migiel, Marilyn, and Juliana Schiesari. *Refiguring woman: perspectives on gender and the Italian Renaissance*. Ithaca, NY: Cornell University Press, 1991.

Miglio, Luisa. *Governare l'alfabeto: donne, scrittura e libri nel Medioevo*. Rome: Viella, 2008.

Miglio, Luisa. "Leggere e scrivere il volgare: sull'alfabetismo delle donne nella Toscana tardo medievale." *Civiltà Communale: Libro, Scrittura, Documento Atti del Convegno Genova, 8–11 novembre 1988*, 364–365.

Milligan, Gerry. "Unlikely heroines in Lucrezia Tornabuoni's Judith and Esther." *Italica*, 88(4) (2011), 538–564.

Minutolo, Ceccarella. *Lettere*, Raffaele Morabito, ed. Naples: Edizioni scientifiche italiane, 1999.

Molho, Anthony. "Deception and marriage strategy in Renaissance Florence," in *Renaissance Quarterly*, Vol. 41(2), n. 2 (Summer, 1988), 193–217.

Morabito, Raffaele. *Lettere e letteratura. Studi sull'epistolografia volgare in Italia*, Alessandria: Edizioni dell'Orso, 2001.

Morandini, Giuliana. *Sospiri e palpiti: scrittrici italiane del Seicento*. Genova: Marietti, 2001, 114–124.

Morata, Olympia. *The complete writings of an Italian heretic*, ed. and transl. by Holt N. Parker. Chicago: University of Chicago Press, 2003.

Morison, Stanley and Nicolas Barker, ed. *Early Italian writing-books: Renaissance to Baroque*. Verona: Valdonega, 1990.

Mostaccio, Silvia. *Osservanza vissuta, osservanza insegnata: la domenicana genovese Tommasina Fieschi e i suoi scritti*. Firenze: L. S. Olschki, 1999.

Muessig, Carolyn, George Ferzoco, and Beverly Mayne Kienzle, eds. *A companion to Catherine of Siena*. Leiden & Boston: Brill, 2012.

Muir, Edward. *The culture wars of the late Renaissance: skeptics, libertines, and opera*. Cambridge, MA: Harvard University Press, 2007.

Murphy, Caroline P. "Lavinia Fontana and *Le Dame della Città*: understanding female artistic patronage in late sixteenth-century Bologna." *Renaissance Studies*, 10(1) (1996), 190–208.

Murphy, Caroline P. *Lavinia Fontana: a painter and her patrons in sixteenth-century Bologna*. New Haven, CT: Yale University Press, 2003.

Najemy, John. "Renaissance epistolarity." In *Between friends: discourses of power and desire in the Machiavelli-Vettori letters of 1513–1515*. Princeton, NJ: Princeton University Press, 1993, 18–57.

Newcomb, Anthony. "Courtesans, musicians or muses? Professional women musicians in sixteenth-century Italy." In Jane Bowers and Judith Tick, eds., *Women making music. The Western art tradition, 1150–1950*. Urbana: University of Illinois Press, 1986, 90–115.

Nicholson, Elizabeth S. G. et al., eds. *Italian women artists: from Renaissance to Baroque*. Milano: Skira; New York: Rizzoli, 2007.

Niccoli, Ottavia, ed. *Rinascimento al femminile*. Rome: Laterza, 1991.

Nico Ottaviani, Maria Grazia. "Nobile sorella mia honoranda: società e scritture femminili: alcuni esempi perugini." In Giovanna Casagrande, ed., *Donne tra Medioevo ed età moderna in Italia: ricerche*. Perugia: Morlacchi, 2004, 153–190.

Nico Ottaviani, Maria Grazia. "Me son missa a scriver questa letera," In *Lettere e altre scritture femminili tra Umbria, Toscana e Marche nei secoli XV-XVI*. Napoli: Liguori, 2006, 39–79, 156–157.

Nigro, Giampiero, ed. *Francesco di Marco Datini: the man, the merchant*. Florence: Firenze University Press, 2010.

Nochlin, Linda. "Why have there been no great women artists?" *ARTnews*, January 1971, 22–39, 67–71.

Nogarola, Isotta. *Complete writings: letterbook, dialogue on Adam and Eve, orations*, ed. and transl. by Margaret L. King and Diana Robin. Chicago: University of Chicago Press, 2004.

Noffke, Suzanne, ed., *Catherine of Siena: an anthology*. Tempe: Arizona Center for Medieval and Renaissance Studies, 2011-2012.

North, Marcy. *The anonymous Renaissance: cultures of discretion in Tudor-Stuart England.* Chicago: University of Chicago Press, 2003, 211–256.

Origo, Iris. *The merchant of Prato: Francesco di Marco Datini.* London: Penguin, 1992 [1957].

Pagden, Sylvia Ferino. *Sofonisba Anguissola: a Renaissance woman.* Exhibition catalogue. Washington, DC: National Museum of Women in the Arts, 1995.

Panizza, Letizia and Sharon Wood, eds., *A history of women's writing*, ed. New York: Cambridge University Press, 2000.

Panizza, Letizia, ed. *Women in Italian Renaissance culture and society.* Oxford: Legenda, 2000.

Parker, Geoffrey, ed. & trans. *At the court of the Borgia, being an account of the reign of Pope Alexander VI, written by his Master of Ceremonies, Johann Burchard.* London: The Folio Society, 1963.

Parker, Holt. "Angela Nogarola (c. 1400) and Isotta Nogarola (1418–1466): thieves of language." In Laurie J. Churchill, Phyllis R. Brown, and Jane E. Jeffrey, eds., *Women writing Latin: from Roman antiquity to Early Modern Europe.* Vol. 3: *Early Modern women writing Latin.* New York: Routledge, 2002, 11–30.

Parker, Holt N. "Latin and Greek poetry by five Renaissance Italian women." In Barbara K. Gold, Paul Allen Miller, and Charles Platter eds., *Sex and gender in medieval and Renaissance texts: the Latin tradition.* Albany: State University of New York Press, 1997, 250–260.

Parker, Holt N. "Women and humanism: nine factors for the woman learning." *Viator*, 35 (2004), 581–616.

Pasolini, Pier Desiderio. *Catherine Sforza*, transl. and prepared with the assistance of the author by Paul Sylvester. Chicago and New York: H. S. Stone and Co., 1898.

Perlingieri, Ilya Sandra. *Sofonisba Anguissola: the first great woman artist of the Renaissance.* New York: Rizzoli, 1992.

Pernis, Maria Grazia, and Laurie Schneider Adams. *Lucrezia Tornabuoni de' Medici and the Medici family in the fifteenth century.* New York: Peter Lang, 2006.

Perosa, Alessandro, ed. *Giovanni Rucellai ed il suo Zibaldone.* London: The Warburg Institute, University of London, 1960–1981.

Petrarch, Francesco. *Letters on familiar matters.* Translated by Aldo S. Bernardo. New York: Italica Press, 2005.

Petrucci, Armando. *Scrivere lettere: una storia plurimillenaria.* Bari, Italy: Laterza, 2008.

Pettegree, Andrew. *The book in the Renaissance.* New Haven: Yale University Press, 2010.

Pezzini, Serena. "Ideologia della conquista, ideologia dell'accoglienza: La Scanderbeide di Margherita Sarrocchi (1623)." *Modern Language Notes*, 120(1) (2005), 190–222.

Phillips, Mark. *The memoir of Marco Parenti: a life in Medici Florence.* Princeton, NJ: Princeton University Press, 1987.

Pighetti, Clelia. *Il vuoto e la quiete: scienza e mistica nel '600: Elena Cornaro e Carlo Rinaldini.* Milan: F. Angeli, 2005.

Pinessi, Orietta. *Sofonisba Anguissola: un "pittore" alla corte di Filippo II.* Milan: Selene, 1998.

Pisana, Camilla. *Lettere di cortigiane del Rinascimento*, ed. Angelo Romano. Rome: Salerno Editrice, 1990.

Plebani, Tiziana. *Il "genere" dei libri: storie e rappresentazioni della lettura al femminile e al maschile tra Medioevo ed età moderna.* Milan, Italy: F. Angeli, 2001.

Pollock, Griselda. "Review of Mary Garrard's *Artemisia Gentileschi.*" *Art Bulletin*, 72(3) (1990), 499–505.

Poss, Richard. "Veronica Gambara: a Renaissance gentildonna." In Katharina M. Wilson, ed., *Women writers of the Renaissance and Reformation.* Athens: University of Georgia Press, 1987, 47–65.

Pozzi, Mario. " 'Andrem di pari all'amorosa face': Appunti sulle lettere di Maria Savorgnan." In *Les femmes écrivains en Italie au Moyen Age et à la Renaissance: actes du colloque international, Aix-en-Provence, 12, 13, 14 novembre 1992*. Centre Aixois de Recherches Italiennes, 1994, 87–101.

Prizer, William F. "Una 'virtù molto conveniente a madonne': Isabella d'Este as a musician." *Journal of Musicology*, 17(1) (1999), 10–49.

Prosperi, Adriano. "Lettere spirituali." In G. Barone, Lucetta Scaraffia, and Gabriella Zarri, eds., *Donne e fede: santità e vita religiosa in Italia*. Rome: Laterza, 1994, 227–251.

Quondam, Amedeo, ed. *Le carte messaggiere Retorica e modelli di comunicazione epistolare per un indice dei libri di lettere del Cinquecento*. Rome: Bulzoni, 1981.

Rabil, Albert, Jr. *Laura Cereta: Quattrocento humanist*. Binghamton, NY: Medieval and Renaissance Texts and Studies, 1981.

Rabil, Albert. "Olympia Morata (1526–1555)." In Rinaldina Russell, ed., *Italian women writers: a bio-bibliographical sourcebook*. Westport, CT: Greenwood Press, 1994, 269–278.

Rabitti, Giovanna. "Le lettere di Chiara Matraini tra pubblico e private." In Gabriella Zarri, ed., *Per lettera: la scrittura epistolare femminile tra archivio e tipografia: secoli XV-XVII*. Rome: Viella, 1999, 209–234.

Rabitti, Giovanna. "Lyric poetry, 1500–1650." In Letizia Panizza and Sharon Wood, eds., Abigail Brundin, transl., *A history of women's writing in Italy*. Cambridge: Cambridge University Press, 2000, 37–42.

Rabitti, Giovanna. "Vittoria Colonna as role model for cinquecento women poets." In Letizia Panizza, ed., *Women in Italian Renaissance culture and society*. Oxford: European Humanities Research Centre, 2000, 478–497.

Ragg, Laura. *The women artists of Bologna*. London: Methuen, 1907.

Raney, Carolyn. *Francesca Caccini, musician to the Medici, and her* Primo libro *(1618)*. PhD dissertation, New York University, 1971.

Ray, Meredith K. "Between stage and page: the letters of Isabella Andreini." In *Writing gender in women's letter collections of the Italian Renaissance*. Toronto; Buffalo: University of Toronto Press, 2009, 156–183.

Ray, Meredith K. "Caterina Sforza's Experiments with Alchemy," In *Daughters of Alchemy: Women and Scientific Culture in Early Modern Italy*. Cambridge, MA: Harvard University Press, 2015, 14–45.

Ray, Meredith K. "Experiments with alchemy: Caterina Sforza in early modern scientific culture." In *Gender and scientific discourse in early modern culture*. Farnham, Surrey, England; Burlington, VT: Ashgate, 2010, 139–163.

Ray, Meredith K. "Letters from the cloister: defending the literary self in Arcangela Tarabotti's 'Lettere familiari e di complimento.'" *Italica*, 81(1) (Spring 2004), 24–43.

Ray, Meredith K. "The pen for the sword: Arcangela Tarabotti's *Lettere familiari e di complimento*." In *Writing gender in women's letter collections of the Italian Renaissance*. Toronto & Buffalo: University of Toronto Press, 2009, 184–213.

Ray, Meredith K. Chapter four, "Scientific Circles in Italy and Abroad: Camilla Erculiani and Margherita Sarrocchi," In *Daughters of Alchemy: Women and Scientific Culture in Early Modern Italy*. Cambridge, MA: Harvard University Press, 2015, 111–155.

Ray, Meredith K. *Writing gender in women's letter collections of the Italian Renaissance*. Toronto & Buffalo: University of Toronto Press, 2009.

Reiss, Sheryl E. and David G. Wilkins, eds., *Beyond Isabella: secular women patrons of art in Renaissance Italy*. Sheryl E. Reiss and David G. Wilkins, eds., Kirksville, Mo.: Truman State University Press, 2001.

Revoltella, Pietro. "Tre lettere di Elena Lucrezia Cornaro Piscopia a Nicolò Venier." In *Il Santo Rivista Antoniana di Storia Dottrina Arte*. Centro Studi Antoniani: Basilica del Santo, Padova, XXVII fasc. 1-2, (1987), 145–155.

Riccardi, Antonio. "The mystic humanism of Maria Maddalena de' Pazzi (1566–1607)." In E. Ann Matter and John Coakley, eds., *Creative women in medieval and Early Modern Italy: a religious and artistic Renaissance*. Philadelphia: University of Pennsylvania Press, 1994, 212–236.

Rice Henderson, Judith. "Erasmus on the art of letter writing." In James J. Murphy, ed., *Renaissance eloquence: studies in the theory and practice of Renaissance rhetoric*. Berkeley: University of California Press, 1983.

Robin, Diana. "Cassandra Fedele's *Epistolae* (1488–1521): biography as effacement." In Thomas F. Mayer and D. R. Woolf, eds., *The rhetorics of life-writing in early modern Europe: forms of biography from Cassandra Fedele to Louis XIV*. Ann Arbor: University of Michigan Press, 1995.

Robin, Diana Maury, Anne R. Larsen, and Carole Levin. *Encyclopedia of women in the Renaissance: Italy, France, and England*. Santa Barbara, CA: ABC-CLIO, 2007.

Robin, Diana. *Publishing women: salons, the presses, and the Counter-Reformation in sixteenth-century Italy*. Chicago: University of Chicago Press, 2007.

Robin, Diana. "The Salt War letters of Vittoria Colonna." In *Publishing women: salons, the presses, and the Counter-Reformation in sixteenth-century Italy*. Chicago: University of Chicago Press, 2007, 79–101.

Rogers, Mary, and Paola Tinagli. *Women in Italy, 1350–1650: ideals and realities: a sourcebook*. Manchester, UK, & New York: Manchester University Press; New York: Distributed exclusively in the USA by Palgrave, 2005.

Rosati, Valeria. *Le lettere di Margherita Datini a Francesco di Marco, 1384–1410*. Prato: Cassa di Risparmi e Depositi, 1977.

Rosenthal, Margaret F. *The honest courtesan: Veronica Franco, citizen and writer in sixteenth-century Venice*. Chicago: University of Chicago Press, 1992.

Ross, Janet. *Lives of the early Medici as told in their correspondence*. London: Chatto & Windus, 1910.

Ross, Sarah Gwyneth. *The birth of feminism: woman as intellect in Renaissance Italy and England*. Cambridge, MA: Harvard University Press, 2009.

Ruggiero, Guido. *The boundaries of Eros: sex crime and sexuality in Renaissance Venice*. New York: Oxford University Press, 1985.

Russell, Rinaldina. "Chiara Matraini nella tradizione lirica femminile." *Forum Italicum*, 34(2) (Fall 2000), 415–427.

Russell, Rinaldina. *Feminist encyclopedia of Italian literature*. Westport, CT: Greenwood Press, 1997.

Russell, Rinaldina. *Italian women writers: a bio-bibliographical sourcebook*. Westport, CT: Greenwood Press, 1994.

Russell, Rinaldina. "Veronica Gambara (1485–1550)." In *A bio-bibliographical sourcebook*. Westport, CT: Greenwood Press, 1994, 145–153.

San Juan, Rose Marie. "The court lady's dilemma: Isabella d'Este and art collecting in the Renaissance." *Oxford Art Journal*, 14(1) (1991), 67–78.

Salvadori, Patrizia, ed. *Lucrezia Tornabuoni. Lettere*. Florence: L.S. Olschki, 1993.

Salvi, Marcella. " 'Il solito è sempre quello, l'insolito è più nuovo': li buffoni e le prostitute di Margherita Costa fra tradizione e innovazione." *Forum Italicum*, 38 (2004), 376–399.

Sarot, Eden. "Ansaldo Cebà and Sara Copia Sullam." *Italica*, 31(3) (September 1954), 138–150.

Sarrocchi, Margherita. *Scanderbeide: the heroic deeds of George Scanderberg, King of Epirus*, Rinaldina Russell, ed. and trans. Chicago: University of Chicago Press, 2006.

Savorgnan, Maria. *"Se mai fui vostra": lettere d'amore a Pietro Bembo*, ed. Monica Farnetti. Ferrara: Edisai, 2012.

Savorgnan di Brazzà, Fabiana. *Scrittura al femminile nel Friuli dal Cinquecento al Settecento*. Udine: Gaspari, 2011.

Scarpati, Claudio. *Le rime spirituali di Vittoria Colonna nel codice vaticano donato a Michelangelo*. *Aevum*, 78, 2004, p. 693, n2.

Schaefer, Jean Owens. "A note on the iconography of a medal of Lavinia Fontana." *Journal of the Warburg and Courtauld Institutes*, 47 (1984), 232–234.

Scott, Karen. "Io Catarina: ecclesiastical politics and oral culture in the letters of Catherine of Siena." In Karen Cherewatuk and Ulrike Wiethaus, eds., *Dear sister: Medieval women and the epistolary genre*. Philadelphia: University of Pennsylvania Press, 1993, 87–121.

Selmi, Elisabetta, ed. *La scrittura femminile a Brescia tra il Quattrocento e l'Ottocento*, with Elisabetta Conti and Maria Moiraghi Sueri. Brescia: Fondazione civiltà bresciana, 2001.

Sforza, Ippolita Maria. *Lettere*, M. Serena Castaldo, ed. Alessandria: Edizioni dell'Orso, 2004.

Shemek, Deanna. "Isabella d'Este and the properties of persuasion." In Jane Couchman and Ann Crabb, eds., *Women's letters across Europe, 1400–1700: form and persuasion*. Aldershot, England, & Burlington, VT: Ashgate, 2005, 108–34.

Shemek, Deanna. "In continuous expectation: Isabella d'Este's epistolary desire." In Dennis Looney and Deanna Shemek, eds., *Phaethon's children: the Este court and its culture in early modern Italy*. Tempe, AZ: Medieval and Renaissance Texts and Studies, 2005, 269–300.

Shemek, Deanna. "Mendacious missives: Isabella d'Este's epistolary theater." In Deanna Shemek and Michael Wyatt, eds., *Writing relations: American scholars in Italian archives: essays for Franca Petrucci Nardelli and Armando Petrucci*. Florence: Leo S. Olschki, 2008, 71–86.

Smarr, Janet L. "A dialogue of dialogues: Tullia d'Aragona and Sperone Speroni." *MLN*, 113 (1998), 204–212.

Smarr, Janet Levarie. *Joining the conversation: dialogues by Renaissance women*. Ann Arbor: University of Michigan Press, 2005.

Smarr, Janet Levarie. "Olympia Morata: from classicist to reformer." In Dennis Looney and Deanna Shemek, eds., *Phaethon's children: the Este court and its culture in early modern Ferrara*. Tempe: Arizona Center for Medieval and Renaissance Studies, 2005, 321–343.

Sobel, Dava. *Galileo's daughter: a drama of science, faith, and love*. London: Fourth Estate, 1999.

Sobel, Dava, transl. and annot. *Letters to father: Suor Maria Celeste to Galileo, 1623–1633*. New York: Walker & Co., 2001.

Solinas, Francesco, ed. *Lettere di Artemisia: edizione critica e annotata con quarantatre documenti inediti*. Rome: De Luca Editori d'Arte, 2011.

Spear, Richard. "Artemisia Gentileschi: ten years of fact and fiction." *Art Bulletin*, 82 (2000), 568–577.

Sperling, Jutta Gisela. *Convents and the body politic in late Renaissance Venice*. Chicago: University of Chicago Press, 1999.

Spini, Giorgio. *Cosimo I e l'indipendenza del principato mediceo*, 2nd edition, Vallecchi, Florence, 1980.

Stampa, Gaspara. *The complete poems: the 1554 edition of the Rime, a bilingual edition*, edited by Troy Tower and Jane Tylus; translated and with an introduction by Jane Tylus. Chicago: University of Chicago Press, 2010.

Stevenson, Jane. "Women and classical education in the early modern period." In Yun Lee Too and Niall Livingstone, eds., *Pedagogy and power: rhetorics of classical learning*. Cambridge, U.K.; New York, NY: Cambridge University Press, 1998, 83–109.

Stevenson, Jane. *Women Latin poets: language, gender, and authority, from antiquity to the eighteenth century*. New York: Oxford University Press, 2005.

Stjerna, Kirsi. *Women and the Reformation*. Malden, MA: Blackwell Pub., 2009, 197–209.

Storey, H. Wayne. *Transcription and visual poetics in the early Italian lyric*. New York: Garland Pub., 1993.

Storey, Tessa. *Carnal commerce in Counter-Reformation Rome*. Cambridge, UK, & New York: Cambridge University Press, 2008.

Stortoni, Laura Anna, ed. *Women poets of the Italian Renaissance: courtly ladies and courtesans*, transl. by Laura Anna Stortoni and Mary Prentice Lillie. New York: Italica Press, 1997.

Stott, Deborah. " 'I am the same Cornelia I have always been': reading Cornelia Collonello's letters to Michelangelo." In Jane Couchman and Ann Crabb, eds., *Women's letters across Europe, 1400–1700: form and persuasion*. Aldershot, England, & Burlington, VT: Ashgate, 2005, 79–100.

Strocchia, Sharon. "Learning the virtues: convent schools and female culture in Renaissance Florence." In Barbara Whitehead, ed., *Women's education in early modern Europe: a history, 1500–1800*. New York: Garland Pub., 1999.

Strocchia, Sharon. "The melancholic nun in Late Renaissance Italy." In Yasmin Haskell, ed., *Diseases of the imagination and imaginary disease in the early modern period*. Turnhout, Belgium: Brepols, 2011, 139–158.

Strocchia, Sharon. "The nun apothecaries of Renaissance Florence: marketing medicines in the convent." *Renaissance Studies*, 25(5) (2011), 627–647.

Strocchia, Sharon. *Nuns and nunneries in Renaissance Florence*. Baltimore: Johns Hopkins University Press, 2009.

Strocchia, Sharon. "Taken into custody: girls and convent guardianship in Renaissance Florence." *Renaissance Studies*, 17(2), 2003, 177–200.

Strozzi, Alessandra. *Selected letters of Alessandra Strozzi*, transl. with an introduction and notes by Heather Gregory. Berkeley: University of California Press, 1997.

Strunck, Christina, ed., *Medici women as cultural mediators, 1533-1–1743*. Cinisello Balsamo, Milan: Silvana, 2011.

Symonds, Margaret. *The story of Perugia*. London: J. M. Dent, 1904.

Tarabotti, Arcangela. "Letter to the Reader from *Paradiso monacale* and Ferrante Pallavicino's Letter 5, To an Ungrateful Woman, from *Corriero svaligiato*." In Letizia Panizza, ed. & transl., *Paternal tyranny*. Chicago: University of Chicago Press, 2004.

Tarabotti, Arcangela. *Women are not human. An anonymous treatise and responses*, transl. by Teresa M. Kenney. New York: Crossroad Publishing Co., 1998.

Tinagli, Paola. *Women in Italian Renaissance art: gender, representation, identity*. Manchester, UK: Manchester University Press, 1997.

Tinagli, Paola, and Mary Rogers, eds. *Women and the visual arts in Italy c. 1400–1650: luxury and leisure, duty and devotion: a sourcebook*. Manchester, UK: Manchester University Press, 2012.

Toccafondi, Diana, and Giovanni Tartaglione, eds. *"Per la tua Margherita…" lettere di una donna del '300 al marito mercante: Margherita Datini a Francesco di Marco, 1384–1401*. Prato: Archivio di Stato di Prato, 2002.

Tomas, Natalie. *A positive novelty: women and public life in renaissance Florence*. Clayton, Vic., Australia: Monash Publications in History, Dept. of History, Monash University, 1992.

Tomas, Natalie. "Commemorating a mortal goddess: Maria Salviati de' Medici and the cultural politics of Duke Cosimo I." In *Practices of gender in late medieval and early modern Europe*, Turnhout: Brepols; Abingdon: Marston, 2008, 261–278.

Tomas, Natalie. "Did women have a space?" In Roger J. Crum and John T. Paoletti, eds., *Renaissance Florence: a social history*. New York: Cambridge University Press, 2006, 311–332.

Tomas, Natalie. *The Medici women: gender and power in Renaissance Florence*. Aldershot, Hampshire, England, & Burlington, VT: Ashgate, 2003.

Tonzig, Maria Ildegarde, ed. *Elena Lucrezia Cornaro Piscopia, prima donna laureata nel mondo. Terzo centenario del dottorato, 1678–1978*. Vicenza: V. Gualandi, 1980.

Treadwell, Nina. *Music and wonder at the Medici court: the 1589 interludes for La pellegrina*. Bloomington & Indianapolis: Indiana University Press, 2008.

Treadwell, Nina. "She descended on a cloud 'from the highest spheres': Florentine monody 'alla Romanina'." *Cambridge Opera Journal*, 16(1) (2004), 1–22.

Tylus, Jane, ed. & trans. *Lucrezia Tornabuoni de' Medici. Sacred narratives.* Chicago: University of Chicago Press, 2001.

Tylus, Jane. *Reclaiming Catherine of Siena: literacy, literature, and the signs of others.* Chicago: University of Chicago Press, 2009.

Tylus, Jane. "Women at the windows: commedia dell'arte and theatrical practice in Early Modern Italy." *Theatre Journal,* 49 (1997), 323–342.

Veen, Henk Theo van. *Cosimo I de' Medici and his self-representation in Florentine art and culture.* New York: Cambridge University Press, 2006.

Veltri, Giuseppe. "Body of conversion and the immortality of the soul: the 'beautiful Jewess' Sara Copio Sullam." In Maria Diemling and Giuseppe Veltri, eds., *The Jewish body: corporeality, society, and identity in the Renaissance and early modern period.* Leiden & Boston: Brill, 2009, 331–354.

Veltri, Giuseppe. *Renaissance philosophy in Jewish garb: foundations and challenges in Judaism on the eve of modernity.* Leiden & Boston: Brill, 2009.

Verdile, Nadia. "Contributi alla biografia di Margherita Sarrocchi." *Rendiconti dell'Accademia di Archeologia, Lettere e Belle Arti di Napoli,* LXI (1989-1990), 165–206.

Viroli, Maurizio. *Niccolò's smile: a biography of Machiavelli.* New York: Farrar, Straus and Giroux, 2000.

Vries, Joyce de. *Caterina Sforza and the art of appearances: gender, art, and culture in early modern Italy.* Farnham, Surrey, England, & Burlington, VT: Ashgate, 2010.

Warnke, Frank J. "Gaspara Stampa: Aphrodite's priestess, love's martyr." In Katharina Wilson, ed., *Women writers of the Renaissance and Reformation.* Athens: University of Georgia Press, 1987, 3–21.

Weaver, Elissa B., ed. *Arcangela Tarabotti: a literary nun in Baroque Venice.* Ravenna: Longo, 2006.

Weaver, Elissa. *Convent theatre in early modern Italy: spiritual fun and learning for women.* Cambridge, UK, &; New York: Cambridge University Press, 2002.

Webb, Jennifer. "Hidden in plain sight: Varano and Sforza women of the Marche." In Katherine McIver, ed., *Wives, widows, mistresses, and nuns in early modern Italy: making the invisible visible through art and patronage.* Farnham, Surrey, England, & Burlington, VT: Ashgate, 2012.

Welch, Evelyn S. "Between Milan and Naples: Ippolita Maria Sforza, duchess of Calabria." In David Abulafia, ed., *The French descent into Renaissance Italy, 1494–5: antecedents and effects.* Aldershot, Hampshire: Variorum: Brookfield, VT: Ashgate Pub. Co., 1995.

Westwater, Lynn Lara. "A cloistered nun abroad: Arcangela Tarabotti's international literary career." In Anke Gilleir, Alicia C. Montoya, and Suzan van Dijk, eds., *Women writing back/ writing women back: transnational perspectives from the late Middle Ages to the dawn of the modern era.* Leiden & Boston: Brill, 2010.

Westwater, Lynn Lara. "A rediscovered friendship in the republic of letters: the unpublished correspondence of Arcangela Tarabotti and Ismaël Boulliau." *Renaissance Quarterly,* 65(1) (Spring 2012), 67–134.

Westwater, Lynn. "Sara Copio Sullam: life and family" and "Sara Copio Sullam: literary life and works." In "The disquieting voice: women's writing and antifeminism in seventeenth-century Venice." Ph.D. dissertation, University of Chicago, 2003.

White, Alain Campbell. "A Translation of the Quaestio De Aqua Et Terra." *Annual Reports of the Dante Society,* 21 (1902), i–59.

Wiesner, Merry E. *Women and gender in early modern Europe,* 2nd ed. Cambridge: Cambridge University Press, 2000.

Wilson, Katharina, ed. *Women writers of the Renaissance and Reformation.* Athens: University of Georgia Press, 1987.

Witt, Ronald G. *In the footsteps of the ancients: the origins of humanism from Lovato to Bruni.,* Leiden &; Boston: Brill, 2000.

Woodward, William Harrison, ed., *Vittorino da Feltre and other humanist educators*. Cambridge: Cambridge University Press, 1912.

Zaggia, Massimo. "Fortuna editoriale delle lettere di Caterina," in Lino Leonardi and Pietro Trifone, eds. *Dire l'ineffabile : Caterina da Siena e il linguaggio della mistica: atti del convegno (Siena, 13-1-14 novembre 2003)*, ed. Lino Leonardi e Pietro Trifone.

Zancan, Marina. "La donna," in *Letteratura italiana*, diretta da A. Asor Rosa, vol. V, Le Questioni, Torino: Einaudi, 1986, 765–788.

Zancan, Marina. *Il doppio itinerario della scrittura. La donna nella tradizione letteraria italiana*. Torino: Einaudi, 1998.

Zarri, Gabriella. "Il carteggio tra don Leone Bartolini e un gruppo di gentildonne bolognesi negli anni del Conciglio di Trento (1545–1563)." *Archivio italiano per la storia della pietà*, 7 (1976), 337–885.

Zarri, Gabriella. "Ginevra Gozzadini dall'Armi, gentildonna bolognese (1520/27–1567)." In O. Niccoli, ed., *Rinascimento al femminile*. Rome: Bari, 1991, 117–142.

Zarri, Gabriella. *La religion di Lucrezia Borgia: le lettere inedite del confessore*. Rome: Roma nel Rinascimento, 2006.

Zarri, Gabriella. "Living saints: a typology of female sanctity in the early sixteenth century." In Daniel Borstein and Roberto Rusconi, eds., *Women and religion in medieval and Renaissance Italy*. Chicago: University of Chicago Press, 1996, 219–303.

Zarri, Gabriella. *Per lettera: la scrittura epistolare femminile tra archivio e tipografia: secoli XV–XVII*. Rome: Viella, 1999.

Zarri, Gabriella. "Religious and devotional writing, 1400–1600." In Letizia Panizza and Sharon Wood, eds., *A history of women's writing in Italy*. New York: Cambridge University Press, 2000, 79–91.

Credits

Index